X-SCM

X-SCM: The New Science of X-treme Supply Chain Management will be developed into a multi-faceted, multi-media set of products to serve as a definitive guide and toolset for executives who must build and operate global supply chain networks in a period of systemic, extreme change. The cornerstone of the project is this book, which includes strategic content and discussion as well as executive templates for strategic decision making and multi-enterprise action-taking.

An experiential web-based X-treme Supply Chain Simulation will accompany *X-SCM: The New Science of X-treme Supply Chain Management*. The simulation energizes and empowers teams online, enabling them to explore supply chain network options and decision making. It will be designed to address the volatile nature of supply chains today, and allow users to test approaches to managing ongoing sets of supply chain upheavals and assess their outcomes.

Lisa H. Harrington is President of the lharrington group, a strategic consulting and marketing communication services firm focused on supply chain management, warehousing, and related technology. She also is a Senior Research Fellow and Adjunct Professor of Supply Chain Management at the Supply Chain Management Center, Robert H. Smith School of Business at the University of Maryland.

Dr. Sandor Boyson has over 25 years of global supply chain management consulting experience in the business and public sectors. He is the co-author (with Dr. Corsi and Ms. Harrington) of two books on supply chain management, including *In Real Time: Managing the New Supply Chain* (Praeger, 2004). Dr. Boyson is founding Co-Director of the Robert H. Smith School's Supply Chain Management Center.

Dr. Thomas M. Corsi is Michelle E. Smith Professor of Logistics at the Robert H. Smith School of Business and founding Co-Director of Smith's Supply Chain Management Center. He has co-authored three books: *The Economic Effects of Surface Freight Deregulation* (Brookings, 1990), and (with Dr. Boyson and Ms. Harrington) *Logistics and the Extended Enterprise: Benchmarks and Best Practices for the Manufacturing Professional* (Wiley, 1999) and *In Real Time: Managing the New Supply Chain* (Praeger, 2004).

X-SCM

The New Science of X-treme Supply Chain Management

LISA H. HARRINGTON

DR. SANDOR BOYSON

DR. THOMAS M. CORSI

Routledge
Taylor & Francis Group

NEW YORK AND LONDON

First published 2011
by Routledge
270 Madison Avenue, New York, NY 10016

Simultaneously published in the UK
by Routledge
2 Park Square, Milton Park, Abingdon, Oxon OX14 4RN

*Routledge is an imprint of the Taylor & Francis Group,
an informa business*

© 2011 Taylor & Francis

The right of Lisa H. Harrington, Dr. Sandor Boyson and Dr. Thomas M. Corsi to be identified as authors of this work has been asserted by them in accordance with sections 77 and 78 of the Copyright, Designs and Patents Act 1988.

Typeset in Minion by
Swales & Willis Ltd, Exeter, Devon
Printed and bound in the United states of America on
acid-free paper by
Sheridan Books, Inc.

Library of Congress Cataloging in Publication Data
X-SCM: the new science of x-treme supply chain management / [edited by] Lisa H. Harrington, Sandor Boyson and Thomas M. Corsi.
     p. cm.
   Includes index.
   1. Business logistics—Management.   2. Risk management.   3. Decision making.   I. Harrington, Lisa H.   II. Boyson, Sandor.   III. Corsi, Thomas M.   IV. Title: Extreme supply chain management.
   HD38.5.X42 2010
   658.7—dc22   2010006457

ISBN13: 978–0–415–87355–0 (hbk)
ISBN13: 978–0–415–87356–7 (pbk)
ISBN13: 978–0–203–84621–6 (ebk)

Please visit the book's companion website at
http://www.routledge.com/textbooks/harrington

Contents

Acknowledgments

Bringing this book and the accompanying toolsets and simulations into being has truly been a community undertaking. We could not have succeeded without the time, energy, commitment, ideas, and perseverance of all of our contributors. We and our team of global contributors never wavered from our mission, despite significant personal and professional challenges that arose during the 18 months it took to birth this project.

As principal authors of the book, I, Sandy Boyson, and Tom Corsi would especially like to thank the following individuals for their contributions:

Richard M. Douglass of Sterling Commerce for believing in the project and for his willingness to fund our efforts.

Rick Blasgen, President and CEO of the Council of Supply Chain Management Professionals (CSCMP), for his willingness to partner with us on the book.

Carlos Alvarenga of Accenture for his ongoing thought leadership in helping us conceptualize X-SCM and map out the book's supporting arguments.

Toby Gooley of CSCMP's *Supply Chain Quarterly* for her tireless and outstanding editing and re-writing.

Perry Trunick for his excellent editing.

Lisa H. Harrington

About the Authors and Contributors

The Authors

Lisa H. Harrington is Senior Research Fellow at the Supply Chain Management Center, Robert H. Smith School of Business, University of Maryland, and an Adjunct Professor of Supply Chain Management. She is also President of the lharrington group LLC, a supply chain management consulting firm. Lisa has served as a supply chain strategy consultant to the U.S. Department of Defense, the U.S. Agency for International Development, the United Nations Population Fund, and numerous Fortune 500 corporations, and has authored hundreds of articles on supply chain management for business and industry publications worldwide. She is co-author of two prior books: *Logistics and the Extended Enterprise* (John Wiley & Sons, 1999), and *In Real Time: Managing the New Supply Chain* (Praeger, 2004). She also served as editor on five other supply chain management books.

Sandor Boyson is Research Professor and Co-Director of the Supply Chain Management Center, Robert H. Smith School of Business, University of Maryland. He holds a Ph.D. in Technology Planning from the University of Sussex. He has served as a technology and strategy consultant to public organizations as varied as the World Bank and the Department of Defense; and numerous private sector organizations. He is co-author of two prior books: *Logistics and the Extended Enterprise* (John Wiley & Sons, 1999), and *In Real Time: Managing the New Supply Chain* (Praeger, 2004).

Thomas M. Corsi is the Michelle E. Smith Professor of Logistics and Co-Director of the Supply Chain Management Center, Robert H. Smith School of Business, University of Maryland. He holds a Ph.D. from the University of Wisconsin-Milwaukee. He has authored more than 100 articles on logistics and transportation, and has consulted for such organizations as the Maryland State Department of Transportation, the National Science Foundation, the U.S. Department of Transportation, United Parcel Service, the U.S. Department of Energy, and the U.S. Army Logistics Agency. He is co-author of three prior books: *Logistics and the Extended Enterprise* (John Wiley & Sons, 1999), *The Economic Effects of Surface Freight Deregulation* (Brooking, 1990), and *In Real Time: Managing the New Supply Chain* (Praeger, 2004).

Project Partner

This book project was accomplished in partnership with the Council of Supply Chain Management Professionals.

Contributor and Project Sponsor

Richard M. Douglass is the Global Industry Executive for Manufacturing and Logistics at Sterling Commerce. He has over 25 years of experience in supply chain management consulting and industry marketing in a variety of manufacturing sectors ranging from chemicals to high tech. He received a B.S. in computer science from Michigan State University and an M.B.A. from the Kellogg Graduate School of Management at Northwestern University.

Sterling Commerce provided the grant money that made this book possible.

Contributors

Carlos Alvarenga is Managing Director, Accenture Supply Chain Services. He is also a Senior Research Fellow at the Supply Chain Management Center, Robert H. Smith School of Business, University of Maryland.

Nathan Birckhead is Service Delivery Leader at Nissan North America in Nashville, Tenn. He holds an M.B.A. from the Robert H. Smith School of Business, University of Maryland.

Ernest Cadotte is a Professor of Marketing at the University of Tennessee. He holds a Ph.D. in Marketing and Logistics from Ohio State University, an M.B.A. in Management Science from the University of Colorado, and a B.S. in Psychology from Michigan State University. As a consultant, he developed a market analysis program for technology transfers at Oak Ridge National Laboratory and has advised a number of technology-based businesses. Ernest developed Marketplace, an integrated business simulation, and adapted the simulation especially for this book to produce a new version—X-treme Supply Chain Simulation.

Gordon S. Cleveland is Radiological Program Analyst at the U.S. Department of Agriculture Animal and Plant Health Inspection Service, Veterinary Services, National Center for Animal Health Emergency Management. Gordon has contributed to the development and delivery of numerous national and state level emergency response exercises and has participated in multiple actual emergency responses which utilized the Incident Command System.

Patricia Cleveland is Associate Dean of Undergraduate Programs at the University of Maryland's Robert H. Smith School of Business. Prior to coming to Smith, she was the Assistant Dean for Student Academic Services at the University of Hawaii's College of Business for six years. Before joining the University of Hawaii, Pat held administrative and faculty positions at Bowling Green State University and the College of Arts & Sciences at the University of Kansas. In addition, she has served on the faculties of Ft. Lewis College in Colorado and Ottawa University in Kansas. Cleveland has a Ph.D. in sociology from the University of Kansas.

Koen Cobbaert is Associate Partner at S&V Management Consultants N.V., headquartered in Belgium. Koen is a specialist in strategic and tactical supply chain management and performance management.

Chaodong Han is Assistant Professor at the College of Business & Economics, Towson University. Dr. Han received his Ph.D. in Logistics from the Robert H. Smith School of Business, University of Maryland. His research focuses on multinational operations and IT in global supply chains.

John R. Macdonald is an Assistant Professor of Supply Chain Management with the Eli Broad Graduate School of Management at Michigan State University. His research interests include supply chain disruptions/risk management, behavioral operations/supply chain management, and research of multiple types involving third-party logistics companies and transportation companies. John has worked on multiple continents with companies such as UTi Worldwide, ConAgra, Union Pacific Railroad, and Ruan Transportation, and has consulted for companies such as SC Johnson, Home Depot, DowCorning, Lion Breweries, and Bluescope Steel.

Kevin McCormack is President of DRK Research and Consulting LLC. He is a Master Instructor for supply chain risk management for the Supply Chain Council and serves on the faculty of the National Graduate School and SKEMA Global Business School.

Hart Rossman is Vice President and Chief Technology Officer for Cyber Programs at SAIC. He is a Senior Research Fellow with the Supply Chain Management Center within the Robert H. Smith School of Business at the University of Maryland in the area of Cyber Supply Chain Assurance. Concurrently, Mr. Rossman is a faculty member with the Institute for Applied Network Security, represents SAIC's Incident Response Team in FIRST, and is a founding member of the Corporate Executive Programme.

John C. Schulte, President of John Schulte Consulting LLC, is a domestic and international consultant with 37 years of experience in disaster and emergency operations response and Incident Command/Incident Management System (ICS) applications and training. John retired in January 2006 from a federal Disaster and Emergency Operations Specialist position. As a federal official and a private consultant John has responded to national and international disasters and presented ICS training courses throughout the United States, Europe, Africa, Southeast Asia, Latin America, and the Caribbean Islands.

Peter Trkman is Assistant Professor of Economics at the University of Ljubljana in Slovenia.

Alexander Verbraeck is Full Professor in Systems and Simulation at Delft University of Technology, and he is the Chair of the Systems Engineering Department. He has an M.Sc. in Mathematics and a Ph.D. in Computer Science from Delft University of Technology in the Netherlands. Alexander also is a part-time Research Professor at the Robert H. Smith School of Business at the University of Maryland in the Logistics, Business, and Public Policy Department. His current research focuses on distributed simulation and gaming, on complex distributed systems such as supply chains, on real-time control and emulation of equipment using simulation, and on the development of generic, object oriented simulation libraries that can be used for modeling of complex systems and for serious gaming.

Peter Verstraeten is Managing Partner at S&V Management Consultants N.V., based in Belgium. Peter is a specialist in strategic and tactical supply chain management and performance management.

Taylor Wilkerson is a Research Fellow with Logistics Management Institute (LMI) where he works in the Supply Chain Management program. He has over 15 years of experience in supply chain management and systems engineering and is a qualified SCOR Model instructor with SCOR-P certification. Taylor has a B.E. from Vanderbilt University and an M.B.A. from the Robert H. Smith School of Business at the University of Maryland.

Part 1
X-SCM Explained

one
Introduction to X-treme Supply Chain Management (X-SCM)

Lisa H. Harrington

This book and its associated online tool kit come at a time of great uncertainty, grave concern, and monumental risk for global supply chains.

The worldwide economic recession and the sudden collapse of financial institutions are only partly responsible for the unprecedented challenges facing supply chain managers today. Volatility and the rate of dramatic change in supply chains have been escalating for some time, as we at the Supply Chain Management Center of the University of Maryland's Robert H. Smith School of Business have been documenting for more than a decade.

In our first book, *Logistics and the Extended Enterprise* (John Wiley, 1999), we examined ways organizations managed risks and extended their capabilities and business boundaries through centralizing management of logistics services. That book came at a time when the prevailing wisdom in consulting circles was that clients should decentralize logistics activities and push the function out to the business units—advice that would have prevented corporations from realizing the opportunities of scale economies and market leverage.

Logistics and the Extended Enterprise also came at a point when the first wave of logistics outsourcing was being met with skepticism from corporate executives. At that time we surveyed 463 companies that had engaged in logistics outsourcing for three years or longer. Our findings were conclusive: carefully targeting, bundling, and outsourcing activities to a third-party logistics firm produced first-year savings of 21.3 percent off the previous year's baseline logistics budget. We noted, however, that the savings appeared to fall off in the second and third years of outsourcing agreements if managerial innovation between the company and its third-party logistics agent was allowed to deteriorate and if relationship risks were not effectively controlled.

In our second book, *In Real Time: Managing the New Supply Chain* (Praeger, 2004), we continued to examine the ways in which organizations managed risks and extended their capabilities and business boundaries in the post-9/11 period. Specifically, we discussed the set of practices required for creating real-time supply chains that link together customers, distributors, producers, and suppliers on a global basis. Through these real-time cyber linkages, organizations could achieve real, sustained productivity gains and cost advantages. Our work in building supply chain portals for the U.S. Department of Defense, Lockheed Martin and others, which we described in the book, led us to a deep conviction that such connectivity and simultaneous processing of information all along the supply chain was a vital component of managing risk:

Real-time systems and rapid-response supply chains have become the basis for business survival and continuity. Given the extreme volatility in the international marketplace, the sudden swing to tighter security/closed borders in the post-9/11 period, and the resultant longer transportation/shipping cycles and more uncertain supply sources, we believe the development of a more complex, adaptive supply chain is imperative.[1]

We then noted that in the post-9/11 world, the real-time supply chain was taking on life-and-death importance for businesses:

> Given the slowdown in demand across many sectors and given longstanding, chronic deflationary pressures on prices and profits, corporate supply chain strategy has had to emphasize establishing more direct, real-time links to demand sources (points of distribution) to avoid the buildup of inventory. This shift involves a core set of activities moving the enterprise from reactive to what we called anticipatory logistics. The volatility of borders and international transport links in the post-9/11 world has meant an adjustment in thinking, away from exclusive emphasis on just-in-time methods to more intelligent techniques for pre-positioning/pre-qualifying of supplies and suppliers to reduce supply chain system response time.[2]

Leading companies were migrating from the old model of "reactive" logistics management to a new practice of "anticipatory" logistics management. The differences between "reactive" and "anticipatory" logistics are presented in Table 1.1.

In this, our third book, we continue our inquiry into how companies survive and indeed prosper in a highly volatile business environment. We argue that the nature of business today requires a new science of supply chain management—one based on rapid risk assessment and response. We call this new science X-Treme Supply Chain Management (X-SCM), and define it as follows:

> *X-treme Supply Chain Management (X-SCM): the science of governing global supply chains experiencing instabilities of unprecedented amplitude, frequency and duration.*

This book brings together an unprecedented array of contributions from world experts in supply chain volatility management. Their collective writings cover the supply chain in all of its forms—physical, financial, cyber, and service—and do so in a way that dials up the science of supply chain management to the next level. To a level capable of taking on the extreme oscillation and change that characterizes our world.

TABLE 1.1.   The shift from reactive to anticipatory logistics

From reactive, just-in-time logistics	To anticipatory logistics
▪ Strategic relationships with Tier I suppliers; Internet auctions for spot buys	▪ Core Tier I supplier relationships plus regionally-based, pre-approved Tier II suppliers and real-time global auctions to help meet spikes in demand
▪ Incremental adjustments to demand planning to ensure smooth supply/demand matching	▪ Strategic scanning systems to spot events on horizon that could cause spikes/dislocations in demand or supply (supply chain control panel technology, knowledge management/data mining)
▪ Ease of cross-border movements of supplies/inventories in the "Age of Globalization"	▪ Pre-positioning of vital stocks in key national markets in the "Age of Security"
▪ Expectations of growth in demand as basis for corporate profit into the distant future; large capital investments in new plants and information technology	▪ Expectations of disinflation and oversupply into the distant future; rationalization and enhancement of existing capital stock and information technology

Source: Sandor Boyson, Lisa H. Harrington, and Thomas M. Corsi, *In Real Time: Managing the New Supply Chain* (Westport, CT: Praeger, 2004): 10.

This book is produced in partnership with the Council of Supply Chain Management Professionals (CSCMP), one of the largest supply chain professional associations in the world, and was supported by a grant from Sterling Commerce.

Our contributing authors come from all walks of the supply chain field: University of Maryland, Sterling Commerce, Cisco Systems, Accenture, Science Applications International Corp. (SAIC), Logistics Management Institute (LMI), U.S. Department of Agriculture, the Supply Chain Council (SCOR), Michigan State University, DRK Research & Consulting, University of Ljubljana, S&V Management Consultants, Towson University, Innovative Learning Solutions, TU-Delft University, and John Schulte Consulting.

Why X-SCM?

Risk and volatility have skyrocketed in the five years since our last book was published. The events of the past two years alone have taken companies and individuals around the world on a wild ride indeed:

- The U.S. housing market collapsed
- Consumers lost billions of dollars in equity and financial resources
- The banking/financial system suffered a meltdown
- Fuel prices soared, then plummeted
- Credit dried up
- A worldwide recession has stressed the global economic system
- Globalization was called into question
- The "green revolution" took hold almost everywhere.

Companies, countries—indeed, the entire world—were caught by surprise by many of these developments. We are now at a new tipping point, one where volatility emerges as a systemic condition, rapid oscillation becomes a business constant, and there no longer are discrete sets of risk events with periods of stability in between. Old supply chain management models begin to break down, bending under the strain of the unknown and the unexpected. There is a need for supply chains to flex at a rapid pace—to sense and respond at a new level.

In short, the time has come for a radical rethinking of supply chain management models.

We need a new science of supply chain volatility management. This new science upends traditional supply chain assumptions of continuous growth, nonstop globalization, and constant demand inflation. It calls on practitioners to abandon the traditional approach to responding to supply chain risk, which follows this predictable pattern:

- Be prepared when events happen
- React—according to plan if possible
- Recover
- Wait for the next event to happen
- Start the cycle again.

The new science of supply chain management—X-SCM—tackles the conditions of systemic volatility, continuous oscillation, and few or no rest or recovery periods. X-SCM recognizes the need for collective, rather than sequential, risk management; and facilitates collaboration on the new scale that is necessary for survival.

Part 1—X-SCM Explained In this chapter and Chapter 2, we explain the concept of X-SCM and put forth the X-SCM Management Framework—the framework that defines what follows in subsequent chapters. The X-SCM Framework addresses volatility on multiple levels: macro-factor, industry, firm and supply chain. It also provides an overview of the set of organizational best practices that are emerging to address this volatility.

In the remaining chapters, we examine in depth the changes that have occurred in various aspects of the "multidimensional supply chain" and offer recommendations for managing in the new environment. We divide our discussion of supply chains into two basic categories: the Tangible Supply Chain and the Intangible Supply Chain.

Part 2—The Tangible Supply Chain The old network design was stable, fixed, long-term, relatively inflexible and founded on the science of predictability. The new, best-practice network design is all about being able to flex in concert with a world that is itself in constant flux, by "flipping the switch" on assets, services, and suppliers when and as needed. In Chapter 3, we present this more integrative approach to dynamic network configuration management and provide rapidly deployable analytic tools for assessing the viability and fitness of global hubs and nodes. In Chapters 4 and 5, we examine the challenges and opportunities that are inherent in managing severe demand and supply flux, and in hedging supplier risk.

Part 3—The Intangible Supply Chain This part discusses aspects of the intangible supply chain— i.e., governance structure as well as the financial, cyber, and services supply chains. Chapter 6 contains a new supply chain risk management model, developed by the Supply Chain Council, that is designed to govern the processes around managing risk.

The case study on Cisco, in Chapter 7, describes how this world leader built a supply chain risk management organization and best practices and rolled them out worldwide. The Cisco case study demonstrates that companies that take a formal, systematic approach to mastering supply chain volatility will be more profitable, and they will have the processes, resources, partnerships, infrastructure, and management capabilities to sense, respond, and adapt to change far more rapidly than their competitors can. They will also capture markets and reduce risk exposure sooner and more successfully.

Next, in Chapters 8 and 9, we delve into the subject of the financial supply chain. The old financial model was based on discrete transactional exchanges. We apply new quantitative methods and tools developed in the fields of finance and financial risk management to supply chain management. This approach incorporates financially optimal solutions to supply chain issues that may—*or may not*—correspond to the answers that traditional physical or information-driven solutions would yield. These chapters discuss an amalgam of finance-based solutions that include risk hedging, tax strategies, and portfolio management. The toolset outlined in Chapter 9 demonstrates how portfolio management theory can be adapted to assessing the lifecycle maturity and profitability horizons of individual products and supply chains.

Part 3 also contains descriptions of groundbreaking new learning tools based on computer gaming, one of which was developed expressly as a companion to this book. Chapter 10, *Gaming X-SCM*, gives readers a glimpse into using gaming systems to simulate and explore risk scenarios. The URLs for these two gaming simulations are listed below.

Next, the book explores the cyber supply chain—i.e., the information/data flows and networks that enable X-SCM. Chapters 11 and 12 address the design and management of risk tolerant cyber supply chains, describing state-of-the-art information technology underpinnings, processes, and practices.

And Chapter 13 presents a model for governing cyber supply chain risk, a subject of increasing urgency with the alarming rise in and severity of cyber attacks on global corporations. The "cyber supply chain assurance model" we present was developed with the cooperation of major federal and private sector players, including the U.S. Department of Homeland Security (DHS), the National Security Agency (NSA), and Pfizer Inc.

Chapter 14—the final chapter in Part 3—looks at minimizing volatility in the service supply chain.

Part 4—When Things Go Terribly Wrong The penultimate section of our book is about managing effectively when the unthinkable happens, when a devastating event up-ends your supply chain. The chapter—written by the incident commander for the federal government at the World Trade Center during the aftermath of 9/11—lays out the operational guidelines and success factors for critical incident management. It is rich with procedures and best practices, fine-tuned through years of actual federal agency disaster response. It has a companion set of online forms to use in critical incident management which can be accessed at http://www.routledge.com/textbooks/harrington.

An online tool kit accompanies this book. This companion tool kit can be found at http://www.routledge.com/textbooks/harrington. In it, we make available a remarkable set of management supports:

- A spreadsheet-based analytic tool that can be used to perform a comparative analysis of total supply chain network costs by country. (Name of tool on website: Comparative Country Supply Chain ROI Analytic Tool.)
- A spreadsheet-based analytic tool that can be used to assess global insourcing vs. outsourcing options in supply chain network design. (Name of tool on website: Insourcing vs. Outsourcing Analytic Tool.)
- A predictive analytic tool designed to assess whether a company is ready to use supply chain risk management technologies and processes. (Name of tool on website: Supply Chain Risk Management Readiness Screener.) The URL and password are listed on the non-password protected section of the book's companion website (http://www.routledge.com/textbooks/harrington).
- An X-SCM risk simulation developed by Interactive Learning Solutions specifically to accompany this book. (Name of simulation: X-treme Supply Chain Simulation.) Access through a link on http://www.routledge.com/textbooks/harrington or directly at http://www.xtremesupplychainsimulation.com/.
- A real-time, multi-player supply chain game developed by the University of Maryland and Tu-Delft University in the Netherlands. To access the *Global Supply Chain Game—Distributor Game,* go to http://www.routledge.com/textbooks/harrington, and click on "Distributor Game." You may also access it directly by going to www.gscg.org, clicking on "Available Game," then "Distributor Games."

As a whole, the multidimensional supply chain requires a well-thought-out **enterprise risk management strategy and roadmap** for change management. Together the book and online tool kit and simulations represent the best multimedia package available today for understanding and learning how to manage extreme supply chain change.

This book is designed for anyone charged with managing part or all of a global supply chain. It represents a compilation of the best thinking on how to approach supply chain management in this era of the extreme. X-SCM is the new science of supply chain management. This book explains that science in theory and in practice, and provides a unique, practical toolset with which to manage the supply chain of volatility.

Notes

1   Sandor Boyson, Lisa H. Harrington, and Thomas M. Corsi, *In Real Time: Managing the New Supply Chain* (Westport, CT: Praeger, 2004), ix.
2   Ibid.

two
The X-SCM Management Framework

Dr. Sandor Boyson

In the past two years, an Army researcher, Steven Burnet, has overseen a study into human perception and bomb detection involving about 800 military men and women. During the study, researchers conducted exhaustive interviews with experienced fighters. They administered personality tests and measured depth perception, vigilance, and related abilities.

Burnet's team found that the men and women who performed best had the sort of knowledge gained through experience, but many also had superb depth perception and a keen ability to sustain intense focus for long periods of time. The ability to pick out odd shapes masked in complex backgrounds—a "Where's Waldo" type of skill that some call anomaly detection—also predicted soldiers' performance on some roadside-bomb simulations.

Researchers found that troops who were good at spotting bombs in simulations tended to think of themselves as predators, not prey. That frame of mind by itself may work to reduce anxiety, experts say.

The brains of elite troops also appear to register perceived threats in a different way from average enlistees. At the sight of angry faces, members of the Navy SEALs show significantly higher activation in the insular cortex than regular soldiers.[1]

Anomaly detection. Predator, not prey. Higher activation level in the face of threats. These traits are the critical success factors not only of bomb-detection units in the military today but also of the vanguard, best-practice commercial organizations that are seeking to sustain success in a global landscape pockmarked with extreme volatility and with countless economic, political, and environmental bombs that are ready to explode.

Thus, we have Cisco and other companies featured in this book committed to "perpetual vigilance," to becoming sense-and-respond supply chains that constantly scan their networks using business intelligence systems and exception reporting to detect anomalies that exceed tolerances. They have shown us that effective real-time risk management is the result not only of better supply chain data but also of breakthroughs in human factors productivity. Corporate supply chain officers exposed to an environment of constant high quality real-time data can hone their expert judgments and make higher quality, more accurate risk management decisions. We have Li & Fung, the legendary Chinese apparel trading company, with its keenly predatory supply chain "antennae" out, sensing for minute cost changes in the countries where it operates and poised to dynamically reconfigure networks to exploit emerging cost advantages. Such companies have shown us that agility in adapting to risk can open up new business opportunities.

We have high-activation supply chains, such as those of Wal-Mart or FedEx, that picked up early storm warnings and freed up managers on the ground in New Orleans to activate, mobilize, and do what was needed during Hurricane Katrina—freedom that is a critical factor in successful grassroots managerial activation in response to potential disruption.

These successes did not come easily. Each of these companies had to overcome a profound, institutional tendency toward denial and face up to a simple truth: The environment had shifted radically, and they had to shift with it to survive.

In the sections ahead, we will demonstrate that, although volatility has been a constant feature of the economy, industry, and supply chains, most firms historically have chosen to treat risk as a strategic and operational "outlier" that has not fundamentally shaped the choices they have made. We will also explain why, as risk and volatility have dramatically increased in recent years, and as the rates of change and variability have progressed exponentially, it has become almost impossible for companies to remain in denial.

In this chapter's final section, we will present a roadmap to the new science of X-treme supply chain management and summarize the set of practices that constitute what we believe is a better way forward.

A. Volatility as a Historical Constant: The Three Tiers of Change Drivers

"Volatility, like the speed of light, is a universal constant independent of the observer's motion."

Einstein's theory of relativity reformulated

Volatility is a constant in the supply chain. The model of ever-present supply chain volatility defined in Figure 2.1 is composed of three nested, interconnected rings. The outermost ring represents the macro factors in economy and society, such as growth or decline of gross domestic product (GDP), that generate oscillations, or waves of change. The next ring inward represents the industry/firm level that both absorbs waves of change and generates its own waves by inventing discontinuous technical innovations or by changing the profile of production or employment. Finally, the innermost ring represents the supply chain itself. It too absorbs waves of change from the economy, industry, and the firm and is molded by these forces, and it too generates waves of change by creating new interdependencies between nations and enterprises.

Volatility can emerge simultaneously in each of the rings and quickly spread in multiple directions across highly porous ring boundaries. It is a simple model in which entities (e.g. sub-systems) within a system interact and impact one another. These interrelationships prove highly consequential in determining attributes and impacts of both the overall system and individual factors or forces. For example, a decline in GDP can trigger a drop in employment, which can lead to lower sales, which can in turn cause "hibernation" behaviors in corporate inventory ordering. Another example would be a fire at a critical supplier's factory creating instability or imbalances that emanate outward from the innermost supply chain ring, disrupting production and sales and hurting corporate profitability.

In the sections below, we will briefly explore how each of these levels of volatility has historically manifested.

Volatility as a Macro-Level Constant

Macro-factor, industry and firm-level volatility have always been a constant of business. This fundamental reality—though often subsumed in the quest for stability—has been a fact of business life for a long time, particularly in those countries that have both pioneered global trade and opened themselves up to trade and competition.

In the United States, volatility has been tied to a 35-year cycle of advanced industrialization, free trade, and globalization. This cycle has triggered oscillatory waves across multiple macro factors, as shown in Table 2.1. In just 30 years, for example, oil imports increased from 48 percent to 78.4 percent of total oil consumption, significantly affecting the country's fiscal stability.

If we look back at history, we find that the increasing volatility faced by the United States as it globalized was not without precedent. Consider the case of England.

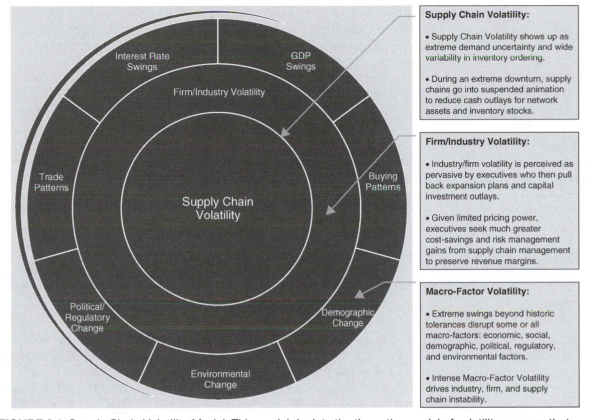

Supply Chain Volatility:

• Supply Chain Volatility shows up as extreme demand uncertainty and wide variability in inventory ordering.

• During an extreme downturn, supply chains go into suspended animation to reduce cash outlays for network assets and inventory stocks.

Firm/Industry Volatility:

• Industry/firm volatility is perceived as pervasive by executives who then pull back expansion plans and capital investment outlays.

• Given limited pricing power, executives seek much greater cost-savings and risk management gains from supply chain management to preserve revenue margins.

Macro-Factor Volatility:

• Extreme swings beyond historic tolerances disrupt some or all macro-factors: economic, social, demographic, political, regulatory, and environmental factors.

• Intense Macro-Factor Volatility drives industry, firm, and supply chain instability.

FIGURE 2.1 Supply Chain Volatility Model. This model depicts the three-tier model of volatility sources that ultimately affect supply chains. The first, and outermost, layer represents macro or systemic forces at work, such as interest rates, trade patterns, political stability, and the like. The second layer incorporates enterprise/business volatility—i.e., sales patterns, product success, company health, etc. The third, innermost, ring represents supply chain volatility, which incorporates those drivers in the two outer rings as well as its own set of variables.

Source: Sandor Boyson, Robert H. Smith School of Business, 2009.

TABLE 2.1. Oscillation nation: measures of volatility in the U.S. business environment

Measure	1977	1981	1989	1993	2001	2009
Real GDP growth	4.9%	8.4%	4.1%	0.5%	−0.5%	−5.5%
Consumer confidence	98.2	83	117.2	58.6	118.9	49.3
Oil imports as % of U.S. oil consumption	48.0%	46.2%	50.3%	55.9%	70.6%	78.4%
Federal reserve outlays as % of GDP	7.04%	5.69%	5.69%	6.20%	6.29%	14.51%
Personal savings rate	8.0%	9.8%	7.9%	5.70%	1.9%	4.3%

Source: Adapted from *Washington Post*, "Obama's Six Month Report Card," July 26, 2009, page A 17 (an extract from www.brookings.edu/index).

England's rise as a dominant international economic player—from the Industrial Revolution of the 1830s up to World War II a century later—began in a triangle formed by London, Liverpool, and Edinburgh that encompassed some 16 million people. Two industries, coal and textile production, were at the forefront of the transformation. By 1850, England had pioneered a shift to an industry-led economy and led the world into a new age of productivity. As its empire and dominance grew, however, so did its business volatility.

During the period of economic activity stretching from the end of 1854 through the middle of 1938, expansion cycles in England ran from 8 to 64 months; contraction cycles lasted from 6 to 81 months; and total business cycles ran from 26 to 135 months. There was no predictability in the country's economic environment. Talk about wild rides![2]

Profound structural change has been a source of tremendous volatility in many nations. Between 1900 and 1950, heavy industrial output increased 126-fold and light industry 40-fold, whereas agricultural output only increased four-fold—evidence of intense structural change in economies everywhere.[3]

This structural transformation has contributed to volatility in other areas as well. For example, the world's population has soared as improved standards of public health have transformed life expectancies. Meanwhile, environmental degradation, which has been inextricably linked to the pace of industrialization, has greatly increased. If we look at the instability of these macro factors in Table 2.2, we see an accelerative pattern of geometric variation.

Volatility as a Constant at the Industry/Firm Level

Wild variations play a cumulative role in markets. They are unexpected only by the fools of economic theory.[4]

The 30-year period of accelerative economic oscillation in the United States described earlier followed a period of relative stability after World War II. The change from stability to pronounced economic fluctuations created managerial anxiety and "C-suite" angst.

This shift in managerial mindset was anticipated by the futurist Alvin Toffler in his largely forgotten work, *The Adaptive Corporation.* Originally written as a secret strategic study for AT&T in the early 1970s, his book pointed to an increasingly competitive global market, rapid technical change and turbulent restructuring in the banking sector. Toffler warned:

TABLE 2.2. Standard reference dates for business cycles: Great Britain

Trough	Peak	Trough	Expansion (Months)	Contraction (Months)	Total (Months)
December 1854	September 1857	March 1858	33	6	39
March 1858	September 1860	December 1862	30	27	57
December 1862	March 1866	March 1868	39	24	63
March 1868	September 1872	June 1879	54	81	135
June 1879	December 1882	June 1886	42	42	84
June 1886	September 1890	February 1895	51	53	104
February 1895	June 1900	September 1901	64	15	79
September 1901	June 1903	November 1904	21	17	38
November 1904	June 1907	November 1908	31	17	48
November 1908	December 1912	September 1914	49	21	70
September 1914	October 1918	April 1919	49	6	55
April 1919	March 1920	June 1921	11	15	26
June 1921	November 1924	July 1926	41	20	61
July 1926	March 1927	September 1928	8	18	26
September 1928	July 1929	August 1932	10	37	47
August 1932	September 1937	September 1938	61	12	73

Source: National Bureau of Economic Research cited in: Clough Bancroft Shepard, *Economic History of Europe*, D.C. Heath and Company, Boston, 1947, page 665.

For many firms, 1955–1970 were years of almost uninterrupted straight-line growth in an equilibrium environment. In such a period, the formula for adaptation is relatively simple. Managers look smart—indeed, they very often are smart—if they simply do "more of the same." Since then, this straight-line strategy has become a blueprint for corporate disaster. The reason is simple. Instead of being routine and predictable, the environment has grown increasingly unstable, accelerative and revolutionary. Under such conditions all organizations become extremely vulnerable to outside forces or pressures. And managers must learn to cope with non-linear forces—i.e., situations in which small inputs can trigger vast results, and vice versa.[5]

In a 1999 article for *Scientific American*, the great mathematician Benoit Mandelbrot brilliantly captured the core reality of volatility that underlies advanced capitalist economies and markets. Mandelbrot said that this reality was swept under the rug by modern portfolio theory, which seeks to normalize risk and minimize the impacts of outlier events that fall outside of the "normal" bell-curve distribution model.

Fortunes are made and lost in sudden bursts of activity when the market seems to speed up and the volatility soars. Last September, for instance, the stock for Alcatel, a French telecommunications equipment manufacturer, dropped about 40 percent one day and fell another 6 percent over the next few days. In a reversal, the stock shot up 10 percent on the fourth day. The classical financial models used for most of this century predict that such precipitous events should never happen. A cornerstone of finance is modern portfolio theory, which tries to maximize returns for a given level of risk. The mathematics underlying portfolio theory handles extreme situations with benign neglect: it regards large market shifts as too unlikely to matter or as impossible to take into account. It is true that portfolio theory may account for what occurs 95 percent of the time in the market. But the picture it presents does not reflect reality, if one agrees that major events are part of the remaining 5 percent. An inescapable analogy is that of a sailor at sea. If the weather is moderate 95 percent of the time, can the mariner afford to ignore the possibility of a typhoon?

The presumption is that all price changes are distributed in a pattern that conforms to the standard bell curve. The width of the bell shape (as measured by its sigma, or standard deviation) depicts how far price changes diverge from the mean; events at the extremes are considered extremely rare. Typhoons are, in effect, defined out of existence.

Do financial data neatly conform to such assumptions? Of course, they never do. Charts of stock or currency changes over time do reveal a constant background of small up and down price movements—but not as uniform as one would expect if price changes fit the bell curve. These patterns, however, constitute only one aspect of the graph. A substantial number of sudden large changes—spikes on the chart that shoot up and down as with the Alcatel stock—stand out from the background of more moderate perturbations. Moreover, the magnitude of price movements (both large and small) may remain roughly constant for a year, and then suddenly the variability may increase for an extended period. Big price jumps become more common as the turbulence of the market grows—clusters of them appear on the chart. The discrepancies between the pictures painted by modern portfolio theory and the actual movement of prices are obvious. Prices do not vary continuously, and they oscillate wildly at all timescales.

Volatility—far from a static entity to be ignored or easily compensated for—is at the very heart of what goes on in financial markets.[6]

Mandelbrot's powerful reminder of the role volatility has continuously played in market economies and how it has affected the industries and firms within those markets has been echoed time and again by academic management theorists. In a seminal review article, "Environmental Volatility: A Reassessment of the Construct," Dugal and Gopalakrishnan trace the development of concepts of environmental volatility as related to organizational strategy.[7]

Dugal and Gopalakrishnan reference various aspects of volatility cited by researchers, including instability, dynamism, variability, stability, turbulence, discontinuity, and environmental change. Their own research examines "a process-based, resources-oriented view of volatility that argues that the volatility experienced by the firm is largely a function of the resources it has available to meet the demands made of it."[8]

Despite all of the studies, analyses and warnings by practitioner and academic researchers, few corporations implemented comprehensive risk programs or sought to take precautions against extreme volatility. Volatility largely remained a sort of background noise in the minds of C-suite executives. It is fair to say that volatility was a sleeping giant in the boardroom—until now.

Volatility as a Supply Chain Constant

Like managers at the industry and firm level, supply chain practitioners have not made systemic risk management a top-of-mind survival issue. Volatility and oscillations at the supply chain level traditionally have been perceived, categorized and sequentially managed as a series of narrowly focused, discrete operational risks. These risks are shared between the community of supply chain partners. This rather narrow interpretation of risk was identified by a literature review conducted for this section by Xiang Wan, a doctoral researcher at the University of Maryland's Robert H. Smith School of Business.

Tang defines supply chain risk management as "the management of supply chain risks through coordination or collaboration among the supply chain partners so as to ensure profitability and continuity."[9] The additional factors of profitability and continuity merit attention; some papers have shown that disruption in supply chains can have very costly repercussions in both the short and the long run. For example, Rice and Caniato cite the case of one company that estimated it suffered a $50 million to $100 million cost impact for each day its supply network was disrupted.[10]

In a competitive environment, many companies have developed supply chains that are complex to manage and are vulnerable to disruptions. In addition, the potential risks in supply chain operations increase exponentially when firms develop cooperative relationships across country boundaries. Political issues, seasonality, natural disasters, and so on all could potentially threaten the normal functioning of a supply chain. Added to these risks are demand risks and financial risks, which emanate from customers, stockholders, and the general vagaries of the market. It is unclear how many of these risks companies can anticipate and plan for; they are more likely, however, to be able to exercise leverage over supply-related risks.

Supply risk is "the potential occurrence of an incident associated with inbound supply from individual supplier failures or the supply market, in which its outcomes result in the inability of the purchasing firm to meet customer demand or cause threats to customer life and safety."[11] The risk includes both the probability of and the potential magnitude of loss.[12]

After the terrorist attacks of September 11, 2001, companies began to reassess commonly accepted strategies for sourcing, transportation, demand planning, and inventory. They recognized that the benefits of practices such as lean management and just-in-time deliveries of supplies and components need to be weighed and balanced against the risk of future disruptions in the timely receipt of materials.[13]

One important topic that has attracted increasing interest from academics and practitioners is how to create a resilient supply chain. Christopher and Heck define resilience as "the ability of a system to return to its original state or move to a new, more desirable state after being disturbed."[14] The notion of flexibility and adaptability are implicit in this definition.

Many scholars have researched ways to reduce the probability of risk and mitigate loss. Their findings offer a structure for understanding the ways in which people handle supply risk: managerial identification of the sources of supply chain risk,[15] managerial perception,[16] assessment and estimation of the risk,[17] and managerial strategies for risk mitigation.[18] The balance of this section will review supply risk, resilience, volatilities, and disruptions in the context of that structure.

Identifying Sources of Supply Chain Risk

Firms that are intent on analyzing and managing their supply chain risk often focus on identifying the sources of that risk. Numerous research papers have investigated the sources of supply chain risk and categorized them into three groups: supplier issues, supply chain collaboration issues, and uncontrollable events. Table 2.3 lists and describes the sub-sources in each category.

"Supplier issues" refers to risks that are mainly caused by the suppliers themselves. They include suppliers' capacity constraints, their ability to constantly keep their costs low, their ability to manage inventory levels, their managerial and decision making skills, and their overall quality.[19]

Blaming all supply risk on suppliers is inaccurate, and it is unfair to them. Supply risk and associated losses may also originate from other parts of a supply chain. If a buyer does not receive

TABLE 2.3. Supply risk sources

Source	Sub-source	Description	Reference
Suppliers' issues	Capacity Constraints	The ability of a system to produce an output quantity in a particular time period.	Lee, Padmanabhan, and Whang, 1997
	Constant low-cost capability	The capability for suppliers to continually lower the cost of the same goods or services.	Steele and Court, 1996
	Suppliers' inventory management	Supplier ability to manage raw materials, work-in-process, and finished goods inventory.	Krause and Handfield, 1999; Tomlin, 2006
	Managerial expertise	Supplier management attitude and ability to foresee market and industry changes.	Zsidisin, 2003
	Lack of qualified suppliers	The limited number of suppliers who can provide a stable, specified, high quality supply.	Noordewier et al., 1990; Zsidisin, 2003
Supply chain collaboration issues	Cycle time	The time between purchase request to a supplier and receipt.	Handfield, 1993; Hult, 1997
	Global suppliers	The ability to source from suppliers located in multiple countries.	Zsidisin, 2003
	Transportation	Methods to distribute, handle, and transport input and output throughout the supply chain	Noordewier et al., 1990; Lee and Billington, 1993
	Compatibility of information system	IS capability to transfer timely, accurate information between firms in supply chain.	Zsidisin, 2003; Lee et al., 2000; Lee, Padmanabhan, and Whang, 2004
	Shipment accuracy	The gap between the actual requests and the quantity shipped.	Steele and Court, 1996
Uncontrollable events	Disasters	Harm caused by natural or human disasters.	Baird and Thomas, 1990; Wagenaar, 1992
	Legal liabilities	Legally enforceable restrictions or commitments relating to the use of the material, product, and service.	Zsidisin and Ellram, 1999
	Market price increase for raw materials	Trends, events, or developments that may increase price of materials.	Steele and Court, 1996
	Technology changes	The unpredictability of changes in product tech	Robertson and Gatignon, 1998; Noordewier et al., 1990; Stump, 1995

an order fulfilled with quality goods delivered on time and in sufficient quantity, it might be because the buyer did not provide complete and correct order information to the supplier. Alternatively, the supplier could have filled the buyer's order on time with satisfactory quantity and quality, but the logistics service provider could be responsible for delays as well as damages to the goods in transit.

Thus we have an example of the second source of supply chain risk: supply chain collaboration issues. Supply chain collaboration issues are related to risks raised by suppliers, logistics service providers and buyers, especially by improper collaboration among participants in a supply chain. They include problems stemming from supply cycle time, global suppliers, transportation, information system compatibility, and shipment quality.[20]

The third group of supply chain risk sources includes uncontrollable events that are hard to predict and can't be controlled, such as natural and human disasters, legal liabilities, market price increases for raw materials, and technology changes.[21]

Factors Influencing Managerial Perception of Risk

The manner in which managers perceive and assess supply chain risks is influenced by any number of factors related to competitive market dynamics and the nature of the goods firms sell to the market. Table 2.4 presents some key research findings on factors that impact how managers perceive the sources of risk identified in Table 2.3. When facing a very unstable market, managers with high-profit items may view the potential sources of supply chain risk much differently than would managers of moderate- to low-profit items in a very stable market. Likewise, a manager of a company that sells high-technology items in a very competitive and volatile market would calculate each of the sources of risk identified in Table 2.3 differently than would a manager in a low-technology, stable environment.

TABLE 2.4. Factors influencing managerial perception of supply risk

Researcher	Results
Zsidisin, 2003	The profit impact of purchased item: high or low The nature of the product: new or old Unstable market price
Steele and Court, 1996	Supply-demand balance Raw materials cost and availability Rate of technology innovation Relationship with suppliers Production, logistics methods
Krajic, 1983	Supply monopoly or oligopoly conditions Pace of technology advancement Entry barriers indicating market concentration Logistics cost
Mitchell, 1995	Buyer demographics Job function Decision-making unit: cross departments or not Product characteristics: innovational or functional Degree of customer-supplier interaction Characteristics of customer-supplier market Firm size Organizational performance Factors in specific country: culture, values

Assessment and Estimation of Supply Chain Risk

After identifying the sources of supply chain risk and the factors that affect managerial perception of these risk sources, the next step is for managers to assess their supply chain risks and measure the potential costs of supply chain disruptions. Risk assessment helps firms to focus on the essential risks and select a strategy to mitigate their risks.

The supply risk assessment deals in large part with the buyer–supplier relationship, and therefore the "agency theory" is a good theoretical basis for this type of analysis. Agency theory explains the relationship between principals and the agents they assign or hire to do work on their behalf. The theory also is concerned with the parties' potential for different understandings of goals and tolerance for risk.[22]

In this context, the purchasing firm serves as the principal and the supplier as are the agent. There are a number of variables that influence the "contract" between the buyer and supplier, as shown in Table 2.5. These variables help us to assess supply chain risk based on agency theory.

Indeed, Table 2.5 outlines the essential elements of agency theory. Suppliers and buyers could potentially have a whole range of relationships, from a completely adversarial relationship to a collaborative one. The nature of their relationship, moreover, depends on any number of factors, such as each side's power in the relationship and the goals of each firm. Table 2.5 also highlights some of the potential areas of conflict or collaboration. Thus, a manager in a collaborative relationship with a primary or sole supplier may have a totally different supply chain risk assessment matrix than would a manager whose relationship with a primary or sole supplier is adversarial.

Even when managers have demonstrated that they recognize the importance of supply chain risk assessment and have assessed their positions relative to their major suppliers, they generally have invested few resources and little time in mitigating supply chain risks. Research has found that is difficult to perform cost-benefit or return on investment (ROI) analyses to justify certain risk-reduction programs or contingency plans.[23] Consequently, passive acceptance is often the default strategy, even when it is not appropriate.[24] Furthermore, as Repenning and Sterman point out, firms rarely invest in improvement programs in a proactive manner because "nobody gets credit for fixing problems that never happened."[25]

Survey research has consistently documented this failure to invest in supply chain risk management. Only 33 percent of respondents to a survey of supply chain executives said that that they paid "sufficient attention to supply chain vulnerability and risk mitigation actions."[26] Moreover, research by Mitroff and Alpaslan on preparing for terrorism found that only between 5 percent and 25 percent of *Fortune* 500 companies are prepared to handle crises or disruptions.[27]

TABLE 2.5. Variables in agency theory

Variable	Description
Information systems	Mechanism to inform the purchasing organization of supplier activities.
Outcome uncertainty	Degree of uncertainty about obtaining desired results.
Goal conflict	Some degree of conflict exists between the goals of the purchasing organization and those of the supplier.
Relationship length	The engagement in a long-term relationship where the purchasing organization will learn about the supplier.
Adverse selection	The misrepresentation of a supplier's abilities that result in its selection.
Moral hazard	Occurs when a supplier fails to expend the required efforts to meet the purchasing firm.

Risk Management Strategies

Even though managers, in general, have not devoted substantial resources to risk mitigation strategies, many such strategies do exist. They can be split into two classes: "risk avoiding" strategies focus on removing or stopping risk sources, while "loss reducing" strategies have the objective of reducing losses caused by the identified risk. Table 2.6 shows some of these strategies for risk mitigation.

It should be noted that these risk mitigation strategies are not additive. In fact, the pursuit of one strategy makes it impossible to pursue an alternative strategy. For example, a single-supplier strategy reduces the potential risks that might arise from global sourcing, but it increases the potential risk from total reliance on a single supplier's capability. Moreover, requiring suppliers to hold inventory may provide a necessary buffer to mitigate the consequences of a disaster, but it also may conflict with the need to deal with suppliers that have low-cost capabilities. Clearly, managers must have a holistic perspective when developing their overall risk mitigation strategies, as opposed to pursuing a single objective.

By developing specific risk mitigation strategies, managers are building resiliency into their supply chains. Rice and Caniato explore this concept and define it through the two components of resiliency: flexibility and redundancy. They assert that redundancy is achieved by maintaining capacity in such areas as inventory, additional production lines, qualifying and maintaining multiple suppliers, and maintaining a dedicated transportation fleet in order to respond to a disruption. They also state that flexibility is achieved by creating the capability to respond by using existing capacity that can be redirected or reallocated. Thus, managers whose supply chains are resilient are in the best position to mitigate risks from supply chain disruptions.[28]

One category of supply chain disruption that has driven the search for resiliency and received increasing attention in recent years results from a security breach and/or a terrorist attack. Lee and Wolfe discuss strategies for mitigating the effects of a security breach:

- comprehensive tracking and monitoring
- total supply network visibility
- flexible sourcing strategies, which include creating a local supply source, developing multiple sources for the same component or input material, and using suppliers with more than one manufacturing site
- balance inventory management
- product and process redesign, including standardization and postponement.[29]

Yossi Sheffi establishes that building redundancies into the supply chain is one possible way for managers to deal with a terrorist attack. However, he identifies and discusses some important trade-offs that must be made when moving forward with this strategy:

- redundancy vs. efficiency
- centralization vs. dispersion
- the lowest bidder vs. the known supplier
- government cooperation vs. direct shareholder value
- managing risk vs. delivering value.[30]

Supply Chain Security Initiatives

Finally, many authors have explained the security initiatives that were developed and launched by the United States government after September 11, 2001, to improve supply chain security. One example is the Container Security Initiative (CSI), launched by U.S. Customs and Border Protection (CBP) in 2002, which involves U.S. and foreign customs teams evaluating and investigating containers overseas prior to loading onboard a vessel destined for the United States. Another initiative is the Customs–Trade Partnership Against Terrorism (C-TPAT), also established in 2002. Companies in this program that have been certified as compliant with specified security measures have the benefit of reduced

TABLE 2.6. Strategies for risk mitigation

Strategy	Description	Source	Reference
"Risk Avoiding" Strategy			
Alliance with supplier	Building a long-term relationship with suppliers aiming to maximize joint profit.	Supplier capability constraint and constant low-cost capability	Smeltzer and Siferd, 1998
Supplier certification	Certifying suppliers that are capable to provide stable, qualified, low cost supply.	Lack of qualified suppliers	Lockhart and Ettkin, 1993; Larson and Kulchitsky, 1998
Communication system supported by IT	Building an efficient channel for information exchange.	Information system compatibility	Marcussen, 1996; Davenport, 1998
Implement quality management programs	Implementing programs to improve the abilities and activities of suppliers to satisfy the quality needs of the purchasing firm.	Supplier capability constraint	Choi and Liker, 1995
Single sourcing	The purchasing firm selects and uses only one supplier, when multiple suppliers are available.	Global suppliers	Newman, 1988; Larson and Kulchitsky, 1998.
Develop target costing with suppliers	Setting a planned selling price and subtracting the desired profit, marketing, and distributing costs, leaving the required manufacturing and procurement costs.	Constant low-cost capability	Newman and McKeller, 1995; Ellram, 1999
Supply contract	Legal constraints to make a supplier more efficient and qualified.	Market price increasing for raw materials	Tsay, 1999; Tang, 2006
Early supplier involvement	Purchasing firms involve suppliers at an early stage in the life cycle of a product.	Supplier capability constraint	LaBahn, 2000; Zsidisin and Smith, 2005
"Loss Reducing" Strategy			
Safety stock	Additional stock for products, supporting activities, and customer service held internally.	Supplier inventory management, shipment quality	Lee and Billington, 1993; Newman, Hanna, and Maffei, 1993
Multiple suppliers	Procurement of a good or service from more than one source.	Lack of qualified suppliers, disasters	Mitchell, 1995; Sheffi, 2001; Kleindorfer and Saad, 2005
Require suppliers to hold inventory	Additional stock for products held at the suppliers' firm.	Disasters	Lee and Billington, 1993; Newman, Hanna, and Maffei, 1993
Risk sharing mechanism	A mechanism that can fairly let purchasing and buying firms share risk.	All sources	Mentzer et al., 2001; Faisal et al., 2006

cargo inspections. These and other supply chain security programs have raised some concerns. For example, Rice and Caniato point out that security requires a continuous commitment and effort by many parties.[31] Additionally, there are continuing concerns that current efforts at inspecting import containers are insufficient and will require significant additional resource allocations if all containers are to be scanned prior to entry into the United States.[32]

Despite this plethora of research on supply chain risk and how to manage it, as well as operational experience and lessons learned, firms do not seem to have changed their posture toward, or investment in, formal risk management programming. Nor has there been much change in the comfort or confidence level of most supply chain managers vis-à-vis risk.

More than three-fourths of respondents in a recent McKinsey and Company study said that supply chain risk had dramatically increased over the past five years. To cope with increasing volatility during that period, 56 percent of the respondents said their companies (most with $1 billion or more in annual revenue) had increasingly centralized supply chain management.[33] This finding is consistent with a study conducted by *World Trade* and the Supply Chain Management Center of the Robert H. Smith School of Business at the University of Maryland in 2007. That survey of more than 300 North American companies engaged in international trade determined that supply chain success is closely associated with the size of a company's revenues. The greater the company's annual revenues, the more global its markets, the greater the centralization of supply chain management, and the greater the investment in and return on investment from supply chain technology and collaboration. The survey revealed a growing distance between the scale and efficiency of these supply chain "super-elite" companies and those that simply do not have the revenue or infrastructure to keep up.[34]

Yet it is ironic that the super-elite companies, which centralized their supply chain management to maximize economies of scale and control, were also the ones most dangerously exposed to the risks of the world market. The concentration of executive power at the headquarters level and the high level of integration of globalized supply chains were constraints on flexibility when disaster struck. In October 2008, when markets around the world froze in panic, the limits of this old supply chain management approach and its governance theories and practices became clearly apparent.

B. Hyper-Volatility: When Accelerative Change Overwhelms the Economy, Industry, and the Supply Chain

Hyper-Volatility in the Economy and Industry

All complex systems experience continuous random motion. Outer limits of normal random fluctuations define a normal range of volatility. An extreme movement beyond the normal range of volatility is called an event. The effect of an event is to put pressure on the norm and perhaps move the norm unless there is an equal balancing event.[35]

In October 2008, the collapse of global financial markets led to a stunningly swift disruption of industrial production and world trade. Those events produced a step-change in the rate of volatility that threatened to overwhelm our slow-moving business and government institutions. It is this type of acceleration to a whole new plane of disequilibrium that we call "hyper-volatility."

Researchers have repeatedly attempted to establish metrics or measures of volatility as a way to assess the intensity of externally induced stressors on an organization's strategic direction, operational processes, and resource base. Tosi, Aldag and Storey developed three indicators of volatility: market, technological, and earnings volatility.[36] Subsequently, Snyder and Glueck validated these indicators, lending support to the use of objective measures.[37] Thus, Dugal and Gopalakrishnan indicated that we can define volatility as "change in the rate of change, and measure it by a coefficient of variations from year to year (in order to abstract away the influences of major trends and to capture discontinuities)."[38]

When we apply this definition of volatility to the current state of the U.S. economy and measure the rate of change on a year-to-year basis, the results are disconcerting, to say the least. Just one example: UPS's second-quarter earnings in 2009 declined 49 percent compared to the same period of the previous year. At that point, package volumes in the United States had fallen for the sixth consecutive quarter as the recession caused businesses to reduce orders amid the highest unemployment rate in 26 years.[39]

When we examine the rate of change or volatility *within the span of a single year*, we are simply astonished:

> Volatility in oil markets in the past year has reached levels not seen since the energy shocks of the late 1970s and early 1980s. In one year, oil went to $145 a barrel, fell to $33 a barrel, and then went up to $70 a barrel.[40]

Clearly, something is different. The speed at which change is occurring is overwhelming us. Extreme or hyper-volatility is taking hold. The evidence of extreme volatility that surrounds us can be seen everywhere in newspaper headlines and website banners:

> The stock market was more volatile last year than in any year since 1933. There were 42 days when the S&P 500 gained or lost more than 3 percent. The previous five years had only five such days.[41]

> The Commerce Department said yesterday in Washington that gross domestic product has shrunk 3.9 percent in the past year, indicating the worst slump since the Great Depression.[42]

> "A lot of things happened, a lot came together, [and] created probably the worst financial crisis, certainly since the Great Depression and possibly even including the Great Depression," Federal Reserve Board Chairman Ben Bernanke said at the start of a town-hall meeting in Kansas City.[43]

In April 2009, Eichengreen and O'Rourke, professors of economics at the University of California at Berkeley and Trinity College Dublin, respectively, presented compelling evidence of the severity of the global economic decline even in comparison to the Great Depression.[44] By analyzing the steepness in decline of world industrial production and trade from peaks in June 1929 and April 2008, they demonstrated (as shown in Figures 2.2 through 2.4) that the current decline has been worse than that experienced in the 1930s.

Eichengreen and O'Rourke found that the declines in global stock markets and in world trade today are steeper and faster than those during the Great Depression. Given the pivotal role the collapse of world trade played in the Great Depression, the latter finding was particularly troubling.

In a September 2009 update, the authors made the following observations:

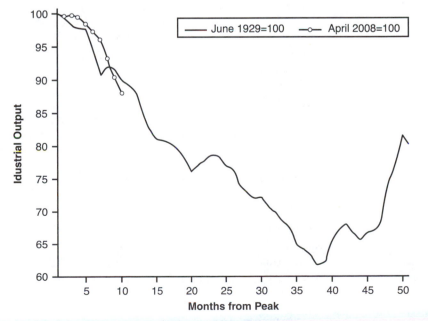

FIGURE 2.2 World industrial output, now vs. then.

Source: Eichengreen and O'Rourke (2009) and IMF.

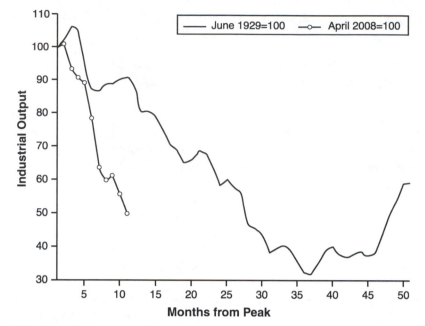

FIGURE 2.3 World stock markets, now vs. then.

Source: Global Financial Database.

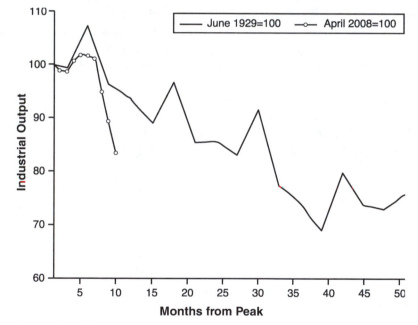

FIGURE 2.4 The volume of world trade, now vs. then.

Source: League of Nations Monthly Bulletin of Statistics, http://www.cpb.nl/eng/research/sector2/data/trademonitor.html

- World stock markets have rebounded a bit since March, and world trade has stabilized, but these are still following paths far below the ones they followed in the Great Depression.
- There are new charts for individual nations' industrial output. The "Big 4" European Union nations divide north–south; today's German and British industrial output are closely tracking their rate of fall in the 1930s, while Italy and France are doing much worse.
- The North Americans (United States and Canada) continue to see their industrial output fall approximately in line with what happened in the 1929 crisis, with no clear signs of a turnaround.

- Japan's industrial output in February was 25 percentage points lower than at the equivalent stage in the Great Depression. There was, however, a sharp rebound in March.[45]

To make matters worse, at the same time that hyper-volatility is hitting the global economy, the world is experiencing accelerative environmental degradation. Concerns about the loss of species and the potential effects of rising temperatures are adding to the sense of crisis.

This radical, interconnected volatility is overwhelming our strategies, our systems, and our processes. Neither we nor our organizations have ever encountered this kind of volatility before.

Hyper-Volatility in the Supply Chain

Rapidly rising connectivity within global systems—both economic and technological—increases the risk of deep collapse. That's a collapse that cascades across adaptive cycles, a kind of pancaking implosion of the entire system as higher-level adaptive cycles collapse, which causes progressive collapse of lower levels [to create a "panarchy."][46]

The Great Recession has shown us the truth of that statement. Nowhere is this interconnectedness more evident than in the ocean shipping industry, which has served as the workhorse of global trade, moving electronics from Asia to North America and Europe, and cars and agricultural products from North America to Asia and Latin America. With the rapid decline of production and demand in those markets, ocean carriers have been forced to remove excess capacity from their fleets. At this writing, there is much talk about the so-called "ghost fleet" of ships moored off the coast of Malaysia some 50 miles from the Port of Singapore. Rumor has it that this collection of idle vessels is at least equal in number and tonnage to the combined navies of the United Kingdom and the United States. They are floating there in suspended animation, waiting for demand to materialize in the West.[47]

A related but less well-known phenomenon has developed on the other side of the world, in the Chesapeake Bay, where in early 2009 ships were waiting until there was enough business to justify entering the Port of Baltimore.

One such ship was the *Hoegh Trekker*, as long as two football fields, which arrived at the anchorage ahead of schedule because it carried fewer vehicles from the Far East than had been expected, according to James Perduto, vice president of marketing for Hoegh Autoliners. At the end of March 2009, the Port of Baltimore was storing 57,000 cars, about 10,000 more than it typically stored before the recession. "People are not purchasing cars at the rate they were pre-recession, which means that dealers are not selling cars," said Richard Scher, spokesman for the Maryland Port Administration. "There's not demand to retrieve those cars at ports like Baltimore," he told a local newspaper.[48]

These similar situations on different sides of the world were directly connected via one overarching supply chain, which has served as a highly efficient central nervous system for quickly transmitting the deflationary effects of lost demand—much as a transverse wave oscillates in two directions simultaneously. A transverse wave is best demonstrated by anchoring one end of a ribbon or string and holding the other end in your hand. Moving your hand up and down and then side to side creates simultaneous, independent wave motions, or transverse waves.[49]

In fact, this transverse wave of hyper-volatility is destabilizing the entire global maritime industry and the related intermodal transportation sector. The effect on these industries is clearly illustrated in the following passage:

Coming off decades of robust growth, freight intermediaries are scrambling to navigate even steeper drops in worldwide trade volumes than during the Great Depression. For example, the giant CMA CGM Group slashed capacity between Asia and South America's East Coast. In order to adjust to the current economic situation and to better adapt its offer to the market demand, CMA CGM Group—together with its partners—has decided to reduce capacity by 35 percent.[50]

We can further track the spread of economic oscillations to the trucking companies that pick up goods from the docks and transport them to customers. In 2008, in the United States alone, over 3,000 trucking companies declared bankruptcy. Those that stayed in business were forced to cut capacity drastically to survive as the contagion of global economic collapse continued to ripple across the supply chain landscape.[51]

These sectoral effects are a subset of the larger, deflationary disequilibria in the global supply chain clearly evidenced by trade statistics. As a result of the "Great Recession" and the contraction in domestic demand in 2008 and 2009, there was a 30 percent drop in Asian goods imported through the largest U.S. port, the Port of Long Beach; a 25.7 percent drop in exports from China to the United States; and a 29 percent drop in exports from China to Thailand, to which China exports electronic components for assembly and shipment back to China for eventual export.

Clearly the international daisy chain of interconnected supply chain functions is driving hyper-volatility in nations and industries around the world.

C. The New Science of Volatility Management: De-Risking from the Multidimensional Supply Chain

> *Managing for resilience involves guarding against collapses even though they might be rare. It implies a precautionary principle.*[52]

The extreme volatility discussed in the previous section is threatening to overwhelm supply chain managers. They have no prior training, experience or operational precedent that could prepare them for managing the degree of volatility and exceptional rate of change we are experiencing today. *In short, our conventional supply chain theories, methods, and tools have failed us.*

Unfortunately, no commonly accepted, next-generation weapon set we can put in the hands of embattled supply chain managers has emerged to take their place. The new science of "X-treme Supply Chain Management" that we propose in this book seeks to fill that gap by addressing the extraordinary challenges and urgent needs of supply chain managers today. These needs include:

1. The need for a wholly new model of supply chain risk management that goes beyond a narrow, sequential identification and management of operational risks. This new model needs to account for systemic risk because of the increasing fragility of interlocked systems and networks. It must also fully recognize that the supply chain itself is a source of extreme volatility for its participants in ways never or seldom openly acknowledged.

Supply chain management, and in particular inventory management, has been cited as being partly responsible for the stability that characterized the U.S. economy in the 1980s and 1990s. Consider this analysis:

> In the 1970s, cycles were volatile and were marked by wild swings. But by the mid-1980s, a period known as the "Great Moderation" had taken hold. With computers helping businesses manage their inventory, policy makers paying more attention to inflation and perhaps just some good luck, business cycles were mild and recessions were shallow.[53]

In a 2008 article, Davis and Kahn attributed the decline in volatility of aggregate economic activity to "a technological story focused on the durable goods sector and in particular on inventory management." They also discussed how improved supply chain management could explain reduced volatility.[54]

Missing from the discussions of supply chain management's contribution to the Great Moderation was an acknowledgment that, as demonstrated earlier, supply chain management practices had increased volatility through the over-integration of supply chain actors, institutions and industries. Now, decades later, supply chain management's role as a destabilizing agent will be further reinforced by the severe cash-conservation strategies and inventory-simplification initiatives that some major companies are launching. To save on shelf space, stock maintenance, inventory, warehousing, and transportation costs, they are reducing product variety and funneling consumer demand into fewer product lines. Walgreens, for example, has reduced its selection of "superglue" products from 25 to 11. Wal-Mart reduced its selection of tape measures from 24 items to just four. And the grocery chain Kroger has cut the number of cereal brands it carries in its stores by 30 percent. Overall, analysts predict a 15 percent reduction in large retail chains' product assortment over the next year.[55]

The important message here is this: new supply chain strategies for survival will themselves act as oscillatory triggers and generate internal waves of volatility. These internally generated disturbances, combined with the even more severe external waves of volatility, will hit companies full-bore and will force supply chain managers to change their thinking.

X-treme Supply Chain Management requires thinking about supply chain management from a systemic risk perspective. How do you map, measure, and balance the probabilities of systemic disruption across the supply chain? This is the core challenge the new science of volatility management seeks to address.

2. The need for a wholly new model of volatility management that spans the "multidimensional" supply chain. The model must encompass not only the traditional product supply chain but also the end-to-end service, financial, and cyber processes to which the supply chain management concept is increasingly being applied. Why is this important? Traditional product supply chains depend to a significant degree on support from service, financial, and information organizations and processes. Without that support, a supply chain's ability to support corporate strategies will be jeopardized. This is a clear and present danger: in our research with dozens of organizations, for example, we found an utter failure to apply supply chain risk management practices to the information systems that constitute the fundamental platform for global supply chain operations.

In addition, each of these supply chain dimensions can exist in a "pure play" version: a service, financial, or IT value chain can serve as a complete and self-contained business ecosystem with its own distinct operational and marketplace risks.

Companies need to apply best practices in risk management across the multiple dimensions that constitute the global supply chain today. In Table 2.7, we briefly define these dimensions and suggest appropriate governance mechanisms. Each of those dimensions is covered by a complete chapter later on in this book.

These seemingly disparate types of supply chains are really facets of a single, multidimensional supply chain. The multidimensional nature of today's supply chains requires a new type of managerial oversight, one that is capable of spanning these dimensions while signaling to customers that the firm has a sophisticated grasp of and control over risk.

The insurance industry's experience highlights the importance of devoting resources to managing risk. Confronted by problems like hurricanes, pandemics, wildfires, identity theft, investment volatility, and more, insurers are hiring chief risk officers (CROs) in an attempt to foresee and manage those risks. Many CRO positions are being created because outside auditors believe it demonstrates recognition of the importance of risk management and an enterprise risk management strategy, according to Terry Fleming, vice president of the Risk and Insurance Management Society's board of directors. "A strong CRO position is a demonstration to the customers of the business that, despite what is going on in the economy, there is a renewed commitment to managing the exposures to loss," Fleming said.[56]

Risk Boards are increasingly being constituted at the C-suite level function as governance and policy-making arms. These boards are bringing together business unit executives to set enterprise-wide risk management objectives; conduct systemic risk assessments; define key performance indicators; and drive supply chain process change through incentive/penalty regimes. In support of Risk Board operations, Corporate Risk Registries are being deployed as shared online databases to capture priority risks and assign them to specific risk owners; to list actions and resources required to address those risks; and to track risk audit schedules and progress toward milestones.

3. The need for a wholly new model of supply chain network efficiency that replaces traditional economies of scale and scope with those that are based on a concept we have named "contingent

TABLE 2.7. Managing volatility across the multi-dimensional supply chain

Supply chain dimension	Business ecosystem characteristics	Key volatility drivers	Priority volatility management actions
Physical/ manufacturing	Ecosystem is composed of connected activity centers for sourcing, processing, and distributing products to end customers	Nodal or inter-nodal disruptions in supply; or wild oscillations in end-customer demand	Risks identified, assessed, registered, and mitigated by Risk Management Board composed of Chief Operations Officer, Corporate Risk Officer, product development and manufacturing managers, supply chain managers and supplier/customer representatives
Service	Ecosystem is composed of connected activity centers for customer interaction, services definition/personalization, aggregation of service/ content modules, and delivery to end customers	Interruptions due to poor quality of service (QOS), unavailability of critical service elements, lack of competitive service pricing or feature sets, and wild oscillations in end-customer demand	Risks identified, assessed, registered and mitigated by Risk Management Board composed of Chief Service Officer, Corporate Risk Officer, internal service providers, and corporate IT managers and supplier/customer service representatives
Financial	Ecosystem is composed of cash/credit flows superimposed upon physical or service supply chain transactions between customers/ payers, institutional intermediaries, and service/product suppliers	Macro-economic turmoil disrupting availability of credit, rapid foreign exchange fluctuations disrupting terms of trade, financial failures by customers or suppliers blocking cash flows or new local tax incentive regimes altering the competitive geography of the supply chain network	Risks identified, assessed, registered, and mitigated by Risk Management Board composed of Chief Financial Officer, Corporate Risk Officer, internal accounting staff, and supplier/customer finance/ trade representatives
Cyber	Ecosystem is composed of connected activity centers for IT acquisition policy, systems integration, network operations, and hardware/ software development	Network outages due to malicious code, denial of service attacks or insider sabotage aimed at undermining critical infrastructure	Risks identified, assessed, registered, and mitigated by Risk Management Board composed of Chief Information Officer, Corporate Risk Officer, internal cyber-security staff and supplier/customer IT representatives

scale." Contingent scale is the ability of the enterprise to rapidly size its assets and services up or down as required by extreme demand fluctuations. These resizing capabilities are executed through flexible contracts with external providers. Contingent scale capability is a critical aspect of best practice supply chains and, indeed, enterprise business volatility management.

Historically, supply chains network development involved the slow buildup of assets and services over time, largely through capital expenditures with long amortization periods or through strategic partnerships. In the past decade and a half, however, the pace of network acquisition has stepped up as "big bang" approaches to globalization have produced explosive international growth. Supply chains, as a result, wildly splay out in all directions as companies source and sell in a rapidly growing complement of markets.

Corporate expenditures on implementing and maintaining these global supply chain infrastructures have been enormous. Companies have hard-wired infrastructure assets into their operations networks in order to meet rapidly growing demand. However, as the global economic crisis has unfolded, the excess capacity built into these hard-wired, asset-heavy networks has saddled companies with huge and burdensome costs.

In the present environment that burden has become a considerable liability. Accordingly, companies are looking for more flexible ways in which to build robust networks that can scale capacity and throughput up or down with speed that matches rapid rate of change in market conditions. These new contingent scale networks have a tremendous competitive benefit to companies: they enable them to hedge financial risks and conserve cash.

In this way, corporate objectives for reducing financial risk and conserving cash can be addressed by converting fixed costs into variable costs through the extension of outsourcing and leasing arrangements for network assets, products, and services. An example we will discuss in Chapter 7 is Cisco's strategy of locking in "first to buy" rights from alternative critical suppliers. The networking systems manufacturer is willing to pay a premium to ensure that it will be able to secure vital products as needed. In this way it can avoid disruptions in product lines that are major revenue generators.

Other examples include companies that rapidly find and lock in distribution center capacity through Internet-based exchanges such as SpaceSpecials.com, which catalogues available specialized warehousing facilities by region and ZIP code. An even more dramatic example is a U.S. company that manufactures laptops in China. This company can completely eliminate its global network of distribution centers by contracting with FEDEX to pick up final products from its factory in Shenzen and deliver them within 24 hours directly to consumers in over 100 U.S. cities. This "China Direct Strategy" (first identified by Ivan Su of Soochow University, Taiwan) enables the manufacturer to achieve contingent scale economies in the face of uncertain demand.

In order to reach contingent scale economies in the supply chain, companies must build capabilities that allow them to search for all available assets, services, knowledge, and capital outside the firm as well as secure "usage rights" to those resources.

"Contingent-scale supply chain networks" in essence are ad hoc, dynamically formed networks created specifically to address the volatile nature of business today. They are a far cry from the fixed, brittle (and easily disrupted) structures of old-style global supply chain designs. These differences are shown graphically in Figure 2.5.

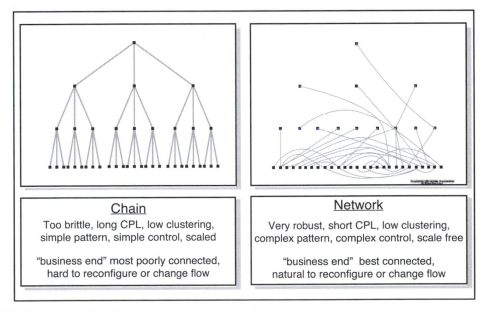

FIGURE 2.5 Chains vs. networks.

Source: Reproduced from Cares, Jeffrey "Distributed Adaptive Logistics," *Information Age Warfare Quarterly*, Winter 2005, Vol. 1, No. 1.

Produced for the U.S. Department of Defense, Figure 2.5 illustrates the difference between the traditional and networked supply chain. The following discussion explains why the flexible networked model is more effective in managing volatility.

> At the left is a prototypical, hierarchical supply chain. This chain is brittle and requires quite a bit of re-routing/retrograding to move commodities from one side of the chain to the other. In addition, although its simple pattern suggests simple control, an enemy likewise has a simple task to understand and influence this network. Since it is not a scale-free network, it will not easily respond to changes in a complex environment. Since it is not a complex network, it cannot exploit the S-curve effect of nimble reconfiguration. In addition, notice a particular feature of using such chains for logistics: the most important nodes—the ones in contact with the enemy—are the least connected.
>
> Contrast this with the network on the right, a scale-free network. This network is very robust and has a short "characteristic path length" (CPL, the average distance from one side of the network to another). It is scale-free, which means it can quite naturally adapt to changes in the competitive environment, and although its complex pattern requires complex control, the network is nonetheless more protected against efforts by an enemy to understand the intent behind its operations. Finally, note how the most important nodes in the network—those in contact with the enemy—are very well connected.[57]

As defined above, the military has cited the need for a new model of supply chain design that can be highly flexible in the face of attack. Its planners have put forward a model of ad-hoc, networked, and scale-free supply chains to address this need. Scale-free, in this context, means fluid rather than fixed supply chain networks; networks that can scale according to need rather than according to a fixed, 5- or 10-year network configuration plan. In confronting the enemy of extreme volatility, corporate managers are similarly seeking new supply chain models and practices as well, such as the contingent scale efficiencies described previously. The lessons of warfighting, in effect, are translatable to the commercial sector. They espouse a culture of extreme and rapid adaptability for networks and business operations—traits that are increasingly necessary in the current and foreseeable business environment.[58]

In summary, a new science of supply chain volatility management is emerging (Table 2.8 summarizes the chief characteristics of new vs. old supply chain science). It is emerging in direct response to the convergence of three needs:

1. The need for a wholly new model of supply chain risk management that goes beyond a narrow and sequential identification and management of operational risks, and accounts for systemic risk;
2. The need for a wholly new model of volatility management capable of spanning the multidimensional supply chain—not only the traditional physical product supply chain but also the financial, the cyber and the service supply chains;
3. The need for a wholly new model of supply chain network efficiency that replaces traditional economies of scale and scope with those based on the "contingent scale" concept, which emphasizes flexibility, and risk hedging.

In the chapters ahead, we will detail the features of this emerging science of supply chain volatility management and make the case that this is the next major evolution of supply chain management, and indeed, business management.

TABLE 2.8. Features of the new vs. old supply chain science

Old Supply Chain Science	New Supply Chain Science
1. *Supply Chain Management Strategy*	**1. *Supply Chain Management Strategy***
Key challenges are managing explosive demand growth and unfettered export-oriented globalization; and an inflationary environment with 10% annual growth rates in key emerging markets.	Key challenges are managing decelerating or steady state demand; a spiral trend to protectionism and inward-oriented regionalization; and a deflationary environment with even key emerging markets not resuming historic growth patterns.
Ever expanding investment in product feature set innovations & distribution across broader geographies and time zones.	Supply chain hibernation/slowdown of spending on product, inventory and distribution to hoard cash.
2. *Supply Chain Network Design*	**2. *Supply Chain Network Design***
Emphasis is on the science of predictability: fixed network of stable long-term hubs and nodes with "optimized" interactions between them.	Emphasis is on the science of adaptability and robustness: scale-free networks organized around risk-hedging.
Network assets such as distribution centers are seen as capital investments to be carefully planned for, acquired and absorbed into a formal network design over a long term period.	Network assets are seen as variable costs; candidate assets and services (e.g. available leased warehouse capacity in a given region) are constantly being catalogued; usage rights are negotiated on an as needed basis.
Achieving long term scale and scope economies are dominant objectives in setting network capacity and throughput targets.	Achieving flexible, contingent scale economies are deemed necessary to respond to a range of high/low requirements posed by alternate planning scenarios.
3. *Demand Management*	**3. *Demand Management***
Forecast-based demand management, with growth expectations and over-ordering routinely built into corporate forecasts (bullwhip effect).	Risk-based demand management, with deflationary expectations and under-ordering routinely built into corporate forecasts.
Demand signals managed separately by channel, with customer interactions recorded and segregated by channel.	Integrated demand signal repository enables 360 degree view of a customer, with multichannel interactions recorded in a single customer record.
4. *Inventory Management*	**4. *Inventory Management***
Inventory as a business necessity with the primary imperative being risk-hedging against spikes in demand through internal holdings of inventory buffer stocks.	Inventory as a business risk shared with supply chain partners through a virtualized multi-echelon inventory system that enables each partner to tap the collective inventory, reduce or eliminate internal buffer stock holdings and avoid financial over-exposure.
Inventory replenishment seen as a tactical response to a very visible short term demand pattern showing in real-time point of sale data.	Inventory replenishment seen as smart strategic response to hidden or emerging demand patterns detected by deep data mining of integrated multichannel demand signal repositories combined with other market intelligence.
5. *Supplier Management*	**5. *Supplier Management***
Rather inflexible supply base. Strong reliance on Tier 1 critical supplier relationships built up over time make it difficult to "unlock" in times of disruption or market volatility. Control of costs and risks often difficult due to "supplier monopoly."	Highly flexible and risk-hedged supply base. Strong reliance on setting up standardized process for pre-qualifying alternate core suppliers and pre-negotiating "first to buy" contracts with them to use as needed to secure critical supplies.
Tier 1 suppliers benefit from Tier 2 sub-suppliers' cost-efficiencies and do not pass along savings to company customer.	Company buys all supplies centrally needed by both its Tier 1 and Tier 2 suppliers, keeping all the volume discount savings for itself.

(Continued Overleaf)

TABLE 2.8. Continued

Old Supply Chain Science	New Supply Chain Science
6. *Supply Chain Collaboration*	**6. *Supply Chain Collaboration***
Visibility between supply chain partners usually limited to one link forward and/or back in the chain.	Visibility between supply chain partners extended 2–4 links backward and forward in the chain.
IT visibility/collaboration systems put into place between core partners to help manage demand/supply transactions.	IT visibility and shared Business Intelligence systems are intensively deployed to manage the collective operations and strategic financial performance of the extended supply chain.
7. *Performance Metrics*	**7. *Performance Metrics***
Supply chain flexibility is presently measured by the ability of the supply chain to respond to an unplanned 20% increase in demand on sustainable basis. This metric has a built-in assumption of/bias toward expecting an upward spike in demand.	Supply chain flexibility can also be measured by the ability of the supply chain to respond to an unplanned 20% decline in demand on a sustainable basis. This measure, intending to address extreme economic uncertainty, might better frame the concept and metric of flexibility.
Production/distribution capacity is measured by the current network of plant, property and equipment; its utilization by the firm and its core suppliers; and volume of product moving through the network or throughput in a given period. Increasing or decreasing throughput is currently considered a time-intensive process to re-balance and achieve new *scale or scope efficiencies*.	Production/distribution capacity includes the capacity held in reserve through pre-negotiated first to buy arrangements with alternate suppliers of products, facilities or services. The ability to rapidly scale up or scale back reserve capacity is a formidable advantage in the face of highly uncertain demand. This can be measured in the speed of time it takes to size up or down network throughput by X% and indicates *contingent scale efficiencies*.
Metrics of supplier management focus on quality and cost.	Metrics of supplier management focus on speed to replace whole sets of suppliers.
8. *Risk Management*	**8. *Risk Management***
Ineffective internal governance: segregation of corporate risk, IT security and supply chain/operations functions.	Risk Board (composed of Corporate Risk, IT Security and Supply Chain/Operations Executives) governs with a unity of command across the product, service, cyber and financial supply chains.
No comprehensive and ongoing assessment of risks across the extended supply chain. Reactive cultural attitude: off-load risk to weaker supply chain partner.	Continuous surveillance of risks across the extended supply chain, with constant re-calculation of highest likelihood/severity risks and recovery time targets for key network hubs and nodes, process flows and specific partners.
No formal registration of priority risks in a supply chain risk registry.	Supply chain-wide formal risk registry that identifies a priority risk and risk owner and defines agreed upon mitigation actions, and monitoring timetables.
Critical incident management is largely based on internal corporate resources and activities.	Critical incidence management techniques mobilize supply chain-wide energy response resources; and coordinate private/public response activities with shared management templates.

Notes

1 Carey, Benedict. "In Battle, Hunches Prove to Be Valuable," *New York Times*, July 28, 2009.

2 National Bureau of Economic Research, cited in: Clough, Bancroft Shepard. *Economic History of Europe* (Boston: DC Heath & Company, 1947), 665.

3 Excerpted from Patel, Surendra. *Technological Transformation* (Helsinki: Routledge Press, 1989).

4 Taleb, Nassim. "The Pseudo-Science Hurting Markets," ft.com, October 23, 2007, http://www.fooledbyrandomness.com/FT-Nobel.pdf

5 Toffler, Alvin. *The Adaptive Corporation* (New York: Bantam Books, 1985), ix.

6 Mandelbrot, Benoit. "How Fractals Can Explain What's Wrong with Wall Street," *Scientific American*, September 15, 2008 (reprint of a 1999 article), http://www.scientificamerican.com/article.cfm?id=multifractals-explain-wall-street

7 Dugal, Mohinder, and Shanthi Gopalakrishnan. "Environmental Volatility: A Reassessment of the Construct," *International Journal of Organizational Analysis* 8, no. 4 (2000): Database: Business Source Premier (1993–2002), 10553185.

8 Ibid.

9 Tang, C. "Perspectives in Supply Chain Risk Management," *International Journal of Production Economics* 103 (2006): 451–488.

10 Rice, James B. Jr., and Federico Caniato. "Building a Secure and Resilient Supply Network," *Supply Chain Management Review* (September 2003).

11 Zsidisin, G.A. "Defining Supply Risk: A Grounded Theory Approach," Proceedings from the Decision Sciences Institute Annual Meeting, San Diego, Calif., 2002.

12 Yates, J.F., and E.R. Stone. "The Risk Construct," in J. Yates (Ed.), *Risk Taking Behavior* (New York: John Wiley & Sons, 1992), 1–25; Mitchell, V.W. "Organizational Risk Perception and Reduction: A Literature Review," *British Journal of Management* 6 (1995): 115–133.

13 Martha, J., and S. Subbakrishna. "Targeting a Just-in-case Supply Chain for the Inevitable Next Disaster," *Supply Chain Management Review* (September/October 2002): 18–23.

14 Christopher, M. "The Agile Supply Chain: Competing in Volatile Markets, Industrial Marketing Management," 29, no. 1 (2000): 37–44. Delporte-Verneiren, D.J.E., P.H.M. Vervest, and E. van Heck. "In Search of Margin for Business Networks," BLED 2005 Proceedings (aisel.aisnet.org).

15 Dean, T., and R. Brown. "Pollution Regulations as a Barrier to New Firm Entry: Initial Evidence and Implications for Future Research," *Academy of Management Journal* 38, no. 1 (1995): 288–303; Walton, S.V., R.B. Handfield, and S.A. Melnyk. "The Green Supply Chain: Integrating Suppliers into Environmental Management Processes," *International Journal of Purchasing & Materials Management* 34, no. 2 (1998): 2–11.

16 Williams, S., M. Zainuba, and R. Jackson. "Affective Influences on Risk Perceptions and Risk Intention," *Journal of Managerial Psychology* 18, no. 2 (2003): 126–138.

17 Zsidisin, G.A., L.M. Ellram, J.R. Carter, and J.L. Cavinato. "An Analysis of Supply Risk Assessment Techniques," *International Journal of Physical Distribution & Logistics Management* 34, no. 5 (2004): 397–413.

18 Tang, "Perspectives in Supply Chain Risk Management."

19 Lee, H.L., V. Padmanabhan, and S. Whang. "Information Distortion in a Supply Chain: The Bullwhip Effect," *Management Science* 43, no. 4 (1997): 546–558; Steele, P.T., and B.H. Court. *Profitable Purchasing Strategies: A Manager's Guide for Improving Organizational Competitiveness Through the Skills of Purchasing* (London: McGraw-Hill, 1996); Krause, D.R., and R.B. Handfield. *Developing a World-Class Supply Base* (Tempe, Ariz.: Center for Advanced Purchasing Studies, 1999); Tomlin, B. "On the Value of Mitigation and Contingency Strategies for Managing Supply Chain Disruption Risks," *Management Science* 52, no. 5 (2006): 639–657; Zsidisin, G.A. "A Grounded Definition of Supply Risk," *Journal of Purchasing and Supply Management* 9 (2003): 217–224; Zsidisin, G.A. "An Agency Theory Investigation of Supply Risk Management," *Journal of Supply Chain Management* 39, no. 3 (2003): 15–27; Noordewier, T.G., G. John, and J.R. Nevin. "Performance Outcomes of Purchasing Arrangement in Industrial Buyer-Vendor Relationships," *Journal of Marketing* 54, no. 4 (1990): 80–93.

20 Handfield, R.B. "The Role of Materials Management in Developing Time-Based Competition," *International Journal of Purchasing and Materials Management* 29, no. 1 (1993): 2–10. Noordewier et al. "Performance Outcomes of Purchasing Arrangement in Industrial Buyer-Vendor Relationships"; Lee, H.L., and C. Billington. "Materials Management in Decentralized Supply Chains," *Operations Research* 41, no. 5 (1993): 835–847.

21 Baird, L.S., and H. Thomas. "What is Risk Anyway?" in R.A. Bettis and H. Thomas (Eds.), *Risk, Strategy, and Management* (Greenwich, Conn.: JAI Press, 1990), 21–52; Wagenaar, W.A. "Risk Taking and Accident Causation," in J. Yates (Ed.), *Risk Taking Behavior* (New York: John Wiley & Sons, 1992), 257–281; Zsidisin, G.A. and L.M. Ellram. "Supply Risk Assessment Analysis," *PRACTIX: Best Practices in Purchasing and Supply Management* 2, no. 4 (1999): 9–12; Steele and Court, *Profitable Purchasing Strategies*; Robertson, T.S., and H. Gatignon. "Technology Development Mode: A Transaction Cost Conceptualization," *Strategic Management Journal* 19, no. 1 (1998): 515–531; Noordewier et al., "Performance Outcomes of Purchasing Arrangement in Industrial Buyer-Vendor

Relationships"; Stump, R.L. "Antecedents of Purchasing Concentration: A Transaction Cost Explanation," *Journal of Business Research* 34, no. 2 (1995): 145–157.

22 http://www.InvestorWords.com

23 Closs, David J., and Edmund F. McGarrell "Enhancing Security throughout the Supply Chain," IBM Center for the Business of Government (2004), available at www.businessofgovernment.org, pp. 52–54; Rice and Caniato "Building a Secure and Resilient Supply Network."

24 Tomlin, Brian, and Snyder, Lawrence, "On the Value of Mitigation and Contingency Strategies for Managing Supply Chain Disruption Risks." Working Paper, Kenan-Flagler Business School, 2006.

25 Repenning, N.P., and J.D. Sterman. "Nobody Ever Gets Credit for Fixing Problems That Never Happened," *California Management Review*, 2001.

26 Poirier, Charles, and Quinn, Frank "How Are We Doing? A Survey of Supply Chain Progress," *Supply Chain Management Review* 8, no. 8 (2004): 24–31.

27 Mitroff, I., and C. Murat. "Preparing for Evil," *Harvard Business Review* 81, no. 44: 109–115, Harvard Business School Publishing Corporation, 2003.

28 Rice and Caniato "Building a Secure and Resilient Supply Network."

29 Lee, H., and M. Wolfe. "Supply Chain Security without Tears," *Supply Chain Management Review* 7, Part 1 (2003): 12–20.

30 Sheffi, Y. "Supply Chain Management under the Threat of International Terrorism," *International Journal of Logistics Management* 12, no. 2 (2001): 1–11.

31 Rice and Caniato "Building a Secure and Resilient Supply Network."

32 Department of Homeland Security, "U.S. Port Safety and Security Survey Report", *Homeland Defense Journal and Market Access International*, February 2007.

33 "Managing Global Supply Chains," *McKinsey Quarterly*, July 2008.

34 *World Trade* and University of Maryland research summarized in Boyson and Sandor, "Supply Chain Globalization: The Era of Revitalized Command is Upon Us," *World Trade*, October 1, 2007.

35 http://nomothetic.net/page2/volatile.html (posted July 29, 2005).

36 Tosi, H., R. Aldag, and R. Storey. "On the Measurement of the Environment: An Assessment of the Lawrence and Lorsch Environmental Uncertainty Subscale," *Administrative Science Quarterly* 18, no. 1 (1973): 27–36 (jstor.org).

37 Snyder, N.H., and W.F. Glueck. "Can Environmental Volatility be Measured Objectively?", *Academy of Management Journal* 25 (1982): 185–192.

38 Dugal, Mohinder, and Gopalakrishnan, Shanthi. "Environmental Volatility: A Reassessment of the Construct," *International Journal of Organizational Analysis* 8 (June 4, 2000): 401–424.

39 Bloomberg News. "U.P.S. Earnings Decline 49%, to $445 Million, as Downturn Saps Demand," *New York Times*, July 24, 2009.

40 Mouawad, Jad. "Swings in Price of Oil Hobble Forecasting," *New York Times*, July 6, 2009.

41 Rogers, John W., Jr. "Thriving in Chaos," *Forbes*, August 2009.

42 Willis, Robert. *Bloomberg Reports*, August 1, 2009: http://www.bloomberg.com

43 http://www.marketwatch.com/story/be. . .cans-2009-07-26

44 Eichengreen, Barry, and Kevin H. O'Rourke. "Comparing the Great Depression to Now for the World, Not Just the U.S.," VoxEU.org, April 6, 2009: http://www.voxeu.org/index.php?q=node/3421

45 Eichengreen, Barry, and Kevin H. O'Rourke. "A Tale of Two Depressions," VoxEU.org, September 1, 2009: http://www.voxeu.org/index.php?q=node/3421

46 C.S. "Buzz" Holling, quoted in Homer-Dixon, Thomas. "Our Panarchic Future," *WorldWatch*, April–May, 2009.

47 Parry, Simon. "Revealed: The Ghost Fleet of the Recession Anchored Just East of Singapore," *London Daily Mail*, September 28, 2009.

48 Arcieri, Kate. "Recession Leads to Backup at Anchorage," *Annapolis Capital*, March 29, 2009.

49 Wikipedia, http://www.wikipedia.com

50 Eyerdam, Rick. "Trial by Logistics: Market and Price Volatility Test Global Freight Carriers," *Latin Trade*, May/June 2009.

51 Metal Bulletin, *Metal Center News*, June 2009.

52 http://rs.resalliance.org/index.php.?s-volatility

53 Cox, Amanda. "Metrics: Turning a Corner?" *New York Times*, July 5, 2009.

54 Davis, Steven, and James Kahn. "Interpreting the Great Moderation: Changes in the Volatility of Economic Activity at the Macro and Micro Levels," *Journal of Economic Perspectives* 22, no.4 (2008): 155–180.

55 Brat, Ilan, Ellen Byron, and Ann Zimmerman. "Retailers Cut Back on Variety, Once the Spice of Marketing," *Wall Street Journal*, June 26, 2009.

56 Goch, Lynna. "Risk's Watchmen," *Best's Review*, April 2009.

57 Lewandowski, Capt. Linda, and Jeffrey Cares. "Sense and Respond Logistics: The Fundamental of Demand Networks," U.S. Department of Defense Office of Force Transformation, unpublished paper (2003); and Cares, Jeffrey. "Distributed Adaptive Logistics," *Information Age Warfare Quarterly* 1, no. 1 (Winter 2005).

58 C.S. "Buzz" Holling, quoted in Homer-Dixon, Thomas. "Our Panarchic Future."

Part 2
The Tangible Supply Chain

three
X-SCM Network Design

Dr. Sandor Boyson, Dr. Chaodong Han, and Dr. John R. Macdonald

Over the past decade, a new approach to the science of network dynamics has deepened our understanding of how networks—ranging from the World Wide Web to biological systems—evolve and become robust. This new thinking has upended the traditional views of network managers everywhere. In particular, it has challenged supply chain managers to examine long-held assumptions about the relative constancy and stability of global supply chain designs.

In his remarkable book, *Linked: The New Science of Networks*, Albert-László Barabási explains the fast-moving field that is defining "the architecture of complexity." Among his main points, Barabási makes several that are directly relevant to the challenges facing today's supply chain manager:

1. The "old network science," pioneered by Erdoz and Renyi and accepted as common sense among network managers since 1959, holds that complex networks are randomly formed, with all of the nodes having a similar number of links,[1] as shown in Figure 3.1(a).

2. The "new network science" emerged from multiple sources. Watts and Strogatz in 1998 discovered that just a few extra links between nodes can form long bridge connections to the other side of a circle, dramatically compressing the distances between vastly separated nodes and offering "short paths to remote areas," as they described them. Another breakthrough discovery came in 1999, when software agents employed by Barabási mapped the structure of the World Wide Web and revealed the critical role of "super-connecting" websites, or Web hubs. As Barabási writes: "Hubs are special. They dominate the structure of all networks in which they are present, making them look like small worlds. Indeed, with links to an unusually large number of nodes, hubs create short paths between any two nodes in the system." These hub-dominated networks are unlike networks where nodes almost randomly connect to each other in haphazard ways (see Figure 3.1(a)). Typically, strong hubs enable networks to be highly agile and scalable in response to sharp fluctuations in demand. A hub-dominated network is shown in Figure 3.1(b).[2] Hub-dominated networks are also called scale-free networks. Unlike randomly connected networks, scale-free networks are characterized by many well-connected hubs that inter-link network nodes and provide short paths from one node of the network to another.

3. Barabási goes on to define the attributes of hub-based network growth, including the *preferential attachment* of nodes to super-connected hubs, and *hub fitness*, or the ability of a hub to compete or thrive based on its distinctive advantages. Finally, he demonstrates that hubs are a source of the *robustness of networks:* as long as the hubs remain intact, a multitude of nodes within a network can be disrupted or extinguished without network fragmentation or failure.[3]

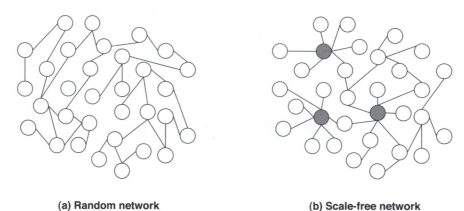

(a) Random network   **(b) Scale-free network**

FIGURE 3.1 Diagrams of random and scale-free networks. Different concepts of network types.

Source: http://commons.wikimedia.org/wiki/File:Scale-free_network_sample.png

For supply chain managers, the new network science provides some compelling messages:

- Supply chain networks are not static. They are continuously evolving and must be treated as dynamic organisms. It is not sufficient to examine network designs every one to three years, as is the practice in most companies today.
- Supply chain hubs are vitally important. The right country hub can make the entire network robust. It can provide an array of short paths to a broad swathe of more remote regional markets, and within a country, hubs connect supply lines to critical customer segments. Given their crucial roles, all current and potential hubs must be constantly assessed for fitness and for distinctive abilities to facilitate preferential attachment by other nodes.
- Short paths opened up by core hub structures must be exploited to gain efficiencies in transportation and communications across the global supply chain.

The new network science can potentially be a powerful tool for managing volatility in supply chains. It can, for example, help supply chain managers to dynamically configure and/or reconfigure supply chain networks in response to endogenous (internally originating) factors, such as shifts in demand or supply patterns within the network; or exogenous (externally originating) factors, such as trade restrictions or natural disasters imposed upon the network. Unfortunately, there is no one solution set for utilizing the new network science to perform rapid supply chain configuration or reconfiguration. The tools available today are generally considered to be separate techniques:

- *Network design and optimization* uses geographic information system (GIS) technology to superimpose the typology of hubs and nodes on a physical map and create "ideal" hub/node configurations based on clustering of priority customers and supply lines.
- *Supply chain-hub analysis/return-on-investment (ROI) measurement* seeks to evaluate candidate country hubs based on comparisons of total logistics cost. Here ROI refers to return on supply chain related investments, such as building warehouses, distribution facilities, and manufacturing plants.
- *Routing/service lead-time options analysis* uses linear programming, mathematical techniques to optimize objective functions and seek "least cost" or "least time" transport options within the network.
- *Total cost of ownership insourcing/outsourcing analysis* seeks to evaluate the costs or benefits of outsourcing the ownership and management of individual hubs, nodes, or network services.

These techniques must be bundled together into a volatility management "tool kit" that helps companies to design a robust network—one that is capable of changing as markets and customer segments shift in terms of strategic priority, or as fitness/risk profiles of operating sites fluctuate over time. This represents a significant departure from current practice, which applies linear programming techniques to identify optimal solutions based on relatively long-term design structures and fixed (or at least static) network nodes.

Today's optimization regimes are no longer viable; to realize promised benefits, they often require a degree of operational stability that is simply unattainable in the present business environment. Accordingly, this tool kit must serve as the basis for a fundamentally new type of network design, which focuses on constant risk-hedging, real-time awareness of available capacity in served markets, and establishment of "contingent" hubs and nodes that can be rapidly activated if needed.

Toward these ends, this chapter proposes a more integrative model that is based on an updated set of premises as well as on the new network science. We call this integrative model "dynamic network configuration management," which we define as the managerial capability to do the following:

- Maintain a dynamic network map that makes it possible for supply chain managers to pinpoint the geographic clustering, at any point in time, of in-store and online customers, the locations of core suppliers (especially suppliers of high-volume items), warehousing assets, and core transportation lanes
- Conduct frequent reviews of baseline costing elements and alternate scenario analyses using this map
- Use rapidly compiled, publicly available data to constantly monitor changes in the relative costs of risk factors and risk-adjusted returns on investment for major country hub locations and intra-country nodal configurations
- Use trade-off analyses to continually adjust transportation modes and routes based on cost or time exigencies
- Use relative-cost comparisons of insourcing and outsourcing to determine the correct, rolling (constantly updated) mix of self-owned and managed vs. partner/vendor-owned and managed assets and capabilities
- Adopt Web-based software to enable highly distributed users to dynamically update the data used in the supply chain map and rolling analysis.

Table 3.1 summarizes the tiers of analysis that constitute dynamic network configuration management.

In the sections ahead, we will review the changing requirements for network configuration; put

TABLE 3.1. Analyzing the international and domestic supply chain network. This table summarizes the tiers of analysis that constitute dynamic network configuration management

Decision tier	Analytic tool used	Organizational benefits
Inter-country hub selection	Spreadsheet-based total logistics-cost analysis	Provides decision makers with best return on investment (ROI) calculation for risk-adjusted supply chain investments
Intra-country nodal configuration	PC or server-based network design/optimization software	Provides decision makers with best network alignment between demand locations, distribution locations and production points
Intra-network transactions management	Web-based cost/service modeling software	Provides decision makers with best routing/transport options to move goods from network locations to customers based on minimization of cost or time
Insource/outsource nodal or transactions management	Spreadsheet-based total logistics-cost analysis	Provides decision makers with best asset- or service-ownership model and most cost-efficient, mixed-ownership network structure

Source: Sandor Boyson, 2009, Robert H. Smith School of Business, University of Maryland.

forward methodologies for international and domestic/in-country network configuration; review transactions management; and conduct an insourcing/outsourcing analysis.

The Benefits of Network Design

Network design has been touted as the best way to balance two competing demands confronting almost every company in recent years: the need to globalize the supply chain and the need to simplify cost and service structures. Indeed, careful network redesign has helped some of the best-known companies in the world to simplify operations while reducing costs and improving service. Just two examples:

- Royal Philips Electronics owned 50 warehouses all over China; when the company conducted a network analysis that analyzed customer locations and service needs, it determined that 80 percent of its customer base was located on China's east coast. With this data in hand, Philips cut the number of warehouses to 20.[4]
- National Semiconductor cut back from five regional distribution centers to a single global center. By doing so, the company reduced its average delivery time from two weeks to four days; switched from using 42 freight forwarders contracting with 14 airlines to one integrated carrier that could provide transportation, freight forwarding, and logistics services; and reduced distribution costs from 2.9 percent of sales to 1.2 percent of sales.[5]

The aggregate success of network design initiatives has been catalogued by a number of observers. In a 1997 article, for example, the consultant Paul Bender describes the typical benefits to be derived from a strategic, worldwide network design effort. Bender uses the example of a semiconductor manufacturer that is based in Japan but has plants and warehouses around the world. Following a network design study, the manufacturer was able to reduce its number of plants from nine to six and cut its warehouses from eight to four. The reduction of facilities significantly reduced all operating costs, with the exception of transportation. Total supply chain costs dropped 14 percent and profits improved by 53 percent because better location of shipping facilities led to improved customer response and increased sales. Bender says that designing and implementing an optimized, consistent worldwide supply chain template—i.e., consistent network design plan—produces savings ranging from 7 percent to 31 percent, with an average cost reduction of 17 percent.[6]

Another consulting organization, the Logistics Bureau, says it has completed more than 100 network design projects across Southeast Asia, Australia, New Zealand, and other nearby regions. The Bureau claims these projects saved between 4 percent and 14 percent of distribution costs, a savings level that is consistent with the ranges cited by Bender and others.[7]

In addition to calculating aggregate savings in supply chain costs, it is possible to document specific functional-area improvements that can be attributed to network design or redesign. Participants in a 2008 survey conducted by the consulting firm Tompkins Associates reported average improvement levels ranging from 0.1 percent to 21.4 percent in 11 functional areas. In several of those areas, individual respondents reported improvements of 30 percent or more, as shown in Table 3.2.

Interestingly, despite these impressive improvements, 40 percent of the survey respondents (who included managers at such big names as Campbell Soup, Hallmark Cards, Target, and Coca-Cola) rated their overall supply chain as "not optimized" or "insufficient." This is not surprising when you consider that network designs and redesigns are not being done often enough to keep pace with today's highly volatile operating environment.

Why Don't We Reconfigure Networks More Often?

There has been a great deal of commentary by supply chain analysts on the need to more frequently utilize network design/redesign tools. Many are now recommending that companies bring this

TABLE 3.2. Business benefits from supply chain network improvements

Network review realized benefits	Average improvement level	Highest improvement level
Improved order fill rate	21.4%	37.5%
Reduced order cycle time	12.1%	37.5%
Investment return (ROI)	10.0%	50.0%
Capacity increase (throughput)	6.6%	30.0%
Reduced transportation costs	5.6%	12.0%
Inventory turns	5.0%	20.0%
Reduced distribution costs	3.8%	12.0%
Incremental change in operating margins	2.0%	3.7%
Capital investment	1.6%	8.0%
Improved profitability	0.2%	1.0%
Reduced supply chain overhead costs	0.1%	1.0%

Source: *2008 Core Benchmarks Report: Getting to the Core of the Problem, Benchmark Your Way to Better Operations,* Tompkins Associates www.tompkinsinc.com/publications/competitive_edge/articles/032608_network_reviews.asp

capability into the operational deployment area and not reserve it for infrequent, strategic planning exercises.

There are good reasons for companies to take a fresh look at their networks more frequently than most do now and to adjust their strategies on at least an annual basis. "The [supply chain] network is very sensitive to changes in business strategy and the operating environment," said Mike Kilgore of the consulting firm Chainalytics in an interview on an industry website. "When you combine the constant changes in business strategy with all the uncertainties in the supply chain right now, including the cost and dynamics of transportation, very few networks are good for more than about 12 months."[8]

In the past, many companies would conduct a network optimization, make changes, and then not think about it again for three to five years, until a major event such as an acquisition occurred. Such a passive approach is a luxury very few companies can afford today, said Jeff Karrenbauer of the software vendor Insight in a separate interview on that website. "You always forecast demand, but now you'll have to forecast costs in much the same way. What could look good in the short term could turn out to be really bad under a different set of cost assumptions. In the past, you could use a fairly static level of costs in the model, but now that's very dangerous. You need to evaluate a number of cost scenarios over multiple periods. That's not often done."[9]

The research firm Gartner Group makes the identical point in a case study of a large cement manufacturer that was seeking to more effectively manage its global network.

> Traditionally, strategic network design has been seen as a strategic tool (often sourced through consultancies) to help companies evaluate their supply chain configurations every few years or so. In more steady-state operating environments, this has been adequate. However, many companies are now finding that they are operating in a different world. They are seeing significantly more variability in raw-material costs, fuel costs, demand levels, and certainty of supply.
>
> These and other factors lead to a more chaotic and unpredictable operating environment. To better understand the new risk levels and determine optimum plans and contingencies, network design tools can be used on a more tactical level, linked to a company's sales and operations planning (S&OP) process.
>
> For years, the use of network design tools was the domain of supply chain and logistics consultancies. End users would periodically call in these consultancies to perform an analysis on the users' manufacturing and distribution networks. The aim of these studies was to verify the existing supply chain configuration and to develop a strategic network plan for the next few years. With companies operating in relatively stable operating environments, this frequency of analysis was often "good enough." However, with the world now in a very different place, and with significant volatility in their operating environments, many companies must evaluate their supply chain configurations far more frequently to ensure they are as close as possible to the optimum cost/service trade-off for their supply chains.[10]

Gartner is not the only one to express such concerns. In a 2009 report, the research firm Aberdeen Group's Nari Viswanathan also questioned why so many companies have failed to make full use of the technological resources at their disposal.

> Network design tools have been available in the industry for the last 10 years, but they have been underutilized. Eighty percent of companies reassess their network at a frequency of less than two times a year. Over 90 percent of companies leverage a spreadsheet-based application or a consulting-based approach rather than an application package for doing network design, and hence are unable to make extensive trade-offs between constraints. This approach is not scalable.[11]

New Modeling Tools Must Account for Volatility

The current toolsets do have limitations; in particular, their modeling techniques focus on "correct optimization solutions" without considering such factors as the potential disruption of nodes or the costs of nodal failure. However, a few modeling tools that build upon the findings of the new network science and seek to account for the risks volatility poses to supply chains are now emerging from the operations research community.

These tools reflect new ideas about building network disruption as variables into models, which were published by the academic operations research community in the late 1990s and mid-2000s. One of those ideas was that companies should consider the *fortification* of their facilities; in other words, they have resources to prevent disruptions at some of their facilities, and thus can partially fortify the associated network. The researchers' model finds the best facilities to fortify, assuming that an interdictor will attempt to disrupt a fixed number of the unfortified facilities.[12] Another model allowed firms to determine whether each facility opened would be reliable or unreliable; reliable facilities would come at a higher cost based on their fortification.[13]

In their well-regarded 2005 paper, "Models for Reliable Supply Chain Network Design," Snyder and Daskin developed trade-off analyses for finding reliable facility locations in a supply chain that is vulnerable to disruptions. These analyses seek to build resilience into the whole network to assure business continuity if a node or nodes should fail:

> Since facility location decisions are costly to implement and difficult to reverse, these strategic decisions permit very little recourse once a disruption occurs, other than re-assignment of customers to non-disrupted facilities. Our goal, therefore, is to choose facility locations proactively so that the system performs well even if disruptions occur.
>
> Consider the following uncapacitated fixed-charge location problem (UFLP)[14] for a 49-node data set consisting of the capitals of the 48 continental U.S. states and Washington, DC. All nodes serve as both potential facility location sites and demand points, with demands proportional to state populations. The optimal UFLP solution entails a fixed cost of $386,900 per year to operate the five opened facilities and a transportation cost of $470,228 per year. Now suppose that the facility in Sacramento, California, becomes unavailable—say, because of a strike or extended power outage. In this case, the West Coast customers served by that facility must instead be served by facilities in Des Moines, Iowa, and Austin, Texas, resulting in a transportation cost of $1,019,065, an increase of 117% from the baseline solution.
>
> We list the "failure costs" (the transportation costs that result after the failure of a facility) for each of the five facilities in the optimal solution, as well as their assigned demands and the transportation cost when no facilities fail. Note that Sacramento serves only 19% of the total demand but generates the largest failure cost because its customers are geographically disparate and the next-closest facility is quite distant. The Harrisburg facility serves customers that are tightly clustered, and good "backup" facilities are fairly close by, but its failure cost is still quite large (a 52% increase in transportation cost) because of the volume of demand that it serves. In contrast, Montgomery serves nearly as much demand as Sacramento, but because it is centrally located, close to backup facilities, its failure cost is smaller than that of Sacramento or Harrisburg. Therefore, the reliability of a facility depends on both the demand served by the facility and the distance of those demands from other facilities.[15]

A Tool Kit for Making Network Decisions

Certainly, enhanced modeling (such as the examples just discussed) is one element of a dynamic network-configuration management system and can be helpful in identifying the vulnerability or fitness of hubs. However, the critical concern for supply chain managers engaged in volatility management today is not how to model the costs of a nodal failure or model the deflecting of traffic from a failed node to an alternate location. Rather, it is how to build robustness into the entire supply chain network as an operational capability.

To address that concern, supply chain managers require a new, more integrative decision tool kit that is capable of dynamically configuring and managing supply chain networks. In the remainder of this chapter, we explore this tool kit and demonstrate in detail how it can be used to make four high-priority network configuration and management decisions: selecting country supply chain hubs, designing intra-country supply chains, analyzing trade-offs for transportation cost and service lead times, and deciding whether to insource or outsource network assets and services.

Decision #1: Selecting Country Supply Chain Hubs

Multinational corporations seek to optimize total logistics costs and return on investment on a global basis. To do so, they need to establish strategic country anchors—large supply chain facilities or capabilities that can efficiently serve regional markets and effectively contribute to attaining corporate ROI objectives.

Despite that need, there currently is a gap in research about national supply chain competitiveness, and—at this writing—no one has developed off-the-shelf, easy-to-use tools that companies can use to analyze the competitive supply chain advantage of locating a hub in one nation over another.

Making that determination today is a difficult and expensive exercise, as one German truck manufacturer learned not long ago. The company engaged a major consulting firm to evaluate which of the BRIC (Brazil, Russia, India, and China) countries could serve as a "source from/sell to" global network hub. The consultants conducted a market-comparison study that involved gathering companywide knowledge about market development, customers, and competition, and included an evaluation of opportunities and threats for each country. The manufacturer plans to update the analysis annually to account for new developments and market changes.

That study cost over $1 million and took many months to complete. Few supply chain managers, though, are able to engage in such a lengthy and expensive endeavor. Indeed, during an economic downturn, even large companies might benefit from a streamlined, rapidly deployable technique for gaining comparative data about candidate supply chain hubs.

In light of this growing need, researchers at the Robert H. Smith School of Business's Supply Chain Management Center (including the authors of this chapter) have initiated and guided a series of studies designed to help companies rapidly assess the relative supply chain competitiveness of possible hub countries. The study subjects included the United States, China, India, Brazil, and Thailand.

Each study began by analyzing the following country-level elements, using readily available, public data:

- Country overview, including basic economic, social, and political facts.
- Physical infrastructure, including ports, airports, roads, and private/public/shared warehouse facilities; and the state of communications and utilities infrastructure necessary for conducting business.
- Supply chain-related policies and regulations, including foreign direct-investment rules, import/export taxation issues, and customs/trade-facilitation processes.
- Third-party logistics providers (3PLs), including availability of full-spectrum service providers, intermodal or mode-specific transportation coordinators, and customs brokers and freight forwarders.
- Company case studies and success factors, including examples of companies that successfully

sourced from or sold to the relevant country, and the key lessons learned in regard to supply chain management.

These analyses were assembled into a summary framework, as shown in Figure 3.2.

Because the new network science mandates the evaluation of supply chain hubs' fitness, the next step was to determine the candidate countries' risk level. We then assigned a risk-adjusted discount rates adjustment figure to calculate the return on investment in supply chain hub based on the results of the country-level situation audits. The risk-adjusted discount rates are critical in calculating the net present value (NPV) of future cash flows generated from supply chain investment projects. (Our methodology will be explained in detail later in this chapter.)

Each country research group then used an Excel spreadsheet model, developed for this purpose, to compare the current supply chain cost structure of the candidate country to those of competitor countries. This spreadsheet was also used to model potential changes in the candidate country's supply chain cost structure and to weigh the impact of those changes on the candidate country's overall supply chain competitiveness. A Comparative Country Supply Chain ROI Analytic Tool is available on the password protected side of the book website at http://www.routledge.com/textbooks/harrington.

Using this same methodology and an Excel spreadsheet model—which is available to purchasers of this book to use in conducting their own modeling exercises—a corporate supply chain strategy group will be able to develop a business case presentation that can

- summarize the advantages and disadvantages of establishing a supply chain hub in a candidate country relative to infrastructure, policies, third-party logistics providers, and supply chain costs;
- summarize the critical success factors and key actions required to establish effective sourcing operations within the candidate country;
- display a modified spreadsheet model that can incorporate the results of the strategy group's recommended actions and provide justification, from a supply chain cost perspective, for investing in the candidate country.

The following discussion explains the supply chain ROI spreadsheet model in detail. It also walks through an example of how we used the model to develop this type of business case.

Rapid Assessment of Risk-Adjusted ROI for Country Hubs

We created an analytical framework for comparing the return on supply chain investment across a spectrum of countries. This comparison was based on country-specific logistics characteristics as well as on the cost implications of a range of supply chain investment factors, including labor productivity and costs, materials sourcing costs, property acquisition and plant investment costs, customs and transportation costs across borders, inventory costs, and perceived supply chain investment risk associated with each country.

Most of those factors have been well documented in the literature. Wu developed a supply chain cost model incorporating material, labor, logistics, inventory holding, and overhead costs.[16] Meanwhile, Lovell, Saw, and Stimson identified the major components of total supply chain costs as manufacturing, transportation, warehousing, and inventory costs.[17] Gordon asserted that hidden wastes also drive supply chain costs.[18]

As for risk-related factors, Moon and LeBlanc applied a risk-adjusted required return to assess the profitability and viability of individual supply chain investments.[19] They suggested that low-risk supply chain projects may justify a lower required rate of return, while riskier supply chain projects may mandate a higher required rate of return. In this exercise, we considered this but also adjusted supply chain investment risk based on country-specific and global supply chain risks. A 2008 AMR Research survey was helpful in this regard; the survey found that the supply chain risk factors of greatest concern to management were energy costs, transportation costs, commodity prices, intellectual property infringement, suppliers' product-quality failures, supply failures, rising labor costs,

	Thailand	China	India	Brazil
Country Overview	•Area: 514,000 sq. km •Capital: Bangkok •Terrain: Central plain •Pop: 65.4M •Gov't: Constitutional Monarchy	•Area: 9,596,960 sq. km •Capital: Beijing •Terrain: mountains, high plateaus •Pop: 1,330M •Gov't: Communist	•Area: 3,287,590 sq. km •Capital: New Delhi •Terrain: mostly upland plain •Pop: 1,147M •Gov't: Federal Republic	•Area: 8,511,965 sq. km •Capital: Brasilia •Terrain: mostly flat to rolling lowlands •Pop: 196M •Gov't: Federal Republic
Economic Development (2007 est.)	•GDP (PPP): $521.5Bn •GDP Real Growth: 4.8% •Labor force: 36.9M •Investment: 26.8% GDP •Inflation: 2.2% •Revenues: $44.14Bn •Expenditures: $49.83Bn	•GDP (PPP): $7,099Bn •GDP Real Growth: 11.9% •Labor force: 800.7M •Investment: 42.7% GDP •Inflation: 4.8% •Revenues: $674.3Bn •Expenditures: $651.6Bn	•GDP (PPP): $2,966Bn •GDP Real Growth: 9% •Labor force: 516.4M •Investment: 33.9% GDP •Inflation: 6.4% •Revenues: $141.2Bn •Expenditures: $172.6Bn	•GDP (PPP): $1849Bn •GDP Real Growth: 5.4% •Labor force: 99.23M •Investment:17.6% •Inflation: 3.6% •Revenues: $244Bn •Expenditures: $219.9Bn
Supply Chain Management	•Goal: enhance efficiency, productive use & management of the road network •Urban transport issues •High cost of transportation: 19% of GDP	•Special Economic Zones (SEZ) to encourage and & minimize supply chain costs •Ability to skip a level of warehousing in American ports •Highways will open rural areas	•Special Economic Zones 2007-2008 exports projected at $17.17B •Procurement issues due to suppliers & infrastructure •Production issues around power reliability	•Supply chain is regulated by 4 main agencies •Finance Sector is most developed in Latin America •Strong domestic demand •huge inventories due to unreliable SCM systems •Unstable Workforce; Frequent Strikes
Infrastructure	•airports: 106 •railways: 4,071km •roadways: 180,053km •waterways: 4,000km •merchant marine: 398 •ports/terminals: 4	•airports: 467 •railways: 75,438km •roadways: 1,930,544km •waterways: 124,000km •merchant marine: 1,826 •ports/terminals: 8	•airports: 346 •railways: 63,221km •roadways: 3,316,452 km •waterways: 14,500km •merchant marine:501 •ports/terminals: 9	•airports: 4,263 •railways: 29,295km •roadways: 1,751,868 km •waterways: 50,000km •merchant marine:136 •ports/terminals: 7
3rd Party Logistics	•"Big 4" major providers present •Major infrastructure investments •High fuel costs: 19% of GDP •Small-Medium sector is huge •Free Trade Zones can be area of growth	•Currently little demand for high-end 3PL services •Many companies handle 3PL functions in-house •Demands vary by region •Comprehensive, reliable information systems needed •Some companies are stated-owned	•Few 3PL logistics providers •Accounts for over 25% of US$ 90B Indian logistics industry •Large, multinational companies are main customers •Projected to grow at a 16% CAGR 16% from 2007-10, with 3PL expanding into integrated players	•Int'l logistics providers present •Much is outsourced •Companies much own logistics infrastructure or outsource
Supply Chain Policies	•Pro-growth •Strict investor protection •FY08-09: "Thai investment year"- focusing on FDI in various industries •Hurdles: policy instability, gov't bureaucracy, gov't instability, inadequately educated workforce	•Most entities are State-owned, JVs, or foreign Wholly-owned •Strict in enforcing contracts •Issues in access to financing, Inefficient gov't bureaucracy, and corruption •Business licenses required for each province •Variety of regulations •Top 5% in import/export costs for a single container,	•Bureaucracy endemic corruption is an issue •To limit FDI takeover, gov't requires investors to obtain permission from Reserve Bank of India (RBI) for equity acquisitions exceeding 30% •Competition Act of 2002 forbids anti-competitive agreements	•Ranked 93rd in overall ease of doing business •Low rank in enforcing contracts •Regulations and regional differences can create burdens for int'l business •40-50% of business is in "informal sector"

FIGURE 3.2 Country Comparative Matrix. The Country Comparative Matrix compares key logistics and supply chain characteristics for the countries studied.

Source: Supply Chain Management Center, Robert H. Smith School of Business, University of Maryland.

and regulatory compliance—all relevant to cross-border investments.[20] And finally, we took into account a proposal by HK Systems, a developer of automated material handling systems, that ROI analyses for supply chain projects should include the identification and evaluation of alternative projects and estimates of the cash flow for each of them.[21]

During the course of our analysis, we assessed the supply chain ROI for individual countries by applying the net present value (NPV) model to our assumptions and comparing them to the U.S. baseline situations. Simply put, NPV assumes that a dollar in the future is worth less than a dollar today due to inflation and uncertainties. The NPV model is used in corporate capital budgeting to analyze the profitability of an investment or project. We also obtained actual data on logistics characteristics and cost parameters for some countries, which we used to assess the robustness of the relative model, which uses assumed comparative data rather than actual data.

As the following case study will show, our approach to conducting a comparative and quantitative analysis of supply chain competitiveness may provide a tool for screening potential locations for supply chain investment and opportunities across the globe. Equipped with this tool, managers may be able to build their own analytical models for a particular set of countries and conduct sensitivity testing for various cost factors, using actual data whenever available.

A Case Analysis

The example we used was a high-tech firm in the United States that needed to determine the best location to build a new cell phone manufacturing plant. The company considered both the United States and emerging economies, including China, India, Brazil, Mexico, and Thailand.

Our example incorporated several assumptions:

1. The investment horizon is five years.
2. An overseas plant would be required to ship 50,000 units annually via the Port of New York/New Jersey to the United States, where the product would be sold.
3. Annual sales are fixed, based on a fixed price and sales volume.
4. Labor costs per unit of product are based on local hourly labor rates and labor productivity.
5. Raw materials are sourced from local channels.
6. Upfront property, plant, and equipment (PP&E) costs are projected according to the general requirements of the cell phone industry and adjusted by overall country-specific economic conditions.
7. The initial investments depreciate over the five-year investment horizon without salvage value.
8. Customs costs are assessed on basic product costs, including labor, materials, and PP&E depreciation costs.
9. Cost parameters (including labor productivity) associated with U.S. domestic manufacturing are the baseline condition. Labor productivity and cost parameters associated with manufacturing in emerging economies are based on those economies' relative strengths and weaknesses as compared to the United States.

Under these assumed business conditions, a baseline relative ROI comparison was developed, as shown in Table 3.3.

The U.S. baseline assumptions included the following: the product sale price is $100 per unit. Sales are $5 million, and selling expenses are $200,000, based on an annual sales volume of 50,000 units. One worker-hour is needed to produce one unit of product in the United States, while labor cost is $20 per hour. Sourcing of raw materials costs $18 per unit if sourced from U.S. local markets. Initial plant investment is $5 million and fully depreciated over a five-year period, without salvage value. U.S. domestic transportation (from manufacturing plant to sales outlets) costs $2 per unit. Safety stock estimates are based on constant demand rates over a year of 365 days and a desired customer service level of 95 percent. The annual cost of safety stocks (e.g., obsolescence, damage and loss, storage and handling) is 20 percent of the original value of safety stocks.

With the above assumptions, annual net cash flows from the manufacturing project could be

TABLE 3.3. Comparison of return on investment across countries. This table shows a comparison of operating and supply chain costs across six countries

Sales and Cost Category	Parameter	USA	China	India	Brazil	Mexico	Thailand
Annual demand (unit)	50,000	50,000	50,000	50,000	50,000	50,000	50,000
Selling price in U.S. market	100	100	100	100	100	100	100
Annual sales in U.S. market		5,000,000	5,000,000	5,000,000	5,000,000	5,000,000	5,000,000
Labor							
Labor hours needed per unit of product (labor productivity)		1.00	2.00	4.00	1.50	5.00	4.00
Total labor hours		50,000	100,000	200,000	75,000	250,000	200,000
Labor cost per hour		20	3	2	7	5	1.5
Total labor costs		1,000,000	300,000	400,000	525,000	1,250,000	300,000
Labor costs per product unit		20.00	6.00	8.00	10.50	25.00	6.00
Materials							
Material costs per unit (assuming sourcing locally)		18	10	8	14	12	8
Total material costs		900,000	500,000	400,000	700,000	600,000	400,000
PP&E Investment (property, plant & equipment)							
Initial plant investment (depreciated over 5 years without salvage value)	5	5,000,000	3,500,000	3,000,000	4,000,000	3,000,000	3,500,000
Annual depreciation cost		1,000,000	700,000	600,000	800,000	600,000	700,000
Allocated depreciation cost per unit		20.00	14.00	12.00	16.00	12.00	14.00
Customs							
Customs value per unit (summing labor, materials and PPE costs)		58.00	30.00	28.00	40.50	49.00	28.00
Customs cost per unit	12%	–	3.60	3.36	4.86	5.88	3.36
Transportation (from origin to sales outlet)							
Estimated transportation cost per unit		2.00	20.00	30.00	14.00	10.00	18.00
Total transportation costs		100,000	1,000,000	1,500,000	700,000	500,000	900,000
Purchasing Cost (=labor + materials + depr + transport costs)							
Total purchasing cost per unit		60	54	61	59	65	49
Inventory							
Unit demand per day during lead time (assuming constant demand)	365	137	137	137	137	137	137
Average lead time (days)		2	30	50	10	5	25
Standard deviation of lead time		1	15	30	5	3	7
Customer service level (z)	1.645	95%	95%	95%	95%	95%	95%
Safety stock requirement (unit)		499	7,489	13,609	2,496	1,361	5,002
Value of safety stocks		29,958	401,433	835,047	148,191	88,295	246,894
Total costs of safety stocks (obsolescence, dammage, etc.)	20%	5,992	80,287	167,009	29,638	17,659	49,379
Cashflows							
U.S. domestic selling expenses		200,000	200,000	200,000	200,000	200,000	200,000
Annual net cashflows		1,794,008	2,219,713	1,732,991	2,045,362	1,832,341	2,450,621
Risk adjusted discount rate		20%	30%	30%	30%	35%	40%
PV of cashflows over 5 years		5,365,183	5,406,267	4,220,819	4,981,621	4,067,726	4,987,416
NPV		365,183	1,906,267	1,220,819	981,621	1,067,726	1,487,416
ROI (return on initial plant investment)		7%	54%	41%	25%	36%	42%

derived by deducting those supply chain costs plus selling expenses from annual sales. The net present value of the net cash flows for the proposed project (building a manufacturing plant in the United States) were calculated based on a 20 percent discount rate for U.S. domestic manufacturing. "Discount rates" were used to adjust the ROIs based on the perceived riskiness of supply chain investment in each country. Once the risk-adjusted rates of return have been factored in, countries with high risk profiles may not be able to demonstrate favorable ROIs.

With all that information in hand, the ROI (return on initial manufacturing plant investment) could be calculated accordingly.

The assumptions for other countries included the following:

Labor productivity and cost: In comparison to the United States, where one worker hour is needed to produce one unit of product, two worker hours are required in China, and the associated Chinese labor cost is $3 per hour; four worker hours are required in India, with a labor cost of $2 per hour; 1.5 work hours are needed in Brazil, and labor costs $7 per hour; five worker hours are required in Mexico, and labor costs $5 per hour; four worker hours are needed in Thailand, and labor costs $1.50 per hour.

Cost of materials: In comparison to U.S. domestic sourcing (with a raw materials cost of $18 per unit), the cost of sourcing materials locally in emerging economies is $10 per unit in China, $8 per unit in India, $14 per unit in Brazil, $12 per unit in Mexico, and $8 per unit in Thailand.

Property, plant and equipment: In comparison to U.S. locations, which require $5 million upfront costs for building a manufacturing plant for this high-tech product, upfront PP&E investment ranged from $3 million in India and Mexico, to $3.5 million in China and Thailand, to $4 million in Brazil. Full depreciation of PP&E cost is allocated over a five-year period, without salvage value.

Customs: Unlike domestic manufacturing, building a manufacturing plant in foreign countries and shipping product back to the U.S. market incurs customs costs. For convenience of analysis, we assumed customs costs of 12 percent of the product value (a sum of labor, materials, and PP&E costs), even though actual customs assessment methods may vary from country to country.

Transportation: Transportation costs from the manufacturing origin to U.S. sales markets are based on distance and the use of ocean and truck transportation. In comparison to U.S. domestic manufacturing, where the transportation cost is $2 per unit, the average shipping cost per unit is $20 for China, $30 for India, $14 for Brazil, $10 for Mexico, and $18 for Thailand.

Inventory: We selected economic order quantity (EOQ) as an inventory policy for optimizing inventory and ordering costs. This simple model assumes constant demand but variable lead times due to the variability of cross-border transportation.

Average lead time estimates were based on the reliability of each country's transportation infrastructure and logistics capabilities, as suggested by research and media reports. In this exercise, lead times from the U.S. manufacturing plant to sales markets average two days, with a standard deviation of one day. Lead times are 30 days for China (inland trucking and ocean transport), with a standard deviation of 15 days; 50 days for India (inland trucking and ocean transport), with a standard deviation of 30 days; 10 days for Brazil (inland trucking and ocean transport), with a standard deviation of five days; five days for Mexico (trucking only) with a standard deviation of three days; and 25 days for Thailand (inland trucking and ocean transport), with a standard deviation of seven days.

When we considered the desired customer service level (assumed to be 95 percent) together with the lead times and their variability, we could calculate safety stock requirements (in units) for each country. Inventory costs, which included obsolescence, theft, damage, storage and handling costs, are assessed as 20 percent of the value of safety stocks maintained in the supply chain system.

Cash flow risks: Discount rates for annual cash flows were adjusted based on the perceived risk of operating in emerging markets. In comparison to the 20 percent discount was applied to U.S. domestic manufacturing, the discount rate for China, India, and Brazil is 30 percent. The discount rate for Mexico is 35 percent; Thailand's discount rate (40 percent) is highest because of political and societal instability at the time of the analysis.

The baseline results, presented in Table 3.3, projected an ROI for locating the manufacturing plant in the United States of 7 percent. The ROI increases to 54 percent for China, 41 percent for India,

25 percent for Brazil, 36 percent for Mexico, and 42 percent for Thailand. The results seem to suggest that locating the manufacturing plant in emerging economies may result in a much higher ROI than locating in the United States.

However, the ROIs for individual countries may change when one or more supply chain cost factors change, affecting the location decision either positively or negatively. To demonstrate how a change in one supply chain cost factor can change the ROI dynamics even when all other factors remain the same—to such a degree that the balance will tip to the U.S. domestic location—we conducted sensitivity analyses. This type of analysis can show the competitiveness of a foreign country relative to specific factors, such as labor productivity, hourly labor rates, material costs, PP&E cost, transportation costs, and discount rates. In general, the higher the cost required to tip the balance of location preference, the more competitive advantages a country will hold in regard to that factor compared to the U.S. location.

Labor productivity: Location in emerging economies often is favored over U.S. domestic locations based in part on the assumption that labor productivity in these countries can be maintained at certain levels. However, if the number of work hours needed to produce one unit of product increases from 2 to 6.37 work hours in China, from 4 to 7.90 work hours in India, from 1.5 to 2.33 work hours in Brazil, from 5 to 6.55 work hours in Mexico, and from 4 to 12 work hours in Thailand, while other factors remain unchanged, then the ROIs in those emerging economies will be less favorable than that of the United States. If that should be the case, then building the plant in the United States would be a financially reasonable choice.

Hourly labor rates: The high cost of labor in the United States is one of the driving forces behind the move to manufacturing offshore. However, we found that if hourly labor rates increase in emerging economies, their location advantages may be undermined. The U.S. hourly labor rate was assumed to be $20. If hourly labor rates increase from $3 to $9.56 in China, from $7 to $10.75 in Brazil, from $5 to $6.52 in Mexico, from $2 to $3.94 in India, and from $1.50 to $4.45 in Thailand, while everything else remains unchanged, then the ROIs across all those emerging economies will fall below 7 percent, resulting in an unfavorable decision in comparison with U.S. domestic locations.

Material costs: The high cost of locally sourced material is one of the factors driving up the total cost of U.S. domestic manufacturing and making offshore production attractive. However, the ROI dynamics across countries may change due to changes in material costs. In our example, the U.S. material cost was assumed to be $18.00 per unit. If material costs per unit increase from $10 to $23.11 in China, from $8 to $16 in India, from $14 to $19.55 in Brazil, from $12 to $19.60 in Mexico, and from $8 to $20 in Thailand, while everything else remains the same, then the ROIs in those emerging economies will be below 7 percent, resulting in an unfavorable decision in comparison with U.S. domestic locations.

Property, plant and equipment investment requirement: We based our location decision on the return on initial PP&E investment. It was assumed that it will cost $5 million to set up a plant that can produce 50,000 units of this high-tech product. We supposed the initial PP&E investment in emerging economies to be much lower, thus justifying a favorable location decision. However, a change in PP&E investment may also change the ROI dynamics across countries. If the PP&E investment requirement rises from $3.5 million to $4.56 million in China, from $3 million to $3.65 million in India, from $4 million to $4.45 million in Brazil, from $3 million to $3.57 million in Mexico, and from $3.5 million to $4.35 million in Thailand, while everything else remains the same, then the ROIs in those emerging economies will be less than 7 percent, resulting in an unfavorable decision in comparison with U.S. domestic locations.

Transportation costs: Transportation costs have been a concern for offshoring manufacturing plants to emerging economies, a factor dragging down supply chain ROIs across foreign countries. In fact, our model shows that if the per-unit transportation cost increases from $20 to $33.16 in China, from $30 to $38.00 in India, from $14 to $19.75 in Brazil, from $10 to $17.65 in Mexico, and from $18 to $30 in Thailand, while everything else remains the same, then ROIs in those emerging economies will fall below 7 percent, resulting in an unfavorable decision in comparison with U.S. domestic locations.

Discount rates: As noted earlier, discount rates are used to adjust the ROIs based on the perceived riskiness of supply chain investment across countries. Locating a manufacturing plant in the United

States was assessed a 20 percent discount rate. If the discount rate increases from 30 percent to 52 percent in China, from 30 percent to 46 percent in India, from 30 percent to 39 percent in Brazil, from 35 percent to 50 percent in Mexico, and from 40 percent to 59 percent in Thailand, while everything else remains the same, then the ROIs in those emerging economies will be less than 7 percent, resulting in an unfavorable decision in comparison with U.S. domestic locations.

A Real-Life Example

Using the same model, we collected actual data for the high-end cell phone manufacturing industry and decided whether the plant should be located in the United States, Thailand, or Singapore. Based on a November 2008 quote from Port-2-Port Shipping, a Singapore freight-rate portal, the total cost of shipping a 20-foot container from Singapore to New York was about $1,945. The shipping cost from Thailand to New York was estimated by Thailand's Board of Investment at $3,092.[22] A 20-foot container can hold 25,580 packaged cell phones.

In our analysis, we used the following assumptions: U.S. annual demand for cell phones is 50,000 units. The retail price is $400 per unit. U.S. labor productivity is two labor hours for one unit of product, and labor cost per hour is $13.61.[23] Material cost is $300, accounting for 75 percent of the retail price. The manufacturing plant costs $5 million to build in the U.S. state of Mississippi.[24] Depreciation is five years without any salvage value. The labor productivity for Thailand is derived using per-worker output comparisons in the industrial sectors. Data suggest that U.S. labor productivity in the industrial sectors may be 9.12 times greater than Thai labor productivity.[25] Thai labor cost in the cell phone manufacturing industry is $1.53 per worker.[26] Transportation lead time from Thailand to New York is 32 days, with standard deviation of 15 days.

The risk discount rate is 40 percent for Thailand due to societal instability and economic vulnerability. Labor productivity in Singapore is derived in the same manner as Thai labor productivity. Data from the same source suggest that U.S. labor productivity may be 1.79 times greater than Singapore's labor productivity. Singapore's labor cost is $8 per worker hour.[27] Ocean shipping from Singapore to New York takes 21 days, with a two-day standard deviation. The risk-adjusted discount rate is 25 percent.

Given these factors, and under normal business conditions, the return on supply chain investment is projected to be 31 percent in the United States, 110 percent in Thailand, and 41 percent in Singapore. However, when business conditions change, the dynamics of ROI across those countries may change as well. A complete breakdown of costs is shown in Table 3.4.

Supply Chain ROI vs. Risk-Adjusted Discount Rate

Our model could be used to develop policy recommendations for foreign countries on how to improve their attractiveness as a manufacturing location by reducing their risk-adjusted discount rates. Figure 3.3 shows how supply chain ROI may vary with the perceived risk of doing business in Thailand.

The baseline risk-adjusted discount rate is 40 percent for Thailand, and the corresponding supply chain ROI is projected to be 110 percent over the five-year investment period, provided other factors remain unchanged. The analysis suggests that when the perceived risk of doing business in Thailand is high enough to warrant a 60 percent discount rate, the projected supply chain ROI decreases from 110 percent to 55 percent over the five-year investment period. On the other hand, if Thailand can improve its business risk profile by reducing its adjusted discount rate from 40 percent to 20 percent, comparable to that of the United States in our example, then the projected ROI will be 208 percent, almost doubling the country's baseline ROI.

Companies seeking to source in Thailand might use this type of analysis to demonstrate the country's perceived risk level and to support requests for risk-reducing incentives (such as trade finance, insurance, or production guarantees) from the investment authorities. Such incentives might cause the ROI to increase dramatically and tip the balance even more sharply in favor of Thailand.

The methodology we have presented is a practical, rapidly deployable approach for evaluating supply chain country hubs and measuring the total risk-adjusted returns from supply chain

TABLE 3.4. Comparison of return on investment across three countries—actual data. This table compares actual ROI investment data across the United States, Thailand, and Singapore

	Parameter	USA	Thailand	Singapore
Annual demand (unit)	50,000	50,000	50,000	50,000
Selling price in U.S. market	400	400	400	400
Annual sales in U.S. market		20,000,000	20,000,000	20,000,000
Labor		90,000	9,873	50,309
Labor hours needed per unit of product (labor productivity)		2.00	18.23	3.58
Total labor hours		100,000	911,577	178,894
Labor cost per hour		13.61	1.53	8.00
Total labor costs		1,361,000	1,395,852	1,431,155
Labor costs per product unit		27.22	27.92	28.62
Materials				
Material costs per unit (assuming sourcing locally)		300	250	275
Total material costs		15,000,000	12,500,000	13,750,000
PPE Investment (property, plant & equipment)				
Initial plant investment (depreciation over-5-years without salvage value)		5,000,000	3,500,000	5,000,000
Annual depreciation cost	5	1,000,000	700,000	1,000,000
Allocated depreciation cost per unit		20.00	14.00	20.00
Customs				
Customs value per unit (assuming labor, materials and PPE costs included)		347.22	291.92	323.62
Customs cost per unit	12%	–	35.03	38.83
Total custom costs			210,180.27	233,008.64
Transportation (from origin to domestic manufacturing plant)				
Estimated transportation cost per unit		–	12.00	8.00
total transportation costs		200,000	600,000	400,000
Purchasing Cost (labor + materials + depr + transport costs)				
Total purchasing cost per unit		347	339	370
Inventory				
Demand per day during lead time (assuming constant demand)	365	137	137	137
Average lead time (days)		2	32	21
Standard deviation of lead time		1	15	2
Customer service level (z)	1.645	95%	95%	95%
Safety stock requirement (unit)		499	7,763	3,327
Value of safety stocks		173,365	2,631,381	1,232,646
Total costs of safety stocks (obsolescence, damage, etc.)	30%	52,010	789,414	369,794
Cashflows				
U.S. domestic selling expenses		200,000	200,000	200,000
Annual cashflow		2,186,990	3,604,553	2,616,042
Risk adjusted discount rate		20%	40%	25%
Present value (PV) of cashflows over 5 years		6,540,440	7,335,856	7,035,270
Net present value (NPV)		1,540,440	3,835,856	2,035,270
ROI (return on initial plant investment)		31%	110%	41%

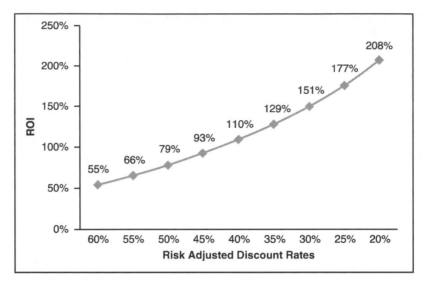

FIGURE 3.3 Supply chain ROI based on discount rates. This figure shows how supply chain ROI may vary with the perceived risk of doing business in Thailand. The horizontal axis reflects the reasonable range of discount rates in reality.

investments in those hubs. The online spreadsheet model that we have made available to readers of this book will provide decision makers with an easy-to-use model that can accommodate most of their "what if" analyses regarding international network design.

Decision #2: Designing the Domestic Supply Chain

In addition to country hubs, companies need to set up domestic (or in-country) networks. By domestic we mean that the scope of the network design and analysis includes changeable variables that are specific to a particular country.

Just like cross-border networks, domestic networks will have risks associated with them. Meanwhile, as supply chains have become longer and more complex, their network designs have become more important and complicated. When we consider both the domestic network and the larger, more complex global network of which it is a component, it becomes apparent that the design of both will have an impact on how companies manage risk and disruption.

In this section, we will first provide a few general principles of network design, and then we will focus on domestic supply chains. We will also examine a key consideration in determining hub fitness: network reach and the ability to collapse distance and open up short paths to remote nodes. This "distance compression" can be measured using the network analysis tools highlighted in this section.

Basic Principles of Domestic Network Design

The recommended steps presented here are very general and are broad enough to allow for considerable leeway in the way they are applied. This basic process will provide a foundation for an examination of how risk, disruptions, and volatility affect the typical network analysis.

An important first step in any network design effort is to scope the problem at hand. The scope of a project encompasses the supply chain attributes or entities that are "in play"; that is, they can be adjusted, added to, removed from the system, or otherwise changed. Since this discussion is focused on domestic supply chains, anything that could be classified as international is automatically classified as being out of scope.

Once the scope of the project has been determined, the data needed to perform the analysis must be sought out. The ideal would be to get as much relevant data as possible and then find an appropriate analysis tool. But for several reasons—the plethora of data that could result, financial limitations on software and human resources, employees' experience using one tool or another—that approach may be impractical or economically infeasible. Accordingly, in many cases, which data are needed will depend on the analysis tool that will be used.

Not every design problem warrants the use of sophisticated network analysis tools, however. Figure 3.4 displays general "rules of thumb," or guidelines, for considering the type of analysis that should be done, using the example of a distribution center or warehouse location analysis. If a number of factors fall into the right-hand column (most complex), then the project may require the use of sophisticated software. If most factors are in the left-hand column, then simpler tools may be sufficient.

The next step is to understand the network well enough to be able to model a baseline that comes within a specified percentage of the actual supply chain cost. In most modeling efforts, some assumptions or generalizations are made to ensure that the model does not get bogged down in the fine details and take far too much time. This is not unlike the so-called "80/20 rule" that is commonly applied in other disciplines: it may take 20 percent of your time to get an 80 percent optimal answer. To get to an answer that is 90 percent or 100 percent correct may take an enormous amount of time to refine the optimization, and ultimately it may not be worth the effort.

There are two main reasons to produce a baseline. The first is to verify that the supply chain is reasonably well understood and the data reflect reality. The second is to provide a basis for comparison among the alternative scenarios that will be produced.

After the baseline is complete, it is important to determine the "what if" scenarios that are to be run during the network analysis. Including the project's sponsors or appropriate decision makers in that discussion can be valuable.

When completed, the analysis should reveal the ideal location, number of suppliers, amount of inventory that should be held, or other answers appropriate to the end goal of the project. The next question is whether the analysis should be revisited and updated, and if so, when that review should be conducted. Many companies have discrete, five-year analysis periods for critical supply chain components and/or echelons. This means that about every five years, they remodel certain components of their supply chains to ensure that the answers generated by their original analyses still hold. Factors such as population shifts, changes in costs and demand, and many others can have a dramatic impact on a revised analysis. Yet companies do not always include these changes when they conduct their periodic analyses.

Least Complex ⟷	*Most Complex*	
Excel + Mapping Tool ⟷	Optimization Software	
One facility under consideration	Two or three facilities under consideration	>3 facilities under consideration
Few sources/destinations	Many sources/destinations	Hundreds of sources/destinations
No inventory space considerations	Major DC inventory considerations	All facility inventory/production considerations
One mode of transportation	Two modes of transportation	All modes of transportation
No manufacturing	Single input/single SKU production	Multiple inputs/multiple production items
Location analysis	Location analysis plus one other selection constraint (service time, transportation mode, etc.)	Network optimization

FIGURE 3.4 Rules of thumb for software choice with location analyses. This figure indicates the level of software sophistication required to model location analysis, based on the complexity of the network to be designed.

This approach, in our view, is no longer effective. The constant volatility confronting supply chains today means that both the scoping of a project and the periodic analysis schedule need to be altered to produce more of a real-time, rolling analysis.

Tailoring the Domestic Supply Chain to Specific Needs and Attributes

There is no one-size-fits-all answer to network design choices. Any design or optimization exercise should aim to tailor the network to the company's specific needs and attributes.

The following two examples are based on real companies and their supply chains, but data, names, locations, and illustrations have been modified to disguise the companies. In the first example, the initial network analysis suggested that a centralized network would be the best choice; in the second, the analysis recommended decentralization. After outlining those scenarios, we will examine how scoping and risk factor into network analyses, and how they can affect the outcome.

Example 1: The Answer Is Centralization

DSM Manufacturing (a pseudonym for the actual company) is a large firm headquartered in a small city in the Midwest. It is looking to contract out packaging of a new product and wants to know in what city the contract packager (CP) should be located in order to reduce network costs outside of the CP's price per package. There are several constraints. First, 15 percent of the product volume would come from Asia, while the rest would come from its core location Marshalltown, Iowa, in the U.S. Midwest. In addition, 10 percent of the Asian volume would have to be routed through Marshalltown for quality control before being shipped to the CP. The CP would then ship the product to one of five regional distribution centers for further handling and shipping to the end customer. Meanwhile, one of the project's sponsors wanted to determine whether Marshalltown, located in an area of the country that was not densely populated, was in fact the optimal location, as indicated by previous network analyses.

The modeling effort that ensued considered possible CP locations around the country, as shown in Figure 3.5. A baseline was validated and scenarios run. To the disappointment of the sponsor, the model recommended that a CP be located in or around Marshalltown. Nearly all of the manufacturing, contract packagers, quality control functions, and 35 percent of the nationwide distribution were centralized around that city. Most network design analyses, in fact, repeatedly showed it as the best location with the lowest inbound and outbound costs.[28]

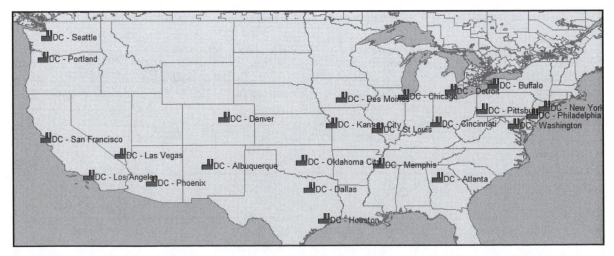

FIGURE 3.5 Sample of possible contract packager (CP) locations in the modeling effort. This figure shows the locations tried in the model by Jim and Phil of alternate contract packager locations.

Source: John R. Macdonald and Kelvin Sakai, "DSM Manufacturing: When Network Analysis Meets Business Reality," published by CSCMP, 2008.

Example 2: The Answer Is Decentralization

Another large manufacturing firm, ABC Corp., was similarly headquartered in an area of the Midwest that was not optimal from a transportation perspective. Nearly 100 percent of its product originated in Asia; the imported goods moved through the Port of Los Angeles/Long Beach and were shipped to the Midwest via rail. The objective of the network analysis was to determine if the city of Milwaukee, Wisconsin, was the best place to locate a distribution center (DC).

A baseline model of this example, with a single DC in Milwaukee, is shown in Figure 3.6. Many scenarios were run, and the best (lowest cost) option recommended three distribution centers: one in Milwaukee to serve the Midwest, one in Ontario, California (near the port of L.A./Long Beach), and one in Atlanta, Georgia. This result is shown in Figure 3.7. This partially decentralized network was the best scenario, given the balance of costs for inventory holding, warehousing, and transportation.

The various scenarios and their outcomes are shown in Table 3.5.

Considering Scoping and Risk in Network Analysis

In addition to the factors discussed above, scope and risk perceptions also played a role in both of these examples.

In the first example, several network factors remained out of scope for various reasons. For instance, an option to produce the 85 percent of the product manufactured in Marshalltown at another location was not allowed because it was deemed to cost too much to move production. This

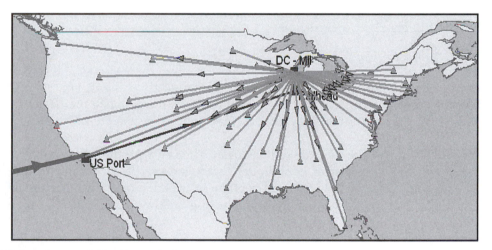

FIGURE 3.6 Baseline model for Example 2.

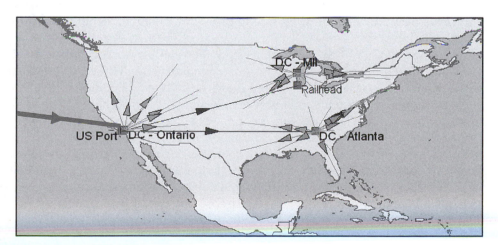

FIGURE 3.7 Best scenario model for Example 2.

TABLE 3.5. Sample scenario calculations

Supply Chain Network Design Worksheet	Baseline	Scenario 1	Scenario 2	Scenario 3	Scenario 4
	Milwaukee	*Milwaukee + Ontario*	*Milwaukee + Dallas*	*Milwaukee + Ontario + Dallas*	*Milwaukee + Ontario + Atlanta*
Transportation costs from Asia to the U.S.A.					
Ocean freight	$1,315,289.00	$939,067.00	$922,754.00	$882,524.00	$892,686.00
Customs duties	$6,551.00	$6,551.00	$6,551.00	$6,551.00	$6,551.00
Facility costs – U.S.A.					
Deconsolidation and warehousing	$65,363.00	$63,671.00	$55,379.00	$55,341.00	$50,710.00
Distribution costs – U.S.A.					
Road freight	$ 714,171.00	$621,285.00	$622,113.00	$506,525.00	$441,717.00
Rail freight	$ 334,000.00	$157,898.00	$241,775.00	$192,333.00	$201,954.00
Air freight	$815.00	$709.00	$715.00	$579.00	$505.00
Inventory holding costs					
Pipeline China – U.S.A.	$72,242.00	$68,801.00	$66,268.00	$64,493.00	$61,753.00
U.S.A. facilities	$65,671.00	$71,805.00	$71,805.00	$77,939.00	$77,939.00
Total	$2,574,102.00	$1,929,787.00	$1,987,360.00	$1,786,285.00	$1,733,815.00

would be considered a "conscious" scoping restriction. However, there also are "unconscious" scoping restrictions—i.e., domino effects that stem from the original decisions. For example, the outbound distribution centers were considered to be out of scope; this also had the effect of placing the service areas (demand regions served by each DC, which affect the volume of product flow) out of scope, too.

This is important because the modeler in this scenario agreed with the sponsor that the location did not seem as if it should be optimal, even though that was the result every time the numbers were run. When the modeler included the service areas in the scope, the modeled volume flowing through each facility changed drastically—enough to justify moving the contract packager location by nearly 1,000 miles.

There are multiple perspectives from which to view risk. From a quality standpoint, DSM Manufacturing was being fairly conservative by requiring 10 percent of its product to first pass through Marshalltown for quality control purposes. But this also had the effect of keeping the CP location in the original analysis near Marshalltown. By locating there, the company could avoid a significant amount of transportation cost.

Risk also affects the volatility of the network itself. Some volatility is created outside of the company. Examples include supplier bankruptcies, strong demand swings, natural disasters, and swiftly changing costs, such as we have seen with oil and diesel fuel. Other sources of volatility are created internally, such as sabotage, accidents, or production failures. When scoping a network analysis, allowing too much of a supply chain network to be in-scope or leaving too much out of the scope could generate additional volatility from these external or internal areas.

Getting the scope of a project right is one of the elements of risk management in network design. A second element is considering whether the network design reflects risk management efforts aimed at preventing some types of disruptions from happening; disruption management that works toward a faster recovery; or a mixture of the two. An example of this would be a case in which a demand population base is located in the U.S. Gulf Coast region. Incorporating a risk management approach in the network scoping would result in a recommendation that manufacturing and DCs move far away from the area due to the threat of hurricanes. A disruption management approach, by contrast, would allow facilities to be located in that region, but would instead include plans for recovering quickly when hurricanes occur.

Yet another element of risk management in network design involves managing trade-offs in such a way as to achieve a company's desired goal. Changing priorities, often spurred by external events, can introduce volatility to a network design. Typical priorities include lowest total cost, excellent customer service, and lowest amount of inventory, among others. A new priority for many companies is supply chain sustainability as it relates to being "green" and having a minimal or carbon-neutral impact on the environment. This is not always voluntary; there are many state and federal government regulations under consideration that might limit emissions or even impose a financial penalty for certain levels of emissions. It is important for managers to be aware of such potential sources of volatility. Having optimized a network for lowest cost, for instance, that network may suddenly be in a vulnerable position when viewed from the vantage point of new priorities.

Points to Ponder

Two main questions arise from a careful consideration of these points and examples. First, if a network is redesigned more frequently, then what is the real baseline? And second, how can dynamic network design actually be achieved?

To answer the first question: the previous optimization model becomes the baseline. Since the network analyses are being done much more frequently, the learning curve associated with understanding the network diminishes. The modeler becomes so familiar with the network, and the "old" model is so recent, that it can be used as the baseline.

As to the second question, there are many ways to achieve the flexibility and agility necessary for implementing possible design changes, and many of these are very specific to the situation, location, company, and industry. One way is to avoid being tied to a given transportation mode. In 2008, when high fuel prices were causing truckload rates to soar, many companies switched some of their shipments to intermodal rail. A second way is to partner with a large third-party logistics provider (3PL) that has warehouse space in many locations. If a network re-optimization indicates that moving a warehouse would reduce costs, it should be possible to make that move within the 3PL's system without having to change the warehouse management system (WMS) or other supply chain information systems.

In short, network design is moving away from discrete projects that occur periodically which aim to achieve a single, optimal solution. Instead, they are moving toward a rolling review of as many network design factors as possible and making adjustments in real time. This type of dynamic network management requires ongoing, frequent analysis. The objective is to adjust to changing priorities and situations by flexibly positioning or repositioning supply chain resources and assets. We need to determine the changes that we can respond to quickly enough and cost-effectively enough to make dynamic network design feasible. At the same time, we also need to determine what risks and analysis results we must ignore so that we move quickly and cost-effectively.

Decision #3: Analyzing Transportation Cost and Service Lead-Time Trade-Offs

Once the supply chain network has been configured—that is, its major country hubs and intra-country nodes have been selected—the work of managing network transactions must be effectively conducted in order to maintain the network's integrity in the face of business volatility. Analyses of the trade-offs between transportation costs and service lead times are crucial for taking advantage of the distance and time compression afforded by robust hubs.

Often, important operational decisions focus on just two major variables: customer time sensitivity—the length of time critical items take to reach key customers; and/or cost sensitivity—the expenditures involved in the routing of a critical item over a particular route. In a volatile demand environment, these decisions frequently are made on the fly, but they have long-lasting repercussions.

Nowhere is this truer than in the military, where network-transactions management decisions can be a matter of life and death. Yet until recently, the U.S. military has not systematically adopted or deployed dynamic network configuration tools, like those used in private industry, to serve the highly dispersed warfighter force. In the case example that follows, we analyze the impact of utilizing a Web-based network-transactions management tool in the supply chain that supported the production and deployment of the military's high-mobility artillery rocket system (HIMARS).

HIMARS Project Background

HIMARS is a multiple-launch rocket system (MLRS) on a wheeled chassis. The system was developed by Lockheed Martin Missiles and Fire Control.

In 2008, Lockheed Martin received a contract to support more than 300 U.S. Army and U.S. Marine Corps MLRS launchers through its Life Cycle Contractor Support (LCCS) system. Under LCCS, a global team of field service representatives feeds records of each unit's launcher operational status, configurations, and component upgrades to a central operations center. That information then becomes immediately available in a networked database that also contains records describing the configuration and maintenance history of every major component and subassembly. Repair facilities and special test equipment are co-located with the operational units to help reduce turnaround times for repair of major components.[29]

Under the contract, Lockheed Martin is responsible for supporting fire-control systems for both HIMARS and the MLRS M270A1 launcher as well as the HIMARS launcher-loader module. The company's responsibilities also include supply, maintenance, and related logistics support, including field service representatives who work alongside the warfighters to provide quick turn-around on repairs. Lives depend on LCCS meeting demanding performance standards. According to Lockheed Martin, at the time the 2008 contract was awarded, LCCS had already been providing a system status-readiness rate for HIMARS that consistently averaged above 99 percent; a mission-capable turnaround time that averaged less than 12 hours for systems based within the United States; and repair turnaround times in the field averaging less than two days.[30]

Risk Profile of the HIMARS Supply Chain Network

LCCS's support performance has been especially strong given the uncertainties and risks surrounding the HIMARS supply chain. Two characteristics of the program create risks that require special attention:

1. LCCS is a relatively new business model that has different requirements than those of the current U.S. Army supply chain. Disconnects between the Army's IT systems and business rules and the IT systems and business rules of Lockheed and its maintenance and repair sub-contractor could pose a significant risk to the HIMARS project throughout its lifecycle. The HIMARS solution must be able to work with commercial industry standards, because Lockheed's maintenance and repair sub-contractor will be managing its order and supply through its own commercial systems, with a major part of the supply chain operated and controlled by the vendor.
2. Because the HIMARS launcher system is new, there are a number of unknowns. However, some aspects of the new HIMARS supply chain can be developed based on experience with the previous generation 270A1 MLRS launcher. For example, predictions for failure rates of common launcher parts, expected demand parameters, safety stock levels and other inventory policies, supplier management requirements, and so forth can all be estimated with some confidence. But other aspects are unpredictable and carry many risks. These include the number of users; unanticipated forward deployments; near-theater and in-theater support resources; pre-positioned stock; logistics; and response times and demands on the supporting supply chain. The level of security, reliability, and availability that will actually be required in a highly volatile military environment worldwide also are unknown.

Designing Network Transaction Management Tools to Overcome Volatility

In response to geopolitical upheavals, the HIMARS supply chain could become severely constrained, and new sources of supply and alternative distribution mechanisms might be urgently needed. For this reason, in the early stage of the project, it was critically important to craft a simulation that could model a range of supply chain scenarios and uncertainties.

Early on in the program development cycle, the Robert H. Smith School of Business Supply Chain Management Center assisted the Army HIMARS Program Management Office and Lockheed Martin in utilizing supply chain network-optimization software to create a HIMARS LCCS Supply Chain Business Model that can:

- Simulate physical, informational, and financial flows across a spectrum of supply chain network configurations. This simulation can also assist in identifying total logistics costs that can form the basis for gain-sharing activities between the HIMARS Program Management Office and Lockheed, and can help to identify key cost drivers that adversely affect readiness.
- Generate optimized inventory, supply, and transportation policies and business rules for the HIMARS supply chain that support readiness goals.
- Be a constantly updated supply chain foundation model in support of ongoing HIMARS operations.

The Smith School and its strategic partner, the consulting firm Operations Associates, worked with the HIMARS Program Office and Lockheed Martin to comprehensively map key supply chain actors, inventory and distribution nodes, and multidirectional material flows. This map of all current and projected production and stocking points included in-theater, forward-positioned stock; depots; and Army/supplier distribution centers.

The map of the projected HIMARS supply chain covers 50 user units; 12 suppliers in Texas, Florida, New Jersey, and Israel; and the Performance Support Integrator Operations Center located in Ft. Worth, Texas, at Lockheed Missiles. This is shown in Figure 3.8.

This map was coded into a geographic information system (GIS) for shared online access, and a rules engine (developed by Radical Logistics) was applied to model optimum supply chain network configurations. We had three purposes for doing so:

- To create a HIMARS supply chain business model that can minimize costs and maximize performance over time;

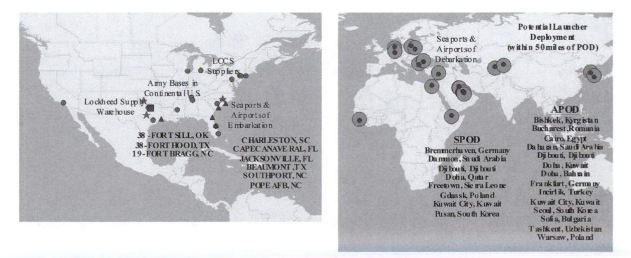

FIGURE 3.8 The global supply chain map for the HIMARS system.

Note: SPOD = seaports of debarkation; APOD = airports of debarkation.

- To compare "as is" performance (financial, operational, and customer service) variables against the model's optimized variables to target improvement initiatives over time;
- To provide decision makers with strategic, long-term visibility over the whole supply chain, guide ordering policies over time, and minimize stock-outs of critical parts.

As shown in Figure 3.9, we modeled all nodes and transit links of the global supply chain.

We also modeled all transit costs from the loading or embarkation points to the unloading or debarkation points; and also modeled times across the network as a prerequisite for creating a decision-support mechanism for supply chain managers, as shown in Figure 3.10.

Drilling down, we defined detailed input rate tables and output displays tables, as shown in Figure 3.11.

This model made it possible for us to develop LCCS supply chain tools to support three things:

- Visibility of cost-effective means of parts delivery;
- Transparency of reasonable LCCS costs based on Army user inputs;
- A potential budgeting tool (using rapid analysis of multiple warehousing and transportation scenarios).

If we look at one aspect, the modeling of parts re-supply options, we can use the software model to determine distance to customer, methods of shipping to customer, transit time and/or cost factors, as shown in Figure 3.12.

Finally, the model lays out the cost-vs.-time options available to the supply chain decision maker, who can choose the fastest or cheapest way to route supplies based on the requirements of the moment. In Figure 3.13, reducing the theater delivery time of 19 launchers from 310 hours to 32 hours involves an almost fourfold increase in cost, which might well be worth the cost differential, depending on the exigencies of the situation.

This case example has demonstrated that a global supply chain network map that defines key locations and transit links between them can be used as a tactical tool to aid decision makers in

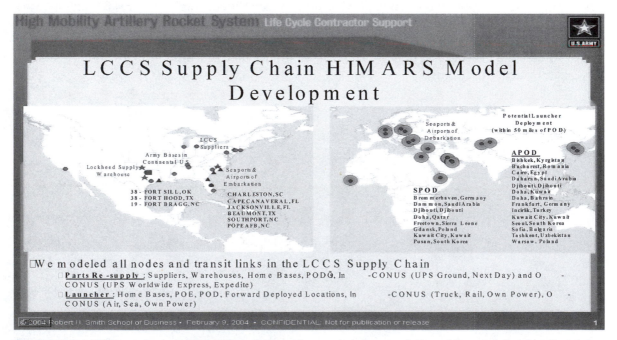

FIGURE 3.9 LCCS supply chain HIMARS model development. A representation of the modeling for all nodes and transit links in the LCCS supply chain.

Note: CONUS = continental United States.

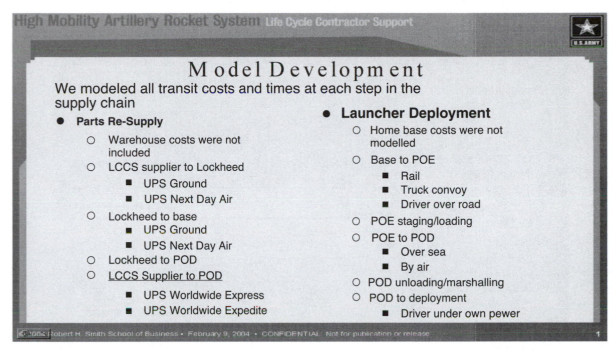

FIGURE 3.10 HIMARS supply chain model development. This figure depicts the supply chain process steps included in the model. POD refers to point of debarkation; POE refers to point of embarkation.

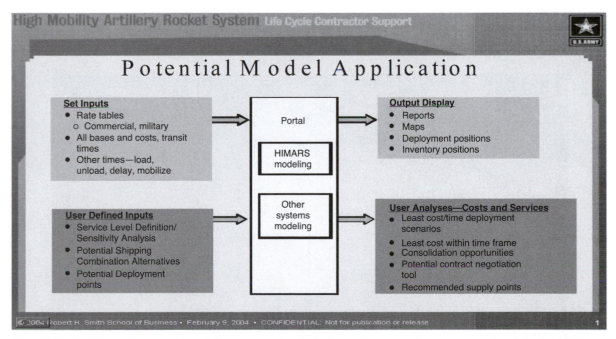

FIGURE 3.11 HIMARS network modeling application. This figure illustrates the components of the HIMARS network modeling application.

managing the costs or service lead times of a very uncertain and volatile supply chain. In the hands of an integrated, lifecycle support contractor (such as those in Lockheed Martin's LCCS program) or a third-party logistics company, such a tool can yield big benefits for the customer by adding dynamism and flexibility to global supply chain networks that historically were treated as fixed-node, relatively static structures. For the U.S. Army and other traditional logistics systems, such an approach can help overcome the inherent risks of globalized operations.

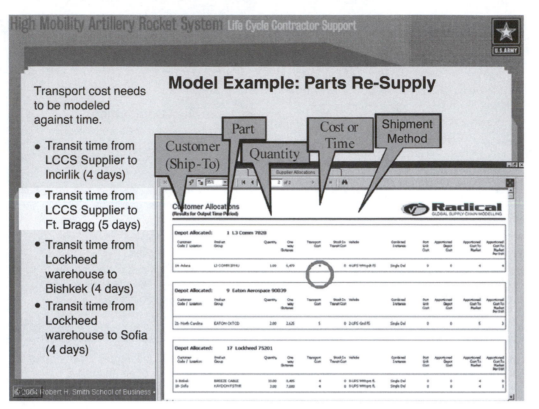

FIGURE 3.12 HIMARS parts re-supply modeling. This figure shows how parts re-supply was modeled across the HIMARS re-supply site network.

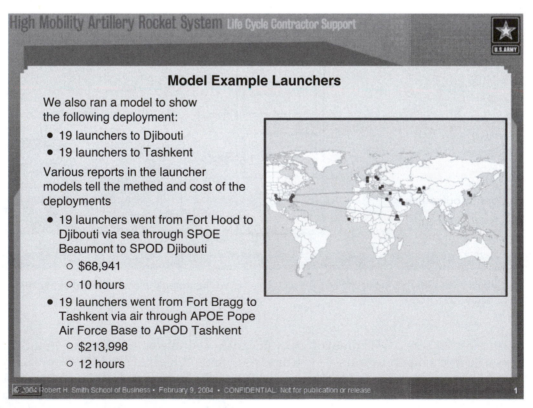

FIGURE 3.13 Delivery-cost model for launchers. This figure shows how delivery times and costs were modeled for launchers.

Decision #4: Insourcing/Outsourcing Network Assets and Services

The final subject of this chapter—ownership of assets or services across the network—has not been explicitly addressed in previous sections of this chapter. It is a very relevant topic, however, as research conducted by the Robert H. Smith School's Supply Chain Management Center has revealed. Our 1999 study of 463 companies that had partnered with external logistics providers for three years or more found concrete evidence that outsourcing of assets and services provides real strategic improvements in flexibility, quality, and cost-efficiency.

Respondents reported cost savings of more than 21 percent in the first year. Moreover, those who had outsourced total logistics lifecycle management enjoyed cost savings of more than 15 percent in the second, third, and fourth years of their 3PL contracts. Table 3.6 details these results.

Although outsourcing can be a valuable arrow in our quiver of managerial solutions, generalities about its utility can be extremely dangerous when dealing with highly volatile situations. What works in many cases may not work for every company's supply chain at all times.

To help them make the right decisions regarding whether or not to outsource, supply chain managers need fast, reliable, off-the-shelf analytic tools. They are not easy to come by, however, and for that reason we are including one as the final component of our network configuration toolset. An Insourcing vs. Outsourcing Analytic Tool to simplify the network insourcing/outsourcing decision exercise is posted online and is available to purchasers of this book at http://www.routledge.com/textbooks/harrington.

The tool we developed uses the comparative analytic approach of measuring aggregate total logistics costs for both insourced and outsourced scenarios. We used it to develop a supply chain strategy to support a U.S. toy distributor's first-phase sales expansion into the following countries: United Kingdom, France, Germany, the Benelux countries (Belgium, the Netherlands, and Luxembourg), Spain, Italy, Scandinavia (Denmark, Norway, Sweden, and Finland), Greece, Poland, and Russia. (The company described in this example is a real company with a masked identity.)

We began the strategy analysis by identifying clusters of potential customer demand in the target countries. This included identifying potential high-volume demand pools in each country, including dense population centers and high-volume demographic segments. We then identified wholesale and retail channels to reach end customers, and we identified and categorized wholesale/retail channels that would serve the high-volume demand pools and demographic segments.

Finally, we proposed a supply chain strategy for Europe, evaluating from a regional supply chain perspective the previously identified retail/wholesale channels and options for serving the population

TABLE 3.6. Cost savings from logistics outsourcing. This table shows logistics cost savings from the outsourcing of logistics functions

Year 1			Years 2, 3, and 4	
Function currently outsourced	Average savings (%)	Standard deviation (%)	Average Savings (%)	Standard deviation (%)
All supply chain functions	21.33	17.34	15.09	14.16
Freight payments and auditing	10.54	13.82	9.44	12.62
Fleet management	10.46	10.15	6.78	4.98
Carrier selection and rate negotiation	10.19	9.19	7.70	7.59
Warehousing operations	9.54	8.42	8.36	8.53
Packaging	8.81	13.71	8.53	12.73
Logistics information systems	7.28	10.09	6.04	5.02
Shipment planning	5.71	8.45	5.35	11.31
Order processing and fulfillment	2.54	11.16	4.50	13.79
Product returns	2.10	2.66	3.10	2.61
Inventory management	3.5	1.91	5.00	3.56

Source: Lisa H. Harrington, Sandor Boyson, and Thomas Corsi, *Logistics and the Extended Enterprise*, John Wiley, 1999, page 137.

centers in the target countries. Our main objective was to specify the right number and location of distribution centers and warehouses to serve the specified countries from both a cost and customer service perspective. Our insourcing/outsourcing analysis focused on determining whether those facilities should be operated by the toy distributor itself or by third-party logistics companies. A discussion of the base situation and the outcomes of our analyses follows.

Situation Analysis

The U.S. East Coast-based Company AlphaA sells toys primarily in the United States. Its toys are mostly manufactured in China, but some are made in South America. Due to current competition in the U.S. market and huge potential in the European market, Company AlphaA decided to expand its presence in Europe. At present, Company AlphaA has generated some sales in the continental Europe with orders primarily shipped via ocean, and in the United Kingdom, which it serves via by air transportation from its warehouse located in Harbor BetaB. However, to sustain efficient and timely supply for the European market while maintaining reasonable logistics costs in the near future, Company AlphaA is considering building a distribution center in continental Europe to serve both its U.K.-based customers and European retailers in its other target markets.

Given Company AlphaA's particular mix of risk and benefit factors, there were three options for logistics network design.

Option I: No distribution center in Europe

Company AlphaA would continue its current practice, in which 60 percent of its European orders are shipped from the warehouse in Harbor BetaB to European retailers by ocean, 20 percent are expedited from Harbor BetaB to Airport CharleyC in Europe and then are transported to retailers by truck, and the remaining 20 percent are shipped directly from suppliers in China by ocean to European retailers. This wait-and-see approach is safe but may risk losing out on expansion opportunities in the European market.

Option II: Third party manages distribution center in Europe

Company AlphaA would outsource its warehouse management to a third-party logistics provider. By doing so, Company AlphaA could avoid having to make an initial, fixed capital investment and could hedge its risk exposure in case sales in Europe do not justify running its own warehouse. This approach would enable Company AlphaA to expand in Europe while leaving open the option of running its own warehouse if business should grow beyond a specified threshold. The negative side is that Company AlphaA would have to pay a premium for warehousing and handling until it decides to manage its own facility.

Option III: Company AlphaA operates distribution center in Europe

Running a distribution center with its own staff, Company AlphaA would be able to build and capitalize on its logistics competency and strongly support its European marketing strategy. However, operational costs, including an enterprise resource planning (ERP) system and labor, are very high. It is uncertain when and whether sales volume would be high enough to justify such a large investment in human resources and technology.

We used the concept of total logistics costs to evaluate these three options and discuss the advantages and disadvantages of each based on cost/benefit and risk/return assessments.

We set up the cost parameters as shown in Table 3.7. In addition, average production cost was set at $10.00 per unit, and import duty is assessed at 12 percent of production cost.

Based on total logistics costs calculations, Option III is the best, lowest-cost option—meaning Company AlphaA should own and manage its own European distribution channel (Table 3.8). Option I (no distribution center in Europe) is the second-best option. Option II (third-party DC) is

TABLE 3.7. Cost parameters for Company AlphaA analysis. This table shows a comparison of transportation costs for company AlphaA

Transportation Costs

Departure	Destination	Mode	Unit cost (USD)
Harbor BetaB	Airport CharleyC in Europe	Air	$1.52
Harbor BetaB	European distribution center	Ocean	$0.22
Harbor BetaB	Retailers in Europe	Ocean	$0.22
Suppliers	Harbor BetaB	Ocean	$0.39
Suppliers	European distribution center	Ocean	$0.22
Suppliers	Retailers in Europe	Ocean	$0.38
Airport CharleyC	European distribution center	Truck	$0.15
European DC	Retailers in Europe	Truck	$0.34
Airport CharleyC	Retailers in Europe	Truck	$0.44

Warehouse Handling Costs

Location	Handling cost (USD)
Warehouse in Harbor BetaB	$0.40 per unit
Warehouse in Europe run by Company AlphaA	$0.50 per unit
Warehouse in Europe run by third party	$1.22 per unit

Percent of Sales by Channel and Capital Cost per Unit of Inventory

	Percentage shipped (by weight)	Capital cost per unit
No DC in Europe		
Supplier→Harbor BetaB→Airport CharleyC→retailers	15%	$0.60
Supplier→Harbor BetaB→retailer	60%	$0.60
Supplier→retailer	25%	$0.00
Third Party or Company AlphaA runs DC in Europe		
Supplier→Harbor BetaB→Airport CharleyC→European DC→retailer	5%	$0.80
Supplier→Harbor BetaB→European DC→Retailer	10%	$0.80
Supplier→European DC→retailer	60%	$0.40
Supplier→retailer	25%	$0.00

the most expensive option. The third-party outsourced option is not tenable given a warehouse cost that is almost double (85 cents per unit) that of a company-owned warehouse (44 cents).

This result should reinforce for supply chain managers the need to be cautious about generalizations. It would have been easy to assume that because the company was new to European logistics, it would benefit from having a third party manage its entry to the continent. In terms of total logistics costs, at least, this clearly is not so.

Owning its distribution channel would also help Company AlphaA enhance its relationships with key customers and get a better handle on demand patterns and service requirements that may be unique to individual country markets. This type of knowledge is particularly important in industries like toys, which have great demand volatility and a very short primary selling season. If Company AlphaA chose to outsource its distribution, it would not get the benefit of this information.

The results of this exercise serve to emphasize the following points:

- Total logistics costs include transportation costs, warehouse handling costs, capital costs for holding inventory, and import duties for international business. Transportation costs may be offset by warehousing costs.

TABLE 3.8. Evaluation of the three options. This table shows that, based on total logistics costs calculations, Option III is the best, lowest-cost option—meaning Company AlphaA should own and manage its own European distribution channel

Warehouse	Handling cost per unit
Company Alpha Managed Warehouse in Harbor Beta	$0.40
Company Alpha Managed European DC	$0.50
Third Party Managed European DC	$1.22

Production Cost	$10.00
Duty rate (% of production cost)	12%

Components of Total Logistics Costs:	
	Transportation Costs
	Warehouse Costs
	Inventory Carrying Costs
	Import Duty

Departure	Destination	Mode	Cost per unit
Harbor Beta	Airport Charley in Europe	Air	$1.52
Harbor Beta	European DC	Ocean	$0.22
Harbor Beta	Retailer in Europe	Ocean	$0.22
Asian and S. American Suppliers	Harbor Beta	Ocean	$0.39
Asian and S. American Suppliers	European DC	Ocean	$0.22
Asian and S. American Suppliers	Retailer in Europe	Ocean	$0.38
Airport Charley in Europe	European DC	Land	$0.15
European DC	Retailer in Europe	Land	$0.34
Airport Charley in Europe	Retailer in Europe	Truck (container)	$0.44

Evaluations of Three Options Distribution Channel	Percentage of Sales Per Channel	Total Transport Costs	Warehouse Costs	Capital Costs Inventory	Duty	Total Logistics Costs
Option I: No Distribution Center in Europe						
Asian and S. American Asian and S. American Supplier – Harbor Beta – Airport Charley – European Retailer	15%	$2.35	$0.40	$0.60	$1.20	$0.68
Asian and S. American Asian and S. American Supplier – Harbor Beta – European Retailer	60%	$0.61	$0.40	$0.60	$1.20	$1.69
Asian and S. American Asian and S. American Supplier – European Retailer	25%	$0.38	$0.00	$0.00	$1.20	$0.40

Total Logistics Costs		$0.81	$0.30	$0.45	$1.20	**$2.76**

Option II: Third Party Managed Distribution Center in Europe

Asian and S. American Supplier – Harbor B – Airport C – European DC – Retailer	5%	$2.40	$1.62	$0.80	$1.20	$0.30
Asian and S. American Supplier – Harbor B – Airport C – Retailer	10%	$2.35	$0.40	$0.80	$1.20	$0.48
Asian and S. American Supplier – European DC – Retailer	60%	$0.56	$1.22	$0.40	$1.20	$2.03
Asian and S. American Supplier – Retailer	25%	$0.38	$0.00	$0.00	$1.20	$0.40
Aggregate Logistics Costs		$0.79	$0.85	$0.36	$1.20	**$3.20**

Option III: Company A Managed Distribution Center in Europe

Asian and S. American Supplier – Harbor B – Airport C – European DC – Retailer	5%	$2.40	$0.90	$0.80	$1.20	$0.27
Asian and S. American Supplier – Harbor B – European DC – Retailer	10%	$0.95	$0.90	$0.80	$1.20	$0.39
Asian and S. American Supplier – European DC – Retailer	60%	$0.56	$0.50	$0.40	$1.20	$1.60
Asian and S. American Supplier – Retailer	25%	$0.38	$0.00	$0.00	$1.20	$0.40
Aggregate Logistics Costs		$0.65	$0.44	$0.36	$1.20	**$2.64**

- Logistics network design serves and depends on a company's marketing and overall business strategy.
- Supply chain network decision making should consider total logistics costs as well as other factors, such as risk exposure, scalability of operations, and market competition, to name a few.

Conclusions

In this chapter, we have argued for a new, more integrative, analytic approach to dynamic network management configuration, and we have provided rapidly deployable spreadsheet tools to help readers apply it. In a world where supply chain cost elements are constantly fluctuating, the tools we have provided for comparing total logistics costs when selecting and managing supply chain hubs are critically important.

In addition to being evaluated based upon cost-efficiencies, supply chain hubs must also be evaluated for fitness, since they are the anchors and mainstays of network robustness. A key dimension of supply chain hub fitness is risk level. This risk level is handled in two ways in our analysis: our country-level situation audit assesses the supply chain "business climate" and infrastructure; and then we assign a risk-adjustment figure to the supply chain return on investment based on this assessment.

Another key dimension of hub fitness is network reach and the ability to collapse distance and open up short paths to remote nodes. This dimension of distance compression is measured using the network analysis tools highlighted in our sections on domestic network design and transport cost/ service lead-time trade-off analyses.

We believe this integrative analysis reflects advances in the new network science and will help supply chain managers to meet the challenges of volatility through more frequent and more holistic reconfiguration of their network's hubs and nodes.

Notes

1 Barabási, Albert-László. *Linked: The New Science of Networks* (Cambridge: Perseus Publishing, 2002), 14–17.

2 Ibid., 14–17.

3 Ibid., 14–17.

4 Philips China example interviews with managers.

5 National Semiconductor example interviews with managers.

6 Bender, Paul. "How to Design an Optimal Worldwide Supply Chain," *Supply Chain Management Review,* 1(1) (Spring 1997).

7 Logistics Bureau Services Matrix. Supply Chain and Distribution Network Design and Optimization, Supply Chain, Logistics and Distribution Network Modeling. http://www.logisticsbureau.com/supply_chain_and_logistics_consulting_services.htm

8 Gilmore, Dan. "Supply Chain Network Design in an Era of Dynamic Costs," *Supply Chain Digest*, March 2, 2006. http://scdigest.com/assets/FirstThoughts/06-03-02.cfm?cid=107

9 Ibid.

10 Payne, Tim. "Case Study: Holcim Uses Network Optimization to Manage Supply Chain Risk and Optimize Costs," Gartner RAS Core Research Note G001659996 (July 2009).

11 Viswanathan, Nari. "Supply Chain Network Design: Architecting a Green Future," Aberdeen Group (February 19, 2009).

12 Scaparra, M.P., and Church, R L. (2005a) "A Bi-level Mixed Integer Program for Critical Infrastructure Protection Planning," Canterbury, Kent, UK; and Scaparra, M.P., and Church, R.L. (2005b) "An Optimal Modeling Approach for The Interdiction Median Problem with Fortification," Kent, Canterbury, UK.

13 Snyder, Lawrence V., and Mark S. Daskin. "Models for Reliable Supply Chain Network Design," in A. Murray and T. Grubesic (Eds.), *Reliability and Vulnerability in Critical Infrastructure: A Quantitative Geographic Perspective* (Springer, 2006).

14 Uncapacitated fixed-charge location problems model the lowest operating cost to serve a given number of customer sites from a given number of product/service sites using x routes. The UFL problems are also called the simple facility location problem, the simple (or uncapacitated) warehouse location problem or the simple (or uncapacitated) plant location problem. In an UFL problem there are a number of sites (n) and a number of customers (m). Each site has a fixed cost (fc). There is a transport cost from each site to each customer (c). There is no limit of capacity for any candidate site and the whole demand of each customer has to be assigned to one site. We are asked to find the *number of sites (facilities)* to be established and specify those sites such that the total cost will be minimized. **Source:** Mehmet Sevkli and Ali Riza Guner, *A New Approach to Solve Uncapacitated Facility Location Problems by Particle Swarm Optimization*, Intelligent Manufacturing Systems, May 29–31, 2006, 237–246.

15 Ibid.

16 Wu, C. (2005) Total Supply Chain Cost Model, Thesis for Leaders for Manufacturing Programs, Massachusetts Institute of Technology, http://dspace.mit.edu/handle/1721.1/34869, accessed September 8, 2009.

17 Lovell, A., R. Saw, and J. Stimson. "Product Value-Density: Managing Diversity through Supply Chain Segmentation," *International Journal of Logistics Management*, 16(1) (2005): 142–158.

18 Gordon, S. (2008). Developing Lean Supply Chains, http://valuechaingroup.com/attachments/File/developing_lean_supply_chains.pdf, accessed September 5, 2009.

19 Moon, G., and L.A. LeBlanc. "The Risk Adjustment of Required Rate of Return for Supply Chain Infrastructure Investments," *Transportation Journal*, Winter, 47(1) (2008): 5–16.

20 AMR Research (2008). http://www.purchasing.com/article/215245-AMR_survey_identifies_top_supply_chain_risks.php, accessed October 2009.

21 HK Systems. Material Handling Industry of America. (2009), HK Systems, Vol. 7, Issue 2, http://www.mhia.org/media/members/14202/128589776863256716.pdf, accessed October 2009.

22 Thailand's Board of Investment (2008). http://www.boi.go.th/english/how/transportation_costs_including_fuel_and_freight_rates.asp

23 U.S. Bureau of Labor Statistics. http://www.bls.gov/oes/current/naics4_334200.htm#b51-0000, accessed November 5, 2008.

24 Numbers are relative to the cost of building a manufacturing plant in Mississippi vs. Thailand. On average, it costs almost 2.7 times as much to build an auto manufacturing plant in the United States than it does in Thailand. The examples used are a $500 million Ford plant in Thailand compared to a $1.3 billion Toyota plant in Mississippi. Selko, Adrienne. "Toyota to Build New Plant in Mississippi," *Industry Week* (February 27, 2007). http://www.industryweek.com/articles/toyota_to_build_new_plant_in_mississippi_13662.aspx. Fuller, Thomas. "Ford

to Build Car Plant in Thailand," *New York Times* (October 10, 2007). http://www.nytimes.com/2007/10/10/business/worldbusiness/10ford.html?ex=1349668800&en=9e345dec5dd288c9&ei=5088&partner=rssnyt&emc=rss.

25 The output per worker in USD in the industrial sector is compared to derive the ratio of labor productivity. http://www.ilo.org/wcmsp5/groups/public/---asia/---ro-bangkok/documents/publication/wcms_099607.pdf, accessed November 5, 2008.

26 Number based on skilled labor figure of US $245/month, assuming 160 hours worked per month. http://www.boi.go.th/english/how/labor_costs.asp, accessed November 5, 2008.

27 See note 25 above.

28 For more details, see the Council of Supply Chain Management Professionals (CSCMP) case study, "DSM Manufacturing: When Network Analysis Meets Business Reality." http://cscmp.org/resources/casestudy.asp.

29 Lockheed Martin. "Lockheed Martin Receives $90 Million MLRS Launcher Support Contract." News release, June 2, 2008.

30 Ibid.

four
Managing Severe Demand and Supply Flux

Dr. Thomas M. Corsi

The global economy is increasingly volatile. Demand patterns fluctuate widely as a reflection of changing customer tastes and preferences along with changes in global economic conditions. In this volatile environment, the challenge facing managers is to integrate their multiple, and often segregated, demand channels into a single repository of demand information. Managers can develop a coherent approach to fulfilling the integrated demand, initially through looking across their inventory positions throughout all levels of the supply chain in real time, i.e., virtualized multi-echelon inventory. Next, relying on sophisticated demand analytics, they establish a set of business rules for accessing available inventory. Managers replenish their inventory pool with automated processes (relying more and more on radio frequency identification, or RFID, technology) and through sophisticated, business intelligence-informed processes.

This chapter begins by exploring the explosion of demand channels in the Internet era. Increasingly, managers must integrate across three important sales channels: the Internet, in-store sales, and telephone orders. The focus will be on documenting the advantages of effectively integrating these three sources of demand, and fulfilling them through the use of sophisticated business analytic capabilities.

This chapter then examines the importance of multi-echelon inventory virtualization as an effective response to a consolidated, multichannel demand picture. The discussion will examine how companies can achieve inventory virtualization and its associated benefits. Examples of successful virtualization strategies will offer readers ideas for implementation.

Finally, the chapter looks at replenishment strategies in an environment of demand volatility. This volatility has prompted a paradigm shift, from a focus on formula-based replenishments driven by economic order-quantity (EOQ) models and sophisticated time-series forecasts, to a focus on automated replenishment based on RFID technology as well as on replenishment informed by business intelligence. The new paradigm provides companies with the capability to respond more quickly to fluctuations in customer demand, and to do so with lower inventory levels throughout the echelons of the supply chain.

Multichannel Demand Integration

During the past decade, there has been an explosion in Internet retail sales. Indeed, as shown in Table 4.1, retail sales over the Internet have tripled from $31.0 billion in 2001 to $128.1 billion in 2007, according the U.S. Census Bureau's Statistical Abstract (2009), and those sales are projected to reach nearly $200 billion by 2011. This surge reflects the widespread diffusion of high-speed Internet

TABLE 4.1. Online retail spending. This table shows the distribution of online retail spending across major retail categories

Category	Online retail spending (billions of dollars)												
	2000	2001	2002	2003	2004	2005	2006	2007	2008 projection	2009 projection	2010 projection	2011 projection	2012 projection
Total	**24.1**	**31.0**	**41.4**	**53.9**	**67.2**	**83.6**	**108.1**	**128.1**	**147.6**	**165.9**	**182.3**	**198.6**	**214.8**
Computer hardware and software	9.3	11.0	12.6	14.5	16.1	18.1	21.2	24.1	26.7	28.9	30.8	32.6	34.1
Consumer electronics	1.1	1.5	2.1	2.6	3.4	4.7	6.8	8.4	10.0	11.5	12.8	14.2	15.5
Books, music, and videos	3.3	3.8	4.5	5.3	6.3	7.5	9.0	9.8	11.1	12.3	13.4	14.4	15.3
Tickets	1.1	1.8	2.5	3.2	3.9	4.6	5.5	6.3	6.8	7.2	7.7	8.1	8.6
Consumer health	0.4	0.4	0.6	1.1	1.8	2.6	3.4	4.2	5.3	6.3	7.2	8.2	9.1
Apparel, accessories, footwear and jewelry	3.4	4.7	6.7	8.7	10.7	14.0	19.1	23.2	27.1	31.1	34.4	37.6	40.7
Grocery and pet food	0.6	0.8	1.3	2.0	3.0	4.1	5.6	7.4	9.1	10.9	12.8	14.8	16.8
Toys and video games	0.8	1.0	1.4	2.1	2.5	2.9	4.1	5.2	5.9	6.5	6.8	7.0	7.9
Sporting goods	0.5	0.7	0.9	1.3	1.6	2.0	2.3	2.5	2.8	3.1	3.4	3.7	3.9
Flowers and specialty gifts	0.9	1.2	1.6	2.1	2.6	3.1	3.9	4.3	4.9	5.4	5.9	6.4	6.8
Home	1.0	1.8	3.1	5.0	7.4	10.0	15.0	18.8	22.7	26.1	29.5	32.9	36.2
Office products	0.3	0.6	1.2	1.8	2.6	3.2	4.1	4.7	5.1	5.7	6.2	6.6	7.1
Other	1.4	1.8	2.9	4.2	5.4	6.7	8.1	9.1	10.1	10.9	11.6	12.2	12.8

Source: http://www.census.gov/compendia/statab/cats/wholesale_retail_trade/online_retail_sales.html

service into U.S. households. With this improved service, it is increasingly easy for consumers to browse the Internet in search of their desired products. Recognizing consumers' increasing reliance on and preference for making purchases online, retailers have plowed significant resources into their websites in order to improve their look and feel as well as to enhance consumers' Web-based shopping experience.

In Table 4.1, the three retail categories accounting for the largest percentage of Internet sales in 2007 were computer hardware and software ($24.1 billion); apparel, accessories, footwear, and jewelry ($23.2 billion); and home products ($18.8 billion). Online sales for these categories are likely to remain strong, but the forecasts project significant growth in a number of other retail sectors. The trend toward the strong development of the Internet demand channel is unmistakable.

The Internet's influence, however, is reaching well beyond direct sales. As shown in Figure 4.1, 66 percent of the respondents in a survey on retail buying patterns reported having made purchases online. More interesting is that, of the 34 percent who said they have not purchased anything online, 45 percent have used the Internet to research items before purchasing them at a store. Indeed, one of every five in-store purchases is now influenced in some way by the Internet.[1] Furthermore, not only are Internet sales increasing at a very fast pace, but retailers are viewing their multichannel buyers as more profitable than their single-channel shoppers.[2] In fact, eMarketer estimates that store sales swayed by online research equaled $471 billion in 2007. This compares with $136 billion in retail e-commerce sales for 2007. Thus, for every $1 in online sales, the Internet has an impact on $3.45 of store sales (reference: Jeffrey Grau, "Multi-Channel Retailing," http://www.emarketer.com/Reports/All/Emarketer_2000476.aspx).

The growth in Internet sales—actual and prospective—has created huge challenges for retailers. First, it adds a significant new demand channel that must be served along with existing demand channels, namely, physical stores and mail orders. Thus, retailers need to develop a total, integrated picture of all the demand channels in real time, or near real time.

The integration of demand across all existing channels represents only the first step in a process designed to both provide more effective customer service and enhance sales to the existing customer base. The integrated, multichannel database of customer orders becomes a huge data warehouse, updated in real time. Companies can achieve a number of important objectives by applying sophisticated business intelligence software to this database. First, they can develop customer profiles and sales histories, which they can use for targeted marketing and sales promotions. Second, they can

FIGURE 4.1 Interplay between online and offline retail sales. The research from Forrester shown in this figure maps the increasing influence online browsing has on offline shopping.

analyze the order patterns and responses to price fluctuations and new-product introductions in order to generate demand forecasts.

Having an integrated, multichannel database that captures historical and real-time information on customer demand patterns is particularly important for dealing with demand volatility. Why? Because the real-time database captures both demand surges and precipitous declines as they occur, functioning as a real-time response or alert system. The business analytic capabilities associated with the data warehouse allow managers to drill down into the database by customer type, geographic region, demand channel, and other classifications. With that information in hand, they can identify problem areas and growth opportunities, and then respond quickly and appropriately to observed volatility. Without a multichannel, real-time data warehouse, response time will be delayed, at significant cost to the firm.

Another reason is that retailers must decide on the best way to achieve a satisfactory experience for customers in each of their demand channels. A fundamental question underlying this decision is whether retailers should have separate supply chains for each demand channel or a single, integrated supply chain for their entire business.

In the early stages of the Internet retail sales explosion, many companies serviced each demand channel independently. Thus, retailers would establish separate distribution centers specifically designed to independently fulfill orders for each demand channel.

Consider the example of Retailer A, which has a central warehouse in Houston, Texas, that handles Internet sales exclusively as well as a series of regional warehouses servicing the "bricks and mortar" stores and mail-order sales. If a customer in Chicago orders an item from Retailer A on the Internet, that order would be filled at the Houston warehouse. While this system does meet the Chicago customer's needs, it is expensive for Retailer A.

If, on the other hand, Retailer A integrated all demand channels into a single supply chain, the customer in Chicago would receive the order directly from a Chicago-area retail store (if the item is in stock at that location). As a result, the customer would receive the order more quickly (achieving a higher level of satisfaction). It would also cost Retailer A less to operate a single supply chain than it would to run separate, nonintegrated supply chains.

Indeed, an Aberdeen Group report based on surveys of 60 national retailers found that 79 percent of the surveyed companies believed that "customer expectations of a seamless purchase and delivery option across all channels are the most critical factor in driving them to integrate their retail operations" across all demand channels. Indeed, the best-in-class retailers "understand the brand value of a multichannel offering: consistency and efficiency across all the channels. Top performers wrap their brand identity around fulfilling customer expectations for seamless purchase and delivery options across all channels." But even the best-in-class retailers, while understanding the importance of achieving multichannel demand integration, face significant obstacles in attaining this goal, the researchers said.[3]

One business that has tackled head-on the assignment of integrating all of its demand channels is Barnes & Noble, the retail bookseller. This company has the challenge of integrating across several distinct demand channels. These include its online, "virtual" bookstore and its bricks-and-mortar retail outlets, which are divided into "normal" stores and very large "superstores." In addition, Barnes & Noble maintains a university bookstore operation. Figure 4.2 provides a snapshot of the company's forecasting program, in which all of its demand channels are integrated to produce a single, multichannel view of its demand for planning purposes.[4]

Multi-Echelon Inventory Virtualization

Clearly, there are significant advantages to servicing multichannel demand with a single, integrated supply chain. There also are many challenges associated with such an endeavor. Despite those obstacles, best-practice companies are moving rapidly to achieve the integrated, single-supply chain concept. One important reason why is that having a single, integrated supply chain implies the existence of a multi-echelon warehousing capacity[5] they can tap into, in real time, to respond expeditiously to the integrated, multichannel demand. Companies define the inventory echelons as locations to

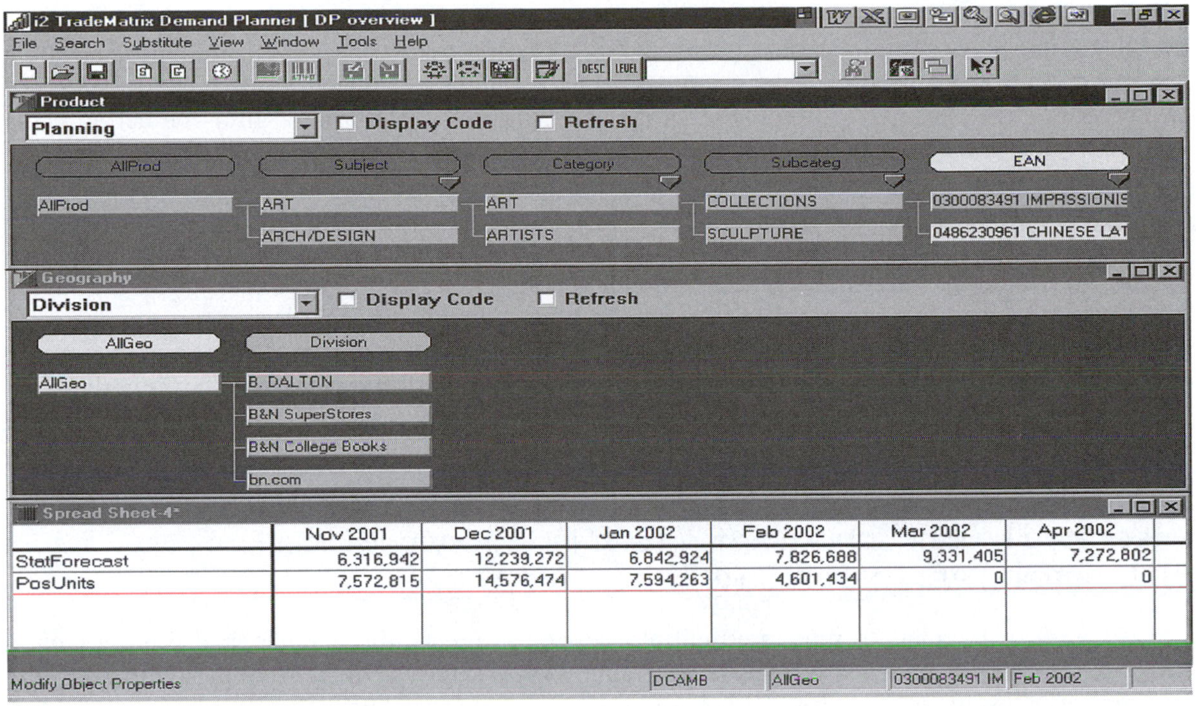

FIGURE 4.2 Barnes & Noble's point-of-sale forecast with multichannel demand integration. Display of Barnes & Noble's integrated forecast of multichannel demand.

Source: Joe Gonnella, VP Inventory Management and Vendor Relations, "Multi-Channel Demand Management in Action," http://www.authorstream.com/Presentation/Techy_Guy-25664-BMI-Mgmt-Conf-May-2005-Gonnella-Management-ConferenceMay-j-as-Entertainment-ppt-powerpoint/

hold inventory. These locations range from the retailers' shelves and warehouses to distributors'/wholesalers' warehouses to the companies' own storage locations.

A single, multi-echelon warehousing capacity provides companies with real-time visibility of inventory positions throughout the entire supply chain—i.e., provides them with a virtualized inventory position. They achieve this visibility by linking the individual inventory positions at each echelon together in a real-time database that can be accessed and drawn down to meet real-time customer demands based on an established set of business rules. For example, if the real-time demand data warehouse shows that a premium customer has a major order, and the inventory needed to fill that order is only available at one echelon in the supply chain, the agreed-upon business rule would assign the available inventory position to the premium customer.

A real-time multi-echelon inventory system provides a number of significant advantages. First, it allows improved levels of customer service, since it provides a real-time picture of all available inventories and enables quick order fulfillment based on business rules. Second, it helps companies control inventory costs. Inventory position throughout all echelons and all channels is known in real time so that new orders will not be placed unless inventory is unavailable.

Relatively few companies have adopted this approach, however. According to an Aberdeen Group report on a survey of 208 manufacturers and distributors, more than 60 percent use "overly simplistic inventory management methods" that result in 15 percent to 30 percent more inventory than they need and in lower service levels. Indeed, only 5 percent of the surveyed companies reported using multi-echelon inventory optimization that takes into account multiple types of demand and supply variability.[6]

Those companies that reported using new optimization methods that manage inventory holistically across multiple stages in the supply chain, including suppliers and downstream partners, saw marked benefits. Those respondents commonly drove 20 percent to 30 percent reductions in on-hand inventory and 10 percent to 20 percent improvements in time to market.[7]

A good example is that of Deere & Company's Commercial & Consumer Equipment Division, which manufactures and markets John Deere lawn and turf care equipment. The division has used multistage inventory planning and optimization (MIPO) software to develop recommended stocking levels at 2,500 North American dealer locations, plants, and warehouses for more than 300 commercial and consumer products. According to the company, it achieved a $1 billion inventory reduction in the first three years since it deployed the software in 2003.[8]

A multi-echelon inventory system places a premium on controlling inventory levels while maintaining or even improving customer service levels, and it allows companies to closely match inventory levels to demand signals. If a company using this type of inventory system faces a rapid decline in demand, it will not be saddled with excess inventory because it has been matching demand and supply in real time through its inventory control system. If there is a rapid surge in demand, a company with a multi-echelon inventory system will know in real time about the potential shortage. As a result, it will be in a position to quickly implement an integrated replenishment strategy that is designed to maximize response to the volatile business environment. Clearly, a multi-echelon inventory system is both appropriate and effective in a volatile demand environment.

Integrated Multichannel Demand and Inventory Virtualization: An Emerging Application Suite

It is not easy for retailers to integrate multiple demand channels into a single, real-time system. If they can master that complex task, however, retailers can achieve significant savings with real-time visibility over inventory at multiple echelons in real time. The retailers' ultimate goal is to establish a single supply chain to meet demand in all channels.

Software vendors have recently brought to market a suite of applications that facilitate multichannel integrated demand/supply systems. One such vendor, NetSuite, has introduced a Multichannel Retail Management Suite of applications designed "to integrate every step of a multichannel retail business, from commerce and order management to marketing, inventory and financials." According to its website,[9] NetSuite's Multichannel Retail Management Suite has the following features: "powerful e-commerce capabilities integrated with other channels; one application to manage a single view of customers across all channels; deep inventory, purchasing and order-management functionality; and real-time visibility across your business with customizable dashboards." With the NetSuite application, "customers can purchase from one channel or location, pick-up from a different one, and return merchandise to another. Retailers can get a complete view of each customer and better understand their needs and behavior."

Indeed, imbedded in the retail management application suite is a powerful tool for business intelligence, which is rapidly becoming an integral part of an overall integrated demand/supply management capability. The real-time business intelligence module can be used effectively as a performance dashboard highlighting key indicators integrated across the multiple channels or isolated by channel. Key indicators regarding real-time inventory levels by echelon, order cycle times by customers in each channel, profitability levels by customer in each channel can alert managers to potential areas of concern in real time so that response strategies can be implemented in a timely fashion.

Replenishment Strategies in an Environment of Demand Volatility

Replenishment strategies have traditionally focused on long-accepted models for determining levels of stock, such as economic order-quantity models. EOQ models have frequently been used in conjunction with time-series forecasts, emphasizing historical sales data as a basis for determining replenishment requirements. EOQ models balance the costs of holding inventory with the ordering costs, along with considerations of lead time and demand patterns, to determine order size and order frequency.

In a highly volatile environment, however, these approaches to replenishment have proved to be inadequate and have resulted in significant inefficiencies. With these policies in place, companies at times have excess inventories; in other circumstances, they are subject to long order cycle times and/or stock-outs and lost sales. This situation has led to a new paradigm for replenishment, consisting of two major components. The first component involves automated replenishment, increasingly driven by RFID technology. The second component involves the use of the business intelligence modules that are an integral part of the integrated, multichannel demand/virtualized multi-echelon inventory software described in the previous section.

Procter & Gamble Co., the world's largest consumer goods company, is at the forefront of adopting automated replenishment, the cornerstone of this new replenishment paradigm. When traditional replenishment policies were in place, P&G experienced significant added costs and inefficiencies. It found that EOQ models and statistical forecasts did not align well with the promotional strategies of Wal-Mart and its other chain-store customers. That lack of alignment has been quite costly: P&G carried companywide, "just in case" inventory representing 65 days' worth of materials and product—in essence, handcuffing some $3 billion daily in rapidly depreciating assets. To address this issue, P&G adopted a new vision: to become what it called a Consumer-Driven Supply Network with "no lost time, never-empty store shelves, and no stationary inventory." To achieve this goal, P&G envisioned the use of actual consumer purchasing information, collected with RFID technology, to increasingly replace unreliable forecasting data and trigger "real-time, simultaneous movement of relevant demand data to all network partners—store, warehouse, retailer, manufacturer, and suppliers."[10]

Figures 4.3 through 4.6 illustrate the implementation of RFID-driven automated replenishment for one P&G product, the Gillette Venus razor for women.[11] Figure 4.3 shows the identification via the RFID tags on each of two boxes of Venus razors that are in stock at the retailer's warehouse (Wal-Mart for illustrative purposes). Figure 4.4 shows a transfer of one box from the warehouse to the store floor, leaving one box remaining in the warehouse; the RFID reader indicates that there is now a single box of razors in the warehouse. In Figure 4.5, the second box of razors is transferred to the retail store, and an automated "out of stock" signal is generated. The RFID reader no longer shows any boxes available in the warehouse. Figure 4.6 shows that the automated "out of stock" signal at Wal-Mart's warehouse is communicated directly to Procter & Gamble's internal enterprise resource planning (ERP) system. According to established business rules, P&G will ship two boxes of razors to replenish the stock at the Wal-Mart warehouse. This replenishment process is automated throughout, resulting in better inventory control and no stock-outs.

Although this capability increasingly is driven by RFID technology, it should be emphasized that its objectives can also be accomplished through integration and linking of the ERP systems of retailers and manufacturers in real time, or in near real time, using point-of-sale data. Concepts like vendor-managed inventory (VMI) and collaborative planning, forecasting, and replenishment (CPFR) are examples of efforts by retailers and manufacturers to facilitate replenishment in a way that minimizes total inventory requirements while maintaining and/or improving customer service levels.

A New Model for Changing Times

As we have seen, leading-edge firms are implementing software applications capable of integrating multichannel demand as well as providing real-time visibility of their inventory position across multiple echelons. Companies with this type of visibility are best positioned to deal with demand volatility. They have a real-time view of demand coming from all available channels, plus they are able to meet customer demand by tapping available inventory across all echelons according to an established set of business rules. Those that have this integrated capability across demand channels and supply echelons are able to create a single, coordinated supply chain that responds in real time to demand fluctuations in either direction.

As part of this integrated system, a huge data warehouse is created, with detailed information on customer demand patterns and the responsiveness of consumers to market promotions and general economic fluctuations. The data warehouse includes demand information by channel and by geographic area; data on inventory levels across all echelons; and data on order cycle times by individual customers and by channel.

What distinguishes best-practice companies is their ability to use this data warehouse to drive their replenishment policies and decisions. They are leading the move from replenishment driven by economic models and time-series forecasts to a replenishment system based on accurate, real-time

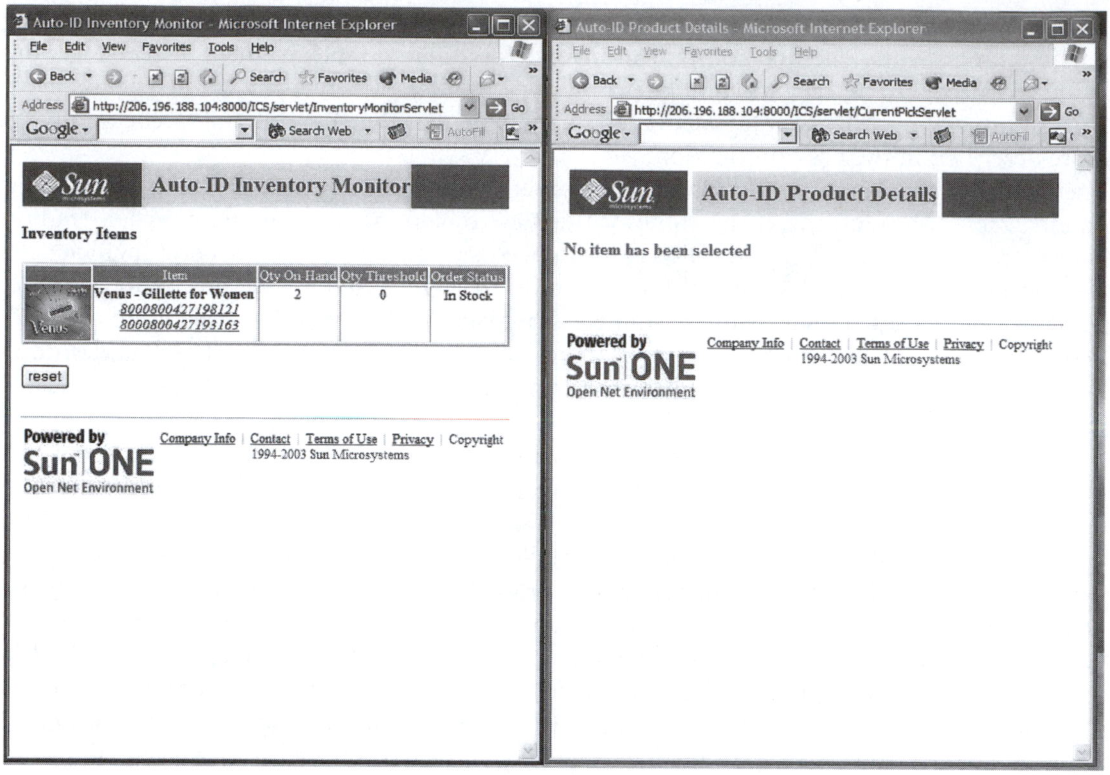

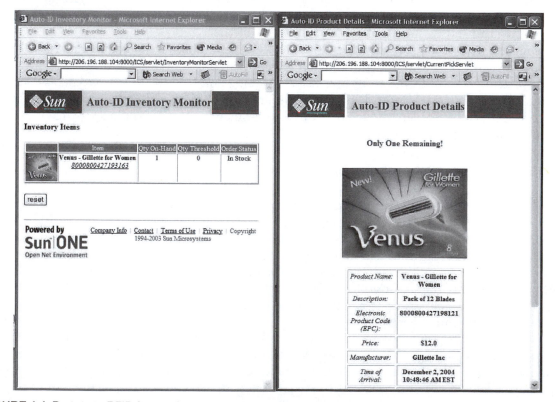

FIGURE 4.3 Prototype RFID for vendor-managed inventory: inventory in-place at retailer warehouse.

Source: Sun Microsystems, I-Force/RFID Center, prototype prepared for Supply Chain Management Center, Robert H. Smith School of Business, 2003.

FIGURE 4.4 Prototype RFID for vendor-managed inventory: inventory draw down at retailer warehouse. Box transfer from warehouse to retail floor; new inventory position at retailer warehouse.

Source: Sun Microsystems, I-Force/RFID Center, prototype prepared for Supply Chain Management Center, Robert H. Smith School of Business, 2003.

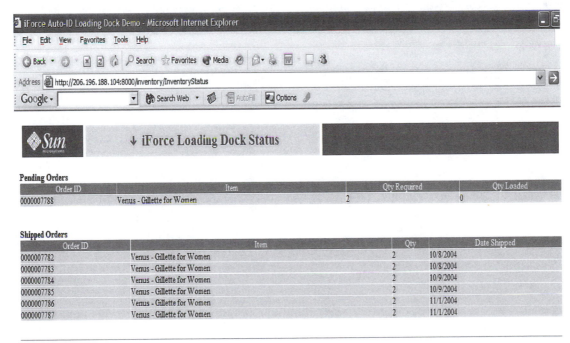

FIGURE 4.5 Prototype RFID for vendor-managed inventory: inventory depleted at retailer warehouse. Out-of-stock signal at retail warehouse.

Source: Sun Microsystems, I-Force/RFID Center, prototype prepared for Supply Chain Management Center, Robert H. Smith School of Business, 2003.

iForce Loading Dock Status

Pending Orders

Order ID	Item	Qty Required	Qty Loaded
0000007788	Venus - Gillette for Women	2	0

Shipped Orders

Order ID	Item	Qty	Date Shipped
0000007782	Venus - Gillette for Women	2	10/8/2004
0000007783	Venus - Gillette for Women	2	10/8/2004
0000007784	Venus - Gillette for Women	2	10/9/2004
0000007785	Venus - Gillette for Women	2	10/9/2004
0000007786	Venus - Gillette for Women	2	11/1/2004
0000007787	Venus - Gillette for Women	2	11/1/2004

Company Info | Contact | Terms of Use | Privacy | Copyright 1994-2002 Sun Microsystems

FIGURE 4.6 Prototype RFID for vendor-managed inventory: ERP signal to vendor for replenishment. Automated reorder communication with producer ERP system.

Source: Sun Microsystems, I-Force/RFID Center, prototype prepared for Supply Chain Management Center, Robert H. Smith School of Business, 2003.

mining of integrated demand/supply data warehouses. The old model generated forecasts from times-series data on retail point-of-sale data, often collected with significant time delays. The new model relies increasingly on customer data collected in real time, to which sophisticated analytics are applied. Those forecasts are far more accurate and detailed, and thus better able to rapidly assess the impact of external events on customer demand.

Notes

1 Nikki Baird, "Trends 2007: Retail IT," *Forrester Research*, January 12, 2007.

2 The Aberdeen Group, "Multichannel Retail Benchmark Report," December 2005. Reported results are based on a survey of 60 major retailers.

3 Ibid.

4 Joe Gonnella, VP Inventory Management and Vendor Relations, "Multi-Channel Demand Management in Action," http://www.authorstream.com/Presentation/Techy_Guy-25664-BMI-Mgmt-Conf-May-2005-Gonnella-Management-ConferenceMay-j-as-Entertainment-ppt-powerpoint/

5 Multi-echelon can be understood a number of ways. It is a concept that has only recently moved out of operations research departments and into software and implementation at companies. While the underlying logic of multi-echelon is quite complex, its business impact is easy to understand. Multi-echelon capability is the ability of software to see the entire supply network and manage the inventory in that network as a "pool," rather than as a group of independent locations. Independent location planning is the assumption that must be dispensed with to understand multi-echelon planning. Multi-echelon planning could just as easily be called "pooled location inventory planning." Source: http://spplan.org/2009/11/02/multiechelon-inventory-optimization-defined/

6 "The Supply Chain Inventory Strategies Benchmark Report," Aberdeen Group, 2005, http://www.allbusiness.com/company-activities-management/operations-supply-chain/4979549-1.html

7 Ibid.

8 Roberto Michel, "Optimization of Inventory," *Modern Materials Handling*, September 2006.

9 http://www.netsuite.com/portal/industries/retail.shtml

10 Sandor Boyson and Chaodong Han, "Eras of Enterprise Globalization: From Vertical Integration to Virtualization and Beyond," Robert H. Smith School of Business, University of Maryland (May 2006).

11 http://us.infores.com/ProductsSolutions/AllProducts/AllProductsDetail/tabid/159/productid/80/Default.aspx

five
Hedging Supplier Risk

Kevin McCormack and Peter Trkman

Part 1: Effective Supplier Risk Management

The risk of disruptions from factors within supply chains and from outside forces is one of the main concerns for both supply chain practitioners and researchers. Many companies have experienced a change in their supply chain risk profile as a result of changes in their business models. Adopting "lean" practices, moving to outsourcing, and a general tendency to reduce the size of the supplier base[1] can all contribute to increased risk.

Broader trends can also increase exposure to risks. These can include globalization, reduced inventory buffers, increased demand for on-time deliveries, or shorter product life cycles. Companies that source globally must also deal with longer distances, increased rules and regulations, currency fluctuations, customs requirements, and language, cultural and time differences along with other operational and strategic issues that amplify supply chain risks.[2]

The recent financial/economic crisis that struck as the first decade of the twenty-first century came to an end has further increased the importance of early identification of risks and disruptions in the supply chain due to deterioration of the performance or even the bankruptcy of suppliers. Supply chain risk management (SCRM) is, therefore, aimed at developing approaches for identification, assessment, analysis, and treatment of areas of vulnerability and risk in supply chains.

Supply chain networks are the dominant competitive model in the current business environment, and this means more risks—each carrying the potential for greater impacts. Supply chain network management, generally understood to be the management of a set of companies that are cooperating to produce a product or service, is the major challenge of procurement and supply chain management groups. Collaborating with and managing the right suppliers is becoming more important. Along with this, the use of strategic partnerships and the involvement of suppliers in product development stages help to achieve a competitive advantage.[3]

Risk management of this network is increasingly critical, since exposure to the supplier-connected risks has severely impacted several companies. Some notable examples include:

- Thomas & Friends Wooden Railway toys which agreed to a $30 million settlement after toy recalls in 2007 due to lead in the paint.
- Chrysler Group LLC., which had to stop production in several factories due to bankruptcy of its supplier Plastech Engineered Products.
- Coal company Peabody Energy that reported $34 million in losses due to contract breach by one of its suppliers.[4]

Preparing for such events is critical. For example, Ericsson suffered a major loss due to a fire at Royal Philips Electronics, its single-source supplier of microprocessor chips for mobile telephony. Ericsson was eventually driven out of the mobile telephony business. Meanwhile, the damage to the competing Nokia supply chain was limited.[5] It is not surprising then that companies, regardless of their industry, rate supplier failure and continuity of supply as their top risk factor.[6]

But, aside from these published stories—how large is the risk connected to a single supplier? The outside environment and the possibility of terrorism, contagious diseases, or worker strikes increasingly reach the headlines of the popular press, and managers often focus attention on many of these high risk-low probability events and ignore smaller risks with high probability of occurrence. The cumulative effect of the latter can also be very detrimental.

The real risks are far more common—late delivery, wrong demand forecast, obsolete inventory, a quality problem. Also, for those taking a more long-term perspective—getting locked into a supplier that loses a market or technology battle with its competitors. The latter can be especially detrimental, since increasing length, complexity, and interdependence in supply chain contracts can mean supply disruptions are more critical and costly when they occur. Procurement is often handled via long-term, fixed-price contracts containing naive terms and clauses in the case of a breach.[7]

Effective methodologies are needed with the capability to evaluate suppliers' current performance and, even more important, to predict the likelihood of future supplier-connected disruption.

Methodology for Supplier Network Risk Management

Currently, SCRM approaches are attempting to measure either supplier attributes or supply chain structure, and then use those measures to compare suppliers and predict disruption. The results are used to prepare mitigation and response strategies. Most often SCRM is a formal process that involves identifying potential losses, understanding the likelihood of potential losses, and assigning significance to these losses.[8] A typical example of such an approach is the procurement risk assessment and mitigation (PRAM) methodology, developed by Dow Chemical Company to measure supply chain risk and its impact.[9]

Due to growing concerns, many companies have initiated various practices aimed at reducing those risks. Systematic supplier performance management[10] is certainly a first step in the right direction.[11] But, as a popular saying warns: "Past performance is no guarantee of future results." With limited visibility, how can you be sure that your important supplier will not experience issues that disrupt deliveries, negatively impact its quality, or even endanger its business continuity and, in turn, the entire supply chain? Do you know if a supplier's strategy is able to cope with technology issues, market turbulence, events from the environment and, importantly, whether it aligns with the strategy of the company for which it is a supplier?

Measuring the risk contribution of the supplier-specific environment to the whole supply chain is vital. First, the supplier characteristics should be studied. According to PRAM, the main characteristics influencing supplier risk are its financial and operational performance, material quality, human resource quality, compliance with work processes, and information technology (IT) system stability. Supplier ethics should also be considered. For example, retail giant Wal-Mart's image suffered due to the use of child labor at one of its suppliers, Kathie Lee Gifford.

Second, the supplier's environment should be studied. This includes market dynamics (customers and competitors), mergers, acquisitions, divestitures, regulatory dynamics, disasters (natural and man-made), and transportation dynamics (routes, borders, modes). While a certain supplier strategy (e.g. ordering large batches to decrease procurement costs or single source suppliers with long contractual commitments) may be acceptable in a non-turbulent environment, it may be detrimental in a more turbulent one (such as the presence of quick technological advances or large commodity price swings).

Additionally, the exogenous uncertainty should be considered both in terms of continuous events (e.g. changes in material prices) and discrete events (terrorism, natural disasters, diseases, etc.). For example, a supplier plant in New Orleans has a high risk of disruption due to hurricanes while a plant in another area can have a high risk of earthquakes. Often, incoming shipments of parts and supplies are disrupted due to political disputes. This was the case at the U.S.-Canada borders for almost two days after September 11, 2001, terror attacks. The delay of the shipments subsequently caused problems for automotive manufacturers.

The final and most important question is whether supplier characteristics will fit with the supply chain structure and strategy of the company that has organized the supply chain network—the supply chain leader. For agile supply chain networks, the supplier flexibility and responsiveness to market turbulence is of utmost importance. For lean supply chain networks, the reliability and low variation in lead times take priority.

The geographic dispersion of the supply chain network plays a vital role as well. Large distances increase the possibility of transport disruption and decrease flexibility in case of high market turbulence. A striking example is the congestion at California ports before Christmas 2004, causing several ships to wait for days to dock and unload. The issue of geography is also connected with the degree of single sourcing employed in the chain. Single-source suppliers of important material or components deserve special attention because they pose a high level of supply risk.

The multitude of factors that should be considered with a large supplier base poses significant challenges to any company attempting to evaluate its suppliers and predict the potential sources of supply chain disruption. The reality is that most companies lack the understanding, capability or willingness to operate at such demanding levels.[12]

In this chapter a model with two aspects is proposed to help in this mission. Various aspects that should be included in the evaluation and their interconnections are shown in Figure 5.1.

The same supplier attributes, strategy, and structure may pose considerably different risks of disruptions in different environments. An assessment of the risk of disruptions based upon a supplier's strategy, structure, performance, and attributes as modified by the turbulence in their specific environment is needed. It is not enough to have a supply chain management professional with a job of "reducing risk."[13] The proper approach towards risk monitoring and mitigation depends on the overall supply chain network strategy of the company. This claim is in line with findings that the role of the procurement office has fundamentally changed in most large organizations. Earlier, interactions with suppliers focused on costs. This led to the perception of procurement as a back-office function, which is still the case in some companies. However, many leaders recognize that

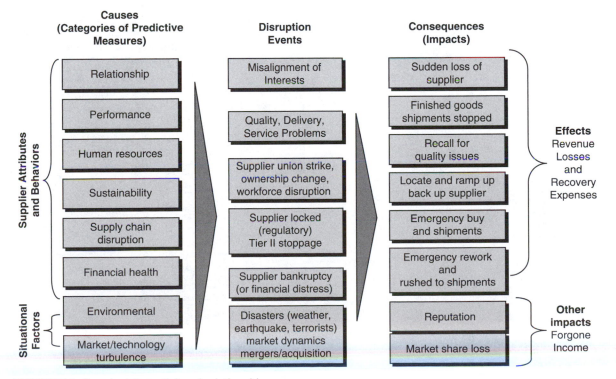

FIGURE 5.1 Supply risk model and relationships.

a high-performing procurement organization can directly contribute to the bottom line and improve shareholder value.[14]

Assessing Supplier Risk

DRK Research LLC., a research and consulting firm focused on supply chain analytics, has created a framework and process to understand the drivers that create supply disruptions and more proactively mitigate the risk. This framework and process consists of a set of disruption predicators developed through several years of research and experience with global supply chains. The process and framework has been used by risk management teams and commodity managers to aid in identifying, predicting, and managing risk on a timely basis or to be alerted to possible risk factors that require their attention.

The assessment approach is to examine the supply commodity network of associated suppliers as a group, measuring the aspects of the model associated with each supplier. Figure 5.2 shows this network view and items from the risk model being measured.

Using online survey methods, the risk assessment model measures the risk-associated characteristics of a company's supply chain based upon several dimensions (shown in Figure 5.2).

The six categories of risk in a supply network are:

1. Supply chain disruption
2. Performance
3. Human resources
4. Environmental
5. Relationship
6. Financial health.

The primary reporting view of the system is the "risk wheel." The diagnostic view of the wheel is

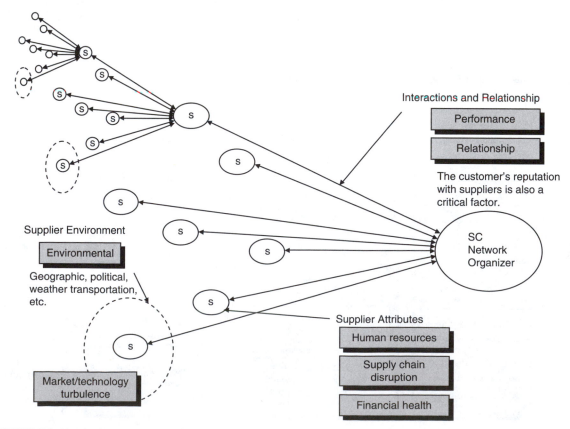

FIGURE 5.2 Network assessment view.

shown in Figure 5.3. The center of the wheel is the Risk Index (RI) for the demographic (supplier, sub-category, commodity, etc.). In the second ring are the risk categories. The outer shows the risk indicators. Each item is *color-coded*. Red indicates a high risk, light red is a medium risk, yellow is low risk, and green is no risk. This report can be used to understand the base factors about the supplier that are driving risk.

The risk distribution matrix, shown in Figure 5.4, is constructed by plotting the Revenue at Risk (Rev Impact) with a supplier vs. the average Risk Index (RI) of that supplier. It is used to view all the suppliers within a commodity group placed within a two-by-two matrix according to their risk and potential impact on your company. The zones are color-coded from red (high risk) to green (no risk). This is a visual sorting mechanism used to help prioritize and focus mitigation actions on the high-risk suppliers.

Supplier Portfolio Management

Typically, a study of a single supplier does not tell the full story. Traditionally, companies adopted strategies which buffer against risks present in their environment by using multiple sources for strategic items and holding safety stock. These buffers, however, restrict operational performances and can negatively impact competitive advantage.[15] The supplier portfolio matrix (Figure 5.5) was developed based on supplier risk rating and the turbulence of its environment. It can help to identify those suppliers where safety stock, multiple sources or even the replacement of the supplier are indeed most needed. (The size of the circle indicates the supplier importance.)

The basic idea of SCRM portfolio management, therefore, should be to have a proper combination of the "stable" classification (that add stability to the chain) and "stars" (that add creativity and the possibility of improvement). A cautionary note: stars are like shooting stars, they can shine brightly but they can also burn out suddenly. Those two types are the main assets of a network and should be properly managed and rewarded.

The "danger" area is a group with immediate risk to the business. You should investigate whether

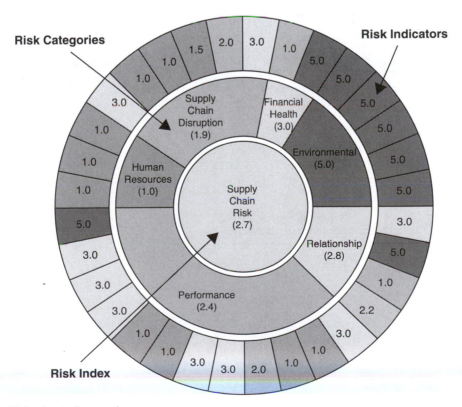

FIGURE 5.3 Risk wheel-diagnostic.

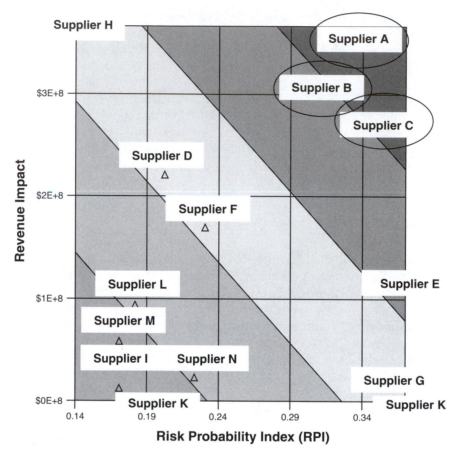

FIGURE 5.4 Risk distribution matrix.

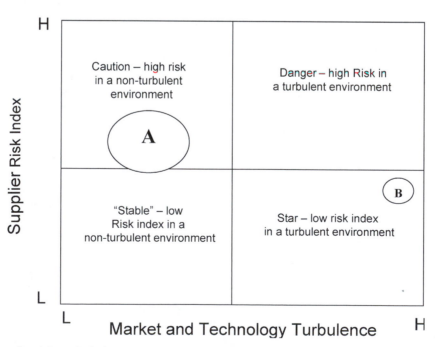

FIGURE 5.5 Supplier risk vs. turbulence.

Source: Trkman and McCormack.

to invest in them (with different supplier development programs, information sharing, etc.) in order to facilitate their move into the star group, or to seek alternative solutions. But, finding alternative solutions is not necessarily easy due to the turbulent environment.

The "caution" area is a decision zone. Although the possibility to improve the suppliers' perform- ance should be investigated, their replacement may be a more desirable option. The most desirable combination of suppliers depends on the operating environment of the supply chain leader, its strategy, and the type of the supply chain.

The implications of the framework can best be described with the analysis of a group of suppliers of a large automotive company. Two of Chrysler's suppliers are chosen as an example (suppliers' names are fictional). Fenton is a low-risk supplier and was in a low turbulence environment and consequently in the "stable" position in the supplier portfolio. Jupiter, on the other hand, had a similar risk rating but was in a highly turbulent environment. This placed it in the "star" position. In addition, Jupiter was the single source of certain parts, which considerably increased the impact of any potential disruption. Since the focus of this supply chain network strategy is on a high level of network reliability,[16] Jupiter's potential risk for Chrysler was too high. Therefore, upon a closer examination, and mainly influenced by the turbulence assessment, mitigation plans were put in place and Chrysler made an investment in qualifying back-up suppliers that could replace Jupiter.

Soon after this, Jupiter, like a shooting star, lost a large customer. This greatly changed its financial position and risk rating. This consequence of the market turbulence caused Jupiter's financial backers to withdraw, resulting in its collapse and liquidation. The back-up suppliers were notified and within one week the production was transferred to those suppliers. Without a consideration of turbulence, the mitigation of this risk may not have been a high priority and an expensive disruption could have occurred.

In summary, all suppliers cannot be rated on a single risk scale; their environments must be considered as a major factor. Basketball superstar Michael Jordan was very dependent on his environment. He shined at basketball but he was less than exciting as a baseball player. Suppliers can be the same way in the context of different supply chains. The secret is to know this and manage your supplier portfolio accordingly.

Free Supply Chain Risk Readiness Screener

According to Aberdeen Research, more than 80 percent of supply management executives reported that their companies experienced supply disruptions within the past 24 months. These supply glitches negatively impacted their companies' customer relations, earnings, time-to- market cycles, sales, and overall brand perceptions.

Aberdeen also found that less than half of enterprises have established metrics and procedures for assessing and managing supply risks. And, many procurement organizations lack sufficient market intelligence, skills, and information systems to effectively predict and mitigate supply risks.

Not every company is in a position to utilize the methodologies of sophisticated supply chain risk management. The *Risk Management Readiness Screener* gives a quick indication if your company is ready for this technology or if other supply chain structural improvements must be addressed first. This readiness test will require about five minutes and should only be taken by someone with in-depth knowledge of your supply chain. A comparison of your company with aggregated readiness results from other companies is presented upon completion. Click on this link if you are interested:

http://www.neurasurvey.com

The Survey Code is: **SCRScreener**

Note: This screening device consists of only ten questions but they are derived from a large data set that spans almost 15 years of research. Like all good indicators they correlate closely with reality because they have been proven in hundreds of real-world case studies.

General Tips Towards Better Supplier Risk Management

— Identify your important suppliers. While the total procurement value might be a good proxy, the suppliers of low-value but high-impact goods should also be included. Long-term suppliers should be included as opposed to those that involve only a one-time commercial transaction.[17]

— Carefully align your supplier mix with your strategy. Is agility and flexibility more important or is the focus on costs?

— Monitor the performance of your important suppliers—not just the averages, but (perhaps even more importantly) the deviations. Consider two suppliers with average lead-time of 14 days: One delivers in 13–15 days, the other in 7–21. The averages are similar, but the deviations vary widely. Which one poses a higher risk? Also monitor the trends in your supplier performance.

— Analyze the environmental turbulence (market, technology) and the potential outside influences on your suppliers. Analyze the operational, financial and human resource quality of your suppliers, but do not forget: the performance of a company and its performance in the chain is not necessary the same.

— Monitor the resilience of your suppliers to outside shocks. Correlate the trends in their performance to the trends in their environment.

— Integrate information systems or engage in joint/supplier development projects. In addition to technological projects, common business process management projects might also be beneficial with those suppliers that bring long-term value and resilience to your company.

Part 2: Supplier Risk Management Case Study

Large Medical Devices Firm (MedDevices) Implementing a Supply Risk Management Program Using a Risk Portfolio Approach

MedDevices, a large medical device manufacturer, has experienced a number of disruptions to operations and customer service as a result of unexpected problems that have occurred within their supply chain. Consequently, the supply management team at MedDevices was tasked with creating a framework to better understand the drivers that create supply disruptions and mitigate the risk more proactively. This process is used by the MedDevices risk management team as well as by the commodity managers to aid in identifying and managing risk on a timely basis. The process also alerts them to possible risk factors that require attention.

The assessment process in this program consists of the preparation, data collection, analysis, and reporting portion of an overall risk management program being implemented by MedDevices and shown in Figure 5.6.

The objectives of this program were to assess all criteria that contribute to supplier risks in the detail level required for identifying critical suppliers and analyzing root causes and implement mitigation steps at identified suppliers. It was also envisioned that changes in suppliers or movement of spend would occur in order to balance the supplier portfolio based upon risk, cost, and spend.

The DRK approach was used within this program in order to quickly and holistically assess supplier risk and build an objective, quantifiable comparison between suppliers.

This approach enables organizations to assess supplier risks holistically within six categories:

1. Relationship
2. Performance
3. Human resources
4. Supply chain disruption
5. Financial health
6. Environmental indicators.

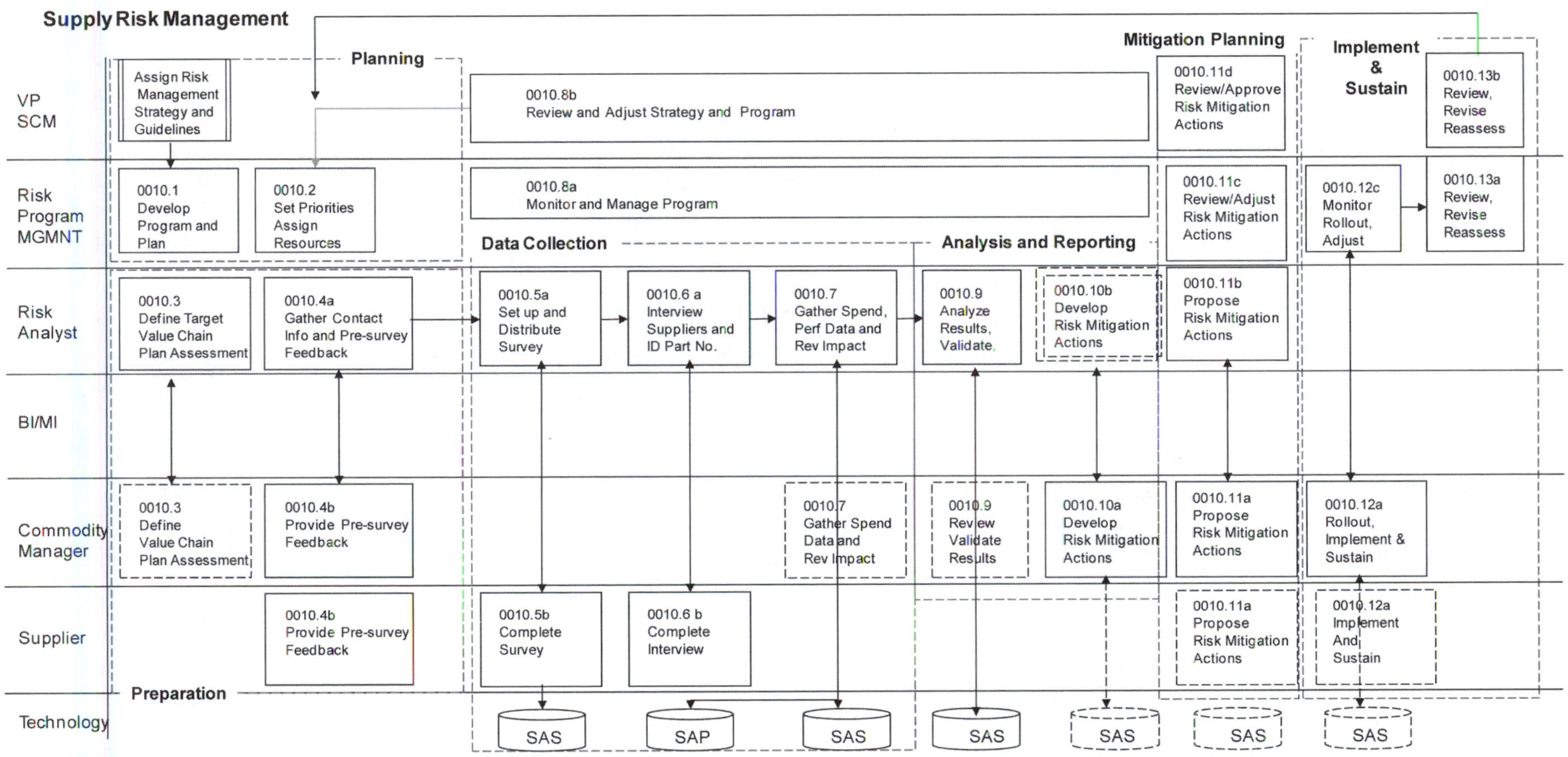

Supply Risk Management

	Planning	Data Collection	Analysis and Reporting	Mitigation Planning	Implement & Sustain
VP SCM	Assign Risk Management Strategy and Guidelines			0010.11d Review/Approve Risk Mitigation Actions	0010.13b Review, Revise Reassess
Risk Program MGMNT	0010.1 Develop Program and Plan / 0010.2 Set Priorities Assign Resources / 0010.8b Review and Adjust Strategy and Program			0010.11c Review/Adjust Risk Mitigation Actions	0010.12c Monitor Rollout, Adjust / 0010.13a Review, Revise Reassess
Risk Analyst	0010.3 Define Target Value Chain Plan Assessment / 0010.4a Gather Contact Info and Pre-survey Feedback / 0010.8a Monitor and Manage Program	0010.5a Set up and Distribute Survey / 0010.6 a Interview Suppliers and ID Part No. / 0010.7 Gather Spend, Perf Data and Rev Impact	0010.9 Analyze Results, Validate, / 0010.10b Develop Risk Mitigation Actions	0010.11b Propose Risk Mitigation Actions	
BI/MI					
Commodity Manager	0010.3 Define Value Chain Plan Assessment / 0010.4b Provide Pre-survey Feedback	0010.5b Complete Survey / 0010.6 b Complete Interview / 0010.7 Gather Spend Data and Rev Impact	0010.9 Review Validate Results / 0010.10a Develop Risk Mitigation Actions	0010.11a Propose Risk Mitigation Actions	0010.12a Rollout, Implement & Sustain
Supplier	0010.4b Provide Pre-survey Feedback			0010.11a Propose Risk Mitigation Actions	0010.12a Implement And Sustain
Technology	Preparation	SAS / SAP / SAS	SAS	SAS	SAS

FIGURE 5.6 Overall risk management process.

The assessment was conducted as a combination of interviews and an online survey that allows organizations to assess a large group of suppliers within a short time frame.

High-level results of the assessment were presented in the form of a supplier portfolio including supplier risk probability and revenue impact of each supplier. See Figure 5.7 (note: all company names and ratings have been changed for this case). This rating is developed from the assessment and performance data using the DRK method. The revenue impact reflects the impact on the company if the supplier suddenly disappears and there was a one-year recovery period.

Alco, a sole source supplier of critical material, was identified with a medium revenue impact and medium to high risks (within the circle). In addition, the details of Alco's risk profile showed that they had several off-shore suppliers that were sole sources and with high-risk profiles, locations, and transportation routes. They also had only minimal risk management processes in place and in conversations concerning these issues reflected no interest in making any changes. MedDevices was a small customer to them (less than 5 percent of their business), and one that required a significant regulatory management and offered a high legal risk from medical lawsuits.

Based on this information, a decision was made to find alternate suppliers for this material and distribute the volume to another supplier. Figure 5.8 shows the results of the actions taken.

Algco, the supplier selected as the alternate supplier of the material, was given the volume from Alco and the company's revenue impact increased to $120 million while its risk profile remained the same. Alco's revenue impact decreased to "0."

The impacts on the supply risk portfolio are very positive. The $120 million of spend that was at Alco was rated at 0.25 RPI (Risk Probability Indicator). When this spend went to Algco, the $120 million was rated at 0.17, a 32 percent reduction in risk.

As a result of the assessment, this company was able to make informed decisions regarding spend and risk as well as potential supply base optimizations including terminations. Mitigation actions

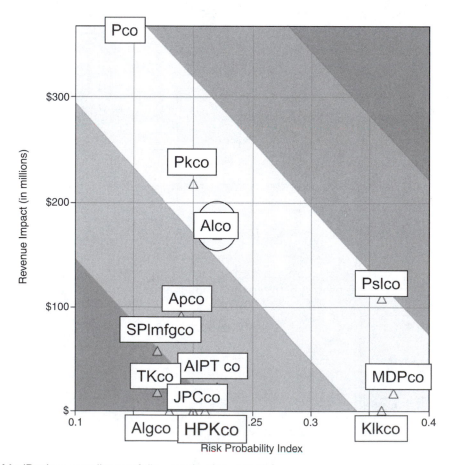

FIGURE 5.7 MedDevices supplier portfolio—packaging material.

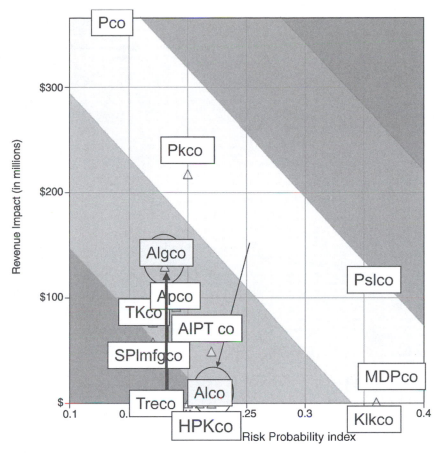

FIGURE 5.8 MedDevices supplier portfolio after changes.

for critical materials were able to improve the risk profile and decrease the potential of supply disruptions.

The following examples show the different mitigation approaches possible in balancing the supply risk portfolio.

1. Taking actions to change the risk profile

This is the first area to examine. What are the attributes of the supplier, the relationship or the interactions that are causing a high risk score and what can be done to change them? For example: a supplier that has a long transportation route (maybe from China) would have a high transportation risk score. If the supplier can store enough inventory to cover a disruption of one or more delivery cycles then their risk score in this area can be substantially reduced, as shown in Figure 5.9. A supplier that is higher risk because of communication issues can be addressed by building a communication process between the supplier and the company. This will reduce the risk profile and move the supplier to the left on Figure 5.9.

2. Distributing spend to several suppliers of a lower risk profile

Figure 5.10 shows the effect of moving all or part of the spend with a risky supplier (1) to less risky suppliers (2, 3 and 4). This can reduce the impact per supplier and reduce the risk for the overall category.

In general, risk mitigation actions can be a combination of changing the risk profile of the supplier, moving spend to less risky suppliers, buffering the company from the impacts (inventory, alternate suppliers available, etc.) or a combination of these. Often the lack of leverage with a supplier is a factor that appears in the assessment. By moving volume from different suppliers and increasing the

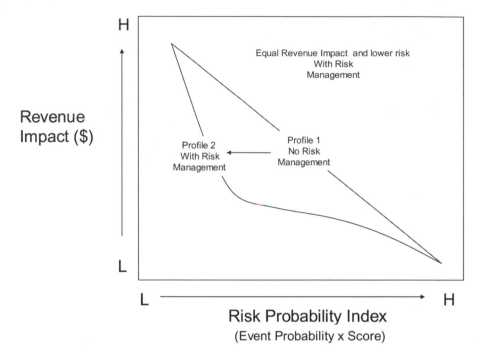

FIGURE 5.9 Equal revenue moved to lower risk supplier.

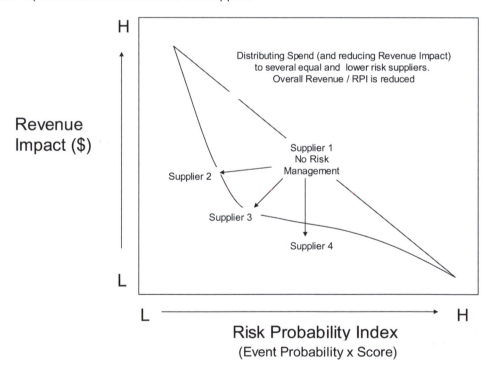

FIGURE 5.10 Distributing the spend to reduce the overall risk.

volume with a key supplier this leverage can be increased but this must be a balance between the risk of reducing sources and being spread too thin to have influence with suppliers.

Notes

1 M. Christopher, and H. Lee, "Mitigating Supply Chain Risk Through Improved Confidence," *International Journal of Physical Distribution & Logistics Management,* 34(5), (2004): 388–396.

2 R.J. Trent, and R.M. Monczka, "Achieving Excellence in Global Sourcing," *Sloan Management Review,* 47(1), (2005): 24–32.

3 C. Araz, and I. Ozkarahan, "Supplier Evaluation and Management System for Strategic Sourcing Based on a New Multicriteria Sorting Procedure," *International Journal of Production Economics*, 106(2), (2007): 585–606.

4 Ç. Haksöz, and A. Kadam, "Supply Risk in Fragile Contracts," *Sloan Management Review*, 49(2), (2008): 7–8.

5 S. Chopra, and M.S. Sodhi, "Managing Risk to Avoid Supply-Chain Breakdown," *Sloan Management Review*, 46(1), (2004): 53–61.

6 An in-depth field study of 89 executives, conducted by AMR, revealed that 28 percent believe that supplier failure poses the most potential threat to their organization; strategic risks (17 percent) and natural disasters (15 percent) were distant second and third. Some 36 percent believe supplier failure risk is increasing, while only 8 percent predict its decrease in the next years (Hillman and Keltz, 2007).

7 Ç. Haksöz, and A. Kadam, "Supply Risk in Fragile Contracts," *Sloan Management Review*, 49(2), (2008): 7–8.

8 L. Giunipero, and R. Eltantawy, "Securing the Upstream Supply Chain: A Risk Management Approach," *International Journal of Physical Distribution & Logistics Management*, 34(9), (2004): 698–713.

9 The procurement risk assessment and mitigation (PRAM) methodology was developed in order to minimize supply disruption within the seven billion raw material portfolio of Dow Chemicals. It uses spreadsheets and visual tools to allow supply managers to create risk profiles of the company's raw materials supply strategies (Hackett Group, 2007).

10 See e.g. A. Rubinson, and J. Jablecki, "Enhancing Supplier Performance Management for More Profit, Less Risk," *Supply Chain Management Review* (2008) for the main principles of supplier performance management.

11 Ibid.

12 R.J. Trent, and R.M. Monczka, "Achieving Excellence in Global Sourcing," *Sloan Management Review*, 47(1), (2005): 24–32.

13 This claim is in line with the recent finding that the role of the procurement office has fundamentally changed in most large organizations. Earlier, interactions with suppliers focused on costs. This led to the perception of procurement as a back-office function, which is still the case today in some companies. Today, however, many leaders recognize that a high-performing procurement organization can directly contribute to the bottom line and improve shareholder value (B. Slobodow, O. Abdullah, and W.C. Babuschak, "When Supplier Partnerships Aren't," *Sloan Management Review*, 49(2), (2008): 77–83).

14 Ibid.

15 Giunipero and Eltantawy, "Securing the Upstream Supply Chain: A Risk Management Approach."

16 High reliability is often a top priority in automotive industry (Demeter et al., 2006).

17 Trent and Monczka, "Achieving Excellence in Global Sourcing."

Part 3
The Intangible
Supply Chain

six
Governing Tangible Risk
The SCOR Model

Taylor Wilkerson

Today's extended global supply chains are highly complex systems, and identifying and managing potential risks throughout these systems is daunting without a structured approach. Managing supply chain risk therefore demands a tool that focuses resources where they are most effective.

For many companies, the Supply Chain Operations Reference (SCOR) model[1] meets that need. The SCOR model has been used by supply chain managers since 1996 to structure and guide supply chain analysis. Its proven utility as an analytical framework for evaluating, improving, and managing supply chain performance has been demonstrated across almost every industry. The SCOR model integrates process definitions with performance and diagnostic metrics and leading practices for improving operational efficiency and customer service.

Recently, the Supply Chain Council (SCC), which owns the SCOR model, formed a project team to investigate the intersection between the SCOR model and supply chain risk management.[2] The team's work resulted in the addition of risk management elements to the model as well as the development of a structured approach for using the SCOR model as a risk management tool. In this section of the chapter, we will briefly explain the SCOR model, and then describe a method for using the model to assess and manage risk.

SCOR Model Overview

The SCOR model is a process framework for defining, analyzing, and improving supply chain performance. Its modular structure allows users to assess the extended supply chain to identify and correct performance shortfalls, leading to cost and customer service improvements.

The model includes three primary elements. The first element is a process structure that facilitates the definition of supply chain processes throughout a network. The second is a metrics hierarchy for measuring supply chain performance and setting targets. The third is a series of best practices for improving supply chain performance. All three of these elements are integrated into a single framework. The metrics, for example, are linked to the processes to allow root-cause analysis of performance gaps. Similarly, the best practices are linked to the metrics and the processes; this allows users to identify implementation requirements and target performance improvements. Together, they form a framework that supports a relatively quick, consistent method for defining supply chain processes and can then be used to manage and improve performance.

The SCOR model defines supply chain operations through five primary processes: Plan, Source, Make, Deliver, and Return. These five processes are the building blocks for defining supply chain operations. Most locations in a supply chain include Plan processes to manage resources and requirements, although in some cases this is done at a central location. Every material handling location has, at a minimum, Source and Deliver processes to order and receive material and to process and ship customer orders. Production locations (or any location that uses the material received to create a new product) will include a Make process as well. Locations that return product to suppliers or handle returns from customers will also have a Return process. Repeating these process elements across the supply chain allows you to quickly describe operations using standard definitions.

For each of the SCOR model processes, there are three levels of detail. Level 1 is the strategic-level view of the five processes (Plan, Source, Make, Deliver, and Return). Level 2, the configuration level, defines how material moves in the supply chain: in response to a forecast, in response to a specific customer order, or in response to design specifications. Level 3, the activity level, identifies the activities involved in completing the process at hand. Together, these three levels provide a view of supply chain processes that allows companies to conduct strategic analysis, along with rapid root-cause diagnosis and correction of problems.

The SCOR model performance metrics are designed to highlight supply chain performance in a business context. Metrics are allocated to five performance attributes: Reliability, Responsiveness, Agility, Cost, and Asset Management. These five attributes align supply chain performance to business objectives of customer service and cost management. The metrics have a diagnostic hierarchy to facilitate root-cause analysis, and each metric is tied to a process or activity to help identify not only the cause of a problem but also where in the supply chain it is occurring. Throughout the hierarchy, the SCOR model metrics maintain the five performance attributes to ensure the entire supply chain is aligned to strategic business objectives.

The best practices in the SCOR model serve as methods for improving supply chain performance. The practices are based on the SCC's research and are proven techniques for enhancing supply chain execution. The SCC continuously updates the best practices in the model to capture current, leading management methods.

Using SCOR for Risk Management

The SCOR model lends itself very well to supply chain risk management for several reasons. First, it allows you to leverage the SCOR framework to quickly define and map your supply chain. This means that you spend less time creating maps and process diagrams and more time on the task at hand—identifying and mitigating risks.

The SCOR model approach is also repeatable, meaning that you can use the same framework, tools, and methods for every supply chain in your portfolio. The model's structure also simplifies the evaluation of elements that are common to multiple supply chains, such as warehouses or suppliers, without having to redefine those elements. Not only is this a time saver, but it also highlights risk events that can impact multiple nodes in your supply chain or multiple supply chains.

Finally, the SCOR framework integrates risk management metrics and best practices with the five supply chain processes. The risk metrics have standard definitions, which facilitate benchmarking of supply chain risk across internal supply chains or with external peers. Because the metrics have standard definitions, they are ideal for sharing information about risk performance and objectives among supply chain partners. Moreover, the linkage of the metrics to processes allows you to quickly identify risk sources and develop appropriate mitigation actions.

As we move through the SCOR model approach for managing risk, you will see how the model provides the structure that is essential for an effective and continuous risk management program.

The SCOR Risk Management Approach

Before you can use the SCOR model to address risk, there must be a risk management program already in place. The initiative must have an executive sponsor who can define objectives for the program as well as provide funding and organizational support for managing supply chain risks. One of the executive sponsor's most important roles is to ensure that the supply chain risk management program is aligned with corporate risk management goals. As with any other supply chain effort, a misalignment between supply chain and corporate priorities is a sure recipe for failure.

The SCOR model, then, is applied within this corporate supply chain risk management program, in five phases:

1. Define the supply chain
2. Analyze the supply chain
3. Assess the supply chain risks
4. Mitigate the supply chain risks
5. Implement the mitigation measures.

This five-phase approach, which is discussed in detail below, is based on the results of research on best practices in supply chain risk management that was conducted by the SCC team. Its basic elements are not necessarily unique; the advantage of the SCOR framework is that it provides the necessary structure for a comprehensive and repeatable program.

Phase 1: Define the Supply Chain

Supply chain risk management starts with a clear definition of the supply chain you will be evaluating. This step is essential for establishing a reasonable project scope. It is also necessary for understanding the risk management requirements of the supply chain. Since supply chains for different product categories—for instance, star performers, steady "cash cows," questionable sellers, and poor performers—will have differing performance objectives in terms of cost and service, it is reasonable to expect that they should also have differing risk objectives.

Once you define the supply chain you will focus on, the next step is to create a map of that supply chain. This exercise starts with locating the relevant supply chain nodes on the appropriate geographic map (or set of maps). Once the nodes have been located, you can depict the direction of material flow between them. Lastly, for each node, you should identify the associated SCOR model processes (Source, Make, Deliver, and Return).[3] An example of this type of geographic map is shown in Figure 6.1.

With the SCOR model structure, you can quickly transform the geographic map into a process or thread diagram showing the SCOR processes identified at each node and the associated material flows. This depiction of your supply chain is very useful for risk management because it lets you visualize the supply chain as a process, complete with the geographic context of operations and the organizational roles involved (that is, the owners and operators of each node). Figure 6.2 shows an example of a thread diagram that is based on the geographic map in Figure 6.1.

The last step in this phase is to define your tolerance for risk in the supply chain you are analyzing. In many cases, the tolerance for risk will be closely linked to corporate priorities for the supply chain. For example, supply chains handling steady-performer, "cash cow" products are likely to be risk-averse in order to protect a major source of income. Star product supply chains, however, probably will accept more risk in an effort to continue capturing market share.

In most cases, the information required for this phase will be readily available; the intent is not for you to start from scratch. At the end of this phase, you should have the information you need to define the scope and intent of the risk management program, and then to start analyzing your supply chain.

Phase 2: Analyze the Supply Chain

The second phase builds on the risk tolerance identified earlier to more specifically define the risk-related requirements for the supply chain. To accomplish this, you need to first define the metrics you will use for quantifying supply chain risks.

The SCOR model uses "value at risk" (VAR) to quantify supply chain risks. VAR's roots are in

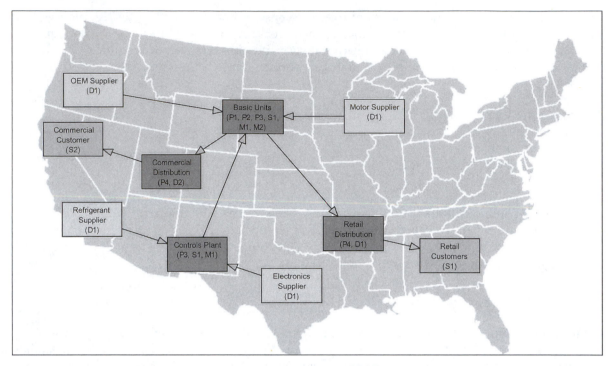

FIGURE 6.1 A geographic diagram of a supply chain using the SCOR model. The diagram depicts the physical locations of supply chain nodes, the SCOR model processes accomplished at each node, the organizations involved in executing those processes, and the material flows between the nodes. This diagram can be used to identify portions of the supply chain at risk due to geographic or political considerations.

Source: Supply Chain Council, 2009.

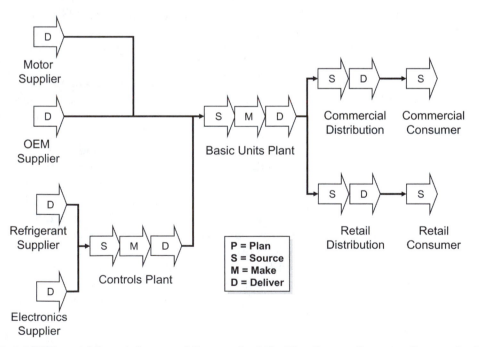

FIGURE 6.2 A SCOR model thread diagram of the supply chain. The diagram illustrates the supply chain as a high-level process flow based on the SCOR model. This process view highlights the roles of organizations in the supply chain and the interactions between them. This diagram can be used to identify which branches of the supply chain are critical for risk management prioritization.

Source: Supply Chain Council, 2009.

measuring and managing financial portfolio risks. It enables equivalent comparisons of different types of risk by putting them all in a financial context.

The VAR for a specific risk is simply the probability of the risk event occurring multiplied by the financial impact that would result if the event should occur. The VAR for an entire supply chain, then, is the sum of the VAR for each risk in the supply chain. The result is an assessment of the likely financial impacts of all risks in the supply chain. This information can be used to develop return on investment (ROI) calculations to guide mitigation efforts.

Before that can happen, however, you need to define the acceptable VAR for the supply chain. There are several ways to arrive at this figure, but the most common are to benchmark peer supply chains or use company-defined risk goals to set a target VAR value. Once the target has been set, it needs to be validated by the project sponsor as well as by key functional managers in the supply chain. Having an agreed-upon supply chain risk target will allow you to better prioritize mitigation efforts.

It is worth noting that although VAR is the preferred metric in the SCOR model, it is not the only way to measure risk. For example, Cisco Systems, among others, uses "time to recover" (TTR) to quantify the risks in its supply chains. TTR is a measure of the expected elapsed time between a risk event occurring and the supply chain recovering to normal operations. By articulating the time to resume normal operations, you can understand the business impacts of that lost capacity in your supply chain.

Whichever risk metric is used, though, it should be meaningful and expressed in a business context that can be understood by all involved, not just supply chain experts. After all, the risks need to be understood across the organization in order to be effectively managed.

Phase 3: Assess the Supply Chain Risks

With the supply chain mapped and risk priorities set, you are ready to assess your supply chain's risks. This phase involves three steps: brainstorming, validation, and documentation.

Brainstorming, or free discussion, starts the risk-identification process. The SCOR model provides a structure for the brainstorming exercise to ensure comprehensive assessments and useful results. Using the geographic and process maps developed earlier, you can start the discussion by asking a series of questions about each supply chain node. Note that the following questions are intended to be general guides; you should add other risk-related questions that would be meaningful for your particular supply chain.

- Are the location and its related material flows subject to natural disasters?
- Is the location in a politically stable region?
- Does the location or the associated material flows indicate a bottleneck or critical failure point in the supply chain?
- Does the location have adequate security? Are the associated material flows adequately secured?
- Are the material flows subject to traffic congestion, border crossings, or other transportation problems? Are transit times consistent?
- Is the location likely to experience significant labor disputes?
- Is the location in an industry or region that is subject to market risks or volatility?
- Is the location financially secure?
- Does the location maintain consistent quality in its operations?
- Is there a risk of product damage along any of the related transportation routes?

As you discuss each node, note any questions that you cannot adequately answer as well as any potential risks that are mentioned.

The more complex your supply chain is, the more brainstorming sessions you will need to identify all of the risks. To keep this manageable, it may be useful to categorize the material flowing through the supply chain by its potential impact if it should be disrupted. For example, if one of your supplier's inputs is a common material that is widely available, you probably can leave that aspect of the supply chain out of your assessment without fear of overlooking a significant risk.

Once the brainstorming sessions have been completed, the next step is to validate the results to be certain that they accurately represent the potential risks to the supply chain. Start by grouping similar risks among the nodes into common risks that have a common cause, or trigger. Then compare nodes to ensure that locations with similar characteristics (geographic location, operations, ownership, etc.) reflect the expected similar risks. This is also the time to research the answers to any questions that could not be fully addressed during the brainstorming sessions. Next, review the overall inventory of risks to identify and remove from consideration any that clearly are highly unlikely to occur or represent a minimal impact. Then do the opposite: identify any significant risks that were overlooked and add them to the inventory.

For each of the risks, assess both the likelihood of the triggering risk event occurring and its potential impact on the supply chain. The information you will need to assess the likelihood of occurrence can come from any number of sources, including insurance actuary data, historical event data, and statistical analysis, to name just a few possibilities. If all else fails, though, you can use an educated guess *with sufficient justification.*

When calculating the potential impact of an event, consider both direct and indirect costs. Direct costs would include the actual damage to property, loss of inventory, idle time expenses, and other costs associated with bringing the supply chain back to full operation. Indirect costs could include lost sales, lost market share, and even lost brand equity due to the disruption. While indirect costs can be difficult to calculate accurately, it is important to include them in your assessment. Without that information, you will not be able to evaluate the full impact of the event.

Lastly, document the risk inventory in a format that can be used in detailed analyses in the future. In most cases, this documentation is best captured in a database system or spreadsheet. Each risk should be identified by location, type of risk, triggering event, likelihood of occurrence, potential impact, and similar considerations.

Phase 4: Mitigate the Supply Chain Risks

At this point, you now have a comprehensive inventory of risks in your supply chain. The next phase, then, is to look for ways to mitigate those risks. Mitigation involves taking action to reduce either the likelihood that a risk will occur or the impact of the event when it does occur. An easy example to understand is theft. Installing locks on your doors will reduce the likelihood that a theft will occur, but it will not change the impact of a theft that does occur. Likewise, buying insurance will reduce the financial impact of a theft, but it will do nothing to prevent it from occurring. Most risk mitigations address some combination of prevention and loss reduction.

How much risk you mitigate will depend on both the risk tolerance of the supply chain (which you have already calculated and expressed in terms of VAR) and the resources available to implement mitigation actions. Using the data collected, you can calculate the VARs of each identified risk and add them together to determine the total potential impact of all of the risks in the supply chain. You can then compare this to the target risk tolerance to determine how much risk must be removed from the supply chain.

It is unlikely that you will be able to actively mitigate every risk you identify; therefore, you need a method for selecting which risks deserve the most attention and effort. A simple and effective way to do that is to plot them in a matrix of likelihood of occurrence and potential impact, as shown in Figure 6.3.

The first priority, of course, should be to address risks with a high potential impact that are most likely to occur. Start with the risks that fall into the upper-right quadrant of Figure 6.3, identifying potential mitigation actions for each. Mitigation actions take many forms and need to be designed

Risk Prioritization

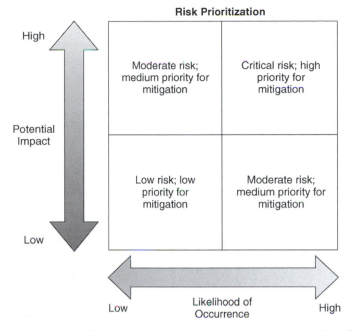

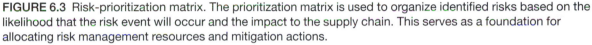

FIGURE 6.3 Risk-prioritization matrix. The prioritization matrix is used to organize identified risks based on the likelihood that the risk event will occur and the impact to the supply chain. This serves as a foundation for allocating risk management resources and mitigation actions.

Source: LMI, 2008.

based on the risk and the operational environment. Just a few of the many possible examples of mitigation actions include redundant supply chain nodes or suppliers, facility relocation, physical security procedures, and active management of potential trigger events.

As you design mitigation actions, be sure to consider how they will reduce the VAR associated with each risk. This serves two purposes. First, it allows you to track how much risk you are taking out of your supply chain. Second, it allows you to start building a business case for the mitigation action by comparing the cost of the action to the value of the risk being removed from the supply chain.

A final word on mitigation: No risk should be left completely unaddressed. At a minimum, you should create a response plan for the less likely and lower-impact risks. While a general response plan will not reduce the likelihood that an event will occur, it will greatly reduce the time to respond to the event and resume normal operations. Remember that the response plan needs to capture a supply chain response, not just your actions. Therefore, the plan needs to include elements that define how you will communicate with suppliers and customers during the risk event and how you will coordinate response actions.

Phase 5: Implement the Mitigation Measures

Now that you have defined your mitigation actions, it is time to implement them. This process begins with the development of an implementation plan and continues through project management and risk monitoring.

The planning stage involves grouping the mitigation actions into common projects for implementation. These projects are then prioritized and put into a project timeline based on such considerations as the availability of resources, project impact, dependencies on other projects, and other implementation factors. Once the project plan has been completed, you can secure the necessary funding and begin implementation. (This topic can only be discussed very briefly here; for more detail and direction, consult standard project management texts.)

A critically important aspect of implementing risk-mitigation measures is having a risk monitoring program. The purpose of such a program is to recognize a risk event or the increased potential for a risk event as early as possible so you can react more quickly and reduce the impact. An effective monitoring program will allow managers to proactively respond to events as they happen, or even take preventive action before they occur. Which monitoring activities you carry out will depend on the risks you have identified in your supply chain; examples include tracking weather patterns, news developments, market trends, and partner companies' financial information, to name just a few.

Monitoring becomes more important when supply chains are extended and event response involves multiple organizations. The sooner you can detect the event, the sooner you can marshal your partners to respond.

Continuous Risk Management

When you have completed all of the steps in the SCOR approach to risk management, you will have identified, prioritized, and mitigated the risks in your supply chain. But this is not the end of your risk management program. In today's economic environment, there is no such thing as a static supply chain—and that means there is no such thing as a static risk profile. As suppliers, customers, and partners are added and removed from your supply chain, you will need to assess the impact of those changes.

That is why it is recommended that you regularly revisit the five-phase process. Just how far back in the process you go, and how often you do so, will depend on your needs and resources. The modular structure of the SCOR model, however, allows you to consider these changes, or even test proposed changes, without reevaluating your entire supply chain. Here is an example of a typical schedule:

- *Monthly*—revisit mitigation plans to ensure that they are being properly implemented and accurately reflect operational needs.
- *Quarterly*—revisit risk assessments, especially those that are subject to market or political conditions, to verify that the VAR for each risk is accurate.
- *Annually*—revisit the supply chain to ensure the supply chain definition and risk priorities accurately reflect the current supply chain configuration.
- *Biannually*—revisit the supply chain definition to ensure that the risk management program reflects both the organizations that are currently involved in the supply chain and the role the supply chain plays in your company's corporate strategy.

A schedule like the one above is important, but in some situations it may be better not to wait for the scheduled review. Specific events may call for a reevaluation of risk in a supply chain. Market shifts, corporate strategy changes, and new technologies are just some examples of developments that should trigger a reevaluation.

A Consistent, Repeatable Approach

Every supply chain faces potential disruptions from multiple sources. The challenge is to understand where your supply chain is exposed to risk and determine how to mitigate the most significant of those risks. The SCOR model provides a framework and structured approach for identifying and managing such risks. The repeatable nature of the SCOR model means that you can use the same approach to manage risks across all of your supply chains and quickly adapt your risk management program to structural changes. The result is a more robust risk management program that is aligned with corporate risk management and business goals as well as with customers' needs.

Notes

1   The SCOR® mark and the contents of the SCOR® model are the exclusive property of, and are used herein with the permission of, the Supply Chain Council Inc. More information about the SCOR model is available from the Supply Chain Council at www.supply-chain.org.

2   Many of the ideas in this section originated with the Supply Chain Council Risk Management Team. I am deeply indebted to my teammates for their contributions to this body of knowledge.

3   For this example, we are using the Level 1 processes to define the supply chain. In many cases, you will want to identify if material is made to stock, made to order, or engineered to order using the SCOR Level 2 processes.

seven
X-SCM Governance Case
Cisco

Lisa H. Harrington

At Cisco Systems, anticipating, preventing, and responding to volatility and risk is a guiding principle of its supply chain operation. The company is in the vanguard of organizations that are embedding volatility management into the very heart of their global supply chain operations. This case study looks at why Cisco's top management—from CEO John T. Chambers on down—considers this approach to be vitally important; what steps the company has taken to make volatility/risk management an integral part of its operation; and how Cisco has benefited from building a highly responsive, flexible supply chain structure.

Why Managing Volatility Is a Top Priority

San Jose, California-based Cisco, a world leader in networking equipment and network management for the Internet, has one of the most complex supply chains in the IT industry, supporting almost 200 product families that require more than 35,000 component parts. The company works with business partners that provide manufacturing, testing, design, transportation, logistics, and other services. Cisco is truly global in scope; it employs nearly 64,000 people in major markets on every continent. Not surprisingly, the company's complex, globally dispersed supply chain is subject to many risks.

From a high-level view, the threats to a company's business can be divided into external and internal risks. Internal risks may be further divided into three subcategories: strategic, operational and financial risks.

- **External risks** include events such as economic downturns, pandemics, natural and man-made catastrophes, acts of war and terrorism, political turmoil, and regulatory concerns.
- **Internal strategic risks** involve threats to the company's business model, product or service portfolio, brands, reputation, and standing in the marketplace.
- **Internal operational risks** are problems that can affect productivity, profit margin, the supply chain, and the physical plant, as well as employee relations and morale.
- **Internal financial risks** have to do with cash flow, equity, stock price, investments, mergers and acquisitions, foreign exchange, interest rates, and other fiscal matters.

Managers must find ways to mitigate, transfer, prevent, or rationally assume all these types of risks. However, they also should address every risk with a view toward mitigating the "fear factor" that can tend to make employees overly cautious, and therefore interfere with business growth and flexibility.

On the supply chain side, risks are inherent in all activities, including:

- Sourcing
- Manufacturing
- Transportation
- Storage.

These risks have always existed, but in recent years they have taken on greater importance for several reasons. For one thing, with Cisco being so large and globally dispersed, the chances are good that a major natural disaster almost anywhere in the world will affect its business in some way. Hurricane Katrina, for example, which devastated New Orleans and the surrounding region, served as a "wake-up call" for Cisco, alerting managers to the need to prepare for unpredictable events, said John O'Connor, Cisco's director, supply chain risk management. Similarly, the earthquake that ravaged the region around Chengdu in China, where Cisco has suppliers, offered another example of a natural disaster that could not be prevented but could be prepared for.

But Cisco's concern is not limited to natural disasters. Managing supply chain volatility and risk is critical for maintaining control in a business world that is changing more quickly than ever. "The velocity of change is picking up dramatically," O'Connor said. "A resilient supply chain is necessary for responding to change in a timely way."

Cisco's management believes the benefits of a resilient supply chain don't stop there. The company sees being a leader in this area translating into new, very real business opportunities. "Any of the [supply chain] volatilities could translate into market opportunities or disruptions," O'Connor observed. "If we don't have a higher level of awareness and acknowledgement of resiliency, they will translate into disruptions." By embracing volatility management, Cisco can capture "market adjacencies," expanding into new product and market opportunities. "Organizations that are anticipating and planning to exploit volatility are going to move ahead," he stressed.

A Worldwide Framework for Managing Risk

To achieve all of those objectives, Cisco needed a cohesive framework and a dedicated team to address risks at the physical network, manufacturing, and component-testing levels, O'Connor said. The risk framework also had to encompass systems processes, applications and data—sitting "under one umbrella, to assess and resolve those risks across all different dimensions," as O'Connor put it.

Any such framework would have to be consistent, replicable, and applicable across not just Cisco's own operations but those of its business partners as well. "When we architect our capabilities, we do it in a manner that anticipates leveraging, reusability, and a common business architecture and framework," O'Connor explained. "What we don't want is to be trapped by 'tribal knowledge.' We want to codify [industry best practices] and have an operating model that sits on top of system architecture framework. We need to talk a common language that is agnostic, and not just a Cisco thing."

To develop the supply chain capabilities that would be needed in order to meet these business continuity and resiliency requirements, Cisco created the Supply Chain Risk Management (SCRM) team. The SCRM team is responsible for ensuring that Cisco has the most resilient supply chain in its industry—ensuring that the company can respond more quickly than any of its competitors in the event of any operational or catastrophic disruption. The team does this by incorporating resiliency requirements into the design and release process for new products, as well as by ensuring product and supply chain risk resiliency for existing products.

The SCRM team is pioneering an approach to managing supply chain risk by defining ways to anticipate and measure risk; building a standards-based Business Continuity Planning (BCP) program that actively measures and improves the ability to recover from disruption; and by developing and executing resiliency programs at the product and supply chain levels. Cisco has developed a unique SCRM process framework, engagement model, set of metrics, and toolset to handle this job.

Program Overview

Cisco's supply chain risk management program consists of three key elements, each managed by teams of experienced professionals:

- **Business Continuity Planning** (BCP) focuses on Cisco's suppliers, manufacturing (EMS) partners, and transportation and logistics providers to document recovery plans, recovery times, and drive resiliency standards. Cisco's BCP program identifies critical business processes, people, and systems associated with over 600 supply chain "nodes" and assesses the time-to-recover (TTR) for each node. TTR is a measure of the time required to restore 100 percent output at a node following a disruption. It is based on the longest recovery time for any critical capability within that node.

    The BCP program is unique in that Cisco has been able to build a BCP dashboard—i.e., a software tool that provides at-a-glance critical information—with data that plays two key roles: (1) It is used by the Crisis Management team to assess the impact of any disruption, and (2) It illuminates vulnerabilities in the supply chain that Cisco can then mitigate.

- **Crisis Management** coordinates proactive and reactive measures through global event monitoring to identify disruptions, assess their possible impact and adopt recovery plans to limit disruption to customers. Cisco's Crisis Management team is responsible for monitoring disruptions globally on a 24/7 basis. In the event a disruption does or could potentially affect Cisco's supply chain, the team uses the BCP dashboard to quickly conduct an impact assessment. It identifies which supply chain nodes are in the affected region, which parts and/or products are made within the affected region, which alternate/fail-over sites should be engaged, and which customers and associated revenue may be affected. The Crisis Management team then engages a cross-functional team to execute response playbooks that have been tailored to the disruption type, location, and anticipated duration. These playbooks include alternate plans by product, trigger points for recovery actions, and advance preparations for known events such as a hurricane.

- **Resiliency** mitigates the use of high-risk components and supply chains for existing products and incorporates resiliency requirements into new products and supply chains. Cisco is concerned with two kinds of resiliency: Product resiliency and supply chain resiliency.

    - **Product Resiliency**: Cisco's Product Resiliency team works closely with its Supply Management team to identify components with TTRs that are outside of Cisco's established tolerances. For such components, Cisco's SCRM and Commodity Management teams develop resiliency plans, which include second/multi-sourcing, alternate site qualification, component risk buffers, and manufacturing rights.

    - **Supply Chain Resiliency**: Cisco's Supply Chain Resiliency team works closely with the company's manufacturing operations, manufacturing partners, and logistics and transportation providers to identify nodes with TTRs that are outside of Cisco's established tolerances. For such nodes, Cisco's SCRM and Manufacturing Operations teams develop resiliency plans that include alternate site qualification, capacity reservations, and semi-finished goods risk buffers.

        Here again, Cisco measures the TTR for the applicable supply chain based on the longest TTR for any node associated with the manufacturing and final delivery of products. It then works to achieve a compliant TTR using a combination of the resiliency options noted above.

The three elements and the activities they include share a common emphasis on time to recover. Clearly, this concept lies at the heart of Cisco's risk management strategy. The company, in fact, considers it a competitive advantage. "We want to be the leader in recovery times for our industry," O'Connor stressed.

In the next sections, we'll look at how Cisco applies this approach to minimize the potential impact of risks in its supply chain.

Assessing Risk

Cisco meets regularly with the contract manufacturers and key component suppliers that build or add value to its products to discuss what risks the company faces and what actions should be taken to mitigate them. In addition, suppliers are asked to complete an annual BCP assessment questionnaire prepared by the Global Supply Chain Management team, which helps Cisco assess suppliers' ability to maintain business continuity.

A key aspect of risk assessment is collecting data and standardizing it, said Lance Solomon, Cisco's manager of supply chain risk management. This allows analysts to score each supply chain node in a standard way. Different types of suppliers—for example, semiconductor suppliers and logistics services providers—receive different sets of questions that reflect their specific roles in the supply chain, but the framework for collecting and analyzing the data is consistent.

To help it standardize and automate risk assessment, Cisco has developed a "risk engine," (software analytic tool) that incorporates many data sets (such as 100-year flood, actuarial, geological, geopolitical, site-incident, and supplier performance data) to assess the likelihood of a disruption. These disruptions are correlated to Cisco's supply chain locations, including supplier sites, contract manufacturing facilities, and logistics centers. The potential impact of a disruption is determined based on the revenue associated with each supply chain node and that node's TTR. Finally, Cisco uses simulation to integrate all of these data sets into a single model that forecasts the likelihood and impact of disruptions and generates "heat maps" identifying potential trouble spots.

These maps identify the portfolio of assets that are at risk, the level of risk, what considerations need to be built into the business model to address the risks, and how the risks should factor into a group's or business unit's decision-making process. For example, the same type of risk could have greater or different potential consequences at different locations. Earthquakes, for instance, are a risk in several parts of the world, but their impact would be different in San Jose, California (company headquarters), Taiwan (where important foundries are located), and Japan (where Cisco purchases parts from a single source).

Cisco has developed its own method of risk probability modeling. When analysts look at the bill of materials (BOM) for a specific product, they know which suppliers are contributing componentry to that product, which manufacturing partners are involved, and who is handling testing, and who is managing subassembly distribution. They consider which customers are buying that product as well as the transportation routing. Thanks to the regular collection and updating of data, all of that assessment can be completed in about an hour, O'Connor said.

Analysts have the ability to isolate the revenue impact of a potential or actual disaster regardless of whether it affects a supplier, contract manufacturer, or Cisco location. They know the products that are affected and their revenue value, as well as their recovery times. For risk management purposes, Cisco prioritizes its products based on their revenue impact, as shown in Figure 7.1. For example, 100 products in 25 product families represent 50 percent of Cisco's revenue; 4,000 products within the 25 product families represent 80 percent of revenue.

This concern about the potential revenue impact of a disruption leads the Risk Management team to focus its efforts on the nodes with the greatest revenue exposure. "If you have $1 billion flowing through a particular node per quarter, and you know that it takes a quarter to relocate the site, [then that's one place to focus on]," Solomon explained.

In addition to revenue, risk analysis also considers the cost of business interruption insurance. O'Connor cited the example of a hypothetical manufacturing node that is responsible for $100 million of product a week. If the time to recover for that manufacturing site is 10 weeks, then Cisco would have to purchase insurance to cover $1 billion of business. If the recovery time is only five weeks, then interruption insurance would only need to cover $500 million.

Supply chain risk in emerging markets and developing economies has been a particular concern. In 2008, the Emerging Countries Supply Chain team revised the analytical processes it had developed for emerging economies in 2007. The new model considers the unique aspects of each country's operating and sales environments when identifying the supply chain changes needed to improve Cisco's

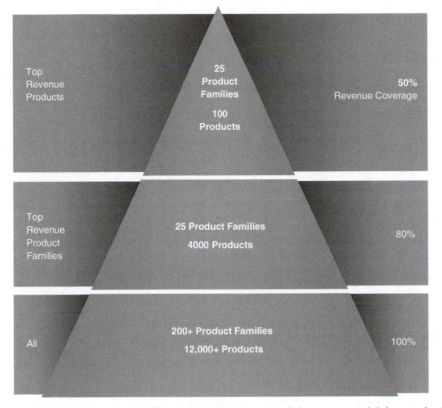

FIGURE 7.1 Products exposure pyramid. Cisco diagrams the potential revenue at risk by product type.

Source: Cisco, 2010.

supply chain performance and customer satisfaction in that country. Figure 7.2 shows the factors that Cisco now takes into consideration.

Institutionalizing Risk Management

Cisco has gone to great lengths to institutionalize its risk management strategy at all levels of the enterprise. Risk management is embedded at the corporate level (the CFO has a risk management function); within the information management system; and at the operations and product levels. All of these areas and managers must coordinate and align their risk management activities.

"We have been working on an enterprise governance model that will have risk and resiliency sponsor groups that work at various levels," explained O'Connor. These include the Risk and Resiliency Operating Committee and several working groups focused on Business Continuity Management, Pandemic Planning, Crisis Management and Risk Governance, and Metrics. "The working groups help us understand how to manage risk and measure our operating level relative to our risk appetite," O'Connor added.

Cisco has a formal risk portfolio management process to manage how it allocates funding to mitigate risks within the supply chain. The process is organized in four phases, proceeding in chronological order:

1. *Program Scope:* Determine which products the team will consider as candidates for risk mitigation. The strategic focus for the team is the highest revenue products for Cisco.

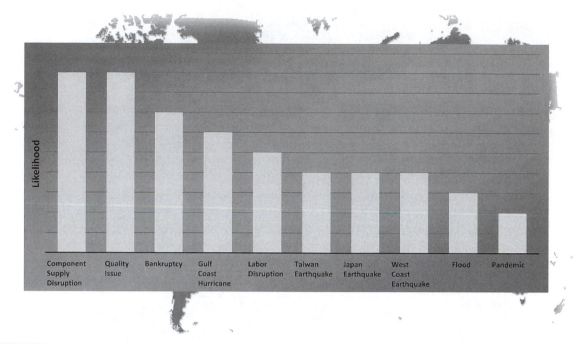

FIGURE 7.2 Understanding supply chain disruptions. Sample disruptions that Cisco factors into its risk analyses.

Source: Cisco, 2010.

2. *Budget Approval Process*: Supplier management teams submit mitigation funding requests which are then allocated based on revenue impact and available budget.
3. *Pipeline Process*: Rank projects based on product revenue ranking; schedule projects for the fiscal year with expense and capital identified by quarter; review quarterly projects to ensure full utilization of SCRM budget.
4. *Project Management Process*: Develop project plans with milestones until the mitigation actions are closed; track and report monthly progress against milestones; release scheduled payments or re-direct funds to next-in-line.

Preparing For and Responding To a Crisis

Crisis management at Cisco consists of four components: global event monitoring, continuity planning, impact analysis, and response playbooks.

Potential disruptions in the supply chain including events at key manufacturing and commodity supplier sites as well as business-critical infrastructure sites, such as airports, are monitored by the Supply Chain Risk Management (SCRM) team using a worldwide alert service.

Cisco's SCRM team also categorizes risk exposure for impact by:

- Type of risk (e.g., weather or natural disaster) ranked by location
- Type of risk ranked by product revenue category (e.g., 100 products represent 50 percent of Cisco's revenue at risk).

Cisco often uses maps and graphic representations to indicate the location and degree of supply chain risk. On a map of the world, for instance, there are red (extreme risk), orange (severe), and yellow (moderate) dots of different sizes. This shows relative risk based on the number of locations (including: supplier, manufacturing, transportation, and logistics), the likelihood of a disruption, and the potential impact of a disruption. Zooming in closer to geographic regions, Cisco can view supply chain risk locations in more detail. Note that, as Figure 7.4 illustrates, Cisco's greatest risk sites are all in Asia.

Cisco leverages the data collected via the BCP program to build maps of its supply chain and graphic representations to indicate the location and degree of supply chain risk. For a specific event or risk,

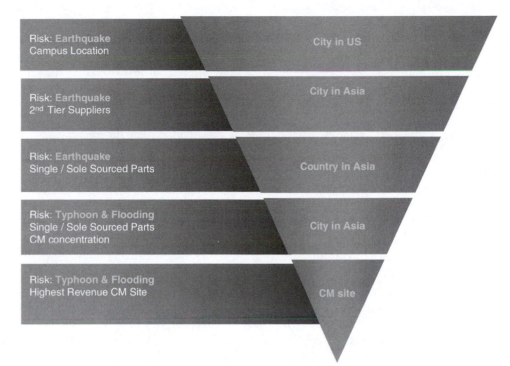

FIGURE 7.3 Event severity exposure by location. Cisco's Supply Chain Risk Management team diagrams the projected impact of natural disasters, such as earthquakes or typhoons, on strategic locations.

Source: Cisco, 2009.

FIGURE 7.4 Global event impact severity map. This map shows an example of how Cisco depicts the location and potential severity of risks, worldwide.

Source: Cisco, 2009.

the team can highlight a region of concern and quickly identify any critical sites within that region. This allows the team to quickly identify locations impacted by an event such as an earthquake, flood, or strike and determine the potential revenue impact. Analysts can click each site on the map and get details about the company, emergency contacts, revenue impact, time to recover, and an alternate source of supply or services.

When the Chengdu earthquake hit in 2008, Cisco's supply chain risk analysts had a wealth of information at their fingertips. Marrying previously collected data about products and revenue exposure with current reports of damage allowed them to quickly assess the impact on other supply chain nodes and on customers. On a satellite map of China, the team could quickly identify any manufacturing sites, logistics centers, and supplier locations that could potentially be affected by the earthquake and the disruptions it could cause in the immediate vicinity as well as in Shanghai, Hong Kong, Guangdong, Macau, and other areas in the eastern half of the country. As it turned out, four suppliers of four products were located within the earthquake zone and were moderately affected. The analysts were able to quickly determine those suppliers' anticipated time to recover and the estimated revenue impact of lost capacity during that period.

When a problem does occur, Cisco's Value Chain Crisis Response team is ready to go. Aided by both a supply chain monitoring capability and a defined set of protocols, the team can quickly respond to events that may impact the supply chain in addition to leveraging predefined ways to communicate with the entire organization. In order to monitor the supply chain, Cisco identified 50 key supplier locations and set criteria for when alarms needed to be sounded (for example, when an earthquake occurs within 200 miles of a site). As backup, the Value Chain Crisis team is also linked into the Global Operations Command Centers that Cisco maintains worldwide to monitor conventional security concerns, such as fires and break-ins.

Ensuring Resiliency in Products and the Supply Chain

Cisco's SCRM program requires a truly collaborative effort to ensure resiliency in the company's highly complex supply chain. Multiple specialized teams are involved in almost every risk management initiative.

As noted earlier, when managers at Cisco discuss resiliency, they are talking about two types: *supply chain resiliency*, which includes supply chain design, manufacturing resiliency, test resiliency, and logistics resiliency; and *product resiliency*, which includes product design, product substitution, strategic inventory, and component mitigation.

The company has a formal, consistent method for measuring supply chain resiliency.

Cisco incorporates risk into its supply chain design process. Minimizing risk and TTR is a consideration when deciding whether to own or outsource infrastructure and capacity, where to locate it, how the company assigns products to suppliers, and how it transports products and manages logistics, O'Connor said. This also includes identifying viable product substitutes for use during a supply chain disruption.

The company also designs for risk in its products. The product design process aims to minimize both product and supply chain risk from the beginning of the product lifecycle. For new product launches, Cisco uses a formal product-lifecycle review to evaluate the resiliency of the product before it is manufactured. Each new product receives a TTR-based risk rating and a BCP requirement, and it must pass muster with the appropriate risk board. All of this affects the time to recover for the product's components. As a result, the product's supply chain is designed with TTR in mind. Cisco also considers supplier TTR when evaluating whether to award business.

Existing products go through what O'Connor calls "de-risking." Analysts consider the product's composition as well as its manufacturing, testing, and logistics aspects from the semiannual BCP assessment. If any of those nodes fall outside of the established risk parameters, the supply chain risk and management groups work to minimize the risk. O'Connor offers this example: If there is a sole-source supplier, they will look for another, qualified source as a backup. But if there is no alternative and a factory is disrupted, then recovery time could be a number of months. The two teams would then work together to implement an inventory buffer that would be segregated and treated as strategic inventory.

For its products, Cisco has developed recovery profiles for each one. These comprise recovery times for manufacturing, test equipment, and the relevant components and pushes them toward established goals, O'Connor said. For manufacturing, this means finding alternate sites that are pre-qualified and can deliver the required capacity within the TTR goal for printed circuit board assembly factories, demand fulfillment sites, raw material warehouses, and finished goods logistics centers.

"In order to bring up a product at an alternate site we need to have test equipment delivered within the TTR goal, and to that end we are focusing on lead-time programs with key suppliers. For example, we have an agreement with one of our chamber suppliers to provide 10 pieces of equipment within 10 weeks," O'Connor said.

Cisco has set TTR goals for manufacturing, testing, and component supply. Goals for manufacturing are shortest, testing is in the middle and component supply has the longest allowable recovery time. These goals reflect the availability of alternate sources.

Resiliency actions apply to inventory (including finished- and semi-finished goods inventory), raw materials, and substitutes. For manufacturing, alternate site readiness, alternate site pre-qualification, capacity options, and finished- and semi-finished goods buffers are the main ways Cisco ensures resiliency. For test equipment, lead-time reduction programs, test standardization and asset visibility help to maintain resilience.

When it comes to components, the first choice is to have a backup source. If there is none, the appropriate team will seek out and identify a second source, verify the alternate site qualifications and possibly establish component buffers.

Aligning Resiliency to Products and Customers

Cisco's approach to risk management focuses on effectively determining the resiliency of the supply chain and leveraging that data to drive crisis monitoring and risk mitigation. This integrated data framework allows the team to make risk management operational by aligning resiliency to what's critical to the business: products and customers. Viewing risk from the product and customer perspective enables the team to drive towards the goal of building resiliency for a specific product or customer. The benefits are that the team can effectively engage with product teams on design for resiliency, building products that are resilient prior to first shipments to customers. The team can explicitly engage in discussion with management on the appetite for risk relative to the cost it would require to build additional resiliency into the supply chain.

Establishing standards for supply chain risk management is one area that requires further development. Toward that end, Cisco became a founding member of the Supply Chain Risk Leadership Council (SCRLC). The organization's purpose is to bring companies together "to advance the discipline of supply chain risk management through best practice sharing and collaboration around specific objectives such as supplier relationships, risk metrics and risk methodology." The group's website is www.scrlc.com; e-mail to info@scrlc.com.

"At Cisco, we define the dimension of risk we were going to solve for. We carve away a collection of risks and manage them across the entire business. The risks occur on a theater, segment, product, supplier, and revenue basis. You'll never be able to solve all risks so the approach needs to combine an organization's appetite for risk with the budget available to mitigate risk" O'Connor said.

Cisco's Risk Management Systems Toolset

To better manage its global risk, Cisco's Supply Chain Risk Management group has developed a toolset that provides visibility into risk exposure, enables risk modeling and analysis, and enables the team to manage resiliency programs for critical components. The toolset includes the following elements:

- **BCP Dashboard**: tabulate and codifies BCP responses into useful data to include part-site mapping (which supplier sites are responsible for making which parts), TTRs, alternate sites, 2nd sources, emergency contacts, recovery plans, etc.
- **Risk Engine**: enables the team to provide comprehensive statistical modeling of supply chain risks (likelihood and impact modeling), provides heat maps as a key input to program priorities, and provides simulation capabilities.
- **Crisis Management Dashboard**: allows the team to monitor supply chain disruptions globally by mapping alerts from a 3rd-party monitoring service to our supply chain nodes, and operates a collaboration workspace for cross-functional crisis management team.
- **Global Component Risk Manager**: this tool has become a central repository for identifying and managing resiliency programs for over 2000 "high-risk" components. The tool enables identification of high-risk components, helps commodity teams identify appropriate resiliency options, tracks implementation activities, tracks the qualification process, etc.

Finally, the SCRM team has developed metrics that enable Cisco to measure resiliency at the product, specific site, city/state, regional and business unit level. In particular, Cisco has developed a "Resiliency Index" which is a composite of resiliency attributes that are calculated and reported by business units at Cisco's semi-annual operations review with senior management. By having resiliency metrics that are shared by the business units and supply chain, Cisco drives a common awareness and understanding of what resiliency means to the organization, as well as a common framework for driving improvements.

Thus far, the program has proven highly effective in response to myriad disruptions—the Chengdu earthquake, the global financial crisis, the factory shutdowns during the Beijing Olympics, Hurricane Ike, and Bangkok airport closures, to name a few. Through these disruptions, Cisco has demonstrated an ability to spot disruptions early on, to conduct rapid impact assessments and to engage cross-functional teams globally to exploit the resiliency programs it has implemented. Key performance metrics such as on-time shipments and customer satisfaction demonstrate the effectiveness of the company's world-class supply chain risk management program.

eight

Financial Supply Chain Risk Engineering

Carlos Alvarenga

"Our business model is one of very high risk: We dig a very big hole in the ground, spend three billion dollars to build a factory in it, which takes three years, to produce technology we haven't invented yet, to run products we haven't designed yet, for markets which don't exist. We do that two or three times a year." — Paul Otellini, CEO, Intel

"Put all your eggs in one basket and then WATCH THAT BASKET." — Andy Grove, Former CEO, Intel

It's difficult, though certainly not impossible, to find a product company today that does not incorporate some elements of the discipline known as supply chain management (SCM) in its strategic thinking and operational execution. From logistics network optimization to strategic sourcing strategies, SCM has transformed the way entire industries operate, along the way enabling operational models that were unthinkable a few decades earlier.

This transformation, for some SCM executives, seems to have run its course. Their companies use sophisticated advanced planning systems (APS) to coordinate global operations and extensive collaborative infrastructures to make and deliver product worldwide. For many people, this is the summit of what SCM is, and they see the next decade of work as one focused on perfecting these models. For others still catching up to these leaders, the goal is to reach either "best-in-class" capabilities or at least industry parity in SCM.

These executives do not see much beyond the current landscape and imagine that perfecting their current models is the order of the day. But is that conclusion correct? Is SCM in a period of "consolidation" or "refinement" as many executives and analysts suggest? This chapter argues that this conclusion is incomplete. Why? Because we are seeing the birth of the third generation of SCM—one focused on expanding techniques developed in the fields of finance and financial risk management and integrating them into what can be called financial SCM (FSCM).

FSCM starts with a radical question: *What if SCM had been invented in finance and not in logistics?* To the theoreticians and practitioners of FSCM, the answer to this question leads to a radically different view of the goals, strategies, and practices that great and good SCM companies should understand and use. In this chapter, we discuss the most important of these ideas and investigate how they can and are being applied to traditional SCM challenges. We also explore the pros and cons of these ideas and present a brief practical framework for applying FSCM that may serve to generate a new debate between SCM and finance executives about these concepts and their applicability to existing strategies and operations. Lastly, the chapter argues that FSCM is a welcome and valuable evolution in the discipline and that, far from entering a static period in its history, SCM is about to be revolutionized yet again by new leaders, ideas, and techniques that daily move from the theoretical into the very real world in which SCM has had such profound impact.

Plans, Trains, and Automobiles

In any discussion of SCM, it is usually a good thing to define its boundaries. For the purposes of the ensuing discussion, we assume a broad definition of the term: one spanning from the initial definition of the business case for a product's creation to the termination of that product, perhaps years or decades later. For such a discussion the common Supply Chain Operations Reference (SCOR) model (with a slight modification to "Deliver" to account for post-sale service activities common to many firms), can be useful to present these activities. To review, the SCOR model (which was discussed earlier in Chapter 6) is a process reference model developed by the management consulting firms PRTM and AMR Research and endorsed by the Supply Chain Council as the cross-industry de facto standard diagnostic tool for supply chain management. SCOR, as the model is known, enables users to address, improve, and communicate supply chain management practices within and between all interested parties in the Extended Enterprise. The SCOR model spans from the supplier's supplier to the customer's customer. SCOR is based on five distinct management processes: Plan, Source, Make, Deliver, and Return.

- *Plan*—Processes that balance aggregate demand and supply to develop a course of action which best meets sourcing, production, and delivery requirements.
- *Source*—Processes that procure goods and services to meet planned or actual demand.
- *Make*—Processes that transform product to a finished state to meet planned or actual demand.
- *Deliver*—Processes that provide finished goods and services to meet planned or actual demand, typically including order management, transportation management, and distribution management.
- *Return*—Processes associated with returning or receiving returned products for any reason. These processes extend into post-delivery customer support.

Figure 8.1 illustrates these areas as they relate to supply chain management.

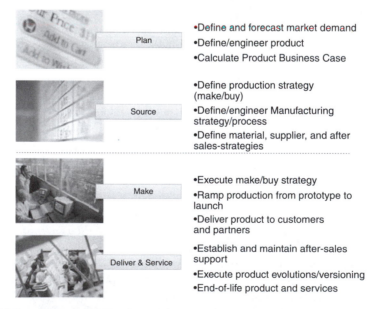

FIGURE 8.1 The SCOR process areas. The figure shows the four basic process areas covered by the Supply Chain Operations Reference (SCOR) model, with a slight modification to "Deliver" to account for post-sale service activities common to many firms.

Source: Alvarenga, 2010.

One can argue that the discipline of SCM, which ties all of these areas together, has progressed through two major phases since its creation in the eighteenth century during the Industrial Revolution and its formalization in Henry Ford's repetitive production lines at the start of the twentieth century. The first of these phases was the "physics phase." During this phase, the aim of the strategists was to optimize the physical flow of materials and goods through a physical world. There were ships to be routed, production lines to be fine tuned, and, later, waste to be minimized.

All of these areas had one thing in common: they were "real" in the sense that they were—and are, of course—tangible parts of the physical world. Consequently, the tools and techniques that this SCM phase valued—from maps, to time and motion studies to "lean"[1] techniques—were those that were focused on and improved *real* things. One could argue that a very common feature of improvement during this SCM phase was that change was "visual" in the sense that often "before" and "after" pictures were the best explanations of what had been improved in the supply chain. This phase eventually became the discipline now called SCM in the early 1980s.

The second evolution of SCM, which began in the 1970s, was the "information phase." SCM's focus began to change, from strictly physical in nature, to incorporating the data used to manage the physical supply chain activities. The rise of companies such as i2 Technologies and the invention of APS brought two profound changes in SCM: (1) technologists and computer scientists began to enter the field in great numbers, and (2) a formal level of abstraction was introduced over the physical world. Let us examine each of these changes.

- The first change—introduction of technologists to the field—meant that people whose basic training had not been in logistics or production were now not only accepted into SCM but, in some cases, actually took over the intellectual leadership of the discipline. This occurred in software companies, academic departments, and product companies alike. The "physicists" did not go away, but they did have to learn the language of IT and irreversibly incorporate IT systems into their operations.
- The second, and more profound, change meant that it became acceptable for SCM teams to focus on abstractions of physical problems. For example, the creation of multiple demand simulations and lifecycle models became routine. Many companies created teams to model non-existent supply chains in their quest to optimize the real one.

These two changes—information optimization and abstraction of the physical supply chain—laid the groundwork for the third evolution of SCM: the "finance phase" or financial supply chain management (FSCM). These three phases are illustrated in Figure 8.2.

Though admittedly early in its trajectory, the third phase can be defined by the following three characteristics:

- Intense focus on quantitative methods and tools borrowed from finance and financial risk management
- Intense focus on financially optimal solutions to real and virtual SCM problems that may—*or may not*—correspond to the answers "physics" or "information"-driven solutions would yield
- Increased abstraction away from the physical SCM world toward what eventually will become two parallel SCM worlds—the physical and the abstract world—similar to that which exists in the banking and finance industries today.

This final bullet highlights an analogous transformation that illuminates this chapter's hypothesis. In banking one finds two parallel worlds: a physical world where people still walk into a bank, apply for a home loan, and then carry a checkbook to a settlement office to buy a house, and a financial world in which analysts and traders are making multi-billion dollar decisions on the likelihood those same people—and millions like them—will ever repay that loan. Indeed, this parallel world creates value through levels of abstractions that, to a lay person, may seem totally removed from the physical world and, in many cases, are nothing more than instruments that allow one to speculate on the probabilities

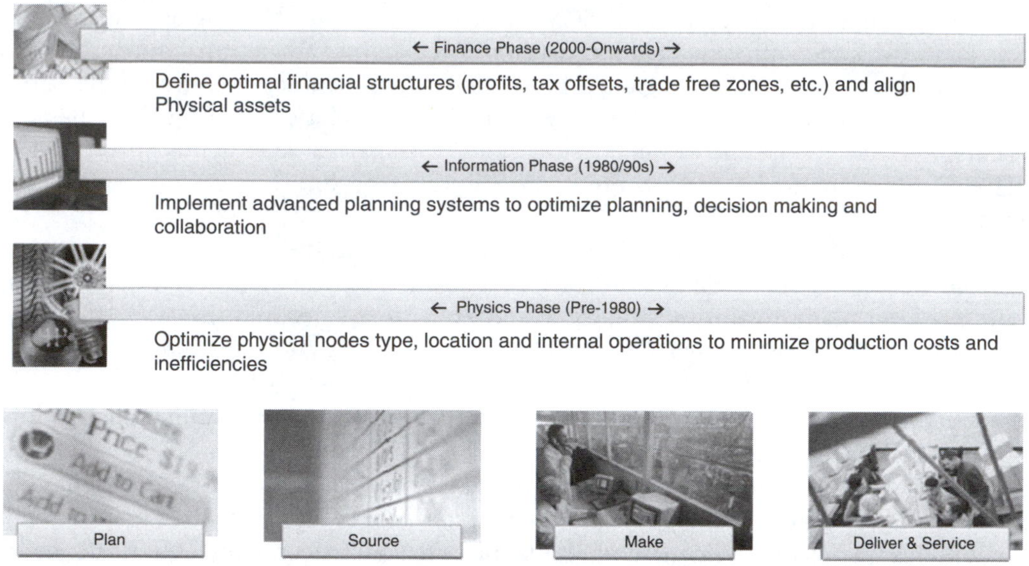

FIGURE 8.2 The evolution of supply chain management. This figure illustrates the three phases of evolution for supply chain management, from the physics phase, which focused on physical flows, through the information phase, all the way to the newly emerging finance phase. The finance phase blends the principals of finance into the other two evolutionary areas of SCM.

Source: Alvarenga, 2010.

of probability itself. Curiously—if ominously for many people—the "virtual" banking world creates and, in some cases, destroys much more value than the physical world. That trend increases every day.

Though it may be hard to see today, the same phenomenon—the laying of the theoretical and applied foundations for a parallel SCM world—is beginning to develop in SCM. The rest of this chapter examines some of the most important elements of this evolution and suggests a basic framework for applying FSCM by companies that want to start moving toward this level of sophistication.

Against the Gods and Other Strange Ideas

Talk to almost anyone involved in the area of FSCM and one book, above others, seems to be common reading. This is Peter L. Bernstein's insightful analysis of the history of risk, *Against the Gods: The Remarkable Story of Risk*.[2] Bernstein's basic thesis: that once one understands good and bad outcomes are the result of risk and not supernatural forces, one's view of the world (and its gods) changes completely. People may take things like fire insurance and credit cards for granted but they exist only because brilliant people moved away from divine causes for everyday events and began to think of good and bad outcomes as the result of quantifiable (and non-quantifiable) uncertainties that are inherent in our world.

Moreover, Bernstein describes how one brilliant mathematician after another pushed the ideas of uncertainty, probability, and utility forward—each one adding a critical element to what would become the modern science of risk management. For example, speaking of the Swiss mathematician Daniel Bernoulli, Bernstein writes:

> He suggests a systematic approach for determining how much each individual desires more over less: the desire is inversely proportional to the quantity of goods possessed.
>
> For the first time in history Bernoulli is applying measurement to something that cannot be counted. He has acted as go-between in the wedding of intuition and measurement. Cardano, Pascal, and Fermat provided a method for figuring the risks in each throw of the dice, but Bernoulli introduces us to the risk-taker—the player who chooses how much to bet or whether to bet at all. Bernoulli laid the intellectual groundwork for much of what was to follow, not just in economics, but in theories about how people make decisions in every aspect of life.[3]

Every aspect of life includes SCM. Take for example when a large cosmetics company launches a new perfume and in doing so does not inform its suppliers that its sales forecast could be off by as much as +/− 70 percent—not unheard of in this industry. This absolute forecast error in a new product launch might be a minor worry for a big cosmetics company but a life or death problem for a small box supplier to that same company. In other words, as Bernoulli postulated, the solution to the same SCM problem—what is the absolute right forecast—has different value to the cosmetics company and to the box supplier. SCM strategists, of course, have understood this problem for decades, and the physicists have responded by creating smart inventory plans or just-in-time production techniques. The "informationists" have focused on collaborative forecasting systems with the perfume suppliers or a new demand planning system. Both are valid responses and help to varying degrees—though it must be said that in practice most often they ignore the utility variance Bernoulli discovered.

The term utility variance refers to the fact that the same outcome can have different value for different agents. In other words, as Bernoulli postulated, the solution to the same SCM problem—what is the absolute right forecast—has different value to the cosmetics company and to the box supplier. Similarly, a given transport lane may have different value to a carrier, a coal shipper, and a cell phone shipper.

But the cosmetics company example described above begs the following question: How would an FSCM specialist look at this problem?

Before discussing the answers to this question, it is worth noting another critical principle Bernstein illuminates in his book and which is fundamental to anyone who has ever worked as a securities trader: *risk is neither good nor bad* in and of itself. In other words, risk is indifferent and amoral and should neither be embraced nor rejected in ignorance. Indeed, every college finance student knows that risk is a necessary pre-condition of reward.

This basic lesson sometimes seems lost on otherwise sophisticated SCM strategists and analysts, however. This is no academic point, as will be shown later, but one of the more important errors many SCM physicists and informationists make when they look at risk in their supply chains. We deal with this critique in more detail below, but for now, it is sufficient to take away two key SCM lessons from *Against the Gods*. First, our understanding of risk was and is an evolutionary process that is quantitative in nature—abstracting real problems into mathematical forms for analysis and solution. Second, risk is both necessary for reward and indifferent per se to either good or bad outcomes to the risk taker.

Now, returning to the perfume problem, and keeping in mind that the value—the *utility*—of the error correction is very different for the big perfume vendor and for the small box manufacturer: What would an FSCM solution to this problem add to the existing solution set? How would an approach founded not on the physics of SCM or on the information flows around them, be any different?

Before addressing these queries, let us first understand the tools and techniques FSCM specialists are bringing to bear on this kind of problem. Let us also look at from where these tools arise and how they impact SCM problems.

The Birth of SCM Quants

As noted earlier, FSCM has three basic tenets:

- Quantitative methods and tools borrowed from finance
- Increased abstraction away from the physical SCM world toward the parallel abstract world
- Intense focus on financially optimal solutions that can sometimes "override" traditional SCM solutions.

The people who are developing FSCM approach the forecasting problem differently from traditional SCM practitioners because the latter group view problems and their goals differently. Before returning to the perfume case above, let's examine some of the fields from which FSCM "Quants"[4] (to borrow a term from finance) are emerging and what each class of specialists is bringing to the discussion.

Real Options

While the field of accounting has contributed specialists to SCM for decades, their role has been the traditional one of calculators of cost and profit. Finance itself has, until recently, rarely interacted with SCM. As far as this author is aware, there are no professors of "SCM finance" teaching at any major business school, and most MBAs who specialize in SCM take only the standard corporate finance class in order to graduate. However, this situation is changing and the change is coming from both academics and finance practitioners.

In the academic world, the change has centered on fields such as Real Options and Valuation, both of which have major relevance to SCM. To summarize, a real option, as distinct from a financial option, is an option related to the physical world. For example, a firm may or may not build a plant, invest in a new production line, or buy a truckload of plastic. The real is not the new plant or truckload of plastic, but the *possibility* of making either thing real. In other words, when one party sells a real option to another, they do not sell the object of that option but the right to make that option real or not. The option's objects—to buy or not buy, to build or not build—exist in the physical world but the option itself is an abstract creation with value that is different from the option object. Thus, the goal of real option research—which has its origins in the 1970s—is to create analyses and tools that allow real options to be created and priced correctly.

Real options provide flexibility in a variety of ways in the real world. Some allow deferral of an action, some allow for alterations of consumption or production, while others allow switching from one consumption or production method to another. In theory, real options give the SCM strategist an almost infinite variety of possible solutions to real-world SCM problems.

To return to our perfume case, let's apply the theory of real options to the situation. Today, the large cosmetics company can either buy or not buy some minimum number of boxes to support its new product launch. If it sets the buy quantity at zero, because it is too concerned about possible forecast error, the small box company has zero revenue.

A real option specialist, however, would look at that same situation and say that another alternative exists—i.e., the creation of an option to buy the box production without actually buying any boxes. Such a real option, once created, would provide the perfume maker with "optional" capacity to support its launch at a much lower cost than the traditional and riskier "minimum buy" that would have to be made today. It would also give the box maker more revenue than it would get if the perfume maker decides that a possible 70 percent forecast error is too high to support a new product launch.

Such a scenario may seem fanciful, but in reality it is not. Real options have already entered the production world. A high-tech company, for example, buys options on engineering hours from small engineering companies when it launches certain new products, where the key constraint to meeting any higher than expected demand is not physical production capacity but engineering hours spent adjusting its hit products for different countries.[5]

Operations Research

Unlike finance, operations research (commonly known as "OR") is a field that has long had close ties with SCM. Many of the mathematical engines that lie at the heart of advanced planning systems, for example, were created by OR specialists. However, a group of OR researchers have of late turned their attention to the incorporation of real options and risk modeling techniques such as Monte Carlo simulation to production and SCM problems.[6]

In their work, OR specialists look at an SCM problem like the perfume case above and apply their techniques, for example, to the production planning aspects of this situation. In this case, the physicists would do all they could to "lean" the perfume supply chain and prepare it to stop as quickly as possible should the product be launched and then prove to be a failure 60 days later. An informationist approach would focus on improving the forecast error itself, perhaps by an increased round of focus groups with potential customers around the world or a series of collaborative planning sessions with major department stores.

An OR specialist, however, would go beyond the static statement that there is a possibility of a 70 percent forecast error and attempt, perhaps using mathematical methods, to simulate the possible demand outcomes and define an optimal capacity strategy vis-à-vis two possible outcomes: that which is most likely to happen and that which would be most catastrophic. In other words, the OR strategist would prepare the perfume maker for what demand should be, given a mathematical combination not just of past sales history but of the impact of randomness on that sales history (the Monte Carlo part) as well as for the possible impact of the worst case scenario (if the forecast is off by 100 or more percent, for example). Again, this may seem like an academic scenario but this technique, too, is already in use. Several manufacturing firms have created integrated finance–OR teams working on SCM/manufacturing problems. They have adopted Monte Carlo simulation for capacity and production planning—projects that can better align capacity decisions with demand probabilities to a degree that has not been possible with traditional forecast-driven capacity calculation methods.

Risk Management

The third and most radical field driving the FSCM evolution is financial risk management. It also is the most misunderstood field in SCM literature today.

There is no current shortage of articles and seminars addressing the topic of SCM risk. The great majority of them share a major problems, namely that they all approach SCM risk from the physicist point of view and they treat risk as a bad thing to be avoided. Because the majority of the authors and consultants working on SCM risk are physicists by training or inclination, they are limited in their view of SCM risk by the physical world. To them SCM risk management is about "real" SCM elements such as a boat in Shanghai that can sink or a plant that can be destroyed by a tornado.[7]

This phenomenon is best illustrated in an interesting study conducted by ARC Research,[8] in which SCM managers were asked to rate the risk that most concerned them and only two "non-physical" risks (government regulation and currency fluctuation) were listed. Their responses are presented in Figure 8.3.

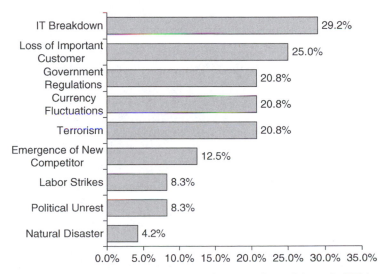

FIGURE 8.3 What macro level events would pose a high risk to your financial results? This figure charts the risks cited by executives as threats to overall corporate financial performance, in a 2005 study conducted by ARC Advisory Group.

Source: *ARC Strategies Series: Risk Management*, Steve Banker, Sid Snitkin, and Adrian Gonzalez, 2005.

The authors note that SCM managers "would see any events that might disrupt reliable availability of materials as serious threats. Poor forecasts of new products and promotions are probably a similar issue. Forecasts can be underestimated or poorly communicated, leading to product shortages that reflect poorly on supply chain managers.[9]

If this view existed in modern finance, then risk management departments on Wall Street would all be outside making sure no robbers get into the building. This is hardly the case because, as noted earlier, in modern finance risk can be both real (bank collapse), directly derivative (securities backed by revenues from that bank), and indirectly derivative (derivatives on the revenues held by parties with no direct relationship to the bank or its direct revenues). The second problem, again related to their training and inclinations, leads them to talk consistently about risk in negative terms. As noted earlier, in finance risk is a good thing as well as bad. Risk creates the opportunity for reward. The job of the risk manager is not to eliminate risk completely, because that would also eliminate rewards, but to manage it. What does it mean to manage risk? It means that risk can only be handled, as the ARC authors correctly note at the start of their analysis, in one of four ways:

- Assumed
- Avoided
- Transferred
- Hedged.

However, most of SCM risk literature today deals with only the first and second options. What about the third and fourth? Can SCM risk really be transferred or hedged? Most top SCM companies understand what risk avoidance and assumption are, and some are even adept at a kind of basic transfer mechanism of it through bi-lateral sourcing or outsourcing arrangements, but very few understand the last, and most powerful, possibility. This chapter deals with this last method in more detail below but it is sufficient to note that the third and fourth options, more than the first two, will transform SCM risk management in the coming decades much as it did modern finance. Again, this is no purely academic discussion. Already, a handful of leading SCM companies in more than one industry use commodity hedging to hedge or transfer supply (and some elements of production) risk, and while these are complex technical strategies, they will become more common as their application is simplified and their value is appreciated.

Financial Optimization

A fourth field currently receiving a lot of attention in FSCM is financial optimization (FO), which refers to the optimization of tax or profitability-related financial flows in a given product supply chain. While this idea is not new, what is new is the arrival of computational and modeling tools that finally enable a systematic and repeatable process for FO. Several companies have created software tools that allow for the modeling and optimization of complex product flows and their associated financial performance that aim to optimize not SCM physical performance in the traditional sense but FSCM performance by reducing taxable exposures and maximizing total SCM profitability. SCM strategists using these tools have developed the ability to rapidly build models of SCM and product-level financial performance and then optimize those models against goals like tax minimization or return on net assets (RONA) or financial contribution. Indeed, often working alongside traditional accounting-advisory firms, these teams are at the vanguard of merging SCM and CFO functions in real, working environments across the world.

Indeed, in the next section, this chapter will present in more detail some of these specific techniques of FSCM that are in use today and which will become more widespread as the FSCM evolution continues.

FSCM In Action: Four Examples

Real Options: How Boeing Uses Real Options in Product Production Decision-making

The commercial aircraft industry is characterized by several exceedingly complex factors that SCM managers must consider when making decisions about product development schedules, technology investments, and strategic sourcing. One major aircraft manufacturer has been at the forefront of incorporating the following finance techniques into these kinds of real-world operations decisions:

- Quantitative technical risk modeling
- Investment and risk modeling metrics
- Real options
- Demand (price and quantity) modeling
- Learning curve optimization (maximize net profits by balancing recurring and non-recurring costs)
- Multi-gate and staged investment processes
- Structured spreadsheet modeling architecture
- Portfolio analysis.

Indeed, this company has recently become a source of patent applications on certain mathematical techniques it developed during the course of its early adoption of FSCM. The most public example of this work has been their incorporation of real option theory into decisions about product development and risk-sharing on new product launches.

In an interview, the leader of the FSCM team notes that his models focus on the following goals:

- Projecting the highest risk variables—price and quantity
- Determining project profitability in an uncertain market
- Capturing variability of future production and cash flows
- Providing forecasts even when market data is sparse
- Designing products and services that help customers manage their own market and operating risks.

This company's approach impacts real-world decisions as follows. Take for example, the decision to subcontract a sub-assembly in an aircraft to a manufacturer in Germany—a decision we label "Project 1." Traditional approaches to this decision would, in essence, determine a quantity, unit price, and delivery schedule. Furthermore, investment and payment terms would be set and executed on a temporal basis as production was started and sub-assemblies delivered.

This manufacturing company, however, approaches the problem differently in that it seeks to (a) understand the risk inherent in this outsourcing decision in a specific, mathematical model, and (b) apply that risk to issues such as contract and payment terms, flexibility models for both buyer and seller, and a continuous adaptation of the risk profile of both the value of Project 1 and the options/ flexibility applied to it throughout its lifecycle. The mathematics for such an approach are no mean feat and, indeed, the technique developed at this company has allowed them to simplify the valuation process so as to make incorporating options techniques easier in operational problems.[10]

Furthermore, the team leader regularly gives multi-day seminars to product managers that explain real option theory and the company's own techniques. The team leader, who is a robotics engineer by training, also notes that the models that he creates are both engineering and financial models. They include variables of aircraft design and financial design, and they can examine each variable's option value in order to make better strategic decisions about the final product. For example, he notes, the company can reduce our unit costs by spending more money on production facilities, by say automation. Where they spend their money depends on what option values they have at any stage of an aircraft design. They can trade off certain design features that may be technically more challenging against the possibility of selling more units by lowering their unit price.

Perhaps the biggest benefit to this aerospace manufacturer of this new approach is that thinking about design and production problems from the point of view of risk and probability has helped the manufacturing company overcome a natural conservative streak in its corporate culture. In other words, understanding risk has helped them make more strategic decisions, incorporating into those decisions not just deterministic scenarios—i.e., those that do not account for randomness in demand—that over time lose their relationship to the real world but a dynamic, constantly revalued perspective of the competitive landscape in which its aircraft and customers must operate.

Operations Research: The Use of Monte Carlo Simulation in Capacity Planning

Capacity modeling is a complex and necessary part of most SCM strategy. Traditionally, this was a purely "physics" problem, in that the goal of the strategist was to match as closely as possible product demand and production capacity. Traditional methods calculated demand for period X and mapped it against capacity for the same period, then adjusted capacity up or down to reach an efficient level of production capability. This approach has several shortcomings, not the least of which is that the forecasts that typically drive capacity requirement analyses are usually deterministic. Because they tend to treat capacity as static capability—i.e., production levels are averaged over a given time period, with temporary variations in capacity typically are "smoothed out" in longer term models.

A leading global semi-conductor manufacturer has begun to address these problems by applying Monte Carlo simulation to the capacity planning questions in what it calls its Next Generation Capacity Model (NGCM). Without diving into the mathematics of their techniques, the company's approach follows four steps:

- Identify the critical capacity constraint (CCR) using techniques based on the theory of constraints[11]
- Introduce a stochastic, i.e., random, element in its demand forecasts using statistical techniques to define peak demand days and standard deviations of historical demand by peak demand days
- Apply the new, risk-adjusted demand patterns to the CCR, which in this case turned out to be warehouse operations throughput, to determine the new risk-adjusted stress/demand-strength/capacity model
- Conduct a safety factor analysis to determine the probability of failure in the new stress-strength model at the facility and processing line levels.

The results of this approach, according to one of their senior production engineers, are several. As he notes in a paper describing their approach:[12]

> Until the development of NGCM, it was not possible to provide capacity forecast recommendations with corresponding levels of certainty. This made it difficult to determine the risks associated with both tactical and strategic capacity decisions. With NGCM, such capability now exists. And while this model was created to address warehouse capacity forecasting challenges, the methods articulated here are applicable to other situations, especially those where TOC/DBR[13] are in use. Operations with fluctuating demand and variable processes will benefit from the application of this capacity model concept as they seek to improve cycle-time performance and reduce work in process inventory.

In an interview, the engineer adds that the increased level of sophistication of the risk techniques being adapted to SCM is changing the role of SCM at his company. As he notes, "manufacturing drives the company but SCM is really being seen as a driver of competitive advantage."

Risk Management: Commodity Hedging at Southwest, Lufthansa, GE, and HP

Perhaps the most publicized FSCM example is the use of hedging strategies in commodity management. A hedge, simply put, is a cost borne in order to reduce the (negative) risk of another existing position. There are many kinds of hedges but some of the most common are financial options such as calls (the right to buy something) and puts (the right to sell something). Many commodities have markets where options on those commodities are traded; one such commodity is aviation fuel, the second-most important direct cost (after labor) in the aviation supply chain.

As has been widely reported in the business and popular press, the majority of procurement departments at U.S. airlines have, in recent years, *not* used commodity hedging strategies to lock in future price protection against the possibility that aviation fuel prices would significantly increase. As a consequence, as with car manufacturers and steel, U.S. airlines have been devastated in the last year as petroleum prices have dramatically increased and they have found themselves forced to buy fuel on spot markets. The consequences of this exposure have been severe: huge losses, layoffs, and route reductions—all at a time when the industry was just starting to show some profitability after several years of terrible performance.

Not all airline procurement teams left themselves un-hedged against this risk, for at least one major U.S. airline and a few European carriers adopted commodity hedging strategies, and in doing so, illustrate FSCM concepts in action. For example, as one article noted, "Southwest was 100 percent hedged for first-quarter 2007, capped at an average crude-equivalent price of about $50 a barrel . . . The locked-in cost is the reason why Southwest's fuel bill is projected to go up only about $500 million this year [2007], one quarter that of US Airways' increase, despite a larger fleet."[14] A 2004 academic paper that analyzed the Southwest hedging program contains an interesting quote from Southwest's Director of Corporate Finance, Dave Carter, who claims that, "If we don't hedge jet fuel price risk, we are speculating. It is our fiduciary duty to try and hedge this risk."[15]

Carter's comment gets to the heart of what some FSCM theorists and practitioners stress about their field: that it is not just a good thing to do but an actual fiduciary responsibility to examine and employ, to the degree possible, certain aspects of FSCM. This is a statement not made lightly, for it has huge ramifications for corporate governance, which are outside the scope of this chapter. Nonetheless, it is hard to argue that if you are a shareholder at a Southwest competitor, and you know that these techniques were available to your procurement and finance teams, you certainly would like to know why they were not exercised. This position would be made all the more urgent by the fact that in Europe, several other airlines deployed the same techniques to more or less the same effect.

Lufthansa, for example, hedged "83 percent of its fuel requirements through the end of this year [2008] and said that it saved 109 million Euros last year through the practice [of hedging], common with European carriers."[16] As the *New York Times* notes:

> The ability to lock into fixed fuel prices months ahead of time—called hedging—can help offset these rising prices. But with the exception of Southwest Airlines, most United States airlines are less hedged than European ones. . . . Air France-KLM has hedged 78 percent of its fuel consumption through March 2009, at $70 to $80 a barrel, Jean-Cyril Spinetta, the chairman and chief executive of the airline, said last month. Through a policy of hedging fuel four years in advance, the company saved about $35 a barrel when oil was at $120 a barrel. . . . Other European airlines have also taken the hedging route. British Airways hedged 72 percent of its fuel needs for the first half of the financial year and 60 percent for the second half. Lufthansa has hedged 83 percent of its fuel requirements through the end of 2008 and said that it saved 109 million Euros ($169 million), last year by doing so.
>
> Even low-cost carriers like Air Berlin, EasyJet, and Ryanair are hedging, with Ryanair recently reversing a longstanding avowal never to do so.

The airlines are not alone in these advanced procurement techniques; companies such as GE have also adopted complex strategies for managing sourcing risk. In 2005, GE's Global Research and

Development Center worked with a small team of business managers to create an arithmetic simulator to analyze a variety of different scenarios for natural gas hedging. To hedge its exposure, GE employs a portfolio approach, relying on swaps,[17] call options and limit orders of varying forms.[18] Similarly, since the 1990s Hewlett-Packard has used a risk management team to analyze and manage commodity purchasing. In 2002, Corey Billington, Blake Johnson, and Alex Triantis described the HP approach in a prescient paper they published years before anyone grasped the power of their pioneering approach:[19]

> To begin with, a systematic analytic process was developed to optimize HP's value-risk objectives for the procurement portfolio. Proprietary software (HPRisk) is now used to examine the impact of different mixes of fixed and flexible quantity contracts (each of which may have caps, floors, or other structured price features) on expected cost and percentile cost levels. A scenario forecasting module feeds into the optimization program to provide distributions of demand, availability, and price, and these are updated through time based on newly collected data. HP's web-enabled software also supports the valuation, monitoring, and management of its contracts.

When airlines hedge their principal raw material—aviation fuel—and companies such as GE and HP do the same with gas, copper, steel, and other basic commodities—they demonstrate the FSCM's tenet of solving a physical problem—availability of a raw material—with a non-physical financial solution. These examples are simple in concept yet complex in execution, of course; and had fuel not increased so dramatically, Southwest, Lufthansa, and the others might have been criticized for making "unnecessary" expenditures in "exotic" risk instruments. After all, fuel hedging has existed without much attention in one way or another in the U.S. aviation industry since it was deregulated in 1978.

Financial Optimization in High-Tech Consumer Electronics

The typical consumer electronics manufacturing company has contract manufacturers making products for it (mostly in Asia) and sells those products through a variety of channels all over the world. When these companies launch a new product, they typically rely on physics-based SCM modeling to map out physical flows and distribution nodes. The tax implications of these product flows were a secondary or tertiary consideration at best.

This changed for one major consumer electronics manufacturer when it purchased software that allowed it to model its products' flows from creation to sales, and also model the cost, financial, and tax flows of its supply chain. In a multi-year effort that should serve as a benchmark for others in the industry, this company saved over U.S.$2 billion through tax optimization and cost avoidance.

This case offers two key lessons. First, it took collaboration between the company's SCM and finance teams to create the data sources and implementation methods to achieve the results noted. Second, the optimized FSCM flow is not always the same as the optimized SCM flow. Indeed, as one of the founders of the software company explained in an interview, everyone understands the physics of these problems, but getting the financial flows right requires a real philosophical change: one has to separate the two problems, be willing to override the physical answer, and trust that the financial models are accurate optimization environments.

This raises the issue as to what consideration ultimately will drive the final SCM model adopted by companies. When that model is the FSCM model—when a finance solution overrides a physics solution—then, we see in action the evolution that this chapter has described.

It is not too far a stretch for SCM executives, with their typically global perspectives, to understand how taxation and product contribution could change their physically optimized SCM models. Most will admit that, if tax and profitability were fully understood, their supply chains would look a lot different than they do today.

There are other finance-based techniques, though more complex and more revolutionary, that will have an even greater impact on SCM. While still theoretical, they are worth noting because they suggest what the third evolution of SCM could look like in the coming decades.

At the Efficient Frontier: The Future of FSCM

In order to move beyond the currently applied level of FSCM, it's necessary to leave behind the constraints of traditional physical and even information-based SCM techniques and look at what is possible from a completely different perspective. Consider, for example, a company that makes grass seed. In an interview with the CFO of this company, he casually points out that their grass seed demand is usually pretty stable. Grass seed is grass seed, he jokes and it's hardly an "impulse buy" after all. Further conversation, however, about the factors that drive the demand for his products leads to the observation that demand for grass seed happens to correlate strongly with temperature. When the mean temperature in his customers' cities is within the range of 55° to 85°, the company sells lots of product. When temperature is not within that range—either above or below—sales drop off linearly until a certain point in both directions, at which time they disappear completely. That demand curve is illustrated in Figure 8.4.

This makes sense intuitively of course. Few people buy a lot of grass seed when the ground is so cold the seed cannot penetrate the soil. Nor will they buy a lot of seed when the temperature is very hot. Clearly, the grass seed company is hurt equally by temperatures that are too high and too low. A fatalistic SCM manager either accepts that his business is governed by the random luck of weather (in this case temperature), while another more sophisticated manager may try to lessen the impact of this "weather risk" by better forecasting or outsourcing production.

In contrast, an FSCM strategist would go far beyond these common responses and could—among other possibilities—decide to use what are known as weather derivatives to tackle this problem.[20] After all, lots of industries—from farming to tractors to heating oil—are affected and there exist markets where one can buy weather hedges, which when used correctly can act as a kind of "weather insurance." The scope of this chapter does not allow a discussion of the mathematics involved, but suffice it to say that a "heating degree hedge" could protect the producer against the cold temperature scenario and a "cooling degree hedge" could protect against the opposite extreme event. This hedging strategy is illustrated in Figure 8.5.

Theoretically, by buying the same kind of risk instruments agriculture and other industries use routinely, the grass seed CFO would in effect hedge his weather-driven "demand risk," something that the vast majority of SCM executives do not consider doing today, even theoretically.[21]

Now consider a more complex problem for a large farm equipment manufacturer which sells tractors and other vehicles. Like the seed CFO, the head of supply chain of this industrial company faces demand volatility that derives from a variety of sources: weather, commodity markets, political decisions made in foreign countries. However, an analysis of his demand indicates that a significant portion of the volatility in his demand is *most* closely correlated with certain specific factors: the price

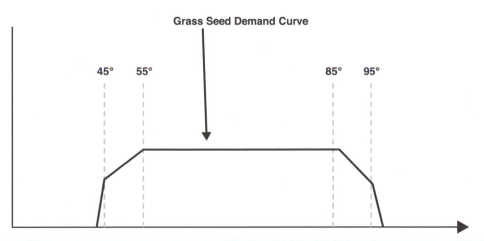

FIGURE 8.4 Grass seed demand curve. This figure illustrates the demand curve for grass seed, driven by temperature range.

Source: Alvarenga, 2010

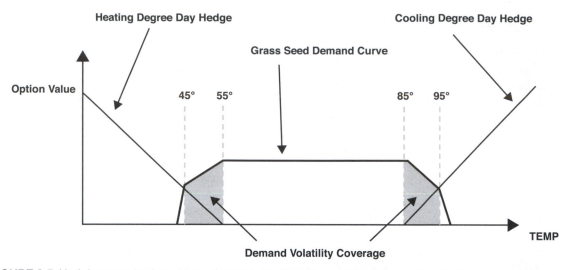

FIGURE 8.5 Hedging out weather-driven demand risk. This figure depicts a possible hedging strategy that the grass seed company could use to insulate itself from volatility. The "heating degree hedge" could protect the producer against the cold temperature scenario (no grass seed consumption) and a "cooling degree hedge" could protect against the opposite extreme event.

Source: Alvarenga, 2010.

of specific commodities, fuel costs, and rainfall. Since these factors are unpredictable this executive carries massive amounts of tractors in lots, much as the "Big Three" U.S. automotive companies are accustomed to doing. The pressure to maintain such high finished goods inventories comes from the corporate VP of sales, who will complain vigorously to his CEO if farmers suddenly want tractors and there are none available. It would seem an intractable problem: the executive has no choice but to carry a vast inventory in huge lots hoping demand will show up, and is seemingly unable to further reduce his inventory costs as a result.

Now, consider the FSCM approach. Given the fact that this company in effect "self-insures" against demand risk and that because its inventory is big and expensive, the head of supply chain decides that his ideal strategy would be to transfer some of the risk of a sudden demand spike to an external entity. In other words, the supply chain executive can lower his inventory if he can buy "demand insurance"—an instrument that, for a fee, will pay him for any lost sales he may incur for having too little inventory in the unlikely case of a sudden and unexpected surge in tractor demand.

The head of SCM contacts various major insurance companies and, in 2010 at least, has no luck finding an insurance company willing to write such a policy. The story does not end there, however. Because there presently is no financial firm that will accept general "market risk," the executive develops an "artificial" or "synthetic" demand curve that (a) "follows" his real demand curve, and (b) is built from items that can be individually, though not collectively, hedged. That strategy is presented in Figure 8.6.

In this scenario, the executive uses a "synthetic" demand curve built on pre-existing risk instruments such as hedges and swaps that collectively "mirror" his real demand curve. These risk instruments effectively "protect" his company against the scenario where demand spikes for any given set of reasons and he has no inventory to sell. The natural evolution of this strategy is that over time the supply chain executive will come to see the hedge instruments as another variable—along with the traditional physical one of spare inventory—to be adjusted against fluctuations in demand.

To FSCM strategists, this company has simply bought a kind of "demand insurance," which, when all is said and done, fulfills the same risk management function as hundreds of millions of dollars of unsold inventory waiting for a demand spike.[22]

As unlikely as the above scenario may seem, such techniques are being developed today by FSCM strategists in industry, consultancies, and a small number of financial services firms. What all these theoretical—but soon possible—strategies have in common is that they are built on a concept called the Efficient Frontier, first laid out by Harry Markowitz in his 1952 paper that launched portfolio theory.[23]

In essence, the Efficient Frontier (see Figure 8.7) is a curve that consists of the optimal risk-reward

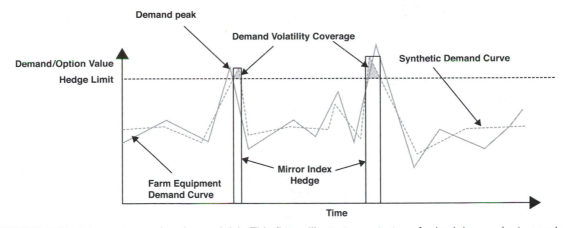

FIGURE 8.6 Hedging out complex demand risk. This figure illustrates a strategy for hedging against complex demand risk in the farm equipment company case example. The strategy involves creating an "artificial" or "synthetic" demand curve that (a) "follows" the company's real demand curve, and (b) is built from items that can be individually, though not collectively, hedged.

Source: Alvarenga, 2010.

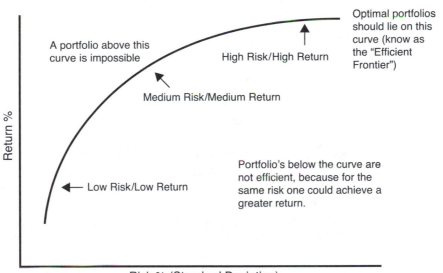

FIGURE 8.7 The Efficient Frontier portfolio theory. This figure diagrams the concept of portfolio risk outlined by economist Harry Markowitz in a groundbreaking paper published in 1952.

Source: Investopedia. http://www.investopedia.com/terms/e/efficientfrontier.asp (accessed June 29, 2008).

portfolios for a given level of risk. This concept from finance is important for FSCM because FCSM aims not just at managing risk, which is the subject of so much SCM risk management thinking today, but of increasing the value of the company, another idea borrowed from finance. Be it by using real option methods to make decisions about airplane features, or reducing profitability by commodity hedging, or by deploying synthetic demand curves to create at least some income in situations where before there were just lost sales—the aim of FSCM is to expand the role of SCM strategy into the world of value maximization, not just delivering products or creating forecasts. If one thinks of a given product's supply chain as really a set of present and future cash flows (again, analogous to a "Project" in finance terms), then as one paper puts it, "by choosing the project to invest in, managers search for efficiency, that is attaining the frontier of possibilities, as well as optimality, that is reaching the point on that frontier that maximizes firm value given the market prices of risk factors."[24] FSCM, by trying at all times to optimize the value of each product's supply chain relative to market risk—something that rarely happens explicitly today— supply chain as a discipline can attain its highest conceptual evolution to date and actually begin an evolution towards becoming closer to a modern corporate finance function, which is what will happen in the coming decades. As the events of 2008 and 2009 have shown, however, such an evolution will not be without its own risks, and there are many lessons to be drawn from finance that FSCM strategists must consider as they evolve their thinking and practices.

When Genius Fails

Perhaps the most interesting public debate in finance at the start of the new century was over the use of risk instruments such as derivatives[25] in the global financial system itself. A decade before the global financial crisis of 2008, far-sighted critics attacked these instruments both from a technical perspective—i.e., that they concentrate risk too narrowly or that they actually do not work when they are most needed; and from a social perspective—i.e., that they are unfair to the poor or that they are a means by which a plutocratic elite manipulate an unwitting public into bearing the cost of poor decisions. For example, Tim Weithers, of the University of Chicago, summarized the most serious worries back in 2007 as follows:

- The sheer size of the derivatives and other instruments vs. the underlying assets on which those derivatives are based. In other words, for any $1 of mortgage debt, there might be $10 of bets on whether that mortgage will ever be paid off.
- The increasing involvement of the hedge fund community in this market, as these institutions are opaque and lightly regulated.
- The operational backlogs and issues surrounding confirmations, clearing, and settlement.[26]

The millions of bankruptcies and foreclosures caused by the collapse of the Western financial system in late 2008 only confirmed Weithers's fears in the minds of most people. Given the economic roller coaster of the last two years, it's worth elaborating on each of these worries and how they might apply to FSCM. The first issue Weithers notes, though couched in arcane finance terms, refers to the "parallel" universe issue discussed earlier in this chapter. The worry is the imbalance between the values of the "real" sources of risk and values of the parallel "derivative" instruments. In an FSCM future, the equivalent might be that Apple could hedge the risk of its next iPod failing in a demand risk marketplace run by, say NYSE Euronext.[27] In this scenario, a large parallel market would exist where thousands of "side bets" were placed on the outcome of the product launch.

The second issue is the involvement of powerful, secretive, and lightly regulated agents using and abusing risk mechanisms, especially as regards "leverage" or the multiplicative impact that leveraged derivatives positions can provide an agent. An FSCM parallel might be if a hedge fund begins to take risk positions on the outcome of certain product cash flows—e.g., iPod sales for the next five years—and by doing so distorts the natural course that launch would have taken.

Direct SCM "speculation" does not exist today formally but that is only because no one has worked out a mechanism to do it—something that today's sophisticated financial services firms could do the moment they set their mind to it. The last issue refers to the mechanics of disposing of derivative instruments, especially in times when the global financial system is "stressed." Given what bankers have done to the world in the recent past, it would be tempting to dismiss FSCM as an idea that, like mortgage-backed securities, is pointless or even dangerous. However, mortgages and hedges did not cause the recent financial crisis—greedy people did. And to dismiss the possibilities and flexibility that FSCM and, say, a functioning demand risk marketplace would provide SCM strategists, is to miss the view of the beneficial forest for the sight of the current mass of rotten trees.

Even if—and this is a very big *if* indeed—the birth of true SCM risk markets experiences some of the same problems seen in the global financial system recently (and that is almost impossible to imagine) the benefits will greatly outweigh the cost. A walk around the acres of unsold inventory in the auto business or a look at the mounds of unsold cosmetics or piles of unsold computers—all a crude form of "self-insurance" against demand volatility—shows just how basic a level at which SCM risk management operates today. Moreover, where lessons can be learned from finance in the regulation of SCM risk instruments and markets—say in accounting treatments or in value at risk (VaR)[28] methodologies—such lessons should also be adopted in FSCM.

As in finance, genius in FSCM will fail when overpowered by greed. But the same can be said of any of the SCM techniques taken for granted today. Indeed, as one leader at Boeing put it when describing the manufacturing challenges in its latest aircraft launch, "nobody inside Boeing thought building the 787 would be easy. After all, the company decided to bet on pushing the boundaries of the possible . . . If everything was going perfect, it [would mean] you weren't trying hard enough."[29]

An FSCM Framework: A Practical Proposal

One of the aims of writing this chapter was to determine if FSCM is at a stage where a basic framework can be discerned from the case studies presented earlier. The answer to this question is a cautious *yes*. The examples presented in this chapter are a first attempt at developing a basic FSCM framework for finance and SCM strategists to consider. It is the hope of this author that a decade from now the FSCM discipline will have evolved in ways unimaginable today.

From an organizational perspective, the first step is to create an FSCM team. The FSCM Framework delineated below suggests a four-step process to create and prepare this team:

1. **Learn.** Create an integrated FSCM team that combines both finance and SCM expertise. Send this team through a comprehensive set of courses on advanced OR, real option, risk management, and financial optimization tools and techniques. They will not find this course set in any one institution; rather, they will have to design a bespoke curriculum from a variety of academic and professional sources. Full course of preparation could take as long as a year or two, though certain industries (such as energy) already boast professionals who understand complex SCM and financial methods. A great product company could do worse than to recruit some of these experts as it builds its first FSCM teams.

2. **Rethink.** As the team evolves, ask them to consider the company's SCM *not only* as a set of physical flows but in the more abstract sense presented above. In other words, instead of thinking only about things such as "safety stock" and "production agility," ask them to think about external drivers of demand volatility, what a synthetic demand curve might look like, sources of financial risk as well as ways in which those risks can be transferred or hedged.

3. **Question.** Ask the team to become familiar with the vendors of the emerging tools in FSCM. All have their pros and cons. In addition, meet with and question thought leaders in FSCM areas and begin to understand the theories behind the tools and techniques, which will make tool evaluation and adoption faster and more effective.

4. **Experiment.** FSCM is a nascent discipline. It is early in its evolution but that process has started. All of the leading companies in this field have at least one thing in common: they are experimenters. Indeed, one should see this exercise as a radical search for SCM innovation that has the potential to completely change the way a company does business—and sooner rather than later. Indeed, what most of these companies also have in common is that once they begin this investigation, they do not abandon it. Despite the rigor of the methods and the intellectual challenge of the perspectives required, the best SCM strategists are stimulated by taking this next step in their thinking and careers. This energy should be harnessed by their companies, with strategists given room to experiment and fail if need be.

From a technical perspective, the FSCM Framework suggests a four-step approach:

1. Understand the financial flows that run parallel to the physical and information flows in the company's supply chain. In this step, the FSCM team creates financial flow and cost models that become the FSCM "world" in which it will strategize and manage.

2. Understand the way risk is created in this parallel world and how, today, it is either being ignored

or managed (i.e., assumed, ignored, transferred, or hedged). This should be done qualitatively at first but then quantitatively as the FSCM team builds its level of sophistication and expertise.

3. Develop two roadmaps. The first roadmap addresses creation of a fully parallel FSCM model that can be used to adjust and, if need be, override the physical SCM model. This covers creation of a risk management tool kit that can be used to (a) evaluate SCM (financial) risk, and (b) manage that risk in complex, multifaceted strategies that fully exploit the innovations of the global financial system in the last three decades.

4. Lastly, deploy the roadmaps and keep a constant qualitative and quantitative alignment between the physical and financial supply chains. Redesign processes such as sales and operations planning to incorporate both worlds concurrently. Work with financial partners to develop new risk management mechanisms for FSCM, where those do not exist today. In the end, transform the SCM team from its current focus to one that is much more externally focused and one which, in a few years, is just at home on a trading floor as a shop floor. It is crucial to note that FSCM in no way eliminates or diminishes the importance of the physical SC and physical SCM; it just shines a new light on those aspects that may reveal heretofore unseen problems and solutions.

Achieving the state described by these four steps will necessarily transform SCM from a function focused only on real product flows and facilities to one that is concerned with corporate-level risk, financial performance, and shareholder risk and returns in the most direct way possible—by controlling the full scope of the products and services that, in the end, are the drivers and determinants of corporate performance in the marketplace.

CFO as Chief SCM Officer

The revolution in FSCM is something the very best SCM companies[30] should embrace, but doing so has many implications. Traditional roles will have to change, as will power over SCM decisions. In the end, what FSCM will do is move SCM into the realm of finance, into the world of the CFO. This means that SCM strategists need to rethink their training and expand their view and knowledge of finance and risk management in the coming years. Just as the original physical evolution and subsequent information evolutions changed SCM forever, so will this next wave of thinkers, tools, and techniques.

Just how long a road this will be is illustrated, again, by the ARC survey cited earlier. When asked to list their top SCM risk management techniques, ARC survey respondents noted the results presented in Figure 8.8.

Not one of the top five solutions is related to FSCM as presented in this chapter. By now, that should be of no surprise. What also will be of no surprise is how many readers will react negatively to this chapter. Many will dismiss FSCM as some fantastic, theoretical view of the future that, if it ever exists at all, will only come into being decades from now. Hopefully, the brief case studies cited here point out the error of that reaction.

It is worth noting that the first outlines for this chapter were laid out in 2005. At that time, only a few people were talking about SCM risk; today it is perhaps the most talked about subject in SCM. A few years ago, real options in contracting were a revolutionary idea; today, they are in use and demonstrating their value. A few years ago, the idea of incorporating Monte Carlo simulation was purely theoretical; today, several software solutions allow you to do just that.

Similarly, the tools for hedging demand volatility may seem fanciful now, but they won't take long to create once the insurance companies, banks, and financial firms that created SCM teams in the last couple of years realize that they sit on the edge of a multi-billion dollar market that is largely ignored today. Indeed, in a recent interview, the head of SCM risk at a major insurance company noted that supply chain as a concept exists at her company and that they are covering certain specific supply chain risks today such as:

- Supplier default/bankruptcy
- Supply quality (i.e., supplier delivers materials but they are unusable because of spoilage or some other defect)

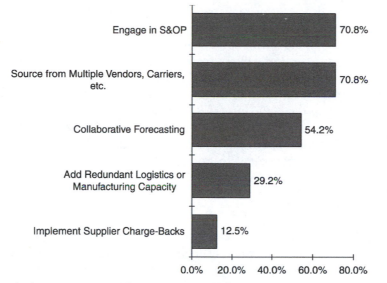

FIGURE 8.8 What are the best ways to avoid supply chain risks? This figure lists the five strategies most cited by ARC survey respondents as ways to avoid supply chain risks.

Source: *ARC Strategies Series: Risk Management*, Steve Banker, Sid Snitkin, and Adrian Gonzalez, 2005.

- Foreign exchange risk on supply contracts
- Gaps between marine and property risk
- Demand concentration risk (i.e., all of a company's demand comes from only a few customers; should one of them fail, the company is severely exposed)
- Weather risk in agricultural industries
- Carbon credit risk (i.e., an enterprise depends on a carbon credit and wants to ensure that, if the credit disappears, it hedges against incremental cost of replacement)
- Risk of government seizure of plant and property.

The insurance executive also noted that in 2008 the company even insured against a few product-income related risks. She added that this is new, and actually a kind of securitization (a structured finance process that distributes risk by aggregating debt instruments in a pool, then issues new securities backed by the pool). However, in the end the issue is "pricing the peril" and this drives the business case to insure or not. The insurance executive also noted that her group is "very entrepreneurial" and is used to "basically creating custom risk solutions from scratch" so that what will be possible in five years may not be imaginable today. This sentiment echoes the thoughts of that group of prescient authors writing in 2002 about the merging of finance and SCM:[31]

> The tools and lessons of financial engineering need to be adapted to these new environments, and embodied in new products and services that enable these emerging capabilities. Similar transformations have already occurred in more traditional commodity-based industries, such as energy, metals, chemicals, or agriculture, where companies purchase primary inputs or sell primary outputs in active markets. As the technology industry, along with other industries, moves towards being more commodity-based, expertise in manufacturing facilities investment and processes—critical competencies of technology firms in the past—will become more peripheral, while expertise in market analysis, contracting, trading, and risk management will become increasingly central to the success of these firms. Companies that develop those competencies will be well positioned to create significant value for their shareholders over the long run.

What they wrote is still accurate and it is time for the wider SCM community to begin to understand the coming FSCM evolution and see it as the next major step in a discipline that has moved from the background to the forefront of globalization.

In closing, think back to the perfume maker and its supplier. In the future, who is to say the supplier will not be able to buy a hedge instrument that would extract that 70 percent forecast error risk and spread it around channel partners or risk-seekers in other industries looking for a high return? Who is to say that the perfume manufacturer will not be able to buy a real option for box production capacity instead of forcing the supplier to accept a risky production commitment that could put it out of business? Who is to say the average investor might not find the ability to invest in specific product cash flows more efficiently than in the companies that bundle them into one corporate stock?

How different SCM would look in that world—a world in which finance and SCM have merged to form an entirely new discipline whose focus is not just warehouses, pallets, and trucks but the most fundamental elements of corporate value creation and preservation.

Acknowledgments

The author wishes to express his gratitude to the following individuals for their time and insights on FSCM: Scott Edwards (Intel), Scott Matthews (Boeing), Alex Triantis and Sandor Boyson (The Smith School, University of Maryland), Scott Koerwer (The Moore School, University of South Carolina), Francis X. Diebold (The Wharton School, University of Pennsylvania), Erwin Hermans (Accenture), Alen Yakar (Garanti Bank International N.V., Istanbul), Herbert Wolf (Alix Partners), and Oliver Scutt (Jonova Inc.).

Notes

1 Lean manufacturing or lean production, which is often known simply as "lean," is a production practice that considers the expenditure of resources for any goal other than the creation of value for the end customer to be wasteful, and thus a target for elimination.

2 Peter L. Bernstein, *Against the Gods: The Remarkable Story of Risk* (New York: John Wiley & Sons, 1996, 1998).

3 Bernstein, 106.

4 The term "quant" was first coined to refer to the mathematicians/physicists who got PhDs in the 1980s and 1990s and rather than go into science, chose much more lucrative careers in finance—a trend that continued until 2008 and will pick up again in 2010.

5 For an example of this field, see Bardia Kamrad and Keith Ord, "Market Risk and Process Uncertainty in Production Operations" (Paper delivered at the Real Options Conference, Columbia Business School), 2006.

6 "A Monte Carlo method is a technique that involves using random numbers and probability to solve problems. The term Monte Carlo Method was coined by S. Ulam and Nicholas Metropolis in reference to games of chance, a popular attraction in Monte Carlo, Monaco (Hoffman, 1998; Metropolis and Ulam, 1949)" (http://www.vertex42.com/ExcelArticles/mc/MonteCarloSimulation.html).

7 See, for example, Patrick Connaughton, "Best Practices: Successfully Managing Security and Risk in a Global Supply Chain," *Forrester Research*, August 3, 2007.

8 Steve Banker, Sid Snitkin, and Adrian Gonzalez, *ARC Strategies Series: Risk Management*, 2005. It's also notable that the number one risk they feared was a breakdown of their IT systems, which speaks volumes about the impact the information phase has had on supply chain management.

9 Ibid., 6.

10 Vinay Datar and Scott Matthews, "European Real Options: An Intuitive Algorithm for the Black-Scholes Formula," *Journal of Applied Finance*, Spring/Summer, 2004.

11 Theory of Constraints (TOC) is an overall management philosophy introduced by Dr. Eliyahu M. Goldratt in his 1984 book titled *The Goal*, that is geared to help organizations continually achieve their goal. The title comes from the contention that any manageable system is limited in achieving more of its goal by a very small number of constraints, and that there is always at least one constraint. The TOC process seeks to identify the constraint and restructure the rest of the organization around it.

12 Scott Edwards, "Capacity Modeling with Monte Carlo Simulation for Finished Goods Warehouses," *Proceedings of the 2006 Crystal Ball User Conference*, 6.

13 "Drum-buffer-rope is the Theory of Constraints production application. It is named after the three essential elements of the solution; the drum or constraint or weakest link, the buffer or material release duration, and the rope or release timing. The aim of the solution is to protect the weakest link in the system, and therefore the system as a whole, against process dependency and variation and thus maximize the systems' overall effectiveness" (http://www.dbrmfg.co.nz/Production%20DBR.htm).

14 Padraic Cassidy, "Southwest Net, Including Fuel-hedging Costs, Dips: Results Match Average of Analysts' Forecasts," *MarketWatch*, January 17, 2007. http://www.marketwatch.com/news/story/southwest-air-net-income-including/story.aspx?guid=%7B557D6875-2B3C-41F8-AA67-E8D63C1038BA%7D (accessed: March 19, 2008).

15 Dave Carter, Dan Rogers, and Betty Simkins, "Fuel Hedging in the Airline Industry: The Case of Southwest Airlines," Oklahoma State University, 2004.

16 "European Airlines Reap Benefits of Oil Hedging,"Caroline Brothers, *New York Times*, June 12, 2008. http://www.nytimes.com/2008/06/12/business/12air.html?_r=1&ref=business&oref=slogin (accessed: June 12, 2008).

17 Swap: "A custom-made and negotiated transaction designed to manage financial risk over a period of 1 to 12 years. Two individuals can create a swap, or a swap may be made through a third party such as a brokerage firm or a bank. Swaps are used to manage risk and often settlements occur in cash, not in delivery of the actual product or financial instruments. Examples of swap transactions include currency swaps, interest rate swaps, and price swaps for a variety of commodities" (http://www.yourdictionary.com/finance/swap).

18 *Treasury & Risk Magazine* Best Practices Summit Awards, 2006. http://www.treasuryandrisk.com/events/06_aha_fr_win.php (accessed: June 30, 2008).

19 Corey Billington, Blake Johnson, and Alex Triantis, "A Real Options Perspective on Supply Chain Management in High Technology," *Journal of Applied Corporate Finance*, Summer 2002, 42–43. This paper, though overlooked by most SCM strategists and consultants, was a visionary work in its analysis and statements about the future of SCM. Indeed, Johnson (Stanford) and Triantis (Maryland) continue to be thought leaders in the FSCM world, in the areas of risk management and real options respectively.

20 A "derivative" simply refers to a financial instrument that "derives" its value/price from some other indicator, in this case temperature (and see note 25 below).

21 There is a lot of literature on weather risk hedging. For an excellent introduction to the topic see, Sean D. Campbell and Francis X. Diebold, "Weather Forecasting for Weather Derivatives," *Journal of the American Statistical Association*, March 2005, Vol. 100, No. 469.

22 In 2005, the author filed for a patent for a method to construct synthetic demand curves for the purposes of hedging out demand volatility.

23 Riskglossary.com, http://www.riskglossary.com/link/efficient_frontier.htm. The Efficient Frontier was first defined by Harry Markowitz in his groundbreaking (1952) paper that launched portfolio theory. That theory considers a universe of risky investments and explores what might be an optimal portfolio based upon those possible investments.

24 M. Boyer, M. Boyer, and R. Garcia, "The Value of Real and Financial Risk Management," *Serie Scientifique*, Centre interuniversitaire de recherce en analyse des organizations, 2005, 21.

25 A "derivative" is a financial instrument that is *derived* from some other asset, index, event, value or condition (known as the underlying asset). Rather than trade or exchange the underlying asset itself, derivative traders enter into an agreement to exchange cash or assets over time based on the underlying asset. A simple example is a futures contract: an agreement to exchange the underlying asset at a future date.

26 Tim Weithers, "Credit Derivatives: Macro-Risk Issues," University of Chicago, April 20, 2007.

27 NYSE Euronext (NYX) is a leading global operator of financial markets and provider of innovative trading technologies. The company's exchanges in Europe and the United States trade equities, futures, options, fixed-income and exchange-traded products.

28 Value at Risk (VaR): "A technique which uses the statistical analysis of historical market trends and volatilities to estimate the likelihood that a given portfolio's losses will exceed a certain amount" InvestorWords.com, http://www.investorwords.com/5217/VAR.html (accessed: July 5, 2008).

29 "The 787 Encounters Turbulence: Technical Glitches and Manufacturing Woes Could Delay Boeing's Breakthrough," *BusinessWeek*, June 18, 2006.

30 And, paradoxically, in some ways the very worst as well.

31 Corey Billington, Blake Johnson, and Alex Triantis, "A Real Options Perspective on Supply Chain Management in High Technology," *Journal of Applied Corporate Finance*, Summer 2002, 42–43.

nine
Supercharging Return on Assets (ROA)

Koen Cobbaert and Peter Verstraeten

Balancing between operational and financial performance, product and service innovation, and proliferation pressure has become a daunting task for most businesses around the globe. In addition, businesses increasingly must deal with volatility and uncertainty as a business certainty for several important reasons. Among them, outsourcing to regions with low labor cost has increased the distance to market and, as a consequence, raised uncertainty of supply. Product customization is no longer an order winner, but rather a qualification to do business. In this environment, enhanced supply chain services (like short lead times, daily deliveries, no stock outs, etc.) have become the new order winners in business. Many of these services are driven by the fact that markets are looking for seamless integration of their virtual supply chains.

Clearly, these and other considerations result in significantly higher business expenses. However, there is a new business reality that compounds the challenges. First, the credit crunch has made the corporate captains think twice about funding the insatiable hunger of their enterprises for more working capital. This has put inventory as well as slack asset capacity on the target list for management. Second, in addition to the credit crunch, the global economic system has been in recession mode for several years. Struggle for survival has focused corporate eyes on costs and profitability.

This combination of the credit crunch and global recession has drawn supply chain costs to the forefront. Indeed, costs and working capital needs are always perceived as too high; service is never high enough. Stated differently, volatility has raised the risk to businesses, but no one is willing to pay for the dual insurance policies: capacity and inventory buffers.

In this environment, managers require robust analytical tools to assist them in the effective management of supply chain costs. Effectively managing these costs is critical to the overall success or failure of the business.

In this chapter, we present Equazion, a business tool that helps managers cope with this new, complex business environment by enabling them to analyze supply chain costs with the goal of cost reduction in combination with needed levels of customer service.

Background

Toward the close of the twentieth century, manufacturers in the process and semi-process industries regularly confronted the challenge of adjusting their supply chains to deal with growing demand volatility and complexity. Many in industries such as food and beverage, performance chemicals, and consumer packaged goods (CPG) had expensive assets requiring, from a financial perspective, maximum capacity utilization. Indeed, these companies, with high-volume items and low production complexity, achieved optimal manufacturing efficiency. However, in their never-ending quest for more demand and sales, the marketing groups introduced many more product versions to open new sales opportunities in business and customer-specific market segments. In addition to this, sales increasingly tried to boost consumer demand by adding promotions and a wider variety of promotional items. Product proliferation and promotion demand complexity did increase total sales volume, but they also triggered an unseen level of demand volatility.

Unfortunately, sales discovered the drawbacks of the law of large numbers.[1] Stated simply, there is greater stability in the behavior of big numbers. Fewer product lines with higher volumes result in more predictable demand. However, the opposite is true when product lines proliferate. The result is unpredictable and erratic demand. The Equazion concept was born as a software application designed specifically to help these companies manage through this proliferation of product lines and the increased volatility of demand by focusing on better management of the supply chain.

Many of these companies faced challenges beyond demand volatility and increased uncertainty. In fact, they found their manufacturing operations also struggled with the product portfolio complexity. All those new recipes, package sizes, and label versions triggered an explosion of changeovers on their production lines. Each changeover drove more asset downtime—from minutes to hours—as well as added scrap, efficiency losses at start of the new batch, and potential for other unplanned issues. As a result, line output volatility increased, with a negative impact on capacity utilization, which prevented maximum asset utilization. The combination of demand volatility from the explosion of product lines and the resulting negative impact on asset utilization had a direct effect on the ability to satisfy customer requests for better service and just-in-time deliveries.

The debate over how the business should cope with these volatility challenges, more often than not, evoked conflicting emotions. Sales claimed market volatility was inevitable and urged operations to provide more flexibility. Operations, under constant pressure for better line utilization and efficiency, claimed that product portfolio rationalization and better forecasts were the ways out of the swamp. And, both sales and operations agreed on the only other alternate solutions—extra capacity to offer more flexibility, and/or raising stock levels to protect the supply chain against the growing demand uncertainty.

This alternate solution was not, however, appreciated by the finance department. Raising stock levels and adding slack capacity meant deterioration of their balance sheet and the profit and loss statement, resulting in a decline in the value of the company.

This fundamental conflict between internal departments presented an opportunity for supply chain consultants to design appropriate tools to resolve these conflicts, i.e., Equazion. Consultants realized that, as a first step, they needed to keep emotions out of the debate. Facts and figures were the right place to begin. The principle question was, "Do we have the information?" The answer was, "We do not have this information readily available." However, many companies, especially those with enterprise resource planning (ERP) systems in place, did indeed have a profusion of detailed data. The necessary information/data to address the problems simply had to be drawn from the ERP wells and turned into meaningful decision support information. These transactional ERP business systems, adopted by many companies in the late 1990s, accurately record any event in the supply chain: from receipt of a customer order to picking, packing, and delivery of each line item (and similarly, any event/transaction that occurs on the inbound side of production). These ERP systems could be referred to as the corporate "Cave of Ali Baba," filled with a treasure of raw data, waiting to be exploited.

However, companies need a way to convert the ERP master data into organized decision support information. The "embryo body" of Equazion is merely a predefined and pre-structured database, filled with ERP master data and supply chain transactions. The Equazion "brain" consists of a number of mathematical and statistical calculations that process the raw ERP transactional data.

We will elaborate in later sections of this chapter on how this Equazion embryo grew into a full-scale decision support tool, enabling managers to cope with volatility and business uncertainty while safeguarding their financial performance. We will also clarify the business reasons behind the Equazion developments.

The Methodology

The Equazion concept and design is built on the foundation of a few axioms. First, there is a sincere belief that business decisions will always be made by people. Computers and software tools can only support those decisions. As discussed above, perspectives differ depending on an individual's responsibility in the company. But regardless of an individual's management responsibility, all business leaders should agree upon creation of shareholder value as their ultimate common objective. Shareholder value is the standard for business performance, and finance is the shared language to discuss this subject.

Finally, we are convinced that sound business decision-making involves analytical thinking. The latter is a closed loop of different steps. It starts with an analysis of the past and, subsequently, an assessment of the current situation.

Based on these analyses and assessments, the options for the future can be evaluated and policies and business decisions can be aligned. Eventually, progress will be measured and monitored to restart the cycle and arrive at a next level of performance improvement. This analytical approach is perfectly reflected in the Six Sigma DMAIC (Define, Measure, Analyze, Improve, and Control) methodology. Therefore, the DMAIC language and methodology was adopted when addressing a business decision-balancing challenge with Equazion. Figure 9.1 shows the different DMAIC steps of a supply chain balance improvement exercise.

DMAIC outlines an efficient and effective way of reaching the right set of management decisions

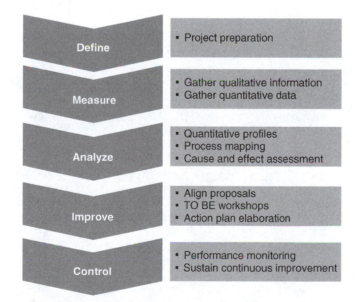

FIGURE 9.1 The DMAIC approach as used in a supply chain balance improvement exercise. DMAIC stands for Define, Measure, Analyze, Improve, and Control and is the standard methodology as propagated in the Six Sigma philosophy for setting up improvement trajectories. The process starts with the Define phase, whose purpose is mainly to assure that the project starts with solid project objective, team, and organization. In the Measure phase, the relevant information is gathered, both in a quantitative way (e.g., a dump of the information available in the ERP system) and in a qualitative way to understand the business and its challenges. In the Analyze phase, the important influence factors are identified and their relation with the relevant key performance indicators (KPIs) is mapped. In the Improve phase, different options and solutions are identified and evaluated, and the valuable options are translated into an action plan. The Control phase assures that improvement initiatives are well embedded in the organization.

Source: Koen Cobbaert and Peter Verstraeten, S & V, 2009.

to obtain a financially healthy and sustainable supply chain in a world of volatility. The direction for this journey is provided by the DuPont model. Figure 9.2 shows a simplified version of the DuPont model.

The DuPont model explains the foundations of the return on net assets (RONA). As a financial performance measure, RONA is the cornerstone for the financial valuation of a business and, consequently, is the best measure to judge shareholder value creation. The example in Figure 9.2 also demonstrates the threefold impact supply chain has on the RONA.

By reducing inventory, the supply chain directors help decrease working capital while reducing the cost of holding inventory. Potentially, this can free some fixed assets by allowing a warehouse to be closed. Moreover, they could try to improve the earnings before interest and taxes (EBIT) by lowering the logistics costs to serve the customers. Ultimately, they can reduce the fixed-asset costs of logistics by outsourcing to an external service provider.

Unfortunately, two buffers against volatility and uncertainty—inventory and slack asset capacity—also reduce the RONA. The supply chain managers face a fundamental dilemma: allow costs to rise as they attempt to serve an ever more demanding market (with the resulting negative impacts on EBIT) or maintain tight control of inventory and asset capacity with the resulting negative impacts on customer service.

The DuPont model actually indicates the odds are against the supply chain directors in this instance. If the supply chain directors affect customer service through a policy of lower inventory and cost-to-serve reductions, they will lose the support of the sales force. Doing the opposite will disappoint the chief financial officer (CFO) and chief executive officer (CEO). The conclusion is that the right set of decisions will need to be made by a cross-functional team, keeping their eyes on the RONA and taking DMAIC as the structured path forward. This is truly making supply chain a business issue.

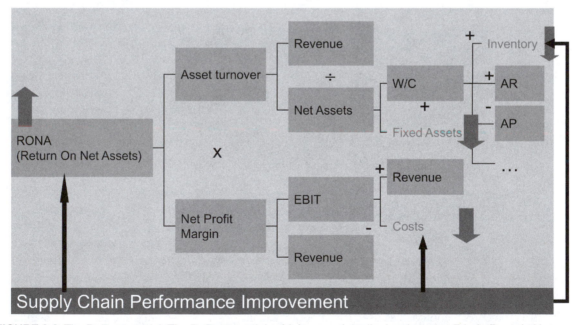

FIGURE 9.2 The DuPont model. The DuPont model, which was originally developed at E.I. du Pont de Nemours, is a model that helps to visualize the influence factors on the return on net assets (RONA). It consists of two parts: the upper part calculates the asset turnover, which is calculated by dividing the revenue by the total net assets. The lower part calculates the net profit margin percentage by dividing the EBIT (earnings before interest and taxes) by the revenue. The multiplication of these two ratios gives the RONA, which is in fact the EBIT divided by the net assets. By splitting further the net assets and the EBIT component, the model helps identify which supply chain factors have an important impact on company performance: higher inventories imply higher net assets, which reduces the asset turnover. Improper use of fixed assets also reduces asset turnover. And obviously, higher costs—e.g., in cost-to-serve—deteriorate EBIT, and, hence, RONA.

Source: Koen Cobbaert and Peter Verstraeten, S & V, 2009.

Measure and Analyze

The "measure" activity in the DMAIC methodology consists of extracting and gathering the ERP transactional details and master data. These are the main raw data from which to start. Built-in calculation routines transform the data into meaningful information. This information is displayed in a variety of graphical and diagnostic tables. Each of these analyses and diagnostics consolidates the expertise and experience of consultants analyzing similar issues in the past.

These diagnostics cover every dimension of the supply chain, from inbound shipments of raw materials and component parts to outbound shipments of finished products. But more importantly, they provide a full 360° perspective of the situation. Diagnostics may reveal that a certain product category could have a detrimental effect on the inventory situation, but equally important are the customers buying from this category. What is the profitability on those customers, and what is their share of the accounts receivable? The diagnostics must address every angle of the cross-functional team's investigation in order to obtain a full picture. That full picture is mandatory to obtain a consensus in the decision process.

The diagnostics have a threefold objective. They should reveal the characteristics of the business in a neutral way. These facts can help to understand the complexity of the business, or they provide elements to consider for further assessments. For example, Figure 9.3 shows that for a particular company, its product portfolio consists of a large tail of small volume items. This tail hardly generates volume or margin, but it does trigger about 40 percent of the finished-product inventory. Small volume items with erratic demand will be hard to forecast and, therefore, will require more safety stock. So, when considering inventory reduction, the first step may be a product portfolio rationalization. Or, these tail products may no longer be offered off-the-shelf but only on a make-to-order basis. It all depends on who is buying these tail products and why. Portfolio diagnostics will trigger a further assessment on the reasons behind this portfolio complexity.

The second objective of the diagnostics is to assess the performance of specific aspects of the broader supply chain. Figure 9.4 proves that the supply chain of a specific supplier-product category combination is quite reliable. Only a small minority of the purchase order lines are received one to three days late. This performance might not be acceptable in a tight just-in-time delivery chain, but, in many other businesses, it will be evaluated as reliable. If so, the diagnostic would argue that supplier reliability is not a root cause of overstocks of raw material. Furthermore, that reliable or non-volatile supply can be applied when calculating the right statistical safety stocks for these materials in the next stage of the supply chain.

The third objective of a diagnostic is to provide a first look at the improvement potential that could be unlocked. Figure 9.5 graphically displays the payment behavior of a specific customer channel. The best possible outcome (BPO) invoice days represent the best possible accounts receivable position one can expect: this is the payment due date and terms printed on each invoice. The "actual" reflects what customers really do. The BPO graph explains that 80 percent of the sales should be paid by customers within 30 days. The actual, however, demonstrates that 80 percent of the payments are received within about 45 days. This diagnostic gives a good indication on the accounts receivable optimization potential if customers would live up to the agreed payment terms.

Although these graphs clearly make a point, some team members will react with disbelief or remain skeptical. Defensive "yes, but" responses often seem to be in our human nature. In some cases, these remarks are pertinent. The question is whether the concern is appropriate or whether it is an effort to avoid a painful truth. To filter and address the arguments appropriately requires the ability to dig into the details quickly. Showing the specific products behind the diagnostic allows the team to validate the analysis or to detect any issues with the raw data.

The set of diagnostics is like a mirror reflecting the reality of the business for the cross-functional team. The view it offers must be accepted by the team to move to the next level. Do we recognize our company in the diagnostics? Can we improve this situation?

Item Profile - ABC on netmargin

<u>Sharpness ABC Classification</u>

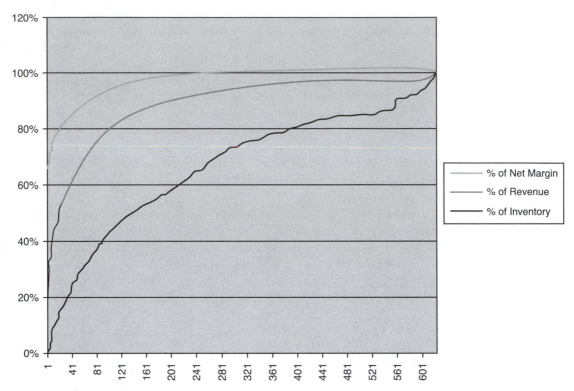

FIGURE 9.3 Product portfolio profile: gaining insight through Pareto-analysis. This picture of profitability contains all products in the portfolio on the horizontal axis, ranked according to the margin they generate. It helps focus the efforts in the company and may help to detect anomalies. Next to the margin graph (the upper curve) the graph also contains the revenue graph (middle curve) and an inventory graph (lower curve). For this case, the graph highlights that:

- The margin graph is much sharper than the revenue graph, meaning that from a high-level point of view, the biggest products seem to have higher relative margins.
- There is a very long tail of products. More than half of the products barely contribute to the company result.
- That long tail of products is responsible for a significant part of the inventory.

As such this is an indication that there might be a considerable portfolio optimization potential.

Source: Koen Cobbaert and Peter Verstraeten, S & V, 2009.

Improve

Can we improve? And if yes, how can we improve and by how much? These are the fundamental questions that should be answered in the "improve" phase. In order to do so, we return to the basics of Six Sigma and DMAIC philosophy and begin to model the situation and its main influencing factors to find the needed answers. The model explains the reasons for the current situation. It shows which factors were drivers in reaching this position. It will also reveal the degree of impact of each factor on the target for improvement. This model also illustrates the potential improvement at the level of the target, when actions positively impact one or more of the influencing elements.

Two recurring supply chain challenges that must be discussed in the context of obtaining a sustainable, financially healthy supply chain are inventory and cost. The first discussion is on right level of inventory to cope with the volatility of business. Simultaneously, we should investigate whether the inventory levels can be reduced and what "right things" should be done to get there. The second challenge is related to the reduction of the supply chain cost-to-serve the market.

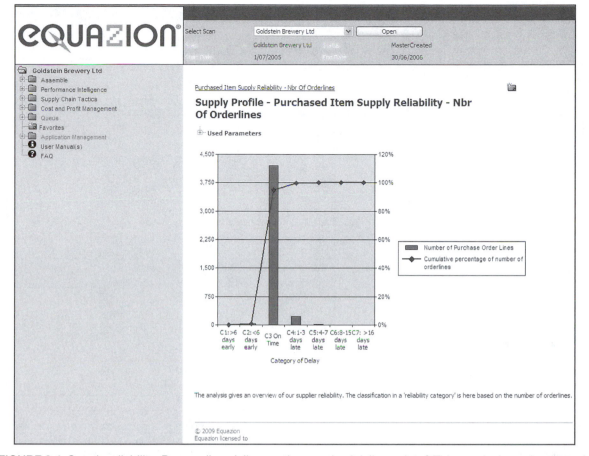

FIGURE 9.4 Supply reliability: Do suppliers deliver on the promised delivery date? This graph shows how supply reliability can be measured. The bars indicate how many purchase order lines have been received in what time delay compared with the promise that the supplier had made. A few order lines were delivered early, the majority (approximately 4,300) was delivered on the promised date, and a small quantity (200 to 300) was delivered between one and three days late. The line graph presents the same data in terms of percentage in a cumulative way.

Source: Equazion, S & V, 2009.

Reducing Inventory Levels

In preparation for tackling the inventory question, it is essential to understand that the finished goods stock consists of different components. Each of these components is the result of a different stocking model with different influencing factors.

Figure 9.6 provides a simplified picture of a number of possible finished goods inventory elements. The speculative inventory is an anticipated stock buildup that could be driven by the expectation of high demand. The level stock is an anticipated stock increase for totally different reasons. The latter is a must when capacity cannot meet demand at certain times of the year. This is a typical case for food and beverage manufacturers that experience a highly seasonal demand. They will raise inventory in spring to meet consumer demand in summer. Both stock types are influenced by a strategic or tactical choice to anticipate a specific situation. The obsolete stock has totally different characteristics and is most likely the result of other influencing factors. This stock is dead if there is no or little expectation for future demand. Various factors could create this situation. Perhaps things went wrong right from the start and the obsolete quantity is left from a failed product introduction. Or it may be the remains of a completely over-forecast promotion effort. Or it may be the consequence of a volatile market, suddenly delisting this product. Obsolete items point to not only marketing and sales; the cause for many obsolete items can be found in supply chain and operations. Perhaps, static planning parameters were no longer in line with a decreasing demand trend. Or, alternatively,

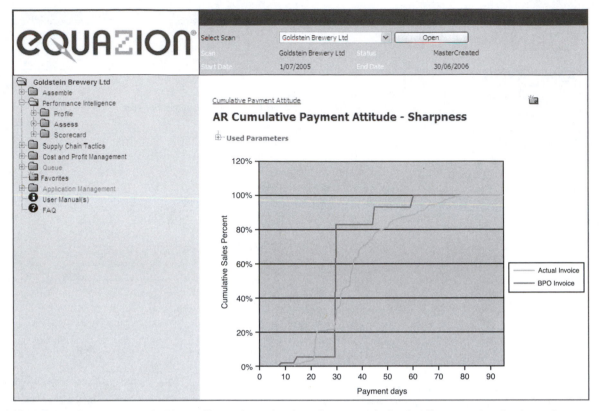

FIGURE 9.5 Accounts receivable profile: an investigation of payment behavior. For every invoice issued, a payment term is specified. Mapping the revenue in a cumulative way according to the associated payment terms gives the gray curve. We see for example that over 80 percent of the sales should be paid within 30 days. In fact, as stated by the gray curve, 80 percent of the sales were paid within 45 to 50 days. This is an indication that there is potential for improving the follow-up of overdue invoices.

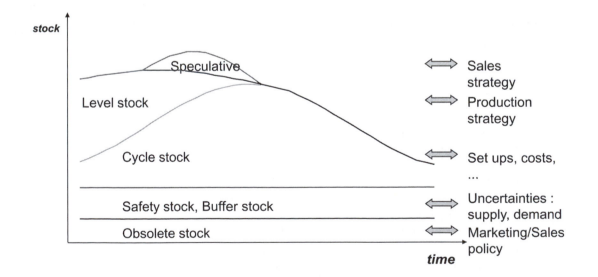

FIGURE 9.6 Inventory components: the reasons for stock-keeping. Inventory is kept for several reasons. Most inventory is kept for dealing with demand and supply uncertainty (safety stock) or for exploiting economies of scale by applying appropriate batch sizes (cycle stock). Next to these inventory types, there is also level stock (to anticipate future demand increases for which we lack sufficient capacity to produce when demand occurs), speculative stock (to anticipate changes in market prices) and obsolete stocks (which are the result of badly anticipated phase-outs, replacements, etc.).

Source: Koen Cobbaert and Peter Verstraeten, 2009.

manufacturing overproduced to defend its efficiency key performance indicators. To do so, they hold on to a minimum batch size, which for small volume items might represent months of demand. Add a change in the market's taste half way down the road and the rest is history.

Many causes link to the phenomenon of obsolescence. A simple way to start the investigation may be a root cause analysis. Begin by asking yourself, "Why?" five times.

A more sophisticated approach starts with a failure mode and effect analysis (FMEA). This technique helps to determine how a process or a product can fail. Engineers in the automotive and aerospace industries are very familiar with the FMEA approach. This technique was also adopted in Six Sigma. It could be used to map all encountered obsolescence disturbances and to distinguish the important ones from the minor ones. This will be the starting point for improvement actions that target systematic avoidances of the obsolescence disturbance.

Two more dynamic inventory components which, when not aligned, can be the source of part of the obsolescence are cycle stock and safety stock. Safety stock protects a company against unexpected demand peaks and/or unreliable inventory replenishment.

The safety stock calculation for fast-moving items is based on a Gauss curve[2] derived from a simple formula in widespread use. The components of this formula can be called the influencing factors. Longer lead-times will invoke high safety stocks, as the period of uncertainty lengthens. Demand volatility or forecast uncertainty will have a similar effect. And the last factor is the desired service level, which is embedded in the formula via the k-factor. The k-factor is a value derived from the normal distribution that indicates how many standard deviations should be used above or below the mean to obtain a certain probability of occurrence. This factor gives the probability that the safety stock will hold against any possible demand volatility. This factor exponentially grows with the desired service level.

The k-factor illustrates that it is not automatic that higher service simply implies greater inventory. Equazion incorporates a specific distribution function, called Package Poisson, which drives the model through a single formula that applies for products with fast, slow, and lumpy demand. The Package Poisson distribution is a derivative of the Poisson distribution, which is a common statistical function that is used for determining optimal inventory parameters for slow moving items.

The cycle stock is the result of the calculation of the Economic Order Quantity (EOQ), which is the quantity that should be ordered when the replenishment level is reached. This is, in essence, the trade-off between higher changeover costs when producing more frequently and the higher inventory holding cost tied to larger batches. The changeover problem can be quite challenging in process and semi-process industries as it can lead to a cascade of major, minor, and micro changeovers, as in a change of bottle format, a change of recipe, and a label switch. The Equazion tactical models allow configuring this complexity and calculating the optimal campaign in these specific circumstances. When the product portfolio changes, this calculation is affected. A changing stock policy that swaps part of the make-to-stock business for a make-to-order operation, or the reverse, will impact the optimal stock levels. Figure 9.7 gives a schematic reflection of some of the Equazion inventory model components and the influencing variables.

The model has a threefold purpose. First, in a given context, it will be the optimal planning parameters per item-location combination. But, more importantly, it allows for a sensitivity analysis of the inventory and its influencing factors. What will be the effect of a product portfolio rationalization, eliminating some of those small volume items? What is the working capital impact of a service level target rise? What is the benefit of a lean changeover program, and is it worth the effort? What are the inventory savings that can be realized by implementing a better forecast process and, thereby, reducing the forecast error? What is the maximum level of volatility we want to prepare for and carry the corresponding buffer costs? This model allows the impact of control variables to be determined (e.g., service level), nuisance variables (e.g., forecast error), and disturbance (e.g., supply failures). Consequently, the potential can be quantified by taking the right decisions and starting the high priority improvement programs.

The impact on the RONA can be quantified. This is where consensus is obtained at the management board on what to do and where to start first. Finally, the model clarifies to management how the factors interactively influence the inventory performance. Therefore, it allows for the definition of a

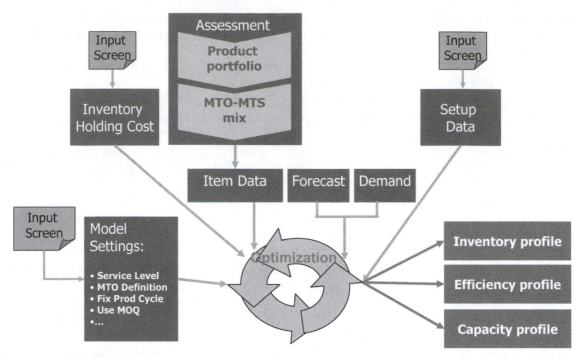

FIGURE 9.7 Equazion inventory model design. The Equazion inventory model optimization takes into account a number of inputs:

- The planning policy of the considered products. What will be the future product portfolio? What products will be kept in stock (make-to-stock) or made to order (MTO)?
- What was the demand variability in the past, or how reliable was the forecast?
- What is the cost for setting up a machine? This cost can be calculated by Equazion based on specification of time required, labor rates, ramp-up profiles, efficiency impact, and capacity type.
- What does it cost to keep inventory? Normally the WACC (weighted average cost of capital) is used to calculate inventory holding costs.
- A number of parameters like production characteristics, service levels, etc.

The result of the optimization run is an impact analysis on inventory (how much inventory is required under these circumstances), efficiency (how much time and money is lost on changing over machines), and capacity.

Source: Koen Cobbaert and Peter Verstraeten, 2009.

balanced set of key performance indicators, i.e., a combination of targets that will drive the company to increase the shareholder value. Target setting and monitoring are part of the control step and close the Six Sigma circle.

Optimizing the Cost-to-Serve: Gaining Insight into the Real Profitability of Your Customers

It is amazing how few companies are able to determine what value a customer really brings to them. And very often, when they think they can, it is doubtful whether their insights effectively reflect the reality. It all comes down to the way traditional accounting systems are set up.

Typically, traditional accounting systems provide a well-elaborated product costing system. This does not necessarily mean the complexity that is being caused by the product is reflected in a correct way. Take a company making a standard blue widget in a quantity of 1,000 per year. However, there is a group of consumers that prefers green widgets. The green widgets sell at a rate of 20 per year. Very rarely can it be derived from the costing system that the cost of this green widget is much higher than that of the blue widget.

The cost for maintaining master data, maintaining price lists, maintaining technical specifications, etc. is exactly the same for both products. But the volume that has to bear these costs is much smaller for the green widget. Also, the green widget is most likely produced in a much smaller batch size than the blue widget. Although the per-unit-cost of changing over the production machinery is much higher for the green widget, most of the time this is not well reflected in the costing system. Despite these deficiencies, when talking about product costing, traditional costing systems often provide a useful starting point.

Traditional costing systems deal with costs which are caused by customer behavior differently, typically in the sales and logistics area. Looking at a profit-and-loss statement, typically the upper part of the statement contains the product-driven costs, which can be specified per product. But below the gross profit level, only the aggregate cost of the sales and the logistics organizations is shown. This point of view is made clear in Figure 9.8.

Often, it is not an easy task to find out which customers are responsible for the bigger chunks of these costs, although everyone in the organization probably has an opinion on this. The fact that these opinions may not always align can be a source of dispute and frustration.

Another element which is completely hidden in traditional accounting systems is the opportunity cost associated with working capital. Both product-driven working capital costs (caused by the inventory) and customer-driven costs (caused by their outstanding payment balances) do not appear in any cost statement. The fact that a customer pays invoices three times later than average does affect the attractiveness of this customer, however.

These considerations call for another approach that ultimately provides this insight that companies are looking for to improve their profitability. When applying the cost-to-serve approach of Equazion to improve these insights, the exercise typically starts with a discussion with the managers responsible for the different departments in the company, based on the profit-and-loss accounts. This discussion allows identification of what causes these costs to occur (what activity is being performed, related to a product, a customer, a brand, etc.) and what drives this activity? A driver can sometimes be derived from simple transactional data extracted from the ERP system, like the number of orders that a customer has placed. Or, it can be more difficult to obtain and may require some specific data collection.

Based on these discussions, a cost calculation model can be set up, in a very different way from the traditional view pictured above. Using activity based costing techniques, the important costs are assigned to products and customers. In order to keep the complexity of the model at an acceptable level, it is important to keep the focus on the important costs. The objective in this type of exercise is not to come to a product cost calculation with extreme precision. When 95 percent of the costs can be assigned in a correct way, the insight will definitely be sufficient. This also improves the sustainability of the model for future re-runs. Translating this approach in a profit-and-loss structure gives a completely different view compared with the traditional accounting view. (Figure 9.9).

This type of profit-and-loss structure can be set up for every individual customer down to the level

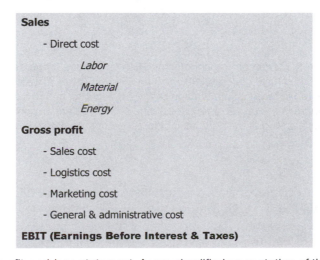

FIGURE 9.8 Traditional profit-and-loss statement. A very simplified presentation of the typical components in a profit-and-loss statement.

Source: Koen Cobbaert and Peter Verstraeten, 2009.

Sales

 - Direct material cost

 - Product driven activity cost

Product margin

 - Customer driven activity cost

Customer margin

 - Other activity costs

EBIT (Earnings Before Interest & Taxes)

FIGURE 9.9 Cost-to-serve profit-and-loss statement. A very simplified presentation of the components in a profit-and-loss statement as it is relevant for cost-to-serve investigation.

Source: Koen Cobbaert and Peter Verstraeten, 2009.

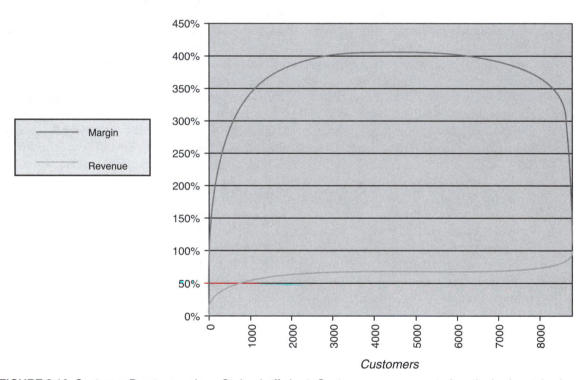

Customers

FIGURE 9.10 Customer Pareto margin or Stobachoff chart. Customers are presented on the horizontal axis according to the margin that they have generated (highest margin on the left, lowest margin on the right). The cumulative margin is presented in terms of percentage by the black curve. In this example a major part of the margin is lost by the customers in the tail. Volume-wise, these customers are important however as can be seen in the gray curve that has an upswing at the right hand side. So getting rid of these customers is not the obvious solution.

Source: Koen Cobbaert and Peter Verstraeten, 2009.

of the customer margin. If a customer ends up with a negative margin at this level, there is really a call for action. This means that keeping the customer the way it is will drag down your profits.

Results coming from these exercises are very often real eye-openers. Where the traditional view often misleads management into thinking that sales costs are equally spread over the entire customer base, this exercise may reveal that a substantial number of customers are simply being subsidized by the other ones. A very clear way to present this is through a Stobachoff chart (see Figure 9.10). This chart is a cumulative mapping of the margin that customers are bringing: customers with the biggest margin are at the left of the chart; customers with the smallest (and most negative) margins are at the right-hand side. The example shows that the margin amounts to 400 percent, to descend afterwards to the level of 100 percent. This means that the margin could have been four times higher if the loss-producing customers had been abandoned.

The real strength of the exercise comes from the identification of why some customers produce a loss for the company. Figure 9.11 illustrates customers may be loss-producing or profit-generating for very different reasons. In this graph—where every customer is represented by a bubble whose size is an indication of revenue—a split is made between the costs driven by the products that the customer purchases (represented by the product mix margin) and the cost-to-serve of the customer. Customers which fall below the diagonal line are loss-producing. This can be for very different reasons, as the dark bubbles illustrate. A customer below the diagonal at the left side of the graph is a customer that pays a very low price for products. Even though the cost-to-serve that customer may be quite low, it simply does not pay enough.

The customer at the right side of the chart may be paying a higher price, but the cost-to-service that customer may be far too expensive for the price it pays. This service may take different shapes: sales representatives paying too much attention, high allowances, coop-advertising, claims, high transportation costs, lots of handling because of small order quantities.

It is important to gain insight into the reason that actually makes a customer loss-generating. Dashboards can identify in a very simple and straightforward way which activities, by customer, are causing an excessive cost and make the cost-to-serve exercise actionable. Figure 9.12 gives an example

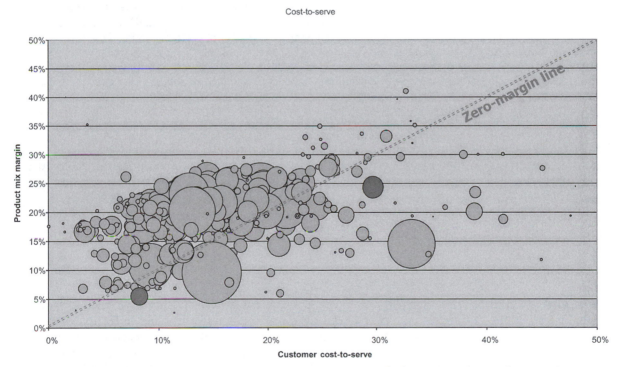

FIGURE 9.11 Cost-to-serve vs. product mix margin. This graph gives insight in how the product margin (sales—product driven costs) relate to the cost-to-serve for every customer. Customers are presented by bubbles (the bigger the bubble, the higher the revenue). The Y-axis expresses the product margin that a customer generates, as a percentage of the revenue. The X-axis presents the cost-to-serve, also as a percentage of the revenue. The diagonal line in the graph separates the profitable customers (above the line) from the non-profitable ones (below the lines). The graph gives an important indication why customers may have a low profitability: the dark bubble in the left-hand corner shows a customer with a low cost-to-serve, but the price he pays for the products is so low that he is still not profitable. The dark bubble on the right-hand side identifies a customer that pays much more for his products, but that has at a same time a much higher service expectation which makes him non-profitable again.

Source: Koen Cobbaert and Peter Verstraeten, 2009.

Profitobject Description	Revenue Value	Margin Tot	Margin Perc	Cost of Capital AR %	Direct Marketing %	Discounts %	EDI Admin %	KAM %	Loading %	Manual Admin %	Picking %	Rebates %	Transport %
Master Cash	1.951.529	-211.674	-10,85%	1,42%	0,00%	0,00%	1,30%	14,40%	1,24%	0,00%	1,66%	14,02%	5,78%
Discount Supermarkets	5.644.522	557.860	9,88%	1,61%	5,30%	0,00%	0,44%	3,32%	1,11%	0,00%	0,76%	0,00%	5,15%
Fryx LTD	657.940	-34.670	-5,27%	2,00%	0,00%	0,00%	4,98%	11,39%	1,58%	0,00%	5,85%	0,00%	7,34%
Fastcheap	5.483.992	-544.796	-9,93%	1,75%	1,04%	2,46%	0,32%	1,02%	1,63%	0,00%	0,80%	0,21%	7,61%
Safe	2.151.064	-535.605	-24,90%	2,85%	0,00%	0,00%	0,00%	3,48%	1,73%	16,27%	2,42%	0,00%	8,04%
Monroy	4.004.721	-147.331	-3,68%	1,18%	4,66%	0,91%	0,00%	2,81%	1,39%	9,03%	1,47%	0,00%	6,45%
Buzzy LTD	11.545.481	471.344	4,08%	1,64%	1,44%	1,86%	0,36%	1,62%	1,29%	0,00%	0,76%	3,64%	6,00%
Arma	3.885.866	-411.364	-10,59%	2,51%	1,98%	3,87%	0,00%	7,23%	1,36%	9,33%	1,50%	1,63%	6,31%
Scott & Lewis	51.625.422	2.226.989	4,31%	2,31%	1,68%	0,43%	0,08%	0,73%	1,26%	0,00%	0,54%	1,33%	5,84%
Walter Burrows	1.040.539	-104.945	-10,09%	2,48%	1,06%	0,00%	2,37%	7,20%	1,84%	0,00%	2,84%	0,00%	8,56%
Maxi	1.838.003	-76.317	-4,15%	2,49%	7,55%	5,28%	1,37%	9,17%	1,20%	0,00%	1,72%	0,00%	5,57%
Sunny's Supermarkets	25.885.403	2.259.465	8,73%	2,50%	1,10%	1,08%	0,10%	1,45%	1,08%	0,00%	0,47%	2,06%	5,03%
Cartleys	339.082	-64.654	-19,07%	2,49%	0,00%	0,00%	7,51%	22,10%	1,79%	0,00%	8,77%	0,00%	8,31%
Texo	16.317.007	-266.769	-1,63%	3,59%	2,86%	5,39%	0,15%	2,30%	1,15%	0,00%	0,53%	0,00%	5,35%

FIGURE 9.12 Cost-to-serve dashboard. The cost-to-serve dashboard provides detailed insights in the cost behavior associated with every customer. In the fourth column the relative margin of every customer is presented. Those customers with the lowest margin are marked in red (mid-gray); the best are marked in green (dark gray). Interesting in this case is the possibility to identify for every cost element which customers are performing good or bad. These cost elements are presented in columns 5 till 14. As an example, we can see that transport costs are very high for Walter Burrows and Cartleys, which explains partially why Cartleys has a low profitability overall. This is indispensable information to identify improvement opportunities in terms of cost-to-serve.

Source: Koen Cobbaert and Peter Verstraeten, 2009.

of what such a dashboard may look like. This table gives the revenue, margin, and margin percentage for some customers. Those customers with the lowest relative margin are automatically colored red (mid-gray). The best are colored green (dark gray). The strongest element, however, lies in the subsequent columns for all groups of cost elements, showing whether this customer is on the high (dark gray) or on the low (mid-gray) side in each. Actions should then be linked to those red (mid-gray) parts of the table that are, volume-wise, most important and that can be influenced.

Conclusion

Management is facing a lot of challenges in these turbulent times. Pressure on cost and working capital is very high, making the need for correct insights indispensable. Given the complex environment in which a lot of companies are operating, a decision support tool is a necessity to find the levers for improvement. Equazion offers this functionality through a sound analytical approach that is fully aligned with the Six Sigma DMAIC approach. This approach starts from readily available ERP data, which are turned into information that is directly addressing the working capital and the cost-to-serve needs. This information is subsequently used to identify the levers for improvement. As shown, the management of supply chain costs becomes critical to the overall success or failure of the business in the current business environment. Above all, the improvement levers discovered with the Equazion tool are very actionable because they identify at the product level or by customer what action is needed. In these turbulent times, correctly identifying the volatility in your business, and gaining the insight needed to act upon it, is a big asset.

Notes

1   In probability theory, the law of large numbers (LLN) is a theorem that describes the result of performing the same experiment a large number of times. According to the law, the average of the results obtained from a large number of trials should be close to the expected value, and will tend to become closer as more trials are performed.

2   The Gauss curve is derived from the normal distribution. The normal distribution is a continuous probability distribution that describes data that cluster around the mean. The graph of the associated probability density function is bell-shaped, with a peak at the mean.

ten
Gaming X-SCM

Ernest Cadotte, Dr. Thomas M. Corsi, and Alexander Verbraeck

Computer simulations offer a powerful tool for virtually exploring business operating and decision-making scenarios without putting real-world operations at risk. In this chapter, we discuss two such simulations that explore risk and volatility in a supply chain management setting.

The two simulations allow users to "game" X-treme supply chain management and thereby gain valuable experience in managing the kind of systemic business volatility discussed throughout this book. The two simulations are: the *X-treme Supply Chain Simulation* and the *Global Supply Chain Game*.

Part 1: X-treme Supply Chain Simulation

The *X-treme Supply Chain Simulation* (www.xtremesupplychainsimulation.com) is a game that develops the risk management skills that are needed in a turbulent supply chain environment. It is a powerful yet entertaining way to learn how to compete and manage risk in a fast-paced market where customers are demanding, relationships with supply chain partners are challenging, and the competition is working hard to take away your business. It is not only a motivational learning experience but a transformational one as well.

Working within the *X-treme Supply Chain Simulation*, you and your teammates will build an entrepreneurial firm, experiment with strategies, develop supply chain partnerships, struggle with business fundamentals, and compete with other participants in a virtual business world. As part of the simulation exercise, you will take control of an enterprise and manage its operations through four decision cycles. During each cycle, you will have to analyze a situation, plan a strategy to improve it, and then execute that strategy with future profitability in mind. Incrementally, you will learn to adjust your strategy and manage your risks as you deal with real-life decisions, threats, conflicts, trade-offs, and potential outcomes.

In short, the simulation provides a "living case" through which you will gain hands-on experience in supply chain management. Along the way, the *X-treme Supply Chain Simulation*:

- Facilitates the learning of important risk management concepts, principles, tools, and ways of thinking within a rapidly changing, and potentially perilous, business environment;
- Enhances your understanding of the critical linkages among members of a supply chain;
- Promotes better decision making by helping you see how your decisions can affect the performance of your firm, your business partners, and the supply chain as a whole;

- Crystallizes the financial implications of your business decisions by linking them to cash flows and bottom-line performance;
- Instills financial accountability and the simultaneous need to deliver supply chain value;
- Internalizes how important it is to use market data, supply chain networking, and competitive signals to adjust a strategic plan and more tightly focus supply chain tactics;
- Provides opportunities to demonstrate supply chain leadership, cross-firm teamwork, and interpersonal skills;
- Excites the competitive spirit and the drive to excel in the market;
- Builds confidence through experience gained through repetitive practice in risk assessment and management.

This simulation exercise should provide you with considerable insight into the management of supply chains in turbulent times—a mindset you can take into the business world, where supply chain disruptions are a fact of life.

Overview: Scenario and Strategies

Rather than start you and your team in the middle of a story (i.e., with a mature firm), the *X-treme Supply Chain Simulation* mimics a start-up venture. The specific scenario in this simulation is supply chain risk management in an emerging technology market. Participants form into teams and compete as either resellers or suppliers. The reseller teams focus on the creation of demand through their efforts to market and distribute microcomputers to end users. They outsource production to other firms that specialize in manufacturing. The supplier teams, meanwhile, focus on achieving economical and reliable production of microcomputers. The suppliers rely on the resellers to create demand for their services and contract with them to market and distribute the computers they produce.

Resellers and suppliers must work together to accomplish their business goals, negotiating both short-term supply contracts and long-term relationship agreements. They also face a series of supply chain threats that originate from competitors, partners, economic conditions, natural disasters, labor strife, distribution channels, and segment preferences. They must anticipate, plan for, and manage such threats while developing a viable, international business.

Whether you are a reseller or a supplier, your firm expands its operations and takes on new tasks and responsibilities during the course of four decision rounds, or quarters. In each round, you evaluate the market opportunity, choose a business strategy, evaluate tactical options, and submit a series of decisions. Your decisions are then weighed against those of your competitors and channel partners in the simulator. Results are quickly fed back to you, and the next round of decision making begins.

As your business grows, the simulation gradually introduces new issues that you must master. Each decision period introduces a dominant activity and a set of decisions that move you through the business lifecycle—from start-up to development, to growth, and to near maturity. As you work through this cycle, the *X-treme Supply Chain Simulation* phases in content that is relevant to the current period. Corresponding readings in the simulation's "help" files explain the nature of the decision you are facing, the issues you must deal with, how they connect with other decisions, and the trade-offs to consider.

By design, the simulation requires that each quarter's activities build upon prior content, so that you have opportunities to learn which actions improve and which ones hurt performance. By doing so, the simulation repeatedly challenges your skill in strategic planning and the tactical matters of cash-flow planning, value creation in product design, production scheduling, supply chain coordination, risk management, and profitability analysis.

The *X-treme Supply Chain* Environment

The *X-treme Supply Chain Simulation* environment has five major components: the game scenario, market setting, chronology of events, supply chain structure, and risk management decisions. The following discussions will introduce you to each component and give you the background you need to get started.

1. The Game Scenario

You are about to start a new company that will enter the microcomputer business during an uncertain period. The international market is in constant flux. Market potential will rise and fall according to local and worldwide economic conditions. In addition, political tensions sometimes emerge as various governing bodies try to do what is best for their own markets. From time to time, natural disasters, such as earthquakes, hurricanes, and floods, disrupt the flow of goods and services to end-user markets. These conditions will affect the ease and cost of managing a supply chain in a global market.

Other firms will be entering the personal computer (PC) market at the same time. In this scenario, the microcomputer industry is in the earliest stage of development. There is no history, and there are no established competitors. All competitors, including your own company, are starting with exactly the same resources and knowledge of the market. Your target market will be direct sales to business customers. You will not be selling to the home market, and you will not sell through retail stores.

In this market, there are resellers and suppliers. Resellers create brands that will satisfy market needs, and then market them on a worldwide basis. Suppliers specialize in the production of microcomputers and represent the source of supply for the resellers. You may choose to be either a reseller or a supplier.

An outside group of venture capitalists provides the seed capital to help you start the business. Your executive team has been hired to get this company off the ground. You have limited financial resources and complete accounting responsibility.

The venture capitalists are expecting you to create a profitable enterprise during the next year in spite of the economic, political, and supply chain risks that you face. If you are able to achieve positive retained earnings over the next four quarters (the decision periods mentioned earlier), then they will reward you with substantial stock options at a fraction of the price they paid for their own stock. To achieve this goal, you must plan for and manage the risks that could emerge during your first year in business.

A balanced scorecard measures your firm's performance and compares your results with those of your competitors. If you choose to be a reseller, the assessment of your business's performance will be based upon financial performance, market effectiveness, marketing performance, investments in the firm's future, human resource management, asset management, supply chain risk, and creation of wealth. If you choose to become a supplier, your firm's total business performance will be assessed based upon financial performance, manufacturing productivity, investments in the firm's future, asset management, supply chain risk, and creation of wealth.

You will receive a quarterly industry newsletter with up-to-date information on current events and projected trends in international business. It is your responsibility to predict how these conditions will affect demand and your supply chain operations.

2. Market Setting

All resellers sell through company-owned sales offices in 12 major metropolitan markets around the world. They can also access business customers through the Internet via three regional "Web centers" located in Mexico City, Shanghai, and Moscow. Web centers are business offices that host the Internet site for the region. The venture capitalists have already set up a sales office in Chicago and the Web center in Mexico City in anticipation of launching the PC industry. Figure 10.1 shows this global sales network.

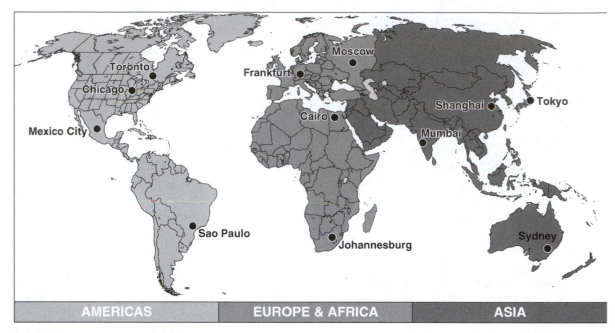

FIGURE 10.1 Available sales office locations.

Suppliers have access to a small factory that the venture capitalists have acquired in Shanghai. They do not have direct access to the end-user market. They must find resellers who want them to produce microcomputers to their specifications and ship the units either to the reseller's warehouse or directly to the final customer.

There are three market segments to serve in the PC market. They are referred to as the "Mercedes," the "Workhorse," and the "Traveler" segments.

- The Mercedes segment is looking for a high-performance computer to use in engineering and manufacturing applications. Mercedes customers are willing to pay extra for high performance.
- The Workhorse segment is the largest group of customers. They want a PC for office use that is easy to use and is also moderately priced.
- The Traveler segment wants a practical computer to use on the road. Traveler customers are executives and salespeople who travel a great deal. This segment is also price-sensitive.

The three segments are portrayed in Figure 10.2. The circles are positioned to indicate the price and performance requirements of each segment. The size of each circle reflects the size of the segment it represents.

Each segment has different needs and wants, and each therefore requires a different market strategy. One of your first decisions is to select initial segments to target. Having selected your target markets, you then develop and execute a strategy to profitably serve those segments.

3. Chronology of Events

Each quarter, or decision period, will include major events requiring you to make critical decisions.

Quarter 1: Organize the Firm, Establish Its Initial Business Strategy, and Go to Test Market

First, name the company and sell $3 million in stock to the venture capitalists. Next, assign corporate responsibilities and establish personal goals, a decision-making process, and team norms. Then, analyze the market survey and supply chain options. With this information in hand, choose to be either a reseller or supplier and establish an initial business strategy.

If you choose to become a reseller, you must (1) choose your target segments; (2) design a brand for

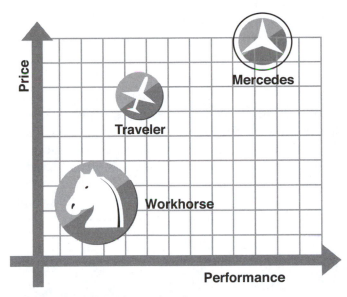

FIGURE 10.2 Market segments arrayed by price and performance.

each target segment; (3) establish brand prices and priorities; (4) design an advertising campaign; (5) hire sales and service personnel; (6) negotiate supply contracts with one or more suppliers; (7) schedule the opening of one or more sales outlets for the next quarter; and (8) purchase market research.

If you choose to become a supplier, you must (1) negotiate sales contracts with resellers; (2) schedule production to meet the resellers' needs; (3) make investments to improve the efficiencies of your production line; (4) initiate a quality-control program; (5) add capacity for the following quarter; and (6) purchase market research.

Finally, begin preliminary assessments of your supply chain risks and tactics for dealing with them.

Quarter 2: Adjustment and Market Expansion

First, sell $2 million in stock to the venture capitalists. Next, review the market, financial and operational data from the test market, and adjust your strategy and tactics as needed. Then, make investments for the future; these include opening new sales outlets (resellers) and adding factory capacity and a quality-improvement program (suppliers). Both resellers and suppliers invest in technology and procedures to streamline the flow of information and inventory from the supplier to the end user.

As the news about economic conditions, world politics, and supply chain partners unfolds, reassess your risks and tactics for dealing with these situations.

Quarter 3: Market Expansion

Continue your expansion plan while coping with the unexpected business conditions that have emerged during your first three quarters in business.

Quarter 4: Push to End Your First Year with Positive Retained Earnings

Even with the challenges you constantly face, everything should be in place for a successful conclusion to your first year in business. Again, adjust your tactical decisions in order to create a strong presence in the market and positive profits and cash flows.

4. Supply Chain Structure

The following descriptions of the roles of resellers and suppliers and how they can work together to achieve their goal will help you understand the overall structure of the business world in which you will compete. As shown in Figure 10.3, both resellers and suppliers have a great deal of freedom to develop relationships.

Supply Contracts

A reseller can negotiate a deal with any supplier to produce one or more of its brands. The entire process begins with a reseller sending a request for proposal (RFP) to a supplier. Next, the supplier runs a factory simulation in order to estimate the costs of different operating conditions. Then, it prepares a proposal and submits it to the reseller. The reseller may accept the terms of the proposal or negotiate for better ones. At some point, the proposal is either finalized and accepted by both parties or completely rejected by one of them. Figure 10.4 outlines the typical negotiation process.

There are many conditions to negotiate in any supply contract, including price, quantity, frequency and mode of delivery, risk-sharing fees, etc. In addition, resellers and suppliers can look beyond individual supply contracts and negotiate longer-term relationships that include management information systems (MIS), electronic data interchange (EDI), and investments in each other's firms. The goal of these longer-term relationships is to improve the efficiency and effectiveness of the supply chain.

Assuming the two parties agree to a supply contract, the supplier then builds and ships the products to the reseller's central warehouse in accordance with the agreement. Once the computers arrive at the reseller's warehouse, they are stored on the shelves and are made available for shipment to customers. Suppliers can ship goods from a factory to a reseller's warehouse via three transportation options: slow, intermediate, and fast.

The Reseller's Role

As a reseller, your primary focus is on the marketing and distribution of microcomputers. You rely on suppliers to produce and ship these microcomputers to a warehouse that you use for distribution. Ultimately, you want to have your suppliers ship directly to your customers, but this path is expensive to set up and requires a close working relationship with one or more suppliers.

Your investors have already set up a central warehouse facility in Shanghai to receive inventory from your suppliers as well as handle and ship inventory to end users. To save money, you lease, rather

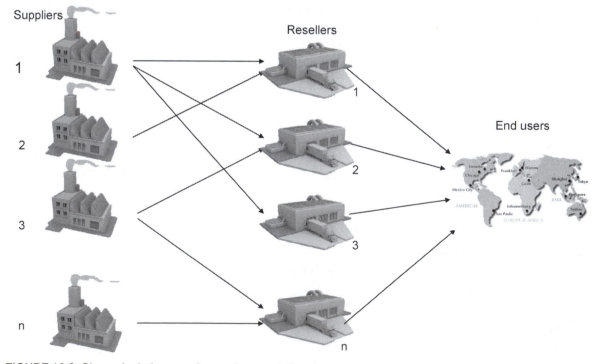

FIGURE 10.3 Channel relations are free to form and dissolve.

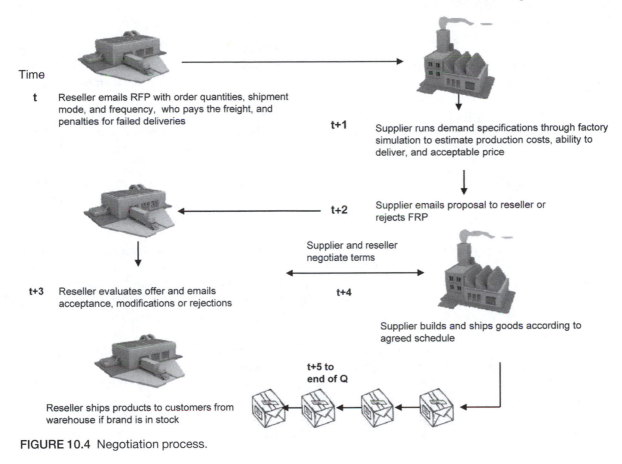

Time

t   Reseller emails RFP with order quantities, shipment mode, and frequency, who pays the freight, and penalties for failed deliveries

t+1   Supplier runs demand specifications through factory simulation to estimate production costs, ability to deliver, and acceptable price

t+2   Supplier emails proposal to reseller or rejects FRP

Supplier and reseller negotiate terms

t+3   Reseller evaluates offer and emails acceptance, modifications or rejections

t+4

Supplier builds and ships goods according to agreed schedule

t+5 to end of Q

Reseller ships products to customers from warehouse if brand is in stock

FIGURE 10.4 Negotiation process.

than own, the warehouse space. As a result, you pay a throughput fee for all goods processed through the warehouse. You also pay an inventory-holding fee for any goods left in the warehouse at the end of each quarter.

You do not have to worry about the size of the warehouse. You can automatically contract for more warehouse space if you need it. Therefore, you only pay for the facilities that you use.

Your marketing and sales departments will need to decide how many units they will need to purchase in order to meet demand for each quarter. It is your job to obtain the necessary inventory to meet that demand. This requires contacting potential suppliers and negotiating contracts that establish conditions under which they will produce and ship computers to you. In the beginning, it will be easier to deal with one contract at a time. However, as you gain experience and get to know more suppliers, it might be prudent to set up longer-term relationships that can benefit both parties.

In any case, the process starts with the request for proposal, or RFP. In order for a supplier to give you a quote on production costs, you need to prepare an RFP that specifies the brands you want to outsource, the quantity you plan to purchase, and the schedule for delivery. You might also want to specify the mode of delivery and who pays the freight, which usually are points of negotiation.

It is very important to verify whether a supplier has fulfilled the terms of the contract. If the products were not shipped as specified in the contract, then you will want to discuss these departures with your supplier. If the supplier failed to deliver some of the units specified in the contract, then your firm might be entitled to a risk-sharing fee for lost profits, assuming you negotiated this condition in the original contract. If you are not satisfied with a supplier's performance, you may need to ask it to make internal changes, or you may have to seek a new supplier altogether.

It is always possible that a supplier's failure to perform may result from inadequate or inaccurate information. Giving suppliers some idea of what to expect in the first and subsequent quarters of sales will affect their decisions regarding how much capacity to build into their factories in Shanghai, and when to add more. This will help to ensure that suppliers have sufficient capacity to meet your projected demand.

The Supplier's Role

The primary focus for your firm is the production of microcomputers. In the beginning, you ship these microcomputers to the resellers' warehouses. Ultimately, you want to ship directly to the end users, but this path is expensive to set up and requires a close working relationship with one or more resellers.

Your goal is to encourage resellers to select your firm as the source for the microcomputers they sell to the end user. You can sit back and wait for the resellers to contact you, or you can take the initiative and pursue them. Obviously, you will find more business opportunities if you take the initiative.

You can also take a short-term or a long-term view in setting up and managing these business dealings. In the beginning, it will be easier to deal with one contract at a time. However, as you gain experience and get to know your resellers, it might be prudent to set up longer-term relationships that can benefit both parties.

In any case, the process starts with the request for proposal. If a reseller is considering working with your firm as a supplier, it submits an RFP that asks you to evaluate whether or not you want to take on this responsibility. In the RFP, your potential business partner specifies which brands it would like you to produce, the quantity, the mode of delivery, who will pay the shipping costs, the frequency of delivery, and a risk-sharing fee that will compensate it for lost profits in the event that you are unable to deliver all of the units specified in the contract.

You must either prepare a contract proposal for the reseller to consider or reject the RFP. Before making a decision, it is wise to evaluate both your costs and your ability to produce the desired brand(s). To determine your production costs and capacity, you can use a factory simulation that has been built into the *X-treme Supply Chain* software.

If you choose to submit a contract proposal, then the most important piece of information is the price you want to charge for producing each brand. As a general rule, pricing is the only term of an RFP that is changeable. If you make changes in these terms relative to the original RFP, they should be noted when the contract is submitted to the reseller for consideration; however, the reseller is not likely to accept these revisions without justification.

After you have signed a contract and some time has passed, you and the reseller may agree to set up advanced management information systems (MIS). If you both have a high-level MIS, you may be able to add certain conditions regarding the reseller's failure to create sufficient demand. That is, you can ask the reseller to specify a minimum contract quantity and agree to pay a risk-sharing fee if it fails to create sufficient demand to meet this minimum. This fee would help to pay for the excess capacity costs that you incurred based upon the reseller's minimum forecast.

Each supplier's ability to attract new business is greatly influenced by its success in fulfilling the promises it made in the prior quarter. It is important, therefore, to continually monitor how well your firm performed in supplying the resellers. Note especially the percentage of on-time deliveries and whether each order ultimately was fulfilled. If you did not achieve a 100 percent rating in both categories, you are certain to face some tough negotiations.

Make the time to review the percentage of contract fulfillment and the percentage of on-time delivery achieved by other suppliers. How do your numbers compare to those of your competition? You always want to be the strongest supplier, and this exercise will help you determine where you may need to improve.

Relationship Development

Supply contracts can take on a very short-term perspective. A reseller might only be concerned with how much the supplier can ship; when it can ship; and what the inventory will cost. The reseller's selection decision might be based solely on which supplier has the lowest delivered cost.

By the same token, the supplier might only be concerned with how much inventory the reseller wants; when it needs to be shipped; and what the price is. Suppliers might accept sales contracts based only on which reseller will pay the highest delivered price.

Furthermore, each contract may have no relationship to the one that came before or the one that will come after. This type of channel strategy offers minimum involvement and efficient negotiations.

There are other strategies that take a longer-term, developmental approach. These strategies often value win/win relationships in which individual contracts are less important than what can be accomplished across the supply chain over a period of time. These strategies require more effort, but they can yield much greater returns than the short-term, one-contract-at-a-time approach.

If you adopt a more comprehensive supply chain and channel strategy, it might include: a clear statement of your intent to work together; the actions you and your supply chain partner will take and a timetable for when you will accomplish them; specification of goals, incentives, and penalties; and sizeable investments in supply chain assets. As you start working with the available supply chain partners, consider the development of a longer-term relationship with one or more of them.

Supply Chain Management Information System for Inventory Management

Regardless of the type of relationship you and your partners develop, you should consider developing an advanced supply chain management information system (MIS). This is an extremely effective method for managing and sharing information about inventory between channel partners because it allows both parties to adjust the number of units ordered to the actual demand in real time as well as to track orders and shipments.

The standard system for fulfilling contracts between a supplier and a reseller is for the reseller to tell the supplier exactly how many units to produce and ship in the coming quarter. This is called a "push" system because it requires the supplier to push the inventory through the supply chain, regardless of the actual number of units that are demanded by the market.

Unfortunately, it is virtually impossible to accurately forecast demand; therefore, the push system is almost never right, and when it is wrong, the consequences may be serious. Overestimates of demand can result in excess inventories that consume large amounts of cash, and underestimates of demand can result in stock-outs, lost sales revenue, and customer ill will.

A better approach, then, is the "pull" system of inventory management. In a pull system, the number of units produced is based upon the actual demand. As units are pulled from the warehouse, the plant produces what is needed to replace the units that were pulled. If demand is less than expected, then fewer units are pulled from the warehouse, and fewer are produced. If demand is greater than expected, more units are pulled from the warehouse, and more are sent to replenish inventory.

To implement a pull inventory system, it is necessary to set up a supply chain management information system. This system will allow you to see exactly: (1) how much inventory a reseller has on hand, and how many units went out with each shipment; (2) if there was insufficient inventory, how many units were not shipped; (3) how many units were shipped late; (4) when the inventory was shipped from the factory; and (5) when it was received at the reseller's warehouse. Without the supply chain management information system, all you will know is the total number of units that were shipped or not shipped.

An inventory push system is the default and so has no additional cost associated with it. An inventory pull system, however, will have a cost because it requires creating a supply chain management information system. There are three options for setting up such a system. Each option adds to the supply chain's pull capability, thus increasing fulfillment levels and reducing inventories and costs.

A Level I supply chain management information system is a modified pull system that allows a reseller to set a minimum and a maximum quantity for each brand in a contract. The reseller predicts the range in which demand should fall. The number of items built and shipped depends upon actual demand, as long as it falls within this range.

A Level II supply chain management information system eliminates the need for either supply chain partner to forecast the number of units to be produced by brand. Instead, the actual demand experienced by the reseller determines the order and shipment quantities. As demand pulls inventory from the reseller's warehouse, the supplier replenishes it, up to its allocated production capacity.

A Level III supply chain management information system shifts inventory management from the reseller to the supplier. The reseller does not stock any inventory; it is all stored at the supplier's factory warehouse. When the reseller receives an order, the shipment paperwork is electronically transferred to the supplier, and the supplier ships the units directly from its factory warehouse to the end customer. The reseller never touches the inventory.

To place an order with a Level II or Level III system, the reseller must provide an estimate of demand, so the supplier can plan its production schedule. However, there is no expectation that the demand for any single brand will exactly match the projected demand. Rather, it is hoped that the estimate will be a reasonable approximation of the total demand across all of the brands that might pass through the factory.

In order to establish a Level II or Level III MIS between two supply chain partners, they must take two steps. First, both the supplier and reseller must purchase the necessary hardware and software to run the MIS system. Second, both parties must also set up electronic data interchange (EDI) between them. If either party fails to make both investments, then the system will resort to the lowest common level. For example, if the supplier has a Level II system and the reseller has a Level I system, then the supply chain management information system will default to Level I.

It will take one quarter to set up the new MIS. If you invest in a new MIS and EDI system in a particular quarter, then you will not be able to use those systems until the following quarter. It is necessary, therefore, for both parties to plan ahead and coordinate their decisions.

It is important to note that there is no carryover benefit from investing in one MIS system versus another. If you start with a lower-level system, it will have to be replaced when you choose to set up a more advanced system. An investment in a lower-level system will not reduce the cost of a higher-level system.

5. Risk Management

Your firm will be a vital part of a complex trading network that can be fragile and prone to disruption from many supply chain risks. Reducing the frequency and impact of these disruptions represents a tremendous opportunity to gain a competitive advantage.[1]

To help manage your supply chain risks, a supply chain risk management (SCRM) template is included in the software. It provides a comprehensive method of identifying, cataloguing, evaluating, and prioritizing the risks that you face. These risks fall into three main categories, each of which has several subcategories:

1. *Strategic risks*

   - business cycle risks
   - social/demographic risks
   - environmental risks
   - political/regulatory regime risks.

2. *Industry risks*

   - product technology risks
   - market uptake/consumer acceptance risks
   - physical/legal infrastructure risks
   - business cycle/capital availability risks.

3. *Company risks*

   - product design/quality risks
   - partner efficiency/stability risks
   - demand/marketing channel risks
   - financial/operating performance risks.

During each quarter of play, your executive team must conduct a comprehensive risk analysis. This analysis maps and prioritizes the risks that your company faces, with the goal of controlling them throughout your first year in business.

Principal risks are those that combine both a high likelihood of occurrence with a high degree of organizational impact when they do occur. These are the key risks your team must focus on managing, in many cases in collaboration with your supply chain partners. To help administer this process, you record these principal risks in a "supply chain risk registry." The registry requires your executive team to: (1) audit each of these principal risks; (2) assign resources to the monitoring and mitigating of these risks; and (3) continually evaluate any change in risk status or urgency level.

Keep in mind that supply chain risk is dynamic. Over time, risks shift and evolve. Some risks will drop off your radar screen completely from one quarter to the next, while others will unexpectedly leap to prominence. You may get valuable clues about evolving supply chain threats from the quarterly newsletter that your company receives. Examine the information in the newsletter carefully.

Finally, your company will be evaluated on its supply chain risk management capabilities as part of its quarterly and cumulative balanced scorecard. This evaluation considers two factors: the level of risk that the firm takes on by being too exclusive or limiting in its business decisions; and the firm's ability to reduce risk by developing good relationships with multiple supply chain partners. Exclusivity increases risk because it gives you few options for addressing problems in the supply chain. In other words, supply chain risk will be great if there is too much exclusivity or dependence upon a limited number of brands, a limited number of markets, and a limited number of supply chain partners. Accordingly, increasing the number of brands, markets, and partners reduces this type of risk.

Another way to reduce risk is to establish meaningful, long-term relationships with business partners and to set up high-level MIS and EDI. Long-term relationships mitigate risk because they reduce the uncertainty of doing business with supply chain partners. MIS and EDI improve the channel's efficiency and effectiveness, and thus boost your firm's performance potential. As a result, any action to formalize relationships with business partners will positively affect supply chain risk.

Evolution of the Market

As you proceed through the simulation game, you will find that the market evolves along the lines of the product's lifecycle. At the outset, brand designs, advertising, media plans, distribution, and pricing are lacking in some respects. During this introductory period (Q1), sales are modest while many customers sit on the sidelines awaiting better offers. As the industry develops, decisions are refined and the market begins to expand (Q2). The rate of growth depends upon how fast the PC industry adapts to the expressed needs of the market, and on how aggressively it pursues that market.

Strong market growth comes as new technology is introduced, prices come down, advertising increases, and distribution becomes more widespread (Q3). The new technology pushes early product designs into decline. The size of the market "pie" grows, but who gets what share of that pie changes depending on the resourcefulness and aggressiveness of each competitor.

Eventually, the maturing market becomes highly segmented, with each market niche being served by a highly focused brand design, advertising campaign, price, and distribution system (Q4 and beyond). Most end users will have entered the market at this stage, and a large share of the sales will represent replacement purchases. Without further stimulation, the market may decline to a steady rate of sales based on such replacement purchases.

At maturity, competition is very stiff. All of the competitors have access to full market knowledge. By this time, they should understand what makes a good brand design, a good price, a good media plan, and a good distribution system. Market share—achieved through heavy advertising, good distribution, and low prices—becomes very important because it drives up production volumes and allows greater economies of scale.

Interestingly, the industry's development in tandem with the product lifecycle occurs naturally in the *X-treme Supply Chain* game. No formula or equation forces this to happen; the market takes on a life of its own once it has been set in motion. The rate of growth, pattern of growth, and ultimate size of the market depend upon the savvy and aggressiveness of the players in the game.

The Simulation's Correspondence to the Real World

The sequence of activities in the *X-treme Supply Chain Simulation* follows the logical way in which an entrepreneurial firm develops a new market in the real world. But although the simulation parallels real market conditions in a number of ways, it (like any simulated environment) is of necessity a simplification. For example, there are no other firms in the market outside of those participating in the simulation; your instructor will specify the number of firms and determine the composition of each team. Still, *X-treme Supply Chain* constitutes the world within which you must learn to compete, and—make no mistake about it—your competitors and supply chain partners are very real.

A word of caution: do not assume that the *X-treme Supply Chain* world behaves *exactly* like the real world. If you have specialized knowledge about the real PC industry, for instance, you may become frustrated that the simulation does not behave in exactly the same manner. First, remember that the *X-treme Supply Chain Simulation* is a simplification of the real world. Second, the *X-treme Supply Chain* PC world is in its infancy, whereas the actual industry is not. Third, the members of your class are essentially entrepreneurs with little experience in working together or within this industry. Finally, your instructor may intentionally alter market parameters to keep each new class on its toes. The best assumption to make, therefore, is that the simulation is a microcosm unto itself.

That is why you should use your knowledge of the real world only as background information to help in your initial planning and decision making. This is not about getting the "right" answers; it is more important to be able to adapt to what the market and your supply chain partners want. Think of it this way: if you changed jobs and moved from the microcomputer business to another industry—say, sporting goods or kitchen appliances—you would find that the "right" answers would be different than those in the computer industry. Every market is unique, and you must learn to adapt to each one.

Finally, keep in mind that, even in the real world, no amount of research can give you the perfect answer. It is almost a given that some aspect of what your customer and supply chain partners want will be misjudged, misunderstood, or overlooked. At times, customers and supply chain partners may even appear to act illogically. That is their prerogative. Your job is to respond to the expressed needs and wants of both. The "right" answer, the "reasonable" response, and the "logical" conclusion are determined by the market—not by what we think they should be.

Textbook + Simulation: An Integrated Set

The structure of this textbook unfolds together with the *X-treme Supply Chain Simulation* game. Its fundamental risk management concepts, principles, and processes are built into the play of the simulation.

But the textbook is intended to do more than provide you with written cues on how to proceed through the risk management aspects of the simulation exercise. It presents you with ideas, ways of thinking, and tools you can use as you deal with the risks that are inherent in business today.

That is why the authors of this book hope that you will not limit yourself to using it only when you play the *X-treme Supply Chain Simulation* game. The more of this textbook's concepts, principles, and processes you can draw upon, the greater your likelihood of success when it is time to assess and manage real supply chain risk.

Part 2: The Global Supply Chain Game

The *X-treme Supply Chain Simulation* featured in the first part of this chapter is designed to provide a learning environment that approximates the challenges of managing a global supply chain. Researchers at TU Delft University in the Netherlands and the Supply Chain Management Center at the Robert H. Smith School of Business, University of Maryland, have developed the *Global Supply Chain Game*[2] that complements the *X-treme Supply Chain Simulation* (www.gscg.org, click on "Available Games," then click on "Distributor Games").

The *Global Supply Chain Game* differs from the *X-treme Supply Chain Simulation* in important ways, however. It simulates the global supply chain environment by operating on a continuous clock, as opposed to the "turn"-based approach featured in the *X-treme Supply Chain Simulation*. In the *Global Supply Chain Game*, supply chain managers respond to ongoing events and challenges.

In the *Distributor Game*—a specific iteration of the *Global Supply Chain Game*—student teams act as distributors, deciding on what mix of computer products (desktops, laptops, multi-media, etc.) they wish to manage and distribute. Computer agents—i.e., decision-making "entities" controlled by the computer—are used to simulate a set of computer suppliers as well as a set of large-lot retailers.

As distributors, teams of players compete through a bidding process to acquire products from suppliers (who vary in physical distance from the suppliers as well as in quality of product and reliability in order fulfillment). The teams must also manage inventories of the different market products at their warehouses based on demand forecasts, and sell their products to market retailers by responding to requests-for-quotes (RFQs).

Rules-based algorithms were developed to control the decisions of large-lot retailers in evaluating multiple distributor teams' responses to their RFQs. Rules-based algorithms also control the response of suppliers to RFQs from the distributor teams to purchase computer products. The rules insure every RFQ from a distributor does, indeed, receive a response from at least one supplier. An incentive to move inventory quickly has been incorporated using a 2 percent depreciation per week on products held in stock—an appropriate figure given the actual market volatility of computers.

The performance of each distributor team is captured in balance and equity sheets that are reported to each team on a regular basis during game play. These reports provide the basis for comparisons with other teams and give teams an opportunity to make appropriate strategy adjustments. The balance and equity sheets take into account cash balances, the value of inventory, outstanding orders, bills to be paid, and payments to be received.

To support the concept of globalization, the distributor game simulation divides the world into three regions: the U.S., Europe, and Asia. (An overview of the European region is illustrated in Figure 10.5.) Each region has player-controlled distributors, agent-controlled suppliers, and agent-controlled markets. The number of players is flexible and can easily be adjusted. During the game, it is possible to buy products from all over the world, thereby allowing global competition both for the distributors buying from global suppliers and for the global markets buying from the global distributor players.

Each team in the simulation controls a distribution company in one of the three regions and must develop and test strategies for global vs. local sourcing, global vs. local sales, inventory levels to be maintained, and product specialization or differentiation. Due to rapid depreciation, unsold items are significantly reduced in value. In the game setting, profit margins are slim because of heavy competition, and making a profit is a challenge for the distributor teams. Customers expect rapid service from the distributor, but they cannot tell in advance when they want to purchase items and what they require.

Facing heavy competition from the other teams, distributors cannot afford to have zero on-hand inventory. Thus, one of the main assignments of the distributor game is for teams to manage the trade-off between maintaining low inventories to decrease inventory costs while simultaneously holding enough inventory to satisfy their customers' dynamic buying patterns.

The player application (Figure 10.6) gives the players an overview of the position of their distributor company and allows them to enter their decisions. Through the application, the players get updates about purchases, sales, finance, and inventory. They can also communicate electronically with other players via a built-in chat functionality.

The *Distributor Game* supports players in learning a number of skills critical to managing global supply chains in real time. These skills include: strategic leadership; operations management; financial management; and information technology.

FIGURE 10.5 *Global Supply Chain Game*: Distributor business network scenario for multiple players. Example of the distributor players in one of the regions in the *Distributor Game*.

In the game, the distributor is constantly struggling to align supply with demand. Internet-based customer inquiries/orders are flooding into the distributor in real time. Simultaneously, orders to suppliers are being triggered to buy computer products to meet market demands. Periodically, the game launches an external event to disrupt the supply chain. Such events include a demand surge; financial crisis/recession and collapse of demand; regional catastrophe knocking out key regional suppliers; a technology shift negating demand for one product type (e.g., Linux machines). The *Distributor Game* puts the teams in the role of a supply chain executive and helps them recognize the need to scan the horizon and constantly balance a portfolio of product and management risks.

Key Learnings

The *Distributor Game* is designed to teach players several important lessons from the dynamic game-play.

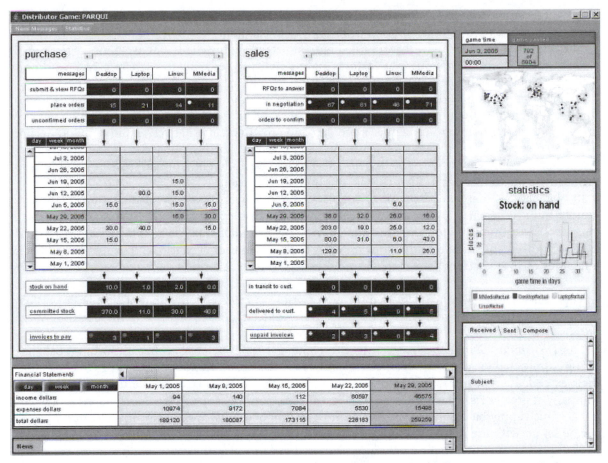

FIGURE 10.6 *Global Supply Chain Game*: distributor dashboard. This figure provides an overview of the distributor company's position and allows the company/player team to enter decisions.

- A distributor must manage the inventory and transportation of its multiple product lines. To be efficient, it must maintain as little inventory as possible to serve total customer demand and yet not miss major sales opportunities due to lack of on-hand inventory.

- The distributor must manage the trade-off between costs in maintaining local in-house stocks of inventory vs. higher transport costs to express ship inventory over greater distances from suppliers as needed. There is the trade-off between using more reliable suppliers who charge higher prices vs. lower-cost but less reliable suppliers. As the game progresses, the distributor can increasingly appreciate the power of real-time information in tracking operational performance and in helping to manage these trade-offs more efficiently.

- Because the electronics industry is a fast-moving one, with constantly shifting pricing and profit margin schemes, the distributor must manage its supply chain to be extremely responsive in terms of price. Through game-play, the distributor teams better understand the competitive pricing dynamics at work in the industry through game play.

- On the buy side, the distributor learns the importance of order size quantities. Order size is a critical determinant of other supply chain costs, such as transportation.

- Finally, the participants experience the powerful imperative to compress the cash-to-cash cycle and effectively manage accounts receivable and accounts payable.

The *Distributor Game* demonstrates for participants (and observers) the web of relationships that technology can help bring together in an accelerated manner to solve supply chain dilemmas. Customer requirements can spark a dramatic "raying out" of messaging and process actions across a web of interrelated enterprises to meet those requirements.

Suppliers from other regions and the whole world can be brought together on an ad-hoc basis using Internet technology to serve the distributor's customers. The participants appreciate the technology infrastructure that supports this supply chain system.

The *Distributor Game* can be incorporated into an overall supply chain management curriculum as a consequence of its continuous-play features and its ability to re-create the dynamic 24/7 world of a real-time global supply chain manager.

Global supply chain leaders are increasingly likely to reach out to a geographically extended set of suppliers for product/component sourcing. The set up of the *Distributor Game* can be changed to provide a teaching point around either rapid demand growth or, alternatively, rapid demand decline. In the former case, the demand order generator can be doubled during game play or, in the latter case, the demand order generator can be halved. This creates very different, but real sets of experiences for the participants to manage in their role as supply chain managers.

In the case of demand expansion, supply chain managers must determine quickly how to rapidly build up their supplier base. Conversely, in the case of demand contraction, supply chain managers must find ways to ramp down quickly. The *Distributor Game* is an effective way to experience such divergent situations, develop strategies to deal with each scenario, and immediately see the outcomes of those actions. The implemented strategies and their results serve as excellent teaching points.

This real-world experience delivered through gaming is more effective than a simple PowerPoint discussion in helping participants more effectively understand how to deal with demand surges or tailspins.

The *Distributor Game* can serve a similar teaching role for a variety of other important challenges facing supply chain leaders. For example, recently there has been a trend for enterprises to consolidate their extended supplier partnerships with a small number of key partners. Naturally, this puts the company at greater risk in the event of supplier failure or outage. *Distributor Game* players can see the impact this supply base concentration has on their supply chains. Specifically, the *Distributor Game* can be set up with the requirement that each distributor player allocate half of total orders to each of two suppliers. After an initial time period has passed in game play, the game administrator can cancel one supplier for each distributor. This will challenge each supply chain manager to respond to the major supply chain disruption. Again, discussion about the impact of losing a core supplier will be much richer and more effective after participants have experienced the situation vs. listening to a presentation delineating the pros and cons of having core suppliers.

These are just two examples of how the *Distributor Game* can be adopted to create situations that supply chain managers must address in a dynamic environment. The game's settings can be adjusted to create transportation bottlenecks and late deliveries due to a country-based crisis that impacts all shipments into and out of that country. In each case, the game provides the participants with the opportunity to deal with the situation in a dynamic environment.

The *Distributor Game* gives gamers the chance to make decisions, see their impact (good or bad), explore different decision scenarios, take risks, and make rapid decisions—all within the safety of a simulated business environment. Managers can see the consequences of their decisions, and learn from them—all without the potential consequences—good or bad—that real-life decision-making carries.

How to Access the *Distributor Game*

To access the *Global Supply Chain Game—Distributor Game*, go to http://www.routledge.com/textbooks/harrington, and click on "Distributor Game." You may also access it directly by going to www.gscg.org, clicking on "Available Games," then "Distributor Games."

Notes

1 Much of the "Risk Management" section has been adapted from material developed for the simulation game by Dr. Sandor Boyson and Dr. Thomas M. Corsi of the University of Maryland's Supply Chain Management Center.
2 Thomas M. Corsi and others, "The Real-Time Global Supply Chain Game: New Educational Tool for Developing Supply Chain Management Professionals," *Transportation Journal*, Summer 2006, Vol. 45, No. 3, 61–73.

eleven
Designing Risk-Tolerant Cyber Supply Chain Communities

Richard M. Douglass

When they think about supply chain volatility, most companies tend to focus on the physical aspects or manifestations of these ups and downs. However, cyber, or information supply chains are equally impacted by volatility and must be designed and managed to account for such oscillation.

In the remaining chapters of this part of the book, we focus on the impact of volatility on so-called cyber supply chains, and how information technology can be and is used not only to mitigate the impacts of volatility, but to take competitive advantage of it. We define the cyber supply chain as all of the information flows, technologies, and IT infrastructure and processes that support the other key types of supply chains—physical, financial, and service.

And we look at how one manages cyber supply chains in the face of ongoing volatility.

Volatility Drivers in the Cyber Supply Chain

To gain an appreciation for the volatility drivers within the cyber supply chain, we first look at the three major elements of any supply chain system: the players, the processes, and the systems.

The Players: Business Collaboration Networks

First, the players. Although we traditionally refer to the supply chain (and others have used the term demand chain, as that implies a more customer-centric view), the reality is that products get made and services delivered by a whole business collaboration network, or community, of trading partners as shown in Figure 11.1. It was Charles Handy[1] who many years ago coined the term the "shamrock" or "cloverleaf" organization, presaging the outsourcing phenomenon that exists today. Handy argued that companies would—or should—over time focus on what became known as core competencies, and then move non-core functions to other organizations for which these functions were indeed core. Thus, each of these outsourced capabilities was a separate leaf on the cloverleaf. That is very much the reality we have today.

Today, Business Collaboration Network (BCN) complexity for manufacturers has continued to increase for a number of reasons. For one, the growing practice of "near shoring," in which companies source from suppliers closer to home for a variety of strategic business reasons, is likely to increase, not decrease, the number of trading partners as a result of pressures for greater regionalization. Furthermore, as emerging markets such as China, Russia, and Brazil become demand centers in their own right, "near sourcing" becomes a relative term. In other words, from a North American

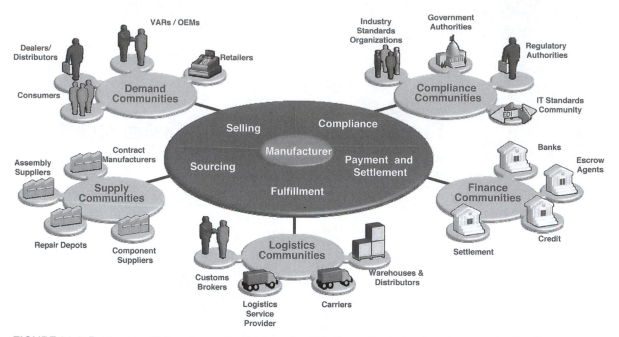

FIGURE 11.1 Business collaboration network diversity. This figure illustrates the diverse set of trading partners in a typical supply chain.

Source: Sterling Commerce, 2010.

or Western European perspective, offshoring meant production in China that was destined to be shipped back home. But for demand originating in China, that *is* home—it is simply domestic production for China.

Near sourcing also is on the rise thanks to increasing logistics costs, uncertain or substandard quality from low-cost production centers, and highly variable and long lead times that result from having geographically far-flung operations.

The upshot of this is that there likely will be more shipments (though not in bulk), more orders, and more trading partners with whom a manufacturer must collaborate. As a direct consequence, there will be more numerous and diverse trade regulations with which to comply, more systems to connect with, more service levels to manage, and so on. In such an environment, consortiums or "virtual communities" must be able to form, evolve, and eventually dissolve very dynamically.

To understand the communities' perspective, just think about how the economic crisis that began in late 2008 will affect the supply chains of the auto industry or high-tech sector. General Motors has just emerged from bankruptcy, a shadow of its former self, and with one new big partner—the U.S. government. GM has shed business units, is in the process of consolidating its dealer base, and also is trying to establish its place among the list of "green" automakers with hybrids and electric cars. One of its major suppliers, and a former business unit, Delphi, has been in bankruptcy, and now it looks as if the creditors will take control of the organization. The Saturn business unit is now defunct, GM unable to find a buyer.

How can all of this upheaval *not* affect GM's collective supply chains? Not to mention the corporation's customers, who undoubtedly wonder how they will get service and spare parts for their cars. If you were the CIO of GM, just imagine how your world has changed in terms of how you need to support the business.

In the high-tech sector, we can expect to see further consolidation upstream in the semiconductor producers and foundries, as they deal with sharply diminished demand and lots of excess capacity. Further downstream with the electronic manufacturing systems (EMS) providers, or contract manufacturers, like Hon Hai, Flextronics, Jabil, Celestica, Sanmina, and so on, we are likely to see a continuing effort on their part to further segment and specialize their business offerings and develop new ways of sharing risk with their OEM partners.

In this current economic climate—and "current" is likely to encompass the next two to three years at least—were EMS providers to focus too heavily on their traditional low-cost-manufacturing value proposition, they would simply destroy their margins and ultimately their market value. So, if you are a CIO at one of these companies, what do you do to support the specialized business offerings that inevitably will shape how you support new, more differentiated supply chain activity?

Logistics companies such as UPS, FedEx, Maersk, DHL, and others also are in an interesting position, not completely dissimilar to the contract manufacturers. While they do not get involved with product design or bottom-up manufacturing, they increasingly are involved in the postponement and returns strategies of their customers. These strategies include outsourcing to logistics providers activities such as final assembly, kitting, private labeling and packaging, returns management, and even simple repairs or refurbishment. Clearly, logistics service providers (LSPs) compete with each other. But where do they draw the line between competing and collaborating with contract manufacturers or EMS providers who offer quite similar, often overlapping supply chain services to their customers?

Global supply chain security issues also add to LSPs operating challenges, as they must deal with increasingly stringent controls over physical movement of goods from one country to another. For example, the recent 10+2 trade regulations[2] that require shippers and carriers to provide additional information on imports to the United States has forced companies to quickly assess how they will collect this data and how they will orchestrate it with other shipment data. If you are the CIO of an LSP or an importing manufacturer or retailer, how do you respond?

This all points to the fact that competition in today's supply chains is becoming increasingly granular and fluid. In a *Harvard Business Review* article, the authors[3] discussed the need for companies to "micro market"—getting much more granular in their selling strategies in order to uncover growth segments (albeit smaller segments, by definition). More recently, others have argued that it is time to "rethink marketing" and get much more customer centric.[4] Among other things, they highlight the growing need to make better use of technologies like CRM (customer relationship management) and Business Intelligence to support this trend. Almost of necessity, this will affect supply chain strategy, both on the planning and the execution side.

From an IT perspective, then, CIOs must be ready to support and enable "micro" business collaboration networks, each with its own rules of operation, service levels, integration and collaboration requirements, and application needs. This creates a whole new dimension of volatility management as these supply chain permutations multiply in order to create competitive distinction.

The Processes: Multi-Enterprise and Market-Specific

The Supply Chain Operations Reference (SCOR) model has become a sort of de facto standard way to describe supply chain processes and their associated inputs, outputs, and metrics. It was initially developed by AMR Research and the consultancy PRTM, along with a consortium of member companies, in response to growing demands for consistent benchmarks of supply chain practices. It is now maintained by the Supply Chain Council, a not-for-profit organization.

What the SCOR model calls "Source" is often referred to as the "procure-to-pay" process. Similarly, "Deliver" is often referred to as the "order-to-cash" process. But one of the key things that this model highlights is the concept that the five core supply chain processes—Plan, Source, Make, Deliver, Return—are inherently *multi-enterprise* processes. One company's Source process links to another's Deliver process. Returns to supplier and customer returns are likewise joined at the hip. Even the Make process involves linkages to multiple companies when outsourced manufacturing, final assembly, or kitting and repairs are concerned.

Like other standards, the SCOR model has gone a long way in helping manufacturers and supply chain participants use a common language to describe not only their internal processes, but also the boundaries of external processes as well. But it also has exposed the inherent complexities of trying to manage multi-enterprise processes. Oh for the good old days when materials requirements planning (MRP) systems[5] first debuted, and companies' chief concern was how to eliminate work-in-process inventory within the cozy four walls of their own plants!

These five basic SCOR processes have significant variability by industry sector, by geographic

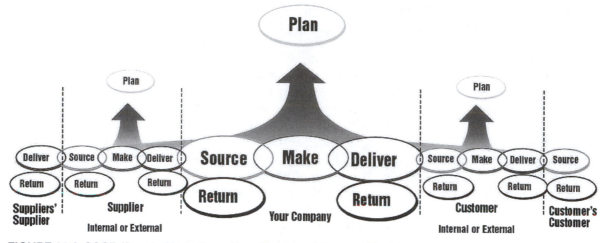

FIGURE 11.2 SCOR (Supply Chain Operations Reference) Process Model.

Source: The Supply Chain Council, 2009

market served, and by the very nature of the products being bought and sold. For example, in the high-tech industry, new product introductions are frequent, product obsolescence often is very rapid, and products are highly complex and require configuration based upon specific customer requirements. Contrast this with the food and beverage sector where, though new product introductions may be more frequent and numerous, the products themselves are much simpler and involve fewer tiers in the supply chain.

Nevertheless, there can be significant complexity in terms of seasonality of demand, special packaging and private labeling, variability of supply, and special logistics requirements such as refrigeration. This creates unique requirements for the information systems that must manage these variants of the basic SCOR-level processes of Plan, Source, Make, Deliver, and Return.

The theme we keep coming back to, therefore, is the fact that not only are these processes highly complex and individualized, but they are seldom *static*. This turbulence in processes leads us to our next topic of discussion: the kinds of information systems and infrastructure that are needed to support the highly volatile mix of players, processes, and market dynamics.

The Systems: Diversity Reigns

Now we turn to the systems—the "cyber" component of the supply chain. If we consider together the players, the processes, and the systems, what we often find in manufacturers is something like the diagram in Figure 11.3.

In truth, this diagram vastly understates the complexities of the underlying systems needed to support the supply chain. The reality is that individual companies often operate with multiple enterprise resource planning (ERP) systems from different vendors, or, at the very least, multiple instances of a single ERP solution dispersed globally. Additionally, organizations rely on one or more best of breed (BoB) software vendors for functions such as supply chain network design, demand forecasting, supply chain planning, and production scheduling. One business unit may have its own custom product lifecycle management tool, whereas other business units may use best-of-breed or ERP capabilities to manage their products. Shop floor and manufacturing execution systems (MES) are likely to vary from plant to plant to accommodate the unique requirements of any given production environment. And, of course, there is the pervasive use of spreadsheets to manage "stuff in the middle"—pulling data from multiple sources, manually manipulating them and then using the results to make decisions or report performance.

All of this information-related complexity is exacerbated by mergers, acquisitions, spin offs, and other business ventures that continuously shuffle the deck for companies. Each new venture brings with it a new set of systems and processes that must eventually be aligned with those of the original enterprise. Thus, even for companies whose intent is to standardize on a single ERP system, the

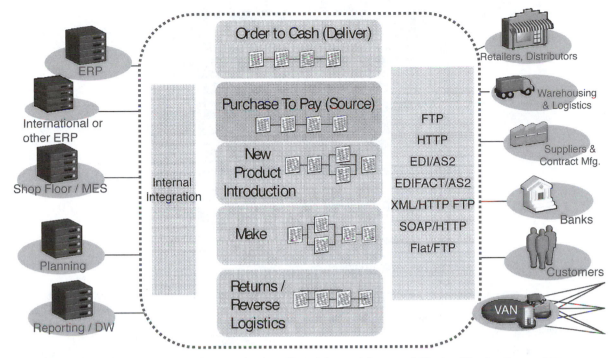

FIGURE 11.3 Typical IT, business process, and trading partner environment. Each of the trading partners described in the Business Collaboration Network section are involved in executing supply chain processes such as order-to-cash or purchase-to-pay. In most cases, a wide array of IT systems such as enterprise resource planning, supply chain planning, etc. is required to enable an end-to-end process such as order to cash.

Source: Sterling Commerce, 2010.

reality of mergers, acquisitions, and new ventures pushes the realization of this goal indefinitely into the future.

To manage the complexity and volatility of these IT systems, companies have deployed, or are considering deploying, a whole cadre of technology solutions that can loosely fall under the umbrella of Business Intelligence (BI). These solutions include:

- Data warehouses
- BI analytics and performance reporting
- Operational BI
- Simulation
- Supply chain visibility, business activity monitoring, and complex event processing.

These systems collect and store in one place various transactional data that flow through a wide range of ERP, CRM, and other systems, including such data as customer orders, shipments, and inventory movements. Their power lies in their ability to "slice and dice" data in a myriad of ways to support analyses of performance and patterns of supply chain behavior.

As supply chains grow more complex, and as process improvements from the so-called "low hanging fruit" become more difficult to identify, these BI tools have continued to advance to provide more real-time, and even predictive, views of supply chain performance (e.g., the so-called operational BI). Their role spans upfront network design to real-time monitoring and alerting to after-the-fact tools for root cause analysis and process improvement. It is rapidly becoming insufficient to report simply on "how did we do?" Organizations also must be capable of assessing "why did we get the results we did?" through tools such as these which help uncover patterns of either desirable or undesirable activity.

For an enterprise to operate at optimum effectiveness, all of these information technologies

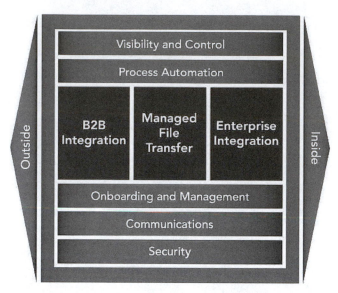

FIGURE 11.4 Core capabilities of an integration platform. This figure depicts the integration platform that underpins corporate IT.

Source: Sterling Commerce, 2010.

must be able to communicate with one another. This requires an integration platform that is the underpinning of all of the lines of communication indicated in Figure 11.4.

Fundamentally, this platform consists of three capabilities: business-to-business (B2B) integration, managed file transfer, and enterprise integration. Collectively, these capabilities enable a company to seamlessly and securely collaborate both internally with various business units and systems and externally with the gamut of trading partners with whom the company transacts business.

Enterprise integration runs the gamut from connecting major applications together, such as ERP customer relationship management (CRM), and various supply chain management applications, to tying together various home-grown systems that have arisen over time to meet very specific needs of the business (or, in many cases, as stop-gap solutions to pressing problems that could not easily be resolved using commercial off-the-shelf software). Too, there is the ubiquitous use of spreadsheets that pull data down from the system of record, and in some cases, feed transactional data back to these same systems.

The integration of all these disparate information systems among external business trading partners—i.e., B2B integration—is all about engaging in electronic commerce with customers, suppliers, contract manufacturers, logistics providers, customs agents, and other entities. Electronic Data Interchange (EDI)[6] has been the de facto standard for how companies have collaborated to simplify and standardize the way they conduct business, but dozens of other standards like RosettaNet, Odette, and CIDX have popped up to deal with the industry-specific needs of high-tech, automotive, and chemical manufacturers, just to cite a few examples. There is a certain irony to the term "standard" in this context, as the inherent differences and ongoing volatility in business requirements have made it quite difficult for companies to keep pace with the rate of change in the technology needed.

Managed file transfer sits in between the internal and external integration technologies as a vehicle to ensure secure movement of data of all kinds, whether they are transactional data, customer proprietary data, or company intellectual property. This could include files ranging from spreadsheets used to summarize intermediate production or financial results to large CAD/CAM (computer aided design/computer aided manufacturing) files to sensitive customer master data.

Operations—Managing Cyber Supply Chain for Volatility

As we talk about volatility and upheaval in today's supply chains, it is perhaps helpful to distinguish between two distinct types of supply chain complexity: competitive and differentiating complexity vs. non-value added, or even value-destroying, complexity. Clearly, your objective should be to exploit the first, and minimize the second form of complexity.

Demand-Side Complexity in the Cyber Supply Chain

On the demand side of the business equation, a multitude of factors drive complexity in forecasting demand as well as in quoting and booking customer orders.

First, most large manufacturers—even those that sell primarily commodity products—sell to numerous distinct market segments. These segments may be based on the industry sectors they serve, as in high tech, where EMS providers like Flextronics and Jabil serve OEMs in consumer electronics, telecommunications and enterprise computing, medical devices and automotive. Or, companies may segment their market based on the type of customer—e.g., distributor, retailer, and end consumer. In each case, the manufacturer's goal is to provide differentiated treatment to its customers according to their unique needs and value.

For many companies, complexity drives such frequency and breadth of change in business requirements that IT organizations find it extremely difficult to respond quickly or cost effectively enough. The result is that business users must either limit the degree to which they support differentiated supply chain responses to different customer segments, or employ various inefficient workarounds based on their existing IT capabilities.

Additionally, companies often lack the sophisticated analytical tools and end-to-end business process integration platforms that enable the collection of factual information on customer buying behavior. As a result, their knowledge of customer buying patterns may be anecdotal and inaccurate. This makes it extremely difficult for organizations to perform true root cause analysis when customer or business issues arise. Lack of data in a readily consumable format, for example, frequently slows down Six Sigma teams. And when companies do not have the data, they either "fudge" a bit in their analyses, spend lots of time manually collecting data, or confine themselves to only those areas where data readily exist. None of these options is optimal.

More Sales Channels

Another source of demand complexity is the variety of sales channels open to customers. In 1980, if you wanted to buy a new car, perhaps you first went to the bookstore to purchase a paper copy of the

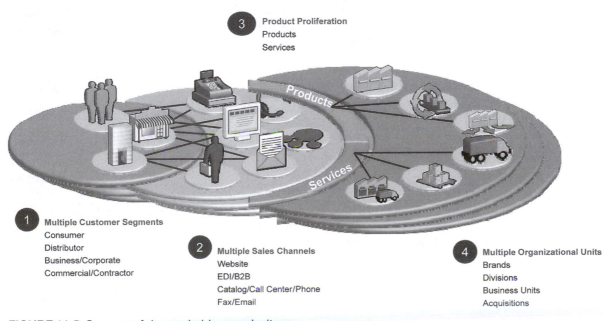

FIGURE 11.5 Sources of demand-side complexity.

Source: Sterling Commerce, 2010.

latest consumer reports that rated that year's models. Then you called and eventually visited various dealers in your area to test drive cars and negotiate a price. You either took what the dealer had on its lot, or you waited weeks for them to get in stock the model you wanted with all of the options you wanted.

Today? With the exception of test driving, you can do all of your car shopping online if you so choose (though filling out that nasty paperwork seems to be a relic of the past that just won't go away). You can view any dealer's inventory, configure your car online, obtain price quotes, etc. And options? If someone in 1980 told you that you could have a handheld device called a mobile phone that could connect to the speakers in your car via something called Bluetooth, a GPS device that would keep you from driving around in circles to find your destination, and a car that could actually park itself—the latter accomplished via voice activation —you would have laughed at them.

The ability of a consumer to order something online, have it shipped directly to them, then return the item to the retail store if they so choose, is a major new phenomenon reshaping traditional buying channels. This kind of cross-channel selling is rapidly becoming the norm in many retail businesses.

The good news from the customer's perspective is that they get things any way they want them, delivered to them via the mode of their choosing, and paid for in a variety of ways. But for the retailer and the manufacturer, it can be quite difficult to have a single view of the customer and what they have ordered, and even more difficult to coordinate replenishment and understand inventory positions. There is also the challenge of effectively coordinating promotions and rebates across these diverse, multi-tiered selling channels.

Proliferation of SKUs

Manufacturers are constantly trying to simplify their list of active end items (SKUs). Try as they might though, mandates for growth as well as region-specific requirements require frequent new product introductions. Products have become increasingly feature-rich in order to satisfy evolving customer demands. This means that, for many companies, SKU proliferation and greater product complexity is a way of life.

Several challenges arise from this product proliferation and increased product complexity. First, even for relatively straightforward products, it can be a nightmare to synchronize catalogs and product information—e.g., pricing changes, special offers, engineering changes—quickly and accurately across all of the channels the company supports when the rate of new product introduction is high. Furthermore, this complexity increase is multiplicative, a function of new products, channels, and customer segments, as different pricing, configuration, and availability regimens may apply.

Rise of Customer Self-Service

More and more companies are pushing customers to do self-service ordering and configuring in an effort to reduce costs while at the same time improving the customer experience. This creates a challenge that affects IT as well as the lines of business around the issue of efficient and accurate configuration of complex products. Not all options are available or suitable for any given product, and the valid options may not always interact in a completely straightforward way. Even when orders are configured by internal sales people or customer service representatives (CSRs), there is the real potential for creating invalid configurations, priced incorrectly. So the trick is for IT to offer systems that smoothly guide the process along, all the while using intelligent configuration engines that make configuration mistakes unlikely—the Japanese "poka-yoke" principle[7] as applied to order taking!

Organizational Complexity

The final area of complexity we will address on the selling side is that of the organizational structure itself. For companies that operate as holding companies or conglomerates of completely unrelated businesses and products, this is not a big issue. It is mostly a financial consolidation issue. But, for companies that have multiple business units that sell to an overlapping customer base, and especially where customers might routinely place orders that call for line items sourced from different business units, the challenge can be substantial. Here the Holy Grail is to present a single face to the customer, where the customer is largely unaware of the underlying organizational structure that is required to support cross-organizational sales execution.

Supply-Side Complexity in the Cyber Supply Chain

Just as the demand side of supply chains is confronted with complexity as a result of volatile demand, rapidly changing product offerings, and channel complexity, the supply side has its own set of complications. As depicted in Figure 11.6, these complexities can include multiple sourcing options, multiple fulfillment channels, and multiple return and aftermarket channels.

As we discussed earlier, the amount of outsourcing of manufacturing and logistics that occurs today has profoundly changed the ways companies fulfill demand. Just look at the Boeing Dreamliner and the problems Boeing has experienced in bringing this innovative new plane to market. The supplier collaboration network established by Boeing with subassembly and component manufacturers is in many ways quite innovative. But this innovation has come at a steep price: a two-year delay in time-to-market.

Granted, there are few manufacturers whose products are as complex as Boeing's. Nevertheless, most manufacturers experience the same types of difficulties in achieving effective collaboration with their suppliers, contract manufacturers, and other third-party providers. And the issues vary depending on where you sit relative to others in the value chain. In some cases, customers simply won't share information such as forecasts and inventory positions at the level of detail or frequency you would like. The resulting uncertainty or lack of knowledge ultimately cascades and intensifies upstream in the supply chain as you hedge your bets in terms of supply/demand balancing.

And finally, the returns process has grown more complex as a result of two factors: increased product complexity, which results in greater repair operations complexity, and environmental "take-back" regulations, which necessitate cradle-to-grave product and component stewardship. Add the

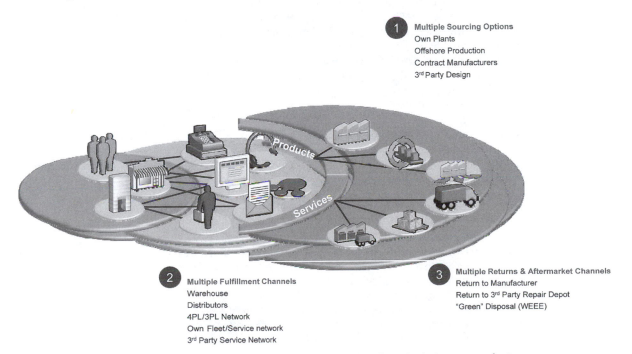

1 Multiple Sourcing Options
Own Plants
Offshore Production
Contract Manufacturers
3rd Party Design

2 Multiple Fulfillment Channels
Warehouse
Distributors
4PL/3PL Network
Own Fleet/Service network
3rd Party Service Network

3 Multiple Returns & Aftermarket Channels
Return to Manufacturer
Return to 3rd Party Repair Depot
"Green" Disposal (WEEE)

FIGURE 11.6 Supply-side complexity. This complexity reflects the diversity in how manufacturers source products, the various routes to market they choose to employ, and how they (and who) will manage returns.

Source: Sterling Commerce, 2010.

fact that returns/repair management in many cases is handled by a third party on your behalf, and you have a recipe for complexity as well as volatility as the rules of the game change.

Given business realities, attempting to eliminate all chaos in the supply chain seems a fool's errand. More realistically, success is about managing the risks that arise from business chaos and constantly morphing operational complexity. We find it helpful to think about this whole issue along two lines: first, How mature is your process? and second, How mature are your IT systems that enable that process?

Take order fulfillment. Maturity in this process is reflected by how well the lines of business responsible for order fulfillment have defined, deployed, and measured what needs to occur to accurately capture an order on the front end, and get it shipped, delivered, and invoiced on the back end. Maturity in the second area—IT support—is reflected in the extent to which your IT organization has made it easy for the lines of business to achieve their mission of delivering the perfect order. If users have to do a lot of manual tasks, and "integrate" with others via email, faxes, or spreadsheets, then there is certainly room for improvement.

The central point here is to get IT and the lines of business in sync about how to achieve the perfect order. Immature systems and processes ultimately lack the ability to effectively respond to volatility in the external supply chain. Why is this so? If processes lack standardization or some unifying framework like the SCOR model, then it is difficult to mount a coherent response to changing requirements. Similarly, inchoate or highly fragmented systems create an environment that is inherently slow to adapt to rapid change in the business.

Notes

1 Charles Handy, born 1932, is an Irish author/philosopher specializing in organizational behavior and management. The so-called "Shamrock Organization" is one in which professional core workers, freelance workers and part-time/temporary routine workers each form one leaf of a three-leaved "shamrock."

2 On January 26, 2009, the new rule titled Importer Security Filing and Additional Carrier Requirements (commonly known as "10+2") went into effect. This new rule applies to import cargo arriving to the United States by vessel. Failure to comply with the new rule could ultimately result in monetary penalties, increased inspections, and delay of cargo. The information submitted in Importer Security Filings improves U.S. Customs and Border Protection's (CBP) ability to identify high-risk shipments in order to prevent smuggling and ensure cargo safety and security. What is an Importer Security Filing? Under the new rule, before merchandise arriving by vessel can be imported into the United States, the "Importer Security Filing (ISF) Importer," or their agent (e.g., licensed customs broker), must electronically submit certain advance cargo information to CBP in the form of an Importer Security Filing. This requirement only applies to cargo arriving in the United States by ocean vessel; it does not apply to cargo arriving by other modes of transportation.

3 Mehrdad Baghai, Sven Smit, and Patrick Viguerie, "Is Your Growth Strategy Flying Blind," *Harvard Business Review*, May 1, 2009.

4 Roland T. Rust, Christine Moorman, and Gaurav Bhalla, "Rethinking Marketing," *Harvard Business Review*, January–February 2010.

5 Materials Requirement Planning (MRP) systems are information systems that determine what assemblies must be built and what materials must be procured in order to build a unit of equipment by a certain date. MRP applications query the bill of materials and inventory *databases* to derive the necessary elements.

6 Electronic Data Interchange is defined as the electronic transfer of business transactions such as orders, invoices, advanced ship notices, and inventory positions using standard data formats. These transactions may be routed through a Value Added Network, or VAN, or sent from company to company via the Internet.

7 *Poka-yoke* is a Japanese term that means "fail-safing" or "mistake-proofing." A poka-yoke is any mechanism in a lean manufacturing process that helps an equipment operator avoid (*yokeru*) mistakes (*poka*). Its purpose is to eliminate product defects by preventing, correcting, or drawing attention to human errors as they occur. The concept was formalized, and the term adopted, by Shigeo Shingo as part of the Toyota Production System. It was originally described as *baka-yoke*, but as this means "fool-proofing" (or "idiot-proofing") the name was changed to the milder *poka-yoke*. More broadly, the term can refer to any behavior-shaping constraint designed into a product to prevent incorrect operation by the user (www.wikipedia.com).

twelve
Managing Risk-Tolerant Cyber Supply Chain Communities

Richard M. Douglass

In managing cyber supply chains, it is critical that platforms and networks are designed to accommodate volatility in an ongoing, ever-changing manner. As such, cyber supply chain networks must be as flexible as their physical or financial counterparts—able to adapt and respond to events that are within normal tolerances, and to those that are outside of normal tolerances.

To this end, we see four key cyber-chain imperatives for manufacturers and other supply chain participants to minimize the downside of supply chain volatility and maximize the upside:

- Provide a global integration platform for dynamic business collaboration networks
- Deploy an integrated supply chain visibility and business intelligence platform
- Create global trade and order management hubs
- Streamline and automate multi-tiered, cross-channel selling.

Provide a Global Platform for Dynamic Business Collaboration Networks

From the perspective of the IT organization, the complexity of the trading partner networks, or business collaboration networks, manifests itself in the difficulty of automating such critical multi-enterprise processes as order-to-cash, procure-to-pay, and returns. A variety of trading partners can be involved across processes and touching different departments within a manufacturing or logistics organization. The most commonly identified trading partners are suppliers and customers. Other trading partners include transportation companies, engineering firms, contract manufacturers, customs agents, dealer networks, distributors, etc. The ability to collect and share real-time information like order status, shipment information, and inventory information directly affects how well an entire supply chain performs and meets customer expectations. Figure 12.1 gives you a sense of the magnitude of the challenge.

The number of trading partners supported on B2B networks has increased dramatically. And this typically reflects just those that the IT group has been able to "onboard," that is, connect with via some sort of transaction exchange mechanism such as electronic data interchange (EDI)—which is generally the tip of the iceberg when it comes to the full number of trading partners that exist for a given company.

Similarly, the communications protocols and standards themselves have proliferated, with numerous variants of EDI, such as RosettaNet (High Tech), CIDX (Chemicals), PIDX (Petroleum), and GUSI (Consumer Goods), just to name a few. Just as ERP and other applications have multiplied in most organizations due to ongoing acquisitions and business ventures, so has the number of

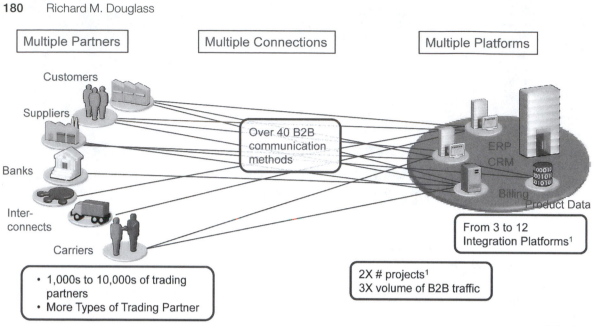

FIGURE 12.1 Increasing complexity in underlying IT platforms. Underlying IT platforms have become increasingly complex.

Source: Sterling Commerce and Gartner, 2009.

integration platforms. As a result, most IT groups are unable to ever quite catch up so that they may standardize.

Ask yourself if the following (fictitious) quote reflects something of the situation you face in your organization:

> We currently have too many groups and platforms doing integration, which is costly, inefficient, and slows down our response to the lines of business. Our company has gone through or is likely to go through a number of acquisitions or new business ventures that makes it imperative for us to have a common integration platform that will simplify and quicken our ability to meet the shifting needs of our business.
>
> Although ERP has given us a standardized approach for major supply chain processes, the reality is that we have multiple supply chains, multiple trading partner communities and multiple scenarios for how we must interact with customers and trading partners. We need a business process platform that makes it relatively straightforward to adapt our standard ERP process flows to the real world.

In fact, when asked what their top challenges were with their current business integration capabilities, a survey of manufacturing executives identified the existence of multiple integration tools and platforms at the top of their list, as shown in Figure 12.2.[1]

In the absence of a comprehensive business integration platform, many key processes and practices are accomplished through varying combinations of manual processes and point products, and through various manual communication media such as fax and email. These multiple, non-standardized, and unconnected operating platforms only impede a company's ability to respond to change.

Best Practice: Rationalize Platforms

This leads us to the first of our suggested best practices to help eliminate waste in business collaboration networks: rationalize your B2B platforms and the integration tools that run on them. The "integration pipeline" of information that spans today's supply chain systems is more critical than ever

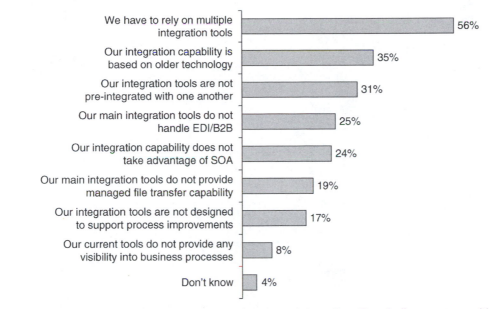

"Which of the following issues limits the effectiveness of your current integration capability? Check all that apply." (n = 260)

FIGURE 12.2 Current constraints to effectiveness of business integration. Top challenges were with their current business integration capabilities.

Source: Forrester Consulting on behalf of Sterling Commerce, 2009.

before given the length and multiplicity of global supply chains today. Integration provides end-to-end visibility in the supply chain that is crucial to managing volatility and risk. Figure 12.3 illustrates a rationalized, integrated business process.

Rationalization and integration of B2B platforms is no easy task. Even standard processes in an ERP system pose challenges to organizations which may come up short in their ability to integrate required supply chain elements. The agility of these systems with regard to integration is debatable as they work to create the needed solutions and connectivity to incorporate all of the supply chain elements.

The importance of this best practice is amplified when companies have engaged in ongoing, substantial merger and acquisition (M&A) activity. A company can tackle the M&A challenge in one of two ways. In one case, it may allow that organization to operate as a largely standalone entity, whereby the parent acts largely as a holding company. More common, though, is where the operations of the acquired company are to be folded in with those of the acquiring company. While this may be a fairly infrequent source of volatility (say, as compared with demand volatility), its effects can be quite far reaching. It affects personnel, procedures, facilities and, of course, systems. It is in the latter case where a common integration platform has proven to yield substantial savings in the time and effort to align cross-organizational processes.

As an example, an automobile parts and accessories manufacturer consolidated integration platforms resulting in accelerated integration of new acquisitions and trading partners. Related benefits included an 81 percent return on investment (ROI) with a one-year payback, reduction in manual processes, and reduced IT costs.

In another instance, a consumer goods manufacturer needed to streamline connectivity with its small to mid-sized trading partners, as a high number of them were not EDI-enabled and still relied on fax and phone communication of orders. The business benefits resulting from this project included improved customer service, enhanced order accuracy, and the ability to eliminate manual processes.

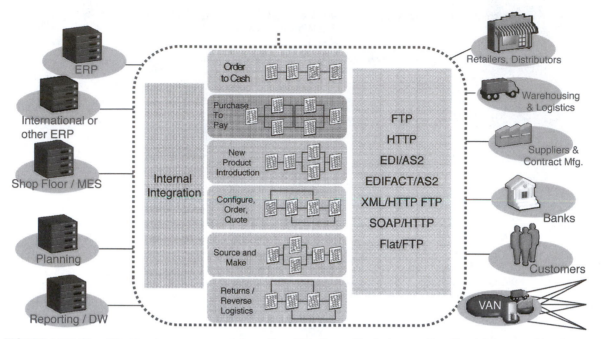

FIGURE 12.3 Simplified business process integration. This figure illustrates a rationalized, integrated business process.

Source: Sterling Commerce, 2009.

A leading hardware distributor outsourced its B2B operations to meet the demand for growing volumes of electronic B2B collaboration and achieve real-time, end-to-end visibility and control over processes shared with customers and business partners. This resulted in lower costs, quicker B2B connectivity with trading partners, and improved customer satisfaction.

To be successful, rationalization and integration of cyber supply chain infrastructure needs to be thought of in terms of more effective supply chain network collaboration, not simply as an IT project. For the external supply chain, an organization's ability to accept various integration protocols from both suppliers and customers creates a positive value perception. This flexibility and the lack of a need to "impose" requirements on trading partners translate into being "easy to do business with," which can drive dollars to the bottom line. In today's economic climate, this is a highly valued capability.

For the internal supply chain, integration brings visibility. For example, an outbound planner (logistics or transportation) will have access to a real-time view of incoming orders and shipments. Effective cross-docking of inbound and outbound shipments depends on this level of visibility. Similarly, the procurement organization will have a clear picture of inbound and outbound transport. This is where the integration of platforms truly answers supply chain volatility by providing end-to-end visibility.

A comprehensive integration solution provides benefits throughout the supply chain. Forrester Research identifies a number of these potential benefits:

- Application development productivity (40 to 60 percent decrease in development time)
- Enhanced process optimization features (process simulations capable of modeling optimums)
- Faster response time to new business requests (lead time to response)
- Increased business/IT collaboration (lead time to final system/process designs)
- Real-time visibility into business processes (graphical representations of processes in operation)
- Lower support costs (reduced maintenance burden, faster, more flexible modifications)
- Increased effectiveness of staff training (training on single strategic tool set instead of many)
- Ability to support M&A activity more effectively (built-in flexibility maximizes operation time).

Streamline Partner Community Management

If the following sounds familiar, then our next suggested best practice for eliminating waste in supply chain collaboration should be helpful to you:

> We have too many exceptions as a result of manual transaction activity with customers and suppliers, driving up our costs and lowering our productivity. We cannot sense and respond quickly enough to changes in demand and/or supply due to lack of automated integration with trading partners.
>
> We have to find a better way to interact with small to mid-sized businesses (SMBs), either customers or suppliers. Our sales channels—call centers, customer service, and direct sales—incur high costs today in managing these interactions. We have to overcome the high initial cost to us in IT of automating the relationship with the SMBs, so that our supply chain can operate more efficiently.
>
> We also need a more automated and comprehensive way to onboard and manage multiple business collaboration networks that consist of various types of trading partners and customers. Currently we have a large backlog of trading partners we would like to onboard but simply cannot due to lack of capacity.

Building value-driven collaborative relationships with customers or suppliers requires that manufacturers or logistics service providers develop new approaches for interacting with them. Today, the myriad variables associated with connecting, integrating, and administering trading partners, especially SMBs, in most cases lead to higher transaction costs, errors, and delays in the supply chain. Achieving electronic connectivity with trading partners can take 45 days or more before parties ever get around to exchanging information electronically. The numerous back and forths to collect the correct information consumes a great deal of time and human capital.

By improving trading community management processes, companies can reduce supply chain process cycle times, error rates, and the ongoing costs of doing business. Simplified and self-service onboarding capabilities for new trading partners can decrease the burden on companies and result in reduced errors and lower costs.

Also, tapping system capabilities to convert fax documents to EDI/XML or EDI/XML to fax documents allows companies to electronically enable less sophisticated partners and reduce manually intensive processes, as shown in Figure 12.4.

For example, Unisource is Canada's single-source distributor of more than 80,000 paper, printing, imaging, graphic arts, packing, and maintenance supplies and equipment. Unisource needed a cost-effective and efficient way of doing EDI with its suppliers, especially SMB suppliers not proficient with EDI. They also wanted to improve their own B2B functionality because their current system no longer met their needs. By using a technology known as webforms, Unisource is able to transact business with its trading partners over the Web without requiring these partners to implement complex and comprehensive e-business programs. This technology makes it easier for partners to provide information to Unisource and only requires an internet connection and a web browser.

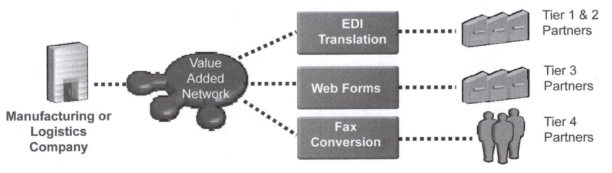

FIGURE 12.4 Hybrid approach for automating B2B commerce. This figure depicts a hybrid approach to automating B2B transactions among trading partners.

Source: Sterling Commerce, 2009.

Outsource B2B Operations

Increasingly, manufacturers and logistics providers are choosing to outsource the development and management of wholly integrated B2B systems as a cost-effective strategy. Outsourcing B2B operations enables organizations to balance the need for a competitive level of in-house expertise, while also evolving systems at the rate of technology acceleration. These companies can select an integrated software set that enables them to refine existing applications and develop new ones as needed with minimum startup time and downtime. Managed services expertise can reduce the total cost of system ownership by:

- Liberating internal IT staff to focus on strategic projects
- Accelerating automated B2B collaboration with partners
- Improving service levels internally and externally
- Gaining competitive advantage in processes, products, and markets.

David Carmichael, product marketing manager at Sterling Commerce, writing in a December 2007 issue of the *Butler Group Review*, observed the following:

> Today's B2B managed services have evolved from technology-based EDI outsourcing to include B2B integration, process visibility, business process management, and community management. This enables an organization to have a single connection to the managed services environment and leverage the economies of scale available to a B2B managed services provider. A B2B integration platform is the core technology behind a B2B managed service and includes the electronic communication medium to send and receive the data in a timely manner.
>
> However, as the focus has moved away from the provision of pure EDI to supporting supply chain and trading partners' activities to enable more effective collaboration with business partners, the B2B integration has evolved also, but it is still based on the VAN. The VAN itself has evolved to meet the needs of its customers into what is now described as integration as a service (IaaS), a collaboration network, integration on demand, or business process network, etc.
>
> For companies with several hundred or indeed thousands of trading partners (both customers and suppliers), responding to their demands and needs dramatically increases the burden for expertise in multiple time zones and languages. Not getting this right can impact customer satisfaction, increase the time required to get new products and services to market, and add significantly to the cost of doing business. Companies should expect their vendor to provide a service to reduce this burden, such as a level 1 trading partner help desk, where the vendor will take calls from all trading partners on their behalf and support them in resolving B2B trading issues.

The basic economic model for B2B operations outsourcing is quite simple, as shown in Figure 12.5.

With a managed services scenario, you derive benefits that are comparable to those described with a cloud computing scenario, whereby you eliminate fixed capital expenditures, and trade it in for a purely variable cost model. The term "cloud computing" is a generic term that refers to a variety of outsourced IT paradigms that include software as a service (SaaS), where customers have access to an application like order management "on demand"; platform as a service (PaaS), where various hardware and system software resources are made available as needed to the user; and IaaS, where a third party takes care of the so-called onboarding process for its customers, whereby B2B transaction links to the customers' trading partners are created and maintained. This is obviously appealing in very volatile economic times, as it shifts what traditionally were up-front capital investments to operational expenses that can be anticipated and budgeted for on a regularized basis.

As Dan Gilmore, editor of *Supply Chain Digest*, said:

> Cash will remain king: Just as with consumers, CEOs and CFOs will not soon forget this period, even as the economy recovers. Credit will *never again* be as easy as it was before the crash (or at least for many,

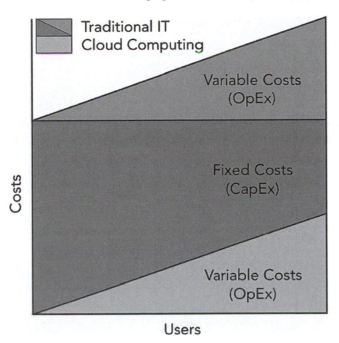

FIGURE 12.5 Economics of traditional IT vs. cloud computing. With traditional IT, companies must make a significant capital investment in IT infrastructure, in addition to incurring variable costs. With cloud computing, there is considerably less capital expenditure involved—most costs are variable costs.

Source: Sterling Commerce, 2009.

many years), and executives will have learned powerful lessons on the value of a strong balance sheet. Cash may not stay king forever, but it will be "prince" at least for a long time.

This has all sorts of ramifications: companies will start to make more supply chain investment "on-demand" software. There will be more (maybe better said—more persistent) attention paid to inventory levels. It also means that with very conservative inventory levels, the supply chain will have to be capable of sensing changes in demand and be able to respond if sales spike above expectations.[2]

There are numerous examples we can point to of outsourced B2B operations as a best practice.

Hirschvogel: Managed Services Case Study

Hirschvogel Inc. manufactures metal components for the automotive industry. The company was established in 1988 to support participation in the North American automotive market for the parent company in Denklingen, Germany. Hirschvogel Automotive Group is one of the world's top manufacturing specialists in metal forming and machining.

In 2007, Hirschvogel manually processed data to and from their ERP system, which was quite labor intensive. Therefore, when their parent company asked them to migrate to SAP as part of a global strategy, they were glad to participate. Hirschvogel had two options: the parent company could invest in additional in-house resources to manage and support B2B integration of multiple automotive standards and protocols or they could outsource the process to a third party. Hirschvogel ultimately decided to outsource its B2B information operations in 2008.

> The decision to outsource our B2B was simple because we knew the return on investment would occur instantly. The outsourcing solution was 90 percent less expensive than our in-house option.
>
> Nico Schuetz, Lead IT Technician, Hirschvogel Inc.

Now Hirschvogel manages its B2B operations by exception. By removing manual processes through the automation of document exchange with the Hirschvogel Inc. ERP system, the managed services option also improves visibility into their supply chain, which helps them better plan production processes.

Big Time Products

Big Time Products is a U.S. manufacturer of work and cleaning gloves sold at such national retailers as the Home Depot, Wal-Mart, and BJ's Wholesale Club. The company processes roughly 8,000 to 10,000 orders per month, ships orders direct-to-store within 48 hours of receipt, and guarantees 98 percent complete and on-time delivery. Like Hirschvogel, Big Time Products decided to outsource its B2B information activities. The solution provides document process management and trading partner support that monitors and manages points of failure in transaction processing, diagnosing problems, and working directly with Big Time Products' trading partners to correct them before they become business-critical, enabling the company to meet its demanding customer delivery requirements.

Protect Intellectual Property and Sensitive Data

Volatility often drives contrarian behaviors to normal security best practices. Businesses in a rush to respond to market conditions may sacrifice information security. They seek to quickly add or remove connections to supply chain partners, integrate business applications, and automate commercial interactions to reduce manual activities—all with the intent to accelerate the velocity of business.

However, security best practices dictate that there be a disciplined, rigorous process for making such changes. These best practices involve normal development practices around system design, coding, integration, testing, and production. They also entail in-depth security design and development that require certificates, tokens, credentials, and other authentication mechanisms.

However, the growth of the Internet and of e-commerce and the increasing reliance on electronic payment systems, data mining, and other information technologies have created a number of new and severe security threats by either creating new and sensitive information about the business, or making that information more widely accessible. These threats include the theft or compromise of sensitive customer data (such as credit card and Social Security numbers) as well as of companies' proprietary financial and intellectual information.

The scope of the potential threat is huge. Every day organizations share megabytes, gigabytes, or even terabytes of data with their business partners around the world using protocols such as FTP, HTTP, S-HTTP, SFTP, and FTPS. If there is no apparent service outage, security breach, or audit failure, most organizations assume these protocols are doing a secure and effective job of file transfer. Only a few years ago, a typical organization shared just a few megabytes of data a month with 10 to 20 partners. Now, it is not uncommon for a large organization to move several gigabytes of data a month to tens of thousands of trading partners.

But each of these communications protocols has serious flaws that are quietly making it harder for organizations to add trading partners, putting their confidential data at risk, and possibly violating privacy and security regulations. High-profile security breaches, such as those at TJX, ChoicePoint, and the National Institutes of Health, continue to occur despite updated industry standards such as the Payment Card Industry Data Security Standard (PCI-DSS) and U.S. government regulations (such as the Health Insurance Portability and Accountability Act of 1996 (HIPAA) Privacy Rule, which protects patients' medical records, and the Sarbanes–Oxley Act of 2002 which set new or enhanced financial management and reporting standards for all U.S. public company boards, management and public accounting firms). These regulations require organizations to safeguard their data. Companies that fail to do so risk not only fines but a loss of customer confidence, lower sales, damage to their brand, and even a reduction in their market valuation.

It is in this environment that the shortcomings of today's commonly used file transfer mechanisms are most severe. Many of the Web-based protocols used today appear to be a bargain because the software can frequently be downloaded from the Web at low or no cost. However, they have inherent risks and weaknesses. Let's take a look at the most well-known protocol—File Transfer Protocol (FTP). Although FTP is widely used, it is an inherently insecure method for transferring files over the Internet.[3] Organizations often use Virtual Private Networks (VPNs)[4] to encrypt the files being transmitted by FTP over the public Internet, thereby making the data more secure.

Another common protocol that most of us use every day, whether we are aware of it or not, is the HyperText Transfer Protocol (HTTP) that is used to send pages over the Web in response to the URLs which users enter into their Web browsers. There are other variations on these, but they all share serious and fundamental limitations that can increase security, compliance, and business risks. These limits fall into four critical areas: Scalability, security, visibility, and compliance.

Scalability refers to the ease with which protocols can accommodate adding new trading partners, and the costs of doing so. In the case of each of the protocols discussed above, none scores well in either the ease or cost categories. For example, if the organization is using these protocols over leased lines, it must buy and manage an additional leased line for each new trading partner. If the enterprise is transferring data over the public Internet, it avoids the cost of additional leased lines but now faces the security risk of sending files over a public rather than a private connection. Therefore, the organization must purchase and manage additional VPNs (Virtual Private Networks) as the number of its trading partners grows.

Security is the ability to grant access to only the information a trading partner should see, while protecting the network from any form of malicious attack. The VPNs used to secure FTP sessions, for example, can encrypt the data being transferred but cannot detect and block any files that contain viruses, worms, or other malware. Each VPN also requires the opening of a hole in the corporate firewall, which provides an avenue for hackers to penetrate internal systems. Finally, these protocols require that the data or files being transferred be stored within the "demilitarized zone," between the outside world and a company's internal servers, where that content is vulnerable to attack.

Visibility refers to the extent to which an organization can monitor data movement and the security of that data. When using VPNs and leased lines, the system administrator can only review events after they happen. This makes it more difficult for them to assure that information was sent or received as needed, to resolve transmission problems as they occur, or to quickly detect and block possible attacks.

Compliance is also a critical limit as the security and visibility shortcomings of these protocols make it more difficult and expensive to achieve and to prove regulatory compliance. In the best case scenario, this forces the organization to spend more money and devote more effort to compliance. In the worst case scenario, it exposes the organization to fines, legal action, and the loss of sales, reputation, and even stock valuation if sensitive data is compromised.

In addition, not only do these protocols impose potential risks to the company's business, but they also create additional costs that are not transparent. For example, even if the software is free or provided at a low cost, the need for additional leased lines and skilled professionals can cause the total cost of ownership to skyrocket. In fact, the actual cost of managing "free" FTP has been estimated to be as high as $500,000 per year at some organizations.

So, companies are looking for community management and integration tools that can provide speed and security, with the flexibility to handle multiple types of data with a range of different protocols. These solutions do exist, but are more readily deployed in other industries. Financial institutions have led the way adopting community management tools because of the extremely large volume and confidentiality of their data exchanges. Their business—in terms of both systems and organizational structure—is built to address data transfer security, and their survival depends on being the best at it.

Manufacturers, retailers, and logistics companies lag behind the financial sector in their cyber security efforts. They must do more in this regard to ensure the security of their global supply chain activities. Their risks in this regard are exacerbated by the level of organizational and business volatility as they engage in increasingly global trade with a fluctuating base of trading partners and end customers.

Any organization that shares information outside the perimeter of its secure network should be aware of these risks and know that another approach—*incorporating an application proxy*[5]—can deliver the security, scalability, and visibility, demanded by today's 24/7 global Web economy. An application proxy also can help the organization meet industry and government compliance regulations by providing audit trails and reports showing that they are in compliance.

Deploying an Integrated Supply Chain Visibility and Business Intelligence Platform

Given the high level of volatility that exists in supply chains today and for the foreseeable future, companies understandably want to minimize risk. On the one hand, you do not want to miss a sale due to lack of inventory or inability to meet the customer's required delivery date. On the other hand, you do not want to get stuck with inventory that may never sell, at least not at your preferred margins.

According to AMR Research,[6] there are six things companies are doing to minimize their risk in their global supply chains:

- Increase IT investment in visibility solutions
- Pursue dual/multi-sourcing strategies
- Institute performance-based contracts
- Collaborate more closely with trading partners
- Outsource manufacturing
- Outsource logistics.

Note that visibility ranks number one among these risk mitigation strategies. Furthermore, if you think about it, visibility is key to the five other risk minimization efforts as well. You need to have a clear picture of actual supplier performance, how it is trending, and what is happening at the moment. If you run a lean production line like Toyota, where deliveries are made to the plant every few hours, you want to know if a key supplier is going to be late. If you have customer performance-based contracts that specify chargebacks or other penalties if you are late, you would like to be notified of any incipient delays in the order-to-cash process, so that you have a chance of taking corrective action. Obviously you do not want to make a habit of expediting orders—you must weigh the costs of expediting against the penalties and ill will you might generate with the customer if you do not.

The other three priorities—collaboration, outsourced manufacturing, and outsourced logistics—simply point out what we have said already. Namely, today's supply chain processes are inherently multi-enterprise, and if you are on the hook for performance to your customer, you can't beg forgiveness if your contract manufacturer or logistics provider did not come through.

Now, at some level, the whole push to achieve greater visibility is not new at all. But the requirements, and the technologies, have matured and gotten much more granular over the years. As Figure 12.6 shows, most companies have fairly decent internal visibility, largely as the result of having ERP in place. However, it is in the external visibility arena where companies often come up short.

The reasons are not hard to understand. A typical order-to-cash process these days involves an OEM, a contract manufacturer, a logistics provider, a distributor or VAR (Value Added Reseller), and, of course, the end customer. Manufacturers often experience "black holes" when it comes to knowing where their shipments are with a logistics service provider (LSP). It is not that LSPs—at least the major ones—do not have their own visibility tools. But usually you, as the customer, have to sign in to their system via the Web, and look for a specific order of yours. This is impractical if you are shipping hundreds if not thousands of orders per day. You need to be proactively *informed* of exceptions, not have to go looking for them.

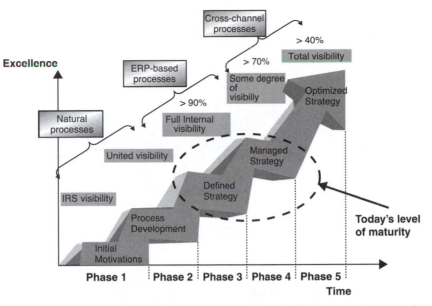

FIGURE 12.6 Maturity model for supply chain visibility. As this figure indicates, most companies have fairly decent internal visibility, largely as the result of having ERP in place.

Source: Manufacturing Insights, an IDC company.

So, the basic problem then is to answer the question, "Where is Waldo?" You remember the puzzle, where an otherwise easy-to-spot guy with overly large spectacles and a bright red and white striped hat and shirt is in fact very difficult to find when surrounded by equally distracting people and goings on. The visibility challenge in today's volatile supply chains is to find a way to filter out the noise that surrounds the events and processes you really care about.

Solving the Problem: Connecting Internally and Externally for End-to-End Process Integration

The general solution to this problem comes in three stages. First, you have to connect the disparate pieces of the supply chain puzzle together. As shown in Figure 12.7, there are the internal systems that must be connected; and there are the connections to external trading partners who participate in your process, be it procure-to-pay, order-to-cash, or returns.

Though ERP applications have done a lot over the years to consolidate and integrate related functions, the reality is that every large enterprise has a plethora of systems that have risen up—including multiple ERP systems—to support special processes, regional requirements, business unit requirements, etc. Many so-called best of breed (BoB) applications such as product lifecycle management, customer relationship management, demand and supply chain planning, transportation management, and warehouse management exist to augment what ERP or similar monolithic systems try to do. And few of these systems are truly independent, standalone solutions to a given process. As a result, an entire class of technology solutions known as enterprise integration has arisen to deal with this situation.

Enterprise integration provides the tools that secure data and processes; provide visibility into data to generate actionable information; enable process design and interface mapping across disparate environments; and manage large file transfers securely and reliably. Quite frankly, this class of technology enablers is far removed from the strategic or even day-to-day concerns of top executives in the supply chain. And yet, it is this kind of "plumbing" that helps to make businesses more nimble and more cost competitive in the market. It is the CIO's job, along with the chief technology architect, to ensure that these foundational technologies are in place, despite the fact that the lines of business just consider this a sort of "black box"—they put things in, and they expect certain things to come out the other side, reliably, quickly.

The other aspect of connecting to achieve end-to-end visibility is to enable B2B integration with

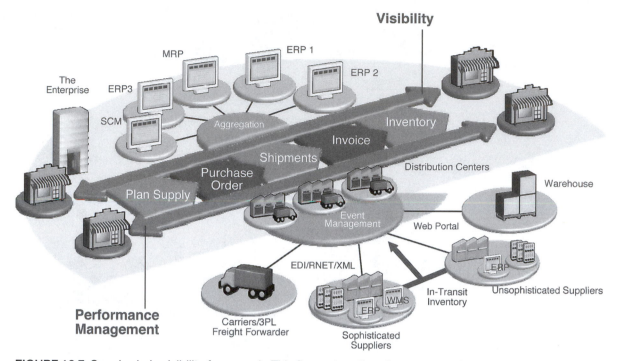

FIGURE 12.7 Supply chain visibility framework. This figure describes the systems, the parties, and the processes involved in supply chain visibility.

Source: Sterling Commerce.

the various trading partners. The most common form of integration technology is EDI (Electronic Data Interchange), whose demise is regularly predicted, but which keeps on humming away supporting billions if not trillions of dollars of commercial activity every year. We went into this capability in much greater depth in the previous section on eliminating waste in supply chain collaboration.

Suffice it to say that without enterprise integration and B2B integration, you simply cannot have an effective multi-enterprise supply chain visibility solution. In the absence of this level of integration, you have people constantly milling about, making calls, updating spreadsheets, all in a frantic effort to keep up with the flow of events and to avoid a serious disruption.

Communicate Inventory and Supply Chain Activity in Real Time

Once you have established the proper internal and external connections, you can do a number of things much more efficiently and accurately. For example, if you are a retailer and a customer comes to your store and is unable to find the item they are looking for, instead of sending them away, you can do an online check of inventory at other stores. For that matter, customers themselves can go on the Internet to see exactly what is available, where, and when they can get it. ATP, or available to promise, is straightforward to calculate, but impossible to do accurately unless you have a complete, global view of your inventory.

When an order is properly booked, supply chain visibility technologies kick in to earn their keep. They go by various names such as supply chain event management and business activity monitoring, but the gist of what they do is the same. You first establish what points or activities in the process you wish to monitor, such as when an ASN (advance ship notice) is sent, when a shipment has cleared customs, when the shipment actually is delivered to the customer's dock, and so on. You then define the conditions under which you wish someone in your organization—or trading partner, for that matter—to be notified should something be late. What often happens is that you want the technology to look for "missed events"—events that should have happened by a particular time, but did not.

This is the reverse of workflow technology, where you do not allow a process to proceed unless a previous step is completed. The goal of supply chain visibility technology is to define what *should be happening* at any given point in time, whereas workflow defines what is *allowed to happen* at any point in time. By its very nature, supply chain visibility technology is exception driven. And most organizations have plenty of exceptions. What supply chain visibility technology does, then, is make these exceptions more readily manageable.

Supply chain visibility technology also gives you clear performance reporting on how the process ultimately fared, such as in Figure 12.8.

Collaborate to Resolve Disruptions and Improve Processes

When you give a kid a new toy, he or she just can't seem to help playing with it in ways you never imagined. For visibility tools to be most effective, you have to give some serious thought as to what you really need to monitor. Otherwise, you can bury yourself in data and, worse, in alerts for which no action is really required, or possible. We can split this information deluge into three categories of data: data about critical events that require intervention should they not happen as planned; data that would likely be useful for subsequent root cause analysis and process improvement; and noise.

Critical event data would include such events as ASN timing. For example, if you do not send the ASN to your customer within a certain window of the expected delivery time, you are subject to a penalty. For such events you need to establish alerts within the supply chain visibility tool, and who will be alerted. This last point is not trivial. Depending on the severity of the issue, you may need to alert several people, across multiple organizations—or you just need to alert Joe in the warehouse. The point is that all such tools must be backed up with proper collaboration procedures, to establish some level of standard for remediation of the problem. You do not want multiple individuals to initiate contradictory responses to an exception.

Distinguishing between potential root cause data and noise before the fact seems somewhat oxymoronic, doesn't it? But the simple fact is that you need to make some intelligent guesses based on experience as to what data represent key indicators of process outcomes. If, for example, you measure a perfect order as one that is delivered on time, in full, and without defect, then what might be the contributing factors to substandard performance? If your on time performance is 93 percent, but your target is 97 percent, what contributes to delayed deliveries? If the item being shipped zips off the production line at the rate of one per minute, then it probably does not make a lot of sense to

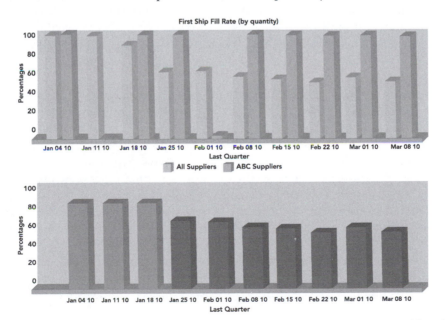

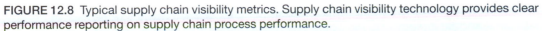

FIGURE 12.8 Typical supply chain visibility metrics. Supply chain visibility technology provides clear performance reporting on supply chain process performance.

Source: Sterling Commerce.

monitor and alert on the production process itself (at least as it relates to a particular customer order). If the item is manufactured in Taiwan and transported by ship to the United States, you probably do not need real-time monitoring there, either.

The great thing about these tools is that your decisions about what to monitor and with what frequency are not set in stone. In most, assuming you have the basic connections talked about earlier, you can change the alerts and change the data that are captured and stored. Other technologies like operational intelligence and complex event processing are providing additional, more robust abilities to identify patterns in data and even create predictive models about likely outcomes given in-the-moment supply chain activity data.

Meet Government Requirements like U.S. Customs (10+2)

Let's look at one very specific situation where visibility solutions can mitigate the risk of volatile supply chains. The U.S. government has always had a role in international customs trade compliance to minimize the security risks of imports into this country. As the global supply chain has prospered over the years, the compliance challenges also have grown, but with the tragedy of 9/11 the risk in global transportation has put everyone on alert, whether moving passengers or freight, to design deterrents to terrorist acts. This has meant a tightening of the physical network with increasing screenings for both passengers (a very large percentage) and cargo (a very small percentage).

Along with these physical screenings, data integration management to identify sources and establish a solid chain of custody across that global supply chain is being demanded by U.S. Customs and Border Protection (CBP) with rules like the Importer Security Filing, otherwise known as "10+2" for the additional 12 pieces of data required by the law, to take full effect on January 26, 2010. There will be 10 data points that must be submitted from the importer of record 24 hours prior to ship departure and 2 data points from the carrier no later the 48 hours after departure from the foreign port of origin. All ISF filings are to be done electronically via vessel Automated Manifest System (AMS) or the Automated Broker Interface (ABI). There will be no paper forms allowed.

As an example, a manufacturer or retailer that is the actual end purchaser of the product also is now the importer of record and has complete responsibility to comply with the "10+2" requirements regardless of who is doing the actual work. Do they have tight control over the chain of custody? Much of this physical chain is the responsibility of other organizations (LSPs, freight forwarders, non-vessel operating common carriers (NVOCCs), customs brokers, carriers, etc.). It is likely that the retailer or manufacturer outsourced the international aspects of its global supply to experts, such as an LSP, which considers this work its core competency. The LSP does not normally own the product. It simply provides a contracted service to manage the complexity of the supply chain partnerships and physical handoffs.

Does your company have the needed visibility or data to comply with the new 10+2 rule? Many research surveys indicate that a majority do not. Non-compliance could mean:

- **Missed shipments creating product delays:** If information is suspicious or incomplete, the U.S. government can dictate that a shipment not proceed at the foreign point of origin.
- **Financial repercussions:** While currently in a test phase that waives any penalties for shippers, the law will impose serious financial penalties when fully enacted.
- **Loss of trusted partners:** Partners in the supply chain (suppliers, carriers, forwarders, etc.) may decide not to risk their business with a company that is not seen in a positive light by the CBP.
- **Loss of customers:** No product to sell, no customer, no business.
- **The law applies to all:** At this time, the requirements apply to everybody unilaterally meaning that companies that have worked hard to be trusted shippers in the eyes of the CBP as members of the Customs–Trade Partnership Against Terrorism will be affected in the same manner.

According to the National Association of Manufacturers, meeting the new 10+2 requirements could cost U.S. businesses about $20 billion a year.[7]

Create Global Trade and Order Management Hubs

Earlier, we discussed three main drivers of volatility in today's supply chains: the players, the processes, and the systems. To briefly recap, by players we mean the manufacturers, suppliers, distributors, logistics providers, contract manufacturers, banks, etc. that are essential to getting products and services delivered to the end customer. Given the level of M&A activity as well as ongoing internal restructuring and "right sourcing" of business processes, the impact of this kind of volatility on the supply chain is profound. Too, this organizational volatility creates an underlying volatility in how business processes, like SCOR's Deliver process, are actually executed, as well as in the disparate systems needed to support them.

Ideally, there would be a "traffic cop" or "conductor" that could sit atop all of this in order to manage the complexity in a way that is transparent to the end customer and cost effective and lean for the manufacturer. We will discuss two such orchestrating technologies: global trade management and order management hubs. Both have existed in some form for a while, but are growing in importance and in capability given the systemic levels of volatility in supply chains that now exist. What is common to both of them is that they do not so much replace existing software applications such as ERP, but rather they pull together in one place all of the functions necessary to streamline and optimize supply chain execution. In essence, they provide a flexible way to decouple the back-end supply-oriented systems from the front-end demand-oriented systems, providing a single hub from which dynamic sourcing decisions, cross-border trade regulations, supply chain finance and other supply chain execution decisions may be efficiently managed.

Global Trade Management

Global trade management (GTM) is another area of logistics where volatility has become firmly embedded. Major drivers of volatility in global trade include:

- Long and highly variable lead times for cross-border movement of goods
- Threats of disruption due to terrorism and regional sources of instability
- Movement of sensitive technologies and proprietary knowledge to restricted parties
- Effects of the global economic crisis on availability of credit and supplier viability
- Regulations designed to ensure more sustainable, "green" commercial activity.

The issue of lead time volatility is largely an outgrowth of the degree to which supply chain activity has been outsourced and moved offshore. If you, as a manufacturer, have key suppliers located nearby, lead time volatility might be measured in hours. But if, for example, your demand base is in the U.S., but most of your manufacturing is done by a contract manufacturer based in Taiwan, your lead time volatility may be measured in days or weeks. Being able, first, to measure and quantify these lead times and their volatility, and second, to identify ways to mitigate this volatility are key requirements of any GTM system.

The threat of terrorism and regional disruptions in a post-9/11 world creates a special challenge for supply chain participants as these kinds of acts cannot be anticipated with any kind of precision. Therefore, companies must have in place contingency plans and alternative sourcing arrangements in cases where they believe that sources of supply might be at risk. Effective GTM must be able to define and have on record these alternative fulfillment arrangements.

In an effort to better secure their safety as well as to avoid exporting goods and services of a highly sensitive, proprietary nature to states or parties considered to be hostile entities, governments have instituted denied or restricted parties lists that forbid the export of such goods. This includes such items as various arms and munitions, specialized encryption software, and advanced computing hardware. Thus, a key requirement for a global trade solution is to actively manage this denied parties list whenever exports are involved.

The global economic crisis that began in late 2008 will have ongoing repercussions for supply chain activity for several years, if not longer. The lack of availability of credit to support global trade as well as questionable viability of various suppliers and carriers makes it incumbent upon manufacturers to have cyber supply chain tools that will help them to quickly evaluate and select options to conduct their business without delay or undue costs.

Finally, companies are looking at ways to operate in a more environmentally sustainable way, both as a matter of sound business practice as well as in response to regulations that seek to maximize sustainable commerce and minimize environmental damage.

Broadly speaking, GTM technologies encompass international transportation and logistics management, compliance, trade content, and supply chain finance. Figure 12.9 highlights some of the specific requirements within each of these broad categories.

In the past, most technology solutions that met these requirements were custom-developed and, in many cases, cobbled together from a patchwork of systems. And, of course, there was and is a high degree of manual intervention required to make this process work. Today, though, solutions have emerged that begin to pull all of these requirements under one umbrella, making it easier and more cost-effective for companies to manage their ever-increasing levels of global supply chain activity.

Global trade visibility is one of the more critical aspects of GTM solutions as it relates to minimizing the risk associated with long lead-time, volatile supply chains. It also poses one of the tougher implementation challenges, simply due to the large number of third parties involved in moving goods globally, including 3PLs, freight forwarders, customs agents, and banks.

Compliance and trade content have become immensely complex due to the ever-changing and burgeoning body of regulations imposed by various countries and supra-national entities. For example, regulations designed to minimize risks of terrorist activities have included requirements for capturing additional data and instituting processes designed to ensure proper chain of custody.

Order Management Hubs

For many companies, the ability to comprehensively and reliably manage orders has actually declined due to the increasingly global nature of their business on both the demand and supply side; ongoing merger and acquistion (M&A) activity that has left them with non-standard, non-connected

Global Trade Management			
International Transportation & Logistics	**Global Trade Compliance**	**Trade Content**	**Finance**
Global Trade Visibility	Export Compliance Screening	FTA Origin Rules & Duty Rates	Import/Private Label LOC
Order Management	Origin/Free Trade Agreement Management	Trade Doc Templates	Open Acct Mgt
Ocean/Air Transportation Management	Parts Catalog & Product Classification	Harmonized Tariffs	Supply Chain Finance
Contract Management	Customs Management	Export/Import License Rules	Export Doc Prep
	Total Landed Cost	Tax & Duty Rates	
		Restricted Parties	

FIGURE 12.9 Global trade management key requirements. This is a generalized set of requirements to manage cross-border trade.

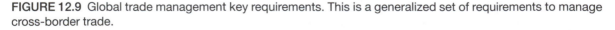

Source: Sterling Commerce, 2010.

organizational and IT capabilities; and the increasing complexity of their products and services. For example, they may receive customer orders from a centralized call center, but line items get fulfilled from multiple business units, each with its own systems. They may outsource some or all of their production to various contract manufacturers, both domestically and offshore. Order line items may get picked from multiple warehouses prior to final consolidation. Finally, the recession has amplified this concern, forcing leaner operations.

Leading companies are addressing this scenario of "slow motion" volatility—the changes are not sudden, but they are systemic—by essentially decoupling the customer's view of their orders from how the manufacturer actually goes about fulfilling that order. Figure 12.10 highlights what we mean by this. The customer simply wants to place an order with a manufacturer. They want to know if the manufacturer can promise delivery at a mutually agreed upon date. They want to have visibility of the order from start to finish.

What the customer does not necessarily need to know—or at least not have to worry about—is if the individual line items are sourced from different business units in the company. Or, as is increasingly common in industries such as high tech, production of the certain line items may be completely outsourced to a contract manufacturer or supplier, and then shipped directly from that third-party source to the end customer.

They are accomplishing this with order management hubs, sometimes referred to as distributed order management solutions due to the fact that line items on the order are "distributed," or sourced, from multiple business units or third parties (Figure 12.10). These systems play a crucial brokering and orchestration role that hides the underlying complexity from the end customer, and greatly streamlines the internal management of these orders by the manufacturer. For example, identifying

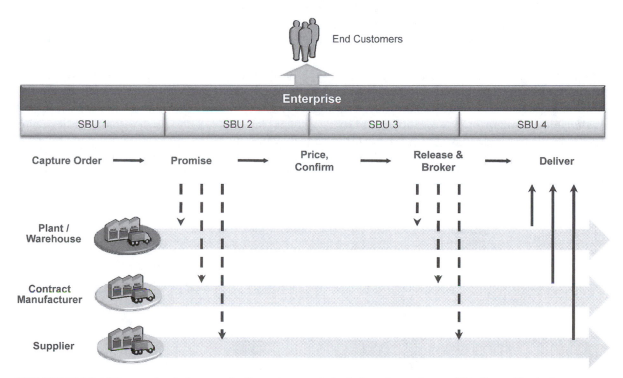

FIGURE 12.10 Hide supply chain complexity and present single face to customer. This figure illustrates a situation in which an end customer places an order with a manufacturer—the "enterprise"—for various line items that are owned and managed by different business units within that enterprise, and that may be fulfilled internally from different manufacturing plants or warehouses, or from third parties such as contract manufacturers and suppliers. An order management hub gives the person placing or taking the order visibility to inventory and scheduled production, regardless of the end source, with committed requirements subsequently being released to each of these sources, and which may then be independently delivered to the end customer. From the end customer's perspective, this is all transparent.

Source: Sterling Commerce, 2010.

what is available-to-promise (ATP) can be done in one pass, because the links exist to available inventory and scheduled supply, regardless of where the supply is coming from.

The coordination of eventual fulfillment similarly is centralized to ensure that all sources of supply are operating in tandem to achieve on-time, in-full shipments to the end customer. This is no simple feat. Traditional ERP systems are seldom up to this task. For example, the basic activity of promising—the so-called ATP check—is often quite difficult to do accurately or in a timely way in the absence of an order management hub. Not surprisingly, companies' perfect order performance metrics—i.e., how often they fulfill an order perfectly based on completeness, timeliness, accuracy, and so on—often suffer from this up-front inability to dependably promise the order.

Outsourcing has introduced additional levels of challenges to these activities. The fact that companies outsource production is not the sole issue. Additionally, it is the frequency and rapidity with which organizations *change* sources that create the difficult-to-manage complexity. Companies constantly make these changes as total cost differentials shift from region to region, as new markets emerge, and as regulatory and political realities dictate that sourcing options be reevaluated. Order management hub technologies mitigate the impact of these changes on the ordering process itself by providing flexible, rule-driven control over the entire order-to-cash process.

Streamline Cross-Channel Selling

Finally, the fourth key to minimizing business volatility through creation of flexible cyber communities lies in streamlining and automating multi-tiered, cross-channel selling (Figure 12.11). Manufactures, like retailers, have discovered that cross-channel selling and fulfillment is very complicated. The many touch points in a cross-channel environment increase the risk for failure, but offer a great opportunity to satisfy the customer. As an example, each touch point is an opportunity for the manufacture to gain valuable insight: the better the manufacturer understands the retailer and end-use customer the better they can satisfy their requirements.

Self-service channels help lower ongoing transactional costs and make it easier to do business with a manufacturer, anytime, anywhere. Today, these channels often rely on subscription-based SaaS models to lower capital outlay. This pay-as-you-go approach not only minimizes upfront investment, but it also enables companies to scale up capability rapidly as demand returns or develops. Additionally, with SaaS, users always have the newest releases of the software.

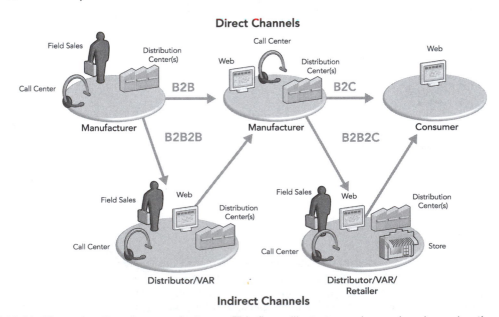

FIGURE 12.11 Channel options for manufacturers. This figure illustrates various sales channel options for manufacturers.

Source: Sterling Commerce, 2010.

Multi-tiered e-commerce solutions give companies a lot more flexibility in how they work with channel partners vs. going direct to the end customer. A key realization for manufacturers of any size is that they have multiple business collaboration networks, each subject to different rules, different modes of operation, etc. The challenge, therefore, is for an organization to take advantage of this complexity by handling it better than its competitors, at lower cost, with greater levels of customer service and with more agility in response to ongoing changes in these networks.

Our experience tells us that there are two major classes of best practices that a manufacturer should consider to help improve its selling process in these difficult economic times:

1. **Go "lean"**—just as you may have done already in your plants, eliminate waste in your quoting, selling, pricing, and configuration processes. Waste that takes the form of errors, delays, unnecessary tasks, repetitive tasks, too much shuffling of orders from one group to another, etc.
2. **Embed your brand in downstream selling partners**—VARs, distributors, retailers, dealers, co-ops, etc. Whenever you have to sell through multiple tiers of partners, you risk the erosion of market share due to lack of attention to your brand on their part, erosion of margin due to incomplete information on ultimate sales and pricing, and loss of revenues and customer retention due to inefficiencies in your downstream distribution chain.

The first best practice category is largely internally focused (though the ideas can certainly be employed for multi-trading partner processes, too). It addresses process improvement through process automation and standardization, while simultaneously allowing for highly configurable and flexible solutions to customer product and service requirements.

The second category of best practices explicitly addresses the concern of multi-tiered distribution networks downstream of your enterprise. As mentioned earlier, we often find that manufacturers will want to consider a continuum of selling options for their customers: EDI, webforms, fax-to-EDI conversion, and e-commerce cross-channel, multi-channel applications. This is exactly the kind of consideration that makes BCNs so complex and where the impact of volatility is keenly felt.

Most manufacturers will have some level of EDI (or similar B2B) capability in place for key customers and some limited Web-based ordering capability. But the bulk of their orders likely come in via phone, fax, email, or mail. Manual order processing is expensive and error-prone. It is especially expensive on a per-transaction basis for the typically large number of customers that constitute a small portion of your prospect's overall revenues. Self-service channels take much of these costs out of the equation.

Self-service channels are not only a lower cost alternative, but they help manufacturers extend their reach to new markets and embed themselves in their various partner channels. Many manufacturers have taken a flexible B2B approach with their retail and distributor partners. By offering multiple ways to receive orders and transmitting information, manufacturers have opened the door to new channels. Their business collaboration network model has had great influence on how performance is measured and how service levels are evaluated.

Manufacturers often have minimal visibility to point-of-sale data downstream of their resellers, including lack of understanding of returns, proof of rebates, etc. The result is inefficient inventory management, charge backs, and added costs from retailers and partners. Retailers are open to sharing POS data where they have an agreement to increase required supply, support promotional activities, and management of price reductions. Self-service retail to manufacture data transfer delivers a win-win situation for both parties.

Manufacturers should capture market share from competitors by being exceptionally easy to do business with, reaching out to new channels, and embedding their brands into downstream resellers' selling channels. Simultaneously, they should create "lean" pricing, quoting, and order capture processes to drive out costs and improve productivity. They should exploit profitable lines such as aftermarket services and parts.

The selling and distribution networks of manufacturers have gotten progressively more complex. While there has always been a concern over disintermediation of channel partners, the reality today is that manufacturers must find new ways to grab market share and boost revenues. This requires a careful analysis of market segments and how end customers can best be served.

In the B2B2B or B2B2C models, the concern is not disintermediation—manufacturers will gladly use their channel partners to sell their products. Rather, the concern is lack of visibility of end-customer demand, lack of proper controls on rebates, and inability to properly guide the quoting and configuration process (where that applies).

Achieving the Benefits of Cyber Communities

Well thought out, well-managed cyber supply chain communities such as those described in this chapter give companies the tools they need to manage business volatility in the most cost-effective manner. Deploying the IT infrastructure to support business collaboration networks, integrated visibility and business intelligence, global trade and order management, and streamlined cross-channel selling gives companies the edge they need to compete and drive advantage.

Notes

1 "The Value of a Comprehensive Integration Solution," commissioned study conducted by Forrester Consulting on behalf of Sterling Commerce, March 11, 2009.
2 Gilmore, Dan, "The New Normal for Supply Chain, Part 2," Supply Chain Digest, July 23, 2009.
3 A plain vanilla FTP (file transfer protocol) session is *not secure*. That is because *your user id and password are sent in the clear* (without any encryption) to the remote server when you log in. Further, the contents of the files you are transferring are sent unencrypted as well. So there is a chance that someone could intercept your login details or snoop inside the file while it is being transferred over the public Internet. Source: http://askbobrankin.com/is_ftp_secure.html
4 A Virtual Private Network is defined as a *network* that is constructed by using public wires to connect nodes. For example, there are a number of systems that enable you to create networks using the Internet as the medium for transporting data. These systems use encryption and other security mechanisms to ensure that only authorized users can access the network and that the data cannot be intercepted. Source: http://www.webopedia.com/TERM/S/security.html
5 *Application proxy* or *application-level proxy*: an application gateway is an application program that runs on a firewall system between two networks. When a client program establishes a connection to a destination service, it connects to an application gateway, or *proxy*. The client then negotiates with the proxy server in order to communicate with the destination service. In effect, the proxy establishes the connection with the destination behind the firewall and acts on behalf of the client, hiding and protecting individual computers on the network behind the firewall. This creates two connections: one between the client and the proxy server and one between the proxy server and the destination. Once connected, the proxy makes all packet-forwarding decisions. Since all communication is conducted through the proxy server, computers behind the firewall are protected. While this is considered a highly secure method of firewall protection, application gateways require great memory and processor resources compared to other firewall technologies, such as stateful inspection. Source: http://www.webopedia.com/TERM/A/application_gateway.html
6 AMR Research, "Supply Chain Risks, Part 1: Taking the Pulse of Global Supply Chain Risks and Mitigation Strategies," July 5, 2008.
7 TheHill.com, October 30, 2008.

thirteen
Governing Intangible Risk
The Cyber Supply Chain Risk Model

Dr. Sandor Boyson, Dr. Thomas M. Corsi, and Hart Rossman

From online shopping to telecommuting, our society and economy have become increasingly reliant on interconnected computer networks. To help foster continued economic growth, improving the security of networked computer systems must be a national priority.

Many of today's tools and mechanisms for protecting against cyber attacks were designed with yesterday's technology in mind. Information systems have evolved from room-size computer workstations shut off from the rest of the world to ubiquitous mobile devices interconnected by a global Internet. In this diverse ecology of communication devices, no cyber security solution works on all operating systems and can protect every type of computer and network component. Operating systems are now composed of millions of lines of code, rather than thousands, and have many more potential holes.

Attackers must find only one hole in a security system for success while security experts must close all potential vulnerabilities of the system.

The nation's critical infrastructure (energy, transportation, telecommunications, etc.), businesses, and services are extensively and increasingly controlled and enabled by software. Vulnerabilities in that software put those resources at risk. The risk is compounded by software size and complexity, the use of software produced by unvetted suppliers, and the interdependence of software systems. Software assurance deals with the root of the problem by improving software security.

Building a secure cyber supply chain becomes more and more challenging every day as the size, complexity, and tempo of software creation increases, and the number and skill level of attackers continues to grow. Attackers have only to find and exploit a single vulnerability to bring chaos to a cyber supply chain.

Given the highly connected global IT market, its economic influence, and its increasingly more hostile threat profile, it was vital to our study to not only look at what our global businesses do right, but where our current programs falter. This review identified three primary problems that collectively support the need for a standardized cyber supply chain reference model.

- The focus of today's supply chain management practice on the physical supply chain, leaving the cyber supply chain highly vulnerable
- There is no defined overarching approach to overcoming functional silos in cyber security
- There is no effective self-regulation and responsibility of the cyber supply chain.

In support of the president's Comprehensive National Cyber Security Initiative (CNCSI) and its urgent mission to protect the nation's cyber assets, Science Applications International Corporation

(SAIC) and the Supply Chain Management Center (SCMC) of the Robert H. Smith School of Business, University of Maryland (UMD) at College Park, collaboratively undertook a research initiative (at the unclassified level) to develop a Cyber Supply Chain Assurance Reference Model. Our research sought to fuse together the fields of cyber security and supply chain risk management by applying proven supply chain practices to this evolving cyber domain. We assessed the dynamics, risks, and management challenges and opportunities of the U.S. cyber supply chain in its role as a critical public system/private infrastructure.

Our intention was not to suggest standards (which are usually developed as a result of long periods of industry experimentation), but to define a model of strategic relationships, its architecture, operational parameters, and scope of practices. In essence, our goal was to develop a cyber supply chain security reference model that would embody the basic goals and concepts behind assuring the ongoing security of the global cyber supply chain.

The research effort focused on two key objectives for the reference model:

1. To establish an end-to-end process view and develop a common language to describe the cyber supply chain, and
2. To help educate leaders about the joint responsibilities all actors across a supply chain share to preserve and enhance the operations of the whole business ecosystem of which they are part.

By studying how global organizations employ highly effective processes to manage highly distributed supply chains and to hedge risk across the end-to-end process, we sought to identify proven models, processes, and management tips that could be fused with cyber-assurance models to achieve better process definition, discipline, and mastery.

Our research study was executed over a concentrated period (September 2008 to March 2009) by faculty and Ph.D. students of the Robert H. Smith Supply Chain Management Center in close consultation with SAIC's Chief Technology Officer (CTO) for Cyber Security.

In this research, we define three main terms.

Cyber infrastructure: The mass of IT systems (hardware, software, and public/private and classified networks) that, together, constitute the backbone of important national and enterprise infrastructure. This infrastructure enables the uninterrupted operations of key government and industrial base actors such as the Department of Defense, the Department of Homeland Security, and their major suppliers.

Cyber supply chain: The entire set of key actors involved with/using cyber infrastructure—system end-users, policy makers, acquisition specialists, system integrators, network providers, and software/hardware suppliers. These users/providers' organizational and process-level interactions to plan, build, manage, maintain, and defend cyber infrastructure.

Cyber Supply Chain Assurance Reference Model: A model that not only defines key actors, processes, and vulnerabilities, but also identifies strategic interdependencies at each node of the international production/sustainment chain.

This initial *Cyber Supply Chain Assurance Reference Model* offers a process discipline-oriented approach built upon three "nested rings." The rings represent levels of planning and operational control designed to address the demand for defense-in-depth within the system development life cycle (SDLC), along with defense-in-breadth across the cyber supply chain.

- *Defense in depth*, in the cyber context, refers to the layering of defense within an organization
- *Defense in breadth*, again in the cyber context, refers to interlocking defenses across a network or supply chain.

The combination of the two defense strategies/approaches results in the holistic approach to security necessary within a complex ecosystem. The three nested rings of the initial cyber supply chain reference model include:

The Governance Ring: This layer addresses the requirement for unity of command; for coherence of cyber supply chain strategic planning and risk management; for effective network design/rule set development; and for acquisition policy to formalize/optimize ecosystem relationships.

The System Integration/Shared Services Ring: This layer addresses the requirement for a rigorous integration function; for the deployment of real-time visibility/monitoring systems of the cyber supply chain; for the continuous conduct of oversight audits; and for highly aggressive interventions to ensure continuous chain of custody/systems quality; and operations continuity.

The Action/Field Ring: This layer addresses the requirement for role-specific best practice processes and integrated cyber/physical asset management. It also incorporates the ongoing identification/collection/dissemination of benchmark practices currently used in organizations exposed to intense and globalized cyber supply chain risk.

Background: The Parallels between the Physical and Cyber Supply Chains

The Physical Supply Chain

The physical supply chain refers to a highly integrated set of activities that facilitate the flow of goods from the point of origin (raw materials, component parts) through production/assembly to various warehouses/distribution centers and, ultimately, to individual customers, often through retail outlets or, increasingly, through direct deliveries to individual residences/places of business. The physical supply chain also involves any product returns for reworking/warranty claims. In addition to the physical flow of goods, the supply chain involves a complex flow of data and financial transactions to facilitate the goods flow.

Increasingly, companies have recognized the importance of supply chains to the overall success of their operations. However, supply chains are complex and involve a number of individual functions. There are suppliers, purchasing, production, and warehouse and transportation managers. There are wholesalers, retailers, and customers. These individual parties each have a critical function as part of the integrated supply chain. Any breakdown or failure in one link in the supply chain results in overall system inefficiency.

Leaders in supply chain excellence manage the entire supply chain from the beginning to the end with an integrated set of software applications that allow supply chain executives to assess the chain's overall performance and to intervene as appropriate when benchmark indicators suggest the need for corrective actions.

In fact, overall supply chain excellence requires managerial oversight of the entire chain to ensure that each function within the chain works properly and completes individual tasks as required, on time and in an integrated fashion that produces best overall end-results for the enterprise. This oversight role extends beyond the four walls of the internal organization to include extended enterprise partners—i.e., suppliers, wholesalers, retailers, and customers.

Excellence in supply chain management requires governance of the entire chain, including extended enterprise partners. It also includes real-time data exchange and appropriate software applications to facilitate, manage, and coordinate individual functions with the chain.

PRTM Management Consultants, Inc.,[1] a global consulting firm with an emphasis on supply chain practice, has developed a Supply Chain Maturity Model that describes and categorizes how far along companies are in achieving a truly integrated, optimized, and holistic supply chain. This maturity model comprises four stages.

- *Stage 1*: Firms start out in Stage 1, whereby each supply chain activity occurs in isolation, with results of one activity passed along "over the wall" to subsequent managers of other activities in a sequential fashion.
- *Stage 2*: Firms achieve internal integration in which independent supply chain functions (demand forecasting, sales ordering, and manufacturing operations) are linked together and

coordinated in near-real time. A netcentric database allows information sharing in real time across all relevant functional departments.

- *Stage 3*: Firms extend their integration beyond their internal walls to allow linkages with external partners.
- *Stage 4*: Firms go beyond information sharing to achieve a level of collaboration and joint decision making with external partners.

Today, best-in-class organizations are moving rapidly from Stage 2 integration to Stage 3 and 4 integration. Actually, the process of achieving Stage 4 integration is extremely challenging. Only a select few companies (Dell, Inc., Wal-Mart, Cisco Systems, Inc., and Hewlett-Packard) have realized Stage 4 supply chains.[2]

To reach Stage 4 maturity, the executive responsible for the supply chain must ensure the integrity of the entire extended supply chain by maintaining a "chain of custody" over all the activities of the chain. This includes such diverse actions as dealing only with trusted prequalified suppliers whose operations are subjected to continuous on-site quality inspections on completed components. It also includes quality checks associated with the manufacturing/assembly processes. Integrity of components in the transportation process, from the assembly/manufacturing points through warehouses and distribution centers to retail outlets and customers, is assured by shipment tracking and tracing.

Risk is a given in the overall management of this complex system. The Supply Chain Risk Literature Review in the Appendix, summarizes the spectrum of sources of supply chain risk. The challenge for the executive responsible for the overall extended supply chain must be to understand the myriad potential risks and develop mitigation strategies to deal with each one.

The Cyber Supply Chain

The cyber supply chain is the mass of IT systems (hardware, software, and public and classified networks) that, together, enable the uninterrupted operations of key government and commercial sector actors, such as the Department of Defense, the Department of Homeland Security, and their major suppliers. The cyber supply chain includes the entire set of key players and their organizational and process-level interactions that plan, build, manage, maintain, and defend this infrastructure. This ecosystem applies equally to public and private sectors. Characterization of roles in the cyber supply chain becomes particularly challenging when assessing the interrelationship between public and private sectors entities in an unregulated or semi-regulated environment.

To further elaborate on the definition of a cyber supply chain, the following list identifies each key actor's role in the cyber supply chain ecosystem:

- *Policy makers* prepare concepts of operation (Con Ops) and determine quality of service (QOS) and supplier performance monitoring standards.
- *Ecosystem acquisition specialists* seek to embed Federal Acquisition Regulation (FAR) changes into procurement contracting in pursuit of greater security.
- *System integrators* act as Tier I coordinators of cross-vendor products and services and seek common criteria for evaluation of Tier II suppliers and more secure cross-vendor transactions/communications platforms.
- *Software developers* manage software pedigree, code integrity, and kernel evaluation and work to carefully screen out human or viral threats to their processes.
- *Hardware/component developers* manage Tier II suppliers, assure production quality, and guard against counterfeits entering the system.
- *Network providers* supply the bandwidth and connectivity for data, video, and voice communications among cyber supply chain actors, and the secure enterprise server networks for applications/service hosting.
- *Operators/end users*, such as intelligence specialists, must maintain the highest trust levels in the system, have clear paths for directing demand signals to the supplier base, and expect a highly responsive supply chain feedback loop.

This ecosystem is displayed in Figure 13.1.[3]

Like a physical supply chain, a cyber supply chain for IT systems is an end-to-end process. It begins with the software developers, whose roles are similar to that of suppliers in the physical supply chain. The roles of purchasing agents, production, and distribution managers in the physical supply chain closely parallel the roles of policy makers and system integrators, hardware/component developers, and network providers in the cyber supply chain. Finally, the physical supply chain customers equate to the operators/end users in the cyber supply chain.

In the physical supply chain, the supply chain manager is charged with ensuring the integrity of the entire process from the supplier through to the customer. This assurance process involves, as noted above, monitoring and assessing the quality of output from each actor in the supply chain.

Gap Analysis: Cyber Supply Chain Management Gaps in Practice

Today, serious issues and threats confront those cyber security professionals who manage our nation's cyber supply chains. As a result of our literature review and interviews with practitioners/experts in the field, we have identified a set of practice gaps in management practices.

As mentioned earlier in this chapter, in spring of 2009, the University of Maryland Robert H. Smith School of Business Supply Chain Management Center, together with SAIC, convened a workshop themed "Developing a Cyber Supply Chain Assurance Reference Model."

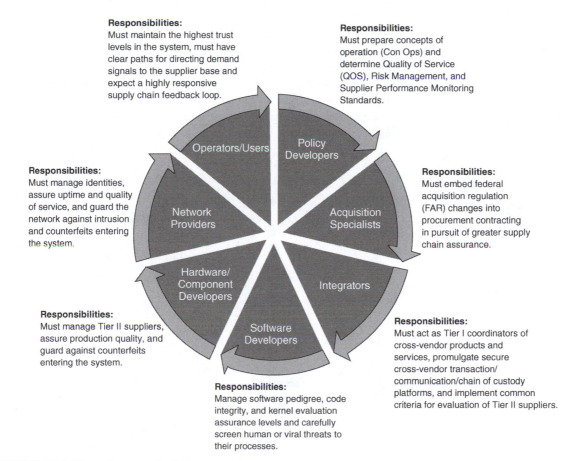

Responsibilities:
Must maintain the highest trust levels in the system, must have clear paths for directing demand signals to the supplier base and expect a highly responsive supply chain feedback loop.

Responsibilities:
Must prepare concepts of operation (Con Ops) and determine Quality of Service (QOS), Risk Management, and Supplier Performance Monitoring Standards.

Responsibilities:
Must manage identities, assure uptime and quality of service, and guard the network against intrusion and counterfeits entering the system.

Responsibilities:
Must embed federal acquisition regulation (FAR) changes into procurement contracting in pursuit of greater supply chain assurance.

Responsibilities:
Must manage Tier II suppliers, assure production quality, and guard against counterfeits entering the system.

Responsibilities:
Must act as Tier I coordinators of cross-vendor products and services, promulgate secure cross-vendor transaction/communication/chain of custody platforms, and implement common criteria for evaluation of Tier II suppliers.

Responsibilities:
Manage software pedigree, code integrity, and kernel evaluation assurance levels and carefully screen human or viral threats to their processes.

Operators/Users, Policy Developers, Acquisition Specialists, Network Providers, Integrators, Hardware/Component Developers, Software Developers

FIGURE 13.1 The cyber supply chain ecosystem.

Source: Robert H. Smith School of Business and JAIC, 2008.

The initial session of the workshop focused on establishing the problem scope and identifying the current strategies being relied on to deter and/or mitigate both real and potential cyber attacks. The workshop included approximately 20 participants from both the private sector and public agencies. Participants held positions within their respective organizations in the cyber supply chain, ranging from software and hardware developers/engineers to acquisition specialists to integrators to network providers to users/policy developers. These participants contributed their thoughts and opinions on a range of issues, setting the stage for the conference. The following pages summarize the results of this initial workshop session.

Setting the Stage: Problem Scope and Current Mitigation Strategies—Participant Responses

Participants initially were asked about whether their organizations had experienced any problems with software malware in the 12 months prior to the conference. As shown in Figure 13.2, participants overwhelmingly reported that their organizations did have to deal with software malware issues recently. In fact, 83.3 percent reported a software malware issue in the previous year.

Participants next were asked about whether their organizations had experienced any problems with counterfeit hardware in the 12 months prior to the conference. As shown in Figure 13.3, the issue of counterfeit hardware was nowhere near as pervasive as was the issue of software malware. In fact, 17.6 percent of the respondents indicated that their organization had to deal with counterfeit hardware in the past year.

Of particular concern is whether the participants perceive the threats from software malware and counterfeit hardware as increasing, decreasing, or remaining the same. The respondents' opinion in this regard is clear and unmistakable. As shown in response to question three (Figure 13.4), they overwhelmingly view the threat as an increasing one. In fact, 68.8 percent of the respondents view the threat as increasing, while none of the respondents view it as decreasing.

Not only are the respondents concerned about the increasing frequency of the threats, they are also concerned about their range of consequences. Indeed, 43.8 percent of respondents view the threats as

Question 1: Has your organization had a problem with software malware in the past year?		Responses
Yes	15	83.33%
No	3	16.67%
Totals	**18**	**100%**

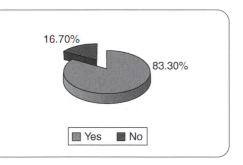

FIGURE 13.2 Focus group response to problem with malware.

Question 2: Has your organization had a problem with counterfeit hardware in the past year?		Responses
Yes	3	17.65%
No	14	82.35%
Totals	**17**	**100%**

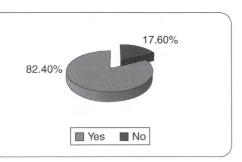

FIGURE 13.3 Focus group response to problem with counterfeit hardware.

Source: Robert H. Smith School of Business and JAIC, 2008.

Question 3: Do you perceive these software and hardware incidents as:		Responses
Increasing in frequency	11	68.75%
Decreasing in frequency	0	0%
Staying about the same	5	31.25%
Totals	**16**	**100%**

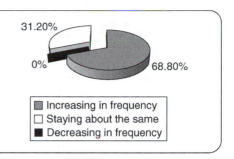

FIGURE 13.4 Focus group response to perception on incidents.

Question 4: How would you categorize the range of consequences of your hardware/software incidents?		Responses
No impact	0	0%
Low impact	4	25%
Moderate impact	7	43.75%
Significant impact	3	18.75%
Severe impact	2	12.50%
Totals	**16**	**100%**

FIGURE 13.5 Focus group response to consequences on incidents.

Source: Robert H. Smith School of Business and JAIC, 2008.

having a moderate impact, 18.7 percent view their impact as potentially significant, and 12.5 percent view the potential impact as severe (Figure 13.5).

Any attempts to mitigate the consequences of both software malware and counterfeit hardware are significantly enhanced if the organization can establish the root causes of the potential disruption. In order to assess the extent to which organizations are making progress in this area, participants were asked about the percentage of incidents they faced in which they were able to determine the root causes. Not surprisingly, the overwhelming majority of the respondents are not doing well in establishing the root causes of the incidents they are facing. According to the respondents, less than half of the organizations are able to establish root causes for 70 percent or more of their incidents. Indeed, over half of the organizations report an ability to determine root causes for less than 50 percent of their incidents (Figure 13.6).

Mitigation attempts are also adversely impacted if organizations do not have visibility into the operations of their IT cyber supply chain partners. According to participants, 53 percent of the organizations have no visibility into the operations of their IT cyber supply chain partners, while 29 percent have some, limited visibility. Only a very small percentage of the organizations have complete, total visibility of their supply chain partners (Figure 13.7).

Participants were then asked to rate the state of cyber security in their organizations. According to the results, 5.9 percent of the participants are very dissatisfied with the state of cyber security in their organizations, while 29.4 percent are somewhat dissatisfied (Figure 13.8).

Participant opinion was also sought on the issue of the adequacy of cyber security tools in the marketplace. Results show that 33.3 percent of the respondents are somewhat dissatisfied

Question 5: Please estimate for what percentage of incidents was your organization able to determine root causes?		Responses
Less than 10%	1	5.88%
10%–20%	3	17.65%
21%–30%	2	11.67%
31%–50%	3	17.65%
51%–70%	0	0%
71% and above	8	47.06%
Totals	**17**	**100%**

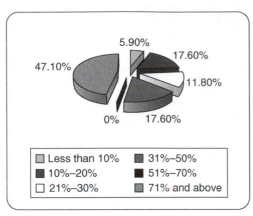

FIGURE 13.6 Focus group response to root cause analysis.

Question 6: How would you rate your visibility into your supply chain partner's operation?		Responses
No visibility	9	52.94%
Some visibility	5	29.41%
Moderate visibility	1	5.88%
High visibility	1	5.88%
Complete visibility	1	5.88%
Totals	**17**	**100%**

FIGURE 13.7 Focus group response to visibility into partners' operations.

Question 7: To what extent are you satisfied with the state of cyber security in your organization?		Responses
Very dissatisfied	1	5.88%
Somewhat dissatisfied	5	29.41%
Neutral	3	17.65%
Somewhat satisfied	7	41.18%
Very satisfied	1	5.88%
Totals	**17**	**100%**

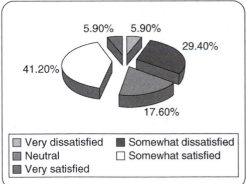

FIGURE 13.8 Focus group response to satisfaction with cyber security.

Source: Robert H. Smith School of Business and JAIC, 2008.

with the cyber security tools presently available, while only 27.8 percent are somewhat satisfied (Figure 13.9).

One effective mitigation strategy to address increasing IT cyber threats would involve the alignment of the IT security organization with the supply chain management team. However, participants indicate that in 47.1 percent of the organizations represented, this alignment does not exist, while in 17.6 percent of them, there is only a slight alignment between them (Figure 13.10).

A final question involved the extent to which a participant's information security operation was aligned with the supply chain risk management center in the organization. Over half of the respondents indicate that such an alignment did not occur in their organization. In fact, less than 12 percent of the respondents said there was a high alignment between IT security and supply chain risk management (Figure 13.11).

Gap 1: The Need to Overcome Functional Silos in Cyber Security

Based on the Supply Chain Management Center-SAIC research study findings, it is clear that functional silos pose a significant threat to cyber security. Indeed, the stovepiped nature of today's cyber supply chains seems to be the single greatest obstacle to cyber security assurance.

We attribute the entrenched nature of these functional silos to the industry's tendency toward

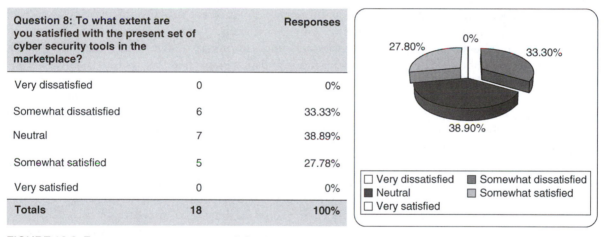

Question 8: To what extent are you satisfied with the present set of cyber security tools in the marketplace?		Responses
Very dissatisfied	0	0%
Somewhat dissatisfied	6	33.33%
Neutral	7	38.89%
Somewhat satisfied	5	27.78%
Very satisfied	0	0%
Totals	18	100%

FIGURE 13.9 Focus group response to satisfaction with cyber security tools.

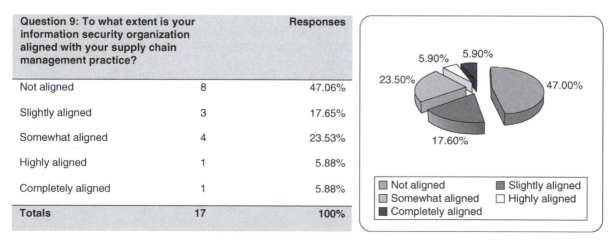

Question 9: To what extent is your information security organization aligned with your supply chain management practice?		Responses
Not aligned	8	47.06%
Slightly aligned	3	17.65%
Somewhat aligned	4	23.53%
Highly aligned	1	5.88%
Completely aligned	1	5.88%
Totals	17	100%

FIGURE 13.10 Focus group response to satisfaction with cyber security alignment with supply chain practices.

Question 10: To what extent is your information security operations (SOC/MSS/TOC) aligned with your supply chain risk management center for joint operations?		Responses
Not aligned	9	52.94%
Slightly aligned	2	11.76%
Somewhat aligned	4	23.53%
Highly aligned	2	11.76%
Completely aligned	0	0%
Totals	17	100%

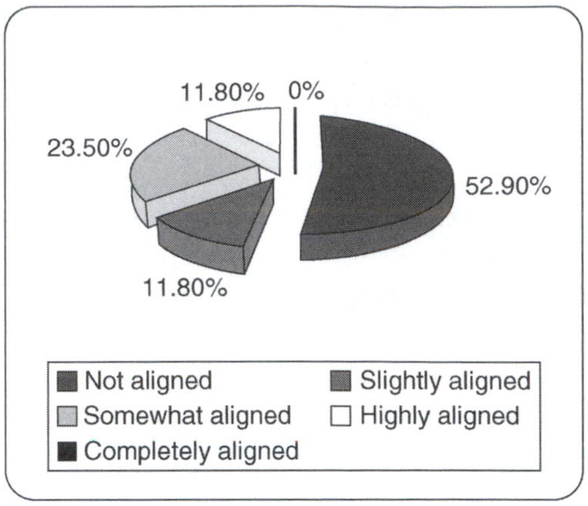

FIGURE 13.11 Focus group response to satisfaction with cyber security operations alignment with supply chain risk management center.

Source: Robert H. Smith School of Business and JAIC, 2008.

increasing specialization and focus narrowing within each domain—e.g., software, hardware, or systems integration. Each specialty area settles into patterns of thought and behavior that become almost like geologic layers over time, patterns often resistant to change.

However, cyber security assurance models in general practice are moving in the exact opposite direction—away from functional stovepiping. More specifically, they have moved from a focus on trust models to a focus on operating systems and applications assurance to a focus on network assurance; and now, hopefully, to a focus on a more holistic perspective that includes system development life cycle (SDLC) and the supply chain.

Figure 13.12 illustrates how the risk management function moves up the technology stack. The initial focus is on product-oriented building blocks—i.e., operating systems, applications, and networks. As the level of sophistication expands, platforms and frameworks must be built to support complementary product providers.

Finally, the paradigm shifts as the role of the risk manager fundamentally transitions from one focused purely on inclusion of security as a functional requirement of a technology to a holistic approach driven by broad business objectives. In short, this broader perspective supports an end-to-end business model—i.e., an SDLC or supply chain model, as illustrated in Figure 13.13.

As the scope of the risk manager changes, so too do the aspects of risk within his or her newly expanded ecosystem. Two features, in particular, have a profound impact on risk and how it is managed in this extended chain: the passive/active nature of the risk management function; and the approach used to conceptualize and resolve threats, vulnerabilities, and predicted impacts of exploitation.

In the first case, it becomes clear that all layers below the SDLC and supply chains take a generally passive approach to risk management. This passiveness is engendered through the widespread use of compliance activities to enforce a particular, generally static, security posture across an organization. In other words, risk management by checklist.

Below the SDLC, most organizations focus on an approach that relies on compliance with a given set of policy, guidance, and practice in which establishing a baseline is easily understood and the system emphasizes managing change control. Once a baseline has been established, most activities focus on ensuring systems do not drift far from it.

Addressing risk management within the SDLC and supply chains, however, requires a more active, continually updated risk management posture. It necessitates a hands-on approach so as to reconcile, on a daily basis, the changing needs of business, as well as the dynamic nature of supply chain relationships. The purpose of this more active approach is to establish a compliance baseline and continually reduce objective and subjective risk hazards to a manageable level.

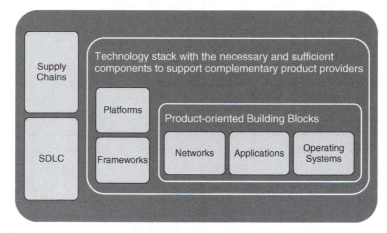

FIGURE 13.12 Paradigm shift to end-to-end business models.

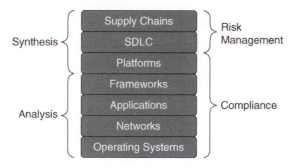

FIGURE 13.13 Cyber market shift in focus from compliance and analysis to synthesis and risk management in moving up the technology stack.

This reduction of risk in a dynamic environment does not just reside in technical mitigation measures such as network intrusion detection systems or specific configuration settings in the operating system on a computer server. Rather, risk reduction measures cut across a deeply striated business environment and should be included and reflected in contracts, economics, finance, and politics.

As an organization moves up the technology stack—from operating systems to total, extended enterprise supply chain management—we see the emergence of a traditional analytic approach to solving problems relating to risk arising from threats, vulnerabilities, or exploitation of a particular component or enterprise. The focus shifts to one of systems thinking and synthesis; an approach that explores the interrelationship and interdependencies between elements in the supply chain ecosystem. In the latter case, organizations train their attention on the products of the interactions between common elements of system and product development life cycles as they intersect across the supply chain.

The combination of synthesis and active risk management make for an interesting domain. The identification and acceptance of shared risk between suppliers and customers, orchestrated by integrators, requires unparalleled vigilance. It also presents untold reward for those ecosystems that develop the adaptive measures to thrive regardless of the nature of the threat.

Clearly, the strength of cyber supply chains relies on the interdependencies between SDLCs across the supply chain. Thus, operational strategies must operate on two axes. Vertically, the ecosystem requires defense in depth within the SDLC. Generally speaking, defense in depth within the SDLC refers to mitigation measures taken that apply solely within the bounds of a single organization's SDLC. This may include having a common system configuration approved by IT security, regular source code reviews, and personnel background checks. Horizontally, the ecosystem needs defense in breadth across the supply chain.

Taking a defense in breadth approach forces you to extend your mitigation measures beyond the bounds of a single SDLC to include your suppliers and customers in the risk management process. This could include security relevant checks within your supply base, collaborative cyber threat and intelligence sharing platforms, or software source code signing that is additive and continually checked and re-checked at every stage in the SDLC across several organizations.

Figure 13.14 illustrates the relationship between major phases in a single actor's SDLC and supply chain and then extends it across a representative ecosystem of nodes of related actors. When viewed independently, a single participants' SDLC does not positively contribute to the management of shared risk for any other actor. If an organization views itself as isolated then it does not positively contribute to the security of products, solutions, or services created and transported by the supply chain in a robust manner. It may contribute to the portions that it directly oversees, though the organization will have little confidence in the effectiveness of this strategy once the product, service, or solution enters a part of the SDLC covered by another actor in the supply chain.

This situation results, in large part, from organizations in the cyber supply chain viewing themselves as the terminus of the chain, rather than a pivot point or orchestrator in a larger multi-player construct. This view drives behaviors such as focusing exclusively on supply chain assurance upstream to suppliers and not downstream to customers. Such uni-directional focus effectively prevents an organization's customers and customer's customers from gaining the benefits of an assured supply chain. The downstream customer-related supply chain is at risk.

Therefore, recognition of this point is critical when it comes to cyber supply chain management. Unlike with many finished goods, cyber systems are procured and developed with a desire to service many classes of customers downstream. These customers often have competing needs, but must be served from a single solution. This is commonly experienced by customers having installed software packages for very simple requirements that, to their bewilderment, have seemingly endless feature sets and configuration options. Such capabilities are available through advanced computing behaviors such as multitasking, netcentric operations, cloud computing, and grid computing.

Recognizing the need to effectively tie together defense in depth and defense in breadth forces the reference model to support mapping specific phases between the SDLC and supply chains of nodes

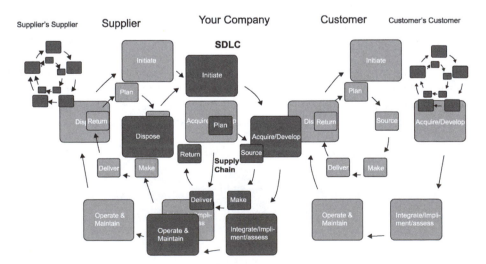

FIGURE 13.14 Relations between single actor's SDLC and supply chain ecosystem.

and actors within the ecosystem. This suggests that using synthesis in the evaluation of the ecosystem from a risk management standpoint, the supply chain orchestrator must apply security mitigation strategies to the supply chain and throughout the supply chain.

Where security is implemented in the cyber supply chain and in what manner is crucial to its effectiveness. The concept of "apply to" and "apply through" is key to understanding the interdependencies between SDLCs across the supply chain. The "apply to" model refers to actively applying security mitigation strategies to the underlying cyber infrastructure that comprises the supply chain. The "apply through" model refers to actively applying security mitigation strategies to both the SDLC and the product, service, or solution as it traverses the supply chain. They drive the need for an evolutionary approach to shared risk management.

"Apply to" security investments impact people, processes, or technologies that embody the supply chain itself. "Apply through" security investments directly impact the components, products, services, and integrated systems created and transported by the supply chains. Utilizing this two-tier model is a key driver in creating the right strategic solutions based upon interdependencies between SDLCs across the supply chain.

Figure 13.15 shows a prototypical mapping highlighting three key phases that synchronize at the intersection between SDLCs and supply chains of nodes/actors. The identification and mapping of these intersections and the interdependencies that drive them allow nodes in the supply chain a greater command of the shared risk involved. In this example, by synchronizing the Initiate-Plan, Integrate-Make, and Dispose-Return stages in the SDLC and supply chain you can effectively adopt and inject security requirements into the ecosystem (Initiate-Plan), ensure they are implemented through the development life cycle (Integrate-Make), and protect the confidentiality of customer data during system disposition (Dispose-Return) regardless of retirement method.

Finally, a reference model must be applied across two dimensions. The first dimension is a series of use cases that articulate how the model can be applied throughout its life cycle. The second dimension identifies vulnerabilities—i.e., how the model might be threatened or abused and, therefore, where one might target risk management strategies and mitigations.

We list several use and abuse cases that flow from the application of our model in Figure 13.16 to illustrate our point.

Each layer of development in the IT stack has created additional complexity and served to further reinforce silo development of standards, assurance practices, and management controls. As an example of this silo effect in cyber security, one has only to look at one domain: software. Automated code-scanning looks only at individual software packages. The Common Criteria for Information Technology Security Evaluation (Common Criteria, National Security Agency) and ISO

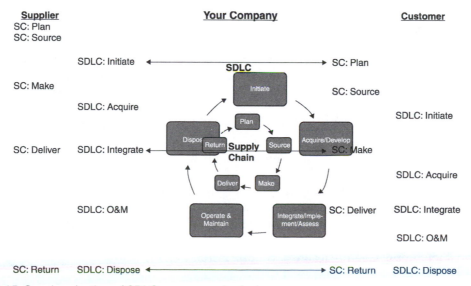

FIGURE 13.15 Synchronization of SDLCs across nodes/actors.

Use Case	Description
Incentives	Develop structured incentives and relationship drivers that facilitate management of shared risk, and facilitate defense in breadth across the supply chain
Improved Visibility	Develop technology and best practices to deepen visibility and add coherence and synchronization across the cyber supply chain
Training	Training and education resources for cyber supply chain professionals, investigators, analysts, and auditors

Abuse Cases	Description
Poor Cyber Manufacturing Hygiene	Introduction of malware to consumer electronics through poor supply chain security practices ("apply to" negatively impacting "apply through")
Supply Chain Denial of Services	Disruption of the supply chain via cyber attack/exploitation
Information Leakage	Industrial espionage that capitalizes on exfiltration of data from supply chain information systems and networks

FIGURE 13.16 List of use cases and abuse cases.

(International Standardization Organization) 15026 capstone standards are focused on analyzing packages of software/code in isolation. Except at the highest levels of assurance, they rely largely on reviewing documents full of compliance claims and warrants provided by the vendor. This is in no small part due to the difficulty in developing assurance standards based on the myriad complexity of real-world computing environments that can be proven repeatable and reliable. What they lack is the requirement and ability to simulate all the possible configuration options and operating environments that the system is likely to encounter and therefore settle on a single instance under a very controlled set of circumstances which are not likely to be reflected in their actual operating environments.

This type of fragmentation and stovepiping of assurance has produced a real need for a common language and framework that can cut across the various domains of cyber security. This need spans different service-provider communities (security professionals, software engineers, hardware manufacturers, system designers, etc.) as well as different governance communities, both public (the National Security Agency, the Department of Homeland Security, the National Institute of Standards and Technology (NIST) and private (SAFECode), etc.).

The search for a common framework has been further spurred by the accelerating globalization and outsourcing of software code and hardware production. These trends present unprecedented assurance challenges to the government, commercial, and vendor communities. These challenges and threats will only continue to grow.

In fact, the fast-moving, emerging nature of the global cyber supply chain means that most corporations and government agencies are constantly improvising and are in "perpetual beta" testing mode—or as one respondent put it, "building an engine while driving the car" or "flying an airplane while building out wings."

There is no question that cyber assets are dispersing across the globe and the pace of systems deployment is intensifying through the use of rapid development methodologies. However, there is still no identified command and control management function across the distributed cyber supply chain. There is no cyber-sector equivalent to the physical supply chain integration function led by an empowered Chief Supply Chain Executive. No one is minding the whole cyber-ecosystem of alliance partners and customers.

Unlike in physical supply chain management, cyber supply chains appear rarely to use end-to-end network visualization/network mapping tools to scope distributed global cyber and physical assets, and the flows/transactions between them. Widespread implementation of a centralized risk analysis/ management function across the extended enterprise cyber supply chain network also appears to be largely lacking.

Finally, no pedigree/chain of custody mechanisms currently span the entire end-to-end cyber supply chain. As one respondent noted: "Security itself is rapidly becoming about proving a negative—the only way to prove no one has inserted anything into the system is to constantly survey the whole of it and keep end-to-end records of custody."

At this point, current cyber supply chain development assurance relies primarily on bill of material tracking for hardware and software configuration. To be truly effective, the cyber supply chain needs a more comprehensive chain of visibility and shared real-time documentation of systems development practices among participants.

Such a chain of custody would mirror that which is now in use in the pharmaceutical industry in the form of e-pedigree initiatives. Under e-pedigree requirements, companies must maintain extensive online documentation and tracking systems to authenticate products in the chain, all the way from material sourcing to end-consumer delivery. This e-pedigree system, mandated by government regulation following a number of high-profile drug counterfeiting and diversion cases, is designed to protect consumers from contaminated medicine or counterfeit drugs. On January 5, 2007, EPCGlobal, an organization dedicated to development of industry-driven standards for the Electronic Product Code (EPC) to support the use of Radio Frequency Identification (RFID) in global trading networks so as to enable visibility and efficiency throughout the supply chain (www.epcglobalinc.org) ratified the Pedigree Standard as an international standard that specifies an XML description of the life history of a product across the highly complex pharmaceuticals industry.

In addition to e-pedigree, the pharmaceutical industry has a strong commitment to supply chain-wide assurance through supplier audits and tracking/tracing technologies such as RFID. This is shown in Figure 13.17, which was provided by an industry leader.

In the pharmaceutical industry, there are party e-pedigree service providers that help companies achieve assurance by auditing end-to-end processes to ensure they are performed in a secure manner and provide chain of custody to both ends of the supply chain These third parties protect company financial and classified information along the chain.

No such mechanism exists in the cyber supply chain.

As a result of these cyber supply chain control gaps, there is a critical need for a next-generation assurance model that spans the disparate layers of the IT platform and protects the whole highly distributed end-to-end supply chain process.

Gap 2: The Need for Effective Self-Regulation and Responsibility

Today, cyber supply chain processes, tools, and management guidance around which to mobilize industry awareness about threats do not exist.

There is a critical need to define a body of best cyber supply chain management practices. This set of practices would serve as an accepted body of knowledge to guide cyber supply chain management across industry segments and among federal regulators and agencies. Such a body of knowledge would provide a foundation to support contractual clauses, claims, and warrants for legal liability

Supply Chain Output	Customer	Delivery Mechanism
Chain of custody evidence of the safety and purity of manufactured output	Regulatory agencies	Application filings, audits, other submissions
Authenticity of manufactured products between the producer and the end consumer as purchased and distributed globally	Distributors, end consumers	Product tagging, cradle-to-grave tracking processes/technologies and reporting structures that verify authenticity

FIGURE 13.17 Pharmaceutical example of supply chain assurance.

protections. It would also create common criteria for third-party evaluation purposes of the cyber supply chain.

A review of activities to date by industry highlights this need:

- MITRE Corporation oversees a number of initiatives including the Common Vulnerabilities and Exposures (CVE) database and the Common Weakness Enumeration (CWE) initiative which has tried to identify a unified, measurable set of software weaknesses. To date, MITRE has identified over 40,000 CVEs and 750 common root causes for these weaknesses documented in the CWE. Clusters of CVE with common threads receive a CWE identification. They also receive a common attack pattern enumeration and classification (CAPEC). CAPEC identifies attack patterns commonly used by cyber attackers and weights or scores the level of threat posed by these attack patterns in terms of confidentiality, integrity, and impact as defined by a common vulnerability scoring system (CVSS). CAPEC is sponsored by the U.S. Department of Homeland Security (DHS) as part of the Software Assurance strategic initiative of its National Cyber Security Division.

This approach is not a dynamic management process, but an assessment tool—mostly applied to assessing code in one isolated software package at a time. It does not span the entire cyber supply chain as an integrated whole.

- NIST and DHS maintain a National Vulnerability Database (NVD), which includes databases of security checklists, security-related software flaws, misconfigurations, product names, and impact metrics.
- Other efforts to manage cyber vulnerability offer a broader approach which aims to gain control over *applications security*. Companies such as Veracode, Inc.,[4] use this database plus MITRE's CWE, NIST's Security Analysis, and the Open Web Application Security Project's (OWASP's) Top 10 list to assemble security flaws that represent top threats.

For most critical business applications, Veracode and its competitors make assessments to determine highest risks. They use intensive methods/techniques, static binary analysis, automated dynamic analysis, and manual penetration testing to perform these assessments. They provide customers with Security Quality Scores (1 to 100) based on accumulation of enumerated weaknesses. Again, this assessment activity does not offer an end-to-end security management process spanning multiple organizations in a shared cyber supply chain.

Recently, with the rise of cloud computing,[5] we are seeing determined efforts to secure *web services infrastructure security*. In the early stages of this innovation, provider companies such as Google located server farms near hydroelectric power sources in remote areas as carrier traffic bandwidth costs pushed Google toward cost economies in services delivery. Today, however, companies such as Amazon are increasingly centralizing cloud computing infrastructure *in/near home headquarters* to better control quality of service and assure security. Physical supply chains followed a similar pattern in the 1990s and early 2000s, decentralizing across the world so as to access low-cost production. Today, companies are returning more operations to the United States and Mexico in order to improve customer service, reduce transportation and inventory carrying costs, accelerate supply chain velocity, and protect production and intellectual property.

- A "new managerial common sense"[6] is emerging for supply chains, based on a more holistic process view, a view that incorporates the need to anchor an end-to-end supply chain stretching from Tier II and III suppliers of code in India up through prime contractors/systems integrators, then injection into critical customer systems.

  Unfortunately for the assurance community, these types of best practices are not being comprehensively gathered across the supply chain, to include software, hardware, and systems-integration domains. Also, they are not being embedded fast enough in Common Criteria Evaluation Assurance Level (EAL) definitions, which form the basis for the depth of evidence to be collected during an ISO 15408 Common Criteria evaluation, to serve as a basis for valid claims or warrants or to provide some legal shielding against unreasonable liability should, for example, the vendor's claims not meet with the performance of the security features of the product.

- Many external observers, including David Rice in "Geekonomics,"[7] argue that the increasing formalization of such best practices provide the basis for corporate accountability through reasonable exposure to liability. This would provide rational incentives for compliance in a way that regulation alone has not been able to do. This might take the form of public shaming or lack of competitiveness in the market due to inferior resilience and security of the IT product or solution.
- Industry representatives in the University of Maryland study and workshop agreed with such observations. They would, however, qualify their agreement with the caveat that the principle of "reasonableness" should apply when reviewing corporate compliance efforts—meaning that cost/benefit considerations should not be excluded from effective assurance models.

The practice gaps and critical issues cited above are the drivers behind development of our Cyber Supply Chain Assurance Reference Model prototype. The prototype can serve as a collecting point for best practices across all the functions and actors of an extended supply chain. It can begin to establish the broad outlines of an ecosystem-wide seal of quality assurance.

The Cyber Supply Chain Assurance Reference Model

The Cyber Supply Chain Assurance Model Purpose

The Cyber Supply Chain Assurance Model has one overriding purpose: to define an organizational architecture and an associated set of principles/practices that, if implemented effectively, could help improve collective control over the integrity and quality of the cyber supply chain. Its main challenge: to overcome the stovepiped nature of the cyber-world today. This is a world where compromised networks, counterfeit routers, malicious code, and insider sabotage are all treated as the problems of separate industries—not as a total supply chain-wide systemic breakdown.

The Cyber Supply Chain Assurance Model endeavors to lay out the common interests of actors to facilitate supply chain-wide cyber security approaches

The Urgency of the Task

Any organization delivering a product or service must efficiently deliver to constituencies or pay the price in loss of prestige, budget, market share, and profitability. The developers and integrators charged with delivering cyber backbones and applications to support supply chains must deliver their systems on time, within budget, and certify that they are secure. In their quest to achieve profitability, however, integrators have outsourced development to third parties in India, China, and elsewhere. The same trend toward outsourcing occurred in the physical supply chain during the 1990s and 2000s.

Deloitte's 2006 "Mastering Complexity" survey[8] of 392 executives in companies based in North America (47 percent) and Europe (53 percent) found that dispersal of assets was far along and that the trends were toward deeply fragmenting supply chains and the whole world as a stage of operations.

Unfortunately, this global dispersion of supply chain assets has had negative repercussions. According to the Smith Supply Chain Management Center/World Trade Magazine Study of 300 companies (2007), this globally distributed approach creates a number of issues:

- Long-distance supply chains inherently require more handoffs among more trading partners—from manufacturers, to carriers, through forwarders, customs, other carriers, etc.
- Handoffs are information-intensive and rarely seamless—even in the most sophisticated IT shops.

Lisa H. Harrington[9] likens the globalized and outsourced supply chain to a conductorless symphony. She notes:

> If the supply chain can be conceived as an orchestra, then imagine 104 musicians; with no conductor; very little sheet music; and what music they have is not shared among musicians. Under such conditions, how can you play a symphony?

Building off this metaphor, Bitran[10] argues that the disintegration of global supply chains is not a sustainable condition and that "mini-maestros" will step into the breach to act as unifying actors who will seek to provide inter-enterprise communications, process discipline, and powerful cross-incentives and communications: "We believe the disintegration of supply networks observed in the automotive, textile, and electronics industry is not sustainable and will be followed by an eventual reintegration." Bitran went on to say that

> One of the dangers of pulling together a final product while sourcing from different players within the network is non-uniformity. The fact that two shirts of different colors on display in a store are from different origins (factories) should be transparent to the end customer. To guarantee this level of transparency, the interfaces in the supply network where parts of these products flow through need to have uniform standards to ensure all players can conform to the same set of requirements. The network itself also needs to be extremely malleable; the players should be "hot-swappable"—weaker players should be easily swapped out with the stronger ones replacing them without disrupting the network. This constant reconfiguration results in optimal productivity and responsiveness.

IT, then, is not a determinant of the network's success; rather, it is an enabler.

Social Contract

A mini-maestro managing a portion of the disintegrated supply network needs to operate with a different social contract. The traditional model of a top-down management approach will not result in an efficient value network. The new social contract should be one that strips away the importance of a hierarchy to allow and encourage individual players to reach their potential. Within a corporate setting, the impact of such a social contract will manifest itself in two ways. First, there will be a sense of equality within different ranks and second, there will be a rooted commitment to allow people to take initiatives and maximize their potential.

The urgency of this situation was revealed in our own research. As mentioned earlier in this chapter, there was a strong sense of anxiety and unease about this situation among participants from the cyber-customer, integrator, and supplier communities who met in the workshop held at UMD at College Park:

- Eighty-three percent of participants had problems with software malware in the past year.
- Seventeen percent had problems with counterfeit hardware in the past year.
- Sixty-eight percent view the threat as increasing; none as decreasing.

Yet, at the same time, this urgency of threat is increasing; only 53 percent reported having visibility into supply chain partner operations, and less than 12 percent reported high alignment between the supply chain and IT system management functions in their organizations.

Cyber Supply Chain Tipping Point

The cyber supply chain has reached a state of fragmentation that urgently requires development of a more effective business model for network orchestration. The current limited visibility of customers and integrators into their global cyber supply chains raises the question: How can they manage and assure what they cannot see? How can they make music together if they're not even playing off the same music score?

Respondents in the Smith Supply Chain Management Center survey defined the problem of software malware and counterfeit hardware as significant in scope, with increasing potential of major disruption. They also indicated that their organizations have not yet adopted some of the best practice strategies they deploy in their physical supply chains to their cyber supply chains—i.e., visibility and transparency of operations across the entire supply chain and alignment of interests between IT security and supply chain risk management.

It is precisely this systemic pattern of cyber supply chain disintegration that creates an imperative for developing a new assurance model. At the same time, the current state of cyber supply chain disintegration calls for a new breed of orchestrators who can envision the holistic end-to-end cyber supply chain and take action to achieve such a state.

The Cyber Supply Chain Management Template

The Cyber Supply Chain Assurance Model uses as its primary management template a "hub" organizational construct. The hub represents a partnership, a coalition of interests spanning the spectrum of players involved in the extended cyber supply chain. These include:

- *Ring No. 1*: Customers who define the cyber supply chain requirements and risk management criteria that will drive the hub organization. Customers (acting in close association with a council of interests from aligned parties) represent the governance function, the innermost ring of the hub.
- *Ring No. 2*: Systems integrators (SIs) represent the cyber supply chain orchestration function, the next closest ring to the center, and act to interpret customer requirements. SIs make up the shared-services arm of the hub. They orchestrate a highly synchronized set of activities that include commissioning, designing, building, maintaining and disposing of supply chains.
- *Ring No. 3*: Cyber-suppliers, which populate the outermost ring of the hub, represent the deployment function. They produce the range of hardware, software, and network products and services that comprise the core building blocks of the cyber supply chain. This ring of suppliers, which encircles the globe, manages a far-flung web of physical facility, workforce, and virtual knowledge assets.

See Figure 13.18 for a diagram of the Cyber Supply Chain Assurance Model.

In the Cyber Supply Chain Assurance Model, these three sets of actors create the cyber supply chain by collectively establishing a charter—a simple, flexible contract, easily amended over time, that binds them together under a shared set of objectives, tasks, authorities, responsibilities, and values. In addition, charter signatories agree to ongoing participation in joint governance, systems design, and educational activities. This is well laid out by William Ulrich, President and Founder of Tactical Strategy Group, Inc. (TSG), in his work, "Organizational Metamorphosis: Becoming the Hub."[11]

Finally, and crucially, the signatories of the charter must establish the *end-to-end risk management framework* that provides community and assurance to the collective workings. This framework derives from looking across the shared cyber supply chain, identifying the key geographic and virtual nodes of activity, and prioritizing the probability/severity of strategic, operational, and human resource risks associated with these nodes and the handoffs among them.

From this risk management framework, the parties establish a *risk registry*. This registry clearly identifies and prioritizes high risks across the chain. The registry assigns specific risks and their management to specific parties. It also describes the actions to be undertaken to mitigate each risk, the resources required for each risk mitigation effort, and the metrics to be used to monitor that risk management effort. The systems integrator in the cyber supply chain then provides the risk monitoring/surveillance across all actors in the chain. This enterprise risk management process is shown in Figure 13.19.

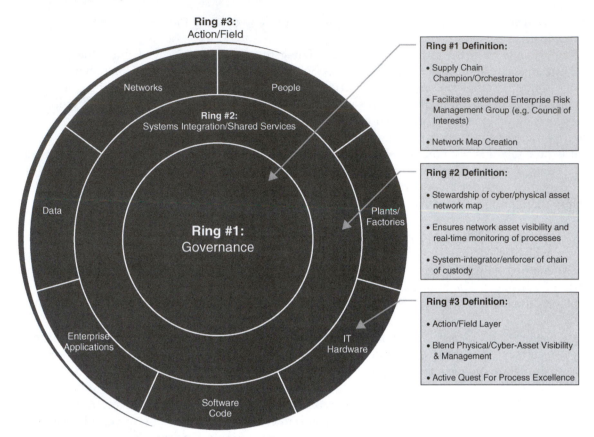

FIGURE 13.18 The Cyber Supply Chain Assurance Model.

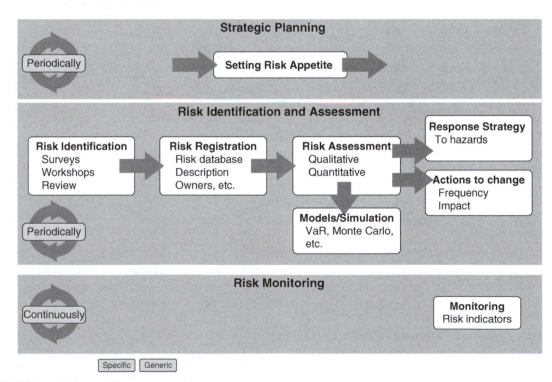

FIGURE 13.19 Managing enterprise risk—process.

Source: SAP AG, 2006.

Each ring layer is deeply involved in managing risk across the cyber supply chain:

- *Ring No. 1* connects and establishes the risk awareness for the whole set of players in and elements of in the outer rings—i.e., people, networks, data, enterprise applications, software code, IT hardware, plants/factories, and people.
- *Ring No. 2* monitors the ongoing set of strategic and operational risks and the efficacy of the cyber supply chain's responses to them.
- *Ring No. 3* focuses on adopting secure practices in deploying assets and processes to manage risk effectively.

Let us be very clear about the nature of the governance function (housed in Ring No. 1) within the proposed model. The governance function does not imply that there is a supply chain czar who centrally manages strategic and operational activities across the rings in a top-down manner. This construct simply will not work in the cyber world. Rather, we envision creation of a "governance" mode, which we define as a form of "flexible coherence" across loosely coupled alliance interests which may be bound economically, by regulation, or in order to provide a common defense (e.g. critical infrastructure identified as vital to national security). Increasingly, these interests would work together to design the virtual cyber supply chain to define its tight/loose inter-linkage structures. At the same time, they would continue—"on the run" and "in real time"—collectively managing the cyber supply chain.

The nested ring structure of our assurance model provides a way to visualize and better understand the extent of virtual integration and interdependency that we believe must be established in order to effectively control the cyber supply chain.

Ultimately, the true challenge of making this model work will be to meaningfully engage a dispersed set of actors, each focused on its own business space, its own precious tasks, in the overarching task of protecting cyber supply chain security. These self-absorbed actors must turn with urgency to the larger work of building the collective supply chain. A "federation of warring tribes" must learn to act as one organism with unity of command to survive.

This is attained through membership in a council of interests that produces a charter, an alliance document that outlines a common assurance vision, analyzes and defines critical risks across the supply chain, and prioritizes those risks for action.

Finally, the integration function in the model—Ring No. 2—does not necessarily represent a separate entity or dedicated systems-integrator company. Instead, the integration function could be performed by a dedicated internal network resource (e.g. an automated sense/response network, a collaboration between nodes within the supply chain network, or driven by contractual obligations).

With these caveats in mind, let us review the nested ring model in its entirety (Figure 13.18).

As stated, each ring or set of players has its own interests and motivations, its own business or operating drivers pushing it to seek greater transparency over the end-to-end cyber supply chain of which it is part. Particularly now, in this acute period of global economic and political instability, each set of players seeks to establish strategic leverage over factors that represent destabilizing elements (e.g. adverse economic conditions, cyber threats, natural disasters). Figure 13.20 depicts the roles and interests of the three groups of players in the cyber supply chain—the cyber supply chain customer, the supplier of IT components, and the systems integrator.

Best Practices within Cyber Supply Chain Rings

As part of the SAIC-Robert H. Smith research study, we interviewed some 30 thought leaders and conducted extensive research into current views on best practices in managing each of the three nested cyber supply chain rings. The participants in our interviews represented a cross-section of leading thinkers on cyber security from both the public and private sectors. Based on our findings, we assembled a set of practices that appear to represent current best practice at each ring layer. Figures 13.21 through 13.26 identify these best practices.

Taking all of these best practices into account, then, how do companies or organizations go about

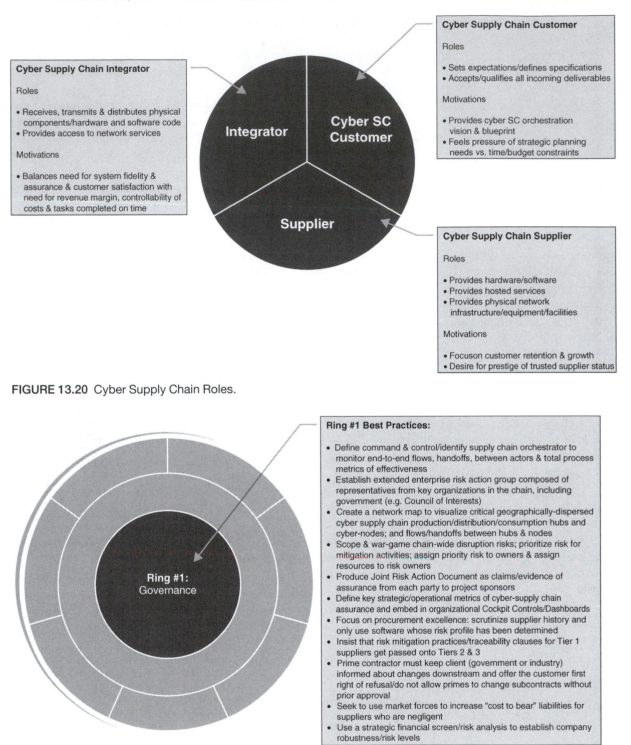

Cyber Supply Chain Integrator

Roles

- Receives, transmits & distributes physical components/hardware and software code
- Provides access to network services

Motivations

- Balances need for system fidelity & assurance & customer satisfaction with need for revenue margin, controllability of costs & tasks completed on time

Cyber Supply Chain Customer

Roles

- Sets expectations/defines specifications
- Accepts/qualifies all incoming deliverables

Motivations

- Provides cyber SC orchestration vision & blueprint
- Feels pressure of strategic planning needs vs. time/budget constraints

Cyber Supply Chain Supplier

Roles

- Provides hardware/software
- Provides hosted services
- Provides physical network infrastructure/equipment/facilities

Motivations

- Focus on customer retention & growth
- Desire for prestige of trusted supplier status

FIGURE 13.20 Cyber Supply Chain Roles.

Ring #1 Best Practices:

- Define command & control/identify supply chain orchestrator to monitor end-to-end flows, handoffs, between actors & total process metrics of effectiveness
- Establish extended enterprise risk action group composed of representatives from key organizations in the chain, including government (e.g. Council of Interests)
- Create a network map to visualize critical geographically-dispersed cyber supply chain production/distribution/consumption hubs and cyber-nodes; and flows/handoffs between hubs & nodes
- Scope & war-game chain-wide disruption risks; prioritize risk for mitigation activities; assign priority risk to owners & assign resources to risk owners
- Produce Joint Risk Action Document as claims/evidence of assurance from each party to project sponsors
- Define key strategic/operational metrics of cyber-supply chain assurance and embed in organizational Cockpit Controls/Dashboards
- Focus on procurement excellence: scrutinize supplier history and only use software whose risk profile has been determined
- Insist that risk mitigation practices/traceability clauses for Tier 1 suppliers get passed onto Tiers 2 & 3
- Prime contractor must keep client (government or industry) informed about changes downstream and offer the customer first right of refusal/do not allow primes to change subcontracts without prior approval
- Seek to use market forces to increase "cost to bear" liabilities for suppliers who are negligent
- Use a strategic financial screen/risk analysis to establish company robustness/risk levels

FIGURE 13.21 Cyber Supply Chain Assurance—Ring No. 1 best practices.

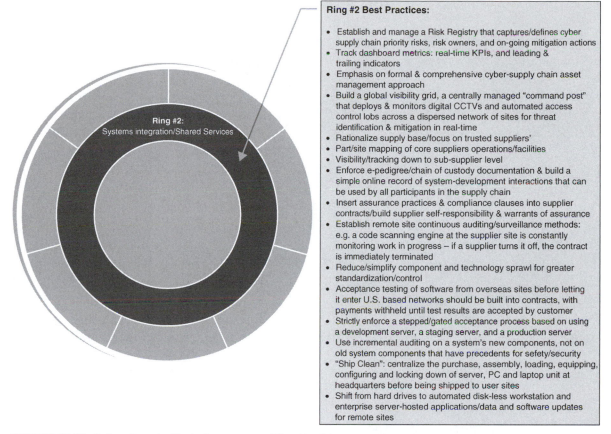

Ring #2 Best Practices:

- Establish and manage a Risk Registry that captures/defines cyber supply chain priority risks, risk owners, and on-going mitigation actions
- Track dashboard metrics: real-time KPIs, and leading & trailing indicators
- Emphasis on formal & comprehensive cyber-supply chain asset management approach
- Build a global visibility grid, a centrally managed "command post" that deploys & monitors digital CCTVs and automated access control lobs across a dispersed network of sites for threat identification & mitigation in real-time
- Rationalize supply base/focus on trusted suppliers'
- Part/site mapping of core suppliers operations/facilities
- Visibility/tracking down to sub-supplier level
- Enforce e-pedigree/chain of custody documentation & build a simple online record of system-development interactions that can be used by all participants in the supply chain
- Insert assurance practices & compliance clauses into supplier contracts/build supplier self-responsibility & warrants of assurance
- Establish remote site continuous auditing/surveillance methods: e.g. a code scanning engine at the supplier site is constantly monitoring work in progress – if a supplier turns it off, the contract is immediately terminated
- Reduce/simplify component and technology sprawl for greater standardization/control
- Acceptance testing of software from overseas sites before letting it enter U.S. based networks should be built into contracts, with payments withheld until test results are accepted by customer
- Strictly enforce a stepped/gated acceptance process based on using a development server, a staging server, and a production server
- Use incremental auditing on a system's new components, not on old system components that have precedents for safety/security
- "Ship Clean": centralize the purchase, assembly, loading, equipping, configuring and locking down of server, PC and laptop unit at headquarters before being shipped to user sites
- Shift from hard drives to automated disk-less workstation and enterprise server-hosted applications/data and software updates for remote sites

FIGURE 13.22 Cyber Supply Chain Assurance—Ring No. 2 best practices.

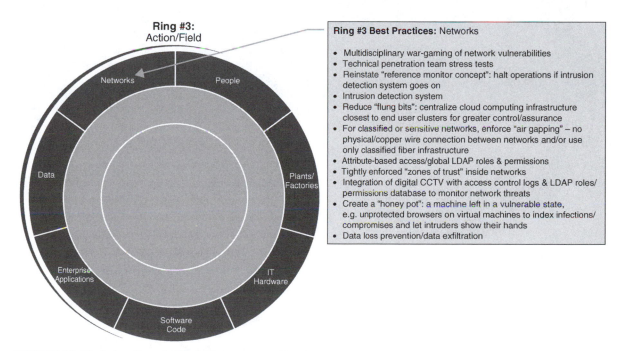

Ring #3 Best Practices: Networks

- Multidisciplinary war-gaming of network vulnerabilities
- Technical penetration team stress tests
- Reinstate "reference monitor concept": halt operations if intrusion detection system goes on
- Intrusion detection system
- Reduce "flung bits": centralize cloud computing infrastructure closest to end user clusters for greater control/assurance
- For classified or sensitive networks, enforce "air gapping" – no physical/copper wire connection between networks and/or use only classified fiber infrastructure
- Attribute-based access/global LDAP roles & permissions
- Tightly enforced "zones of trust" inside networks
- Integration of digital CCTV with access control logs & LDAP roles/ permissions database to monitor network threats
- Create a "honey pot": a machine left in a vulnerable state, e.g. unprotected browsers on virtual machines to index infections/ compromises and let intruders show their hands
- Data loss prevention/data exfiltration

FIGURE 13.23 Cyber Supply Chain Assurance—Ring No. 3 best practices (networks).

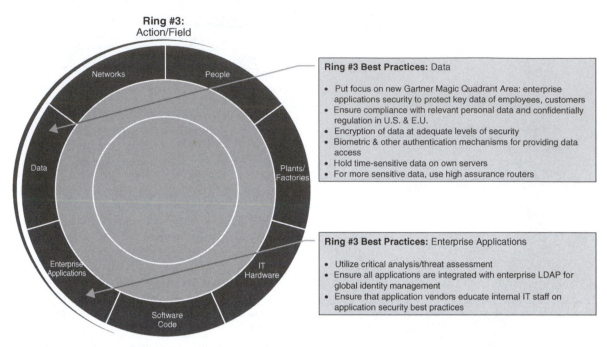

FIGURE 13.24 Cyber Supply Chain Assurance—Ring No. 3 best practices (data and enterprise applications).

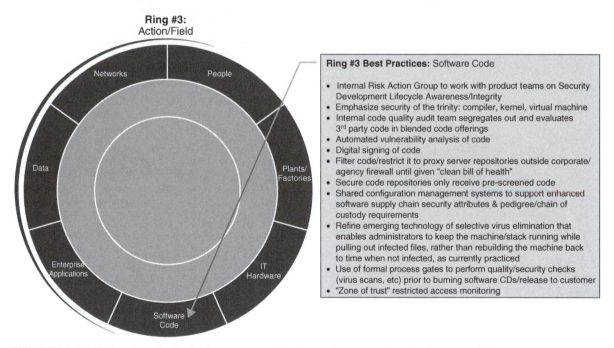

FIGURE 13.25 Cyber Supply Chain Assurance—Ring No. 3 best practices (software code).

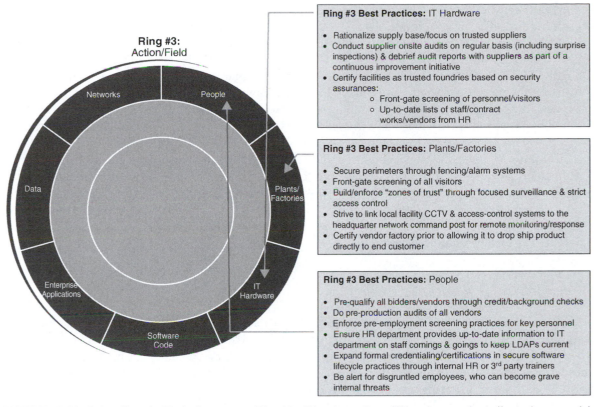

Ring #3 Best Practices: IT Hardware

- Rationalize supply base/focus on trusted suppliers
- Conduct supplier onsite audits on regular basis (including surprise inspections) & debrief audit reports with suppliers as part of a continuous improvement initiative
- Certify facilities as trusted foundries based on security assurances:
  - ○ Front-gate screening of personnel/visitors
  - ○ Up-to-date lists of staff/contract works/vendors from HR

Ring #3 Best Practices: Plants/Factories

- Secure perimeters through fencing/alarm systems
- Front-gate screening of all visitors
- Build/enforce "zones of trust" through focused surveillance & strict access control
- Strive to link local facility CCTV & access-control systems to the headquarter network command post for remote monitoring/response
- Certify vendor factory prior to allowing it to drop ship product directly to end customer

Ring #3 Best Practices: People

- Pre-qualify all bidders/vendors through credit/background checks
- Do pre-production audits of all vendors
- Enforce pre-employment screening practices for key personnel
- Ensure HR department provides up-to-date information to IT department on staff comings & goings to keep LDAPs current
- Expand formal credentialing/certifications in secure software lifecycle practices through internal HR or 3rd party trainers
- Be alert for disgruntled employees, who can become grave internal threats

FIGURE 13.26 Cyber Supply Chain Assurance: Ring No. 3 best practices (IT hardware, plants/factories, people).

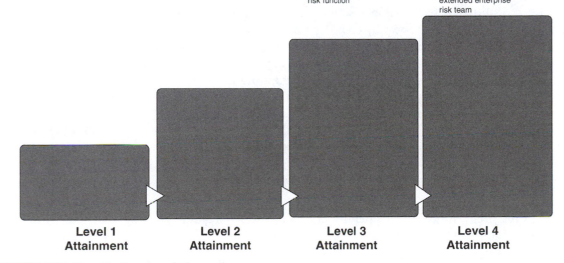

- Internal unit focus only
- Project or software package-specific assurance practices
- No formal cyber supply chain risk program

- Cross-unit internal coordination
- Corporate assurance practices
- Some cyber supply chain risk assessments

- Extend coordination with supply chain partners
- Sharing of assurance practices/information with partners
- Formal corporate cyber supply chain risk function

- Practice/process integration with cyber supply chain partners
- Unified set of chain-wide assurance practices
- Cyber supply chain orchestrator & extended enterprise risk team

Level 1 Attainment   **Level 2 Attainment**   **Level 3 Attainment**   **Level 4 Attainment**

FIGURE 13.27 Organizational evolution pathway.

Source: Supply Chain Management Center – Robert H. Smith School of Business.

achieving the Cyber Supply Chain Assurance Model outlined in this chapter? The attributes defined for each ring layer of the model can serve as the basis for constructing a stepped or phased evolutionary diagram that can serve as a blueprint for how organizations evolve toward management of the total cyber supply chain.

Figure 13.27 characterizes a possible stepped path an organization might follow in its evolution toward a fully integrated cyber supply chain. Each step shows a progressively more robust and holistic approach to linking strategy to task in coupling defense in depth and defense in breadth. Level 1 is typified by an organization that has achieved a certain level of rigor of risk management within its own enterprise. Its practices focus almost exclusively on its own SDLC in isolation and do not take into account a shared risk management strategy by integrating its efforts with the rest of the cyber supply chain. Level 4 organizations, by contrast, exemplify the ability to balance the implementation of defense in depth practices with a defense in breadth strategy that draws in key players in the cyber supply chain ecosystem. A Level 4 organizations' shared risk management strategy reinforces and extends its own internal practices and acts as a force multiplier creating increased resiliency and reliability for each actor in the ecosystem.

Conclusion: The Way Forward

During the course of researching and developing a cyber supply chain assurance reference model, the research team uncovered a fundamental discovery: global cyber supply chains are as fragmented and stovepiped today as global physical supply chains were a decade and a half ago. This is not good news, because the risks inherent in an unsecured cyber supply chain have tremendous ramifications for both the economy and security of the United States and its global trading partners.

In the early 1990s, the Robert H. Smith School of Business Supply Chain Management Center conducted a research study similar to the cyber supply chain initiative discussed in this chapter. In that study, the Supply Chain Management Center looked at hundreds of companies that were undertaking global physical supply chain transformation. There are remarkable similarities between the findings of that mid-1990s study of physical supply chains, and our most recent analysis of cyber supply chains.

During the 1990s, physical supply chain managers struggled to gain visibility over operations and establish more collaborative and robust business ecosystems with customers, distributors, and suppliers on a worldwide basis. Global supply chain managers responded to the challenges of dis-integration and disconnectedness by creating a process map and set of activity definitions to capture and understand the operational complexities they faced. From these process maps and activity definitions, organizations began to build more effective physical supply chains—supply chains based on integration, multi-tiered visibility, and process orchestration.

From these concerted efforts to codify the physical supply chain, a consensus model of supply chain operations emerged—called the Supply Chain Operations Reference (SCOR) model. The SCOR model was developed by the Supply Chain Council, a membership group of over 800 companies. It is now a widely accepted industry standard for enterprise supply chain operations and practices.

Today, the same type of consensus must be forged around the definition and purpose of a cyber supply chain. Further, this model must meet certain critical tests:

- It must deliver "defense in depth" and "defense in breadth" layering practices within each organization while extending security mitigation and risk management practices across the cyber supply chain.
- Provide visibility and coherence across the cyber supply chain, which enables effective orchestration and synchronization across global supply chains, and beyond the four walls of individual organizations.
- Create structured incentives and relationship drivers, which encourage and facilitate management of shared risk. Without such personal incentives, change at the level we are discussing is very unlikely to occur. This could take the form of an industry-wide Code of Practice

designed to ensure cooperation and compliance among key supply chain actors while avoiding unnecessary costs and regulatory burdens for industry.

- Improve communication between the cyber and physical supply chain domains. Lack of communication between the two arenas is constraining advancement—despite the fact that they share many of the same end purposes and goals. A common set of terms and definitions is a starting point with the ultimate goal being interoperable information systems which drive improved command and control of the cyber supply chain delivering timely intelligence and augmented risk-based decision-making capabilities in real time.

- The concepts of "apply to" and "apply through" are key to understanding the interdependencies between SDLCs across the supply chain. These, in turn, drive the need for an evolutionary approach to shared risk management. "Apply to" investments impact people, processes, or technology that embody the supply chain itself. "Apply through" investments directly impact the components, products, services, and integrated systems created and transported by the supply chains. Utilizing this two-tier model is a key driver in creating the right strategic solutions based upon interdependencies between SDLCs across the supply chain.

Information Technology Systems have become increasingly critical to government and enterprise system operations and sustainability. Consequently, we have witnessed more intensive and extensive organizational efforts to minimize systems-risk and to maximize resiliency. At the federal level, the President's Comprehensive National Cybersecurity Initiative is an umbrella strategic framework under which a number of proposals are grouped. These proposals are all intended to enhance the security of the federal government's networks and shield them from intrusion and attack. Coupling these national initiatives with a Code of Practice in industry designed to be enforceable and reassure government that it is effective in raising the level of cyber-supply chain integrity and resilience provides the foundation for an assured ecosystem in which our reference model could be applied and measured in the context of a maturity model. Over time, these practices will be improved upon, such that a common body of knowledge will be available for application in global cyber supply chains, reducing the risk environment for those prescient enough adopt them.

Acknowledgments

The authors would like to thank Robert H. Smith School of Business, University of Maryland, Dean Anand Anandalingam for his endorsement and facilitation of this research; Rodrigo Briito and Xiang Wan for their research support on this project; and Josef Hapli for his work on the report's overall design and graphics. We are appreciative of their effort and contribution.

Notes

1. www.PRTM.com, 2009.
2. Ibid.
3. The Supply Chain Management Center: Robert H. Smith School of Business.
4. Veracode offers the first on-demand, application security solution that provides automated application security testing through an easy-to-use, software-as-a-service delivery model. By providing code analysis and web application security testing as a service, organizations have no software or hardware to purchase, install, maintain, or upgrade.

   With Veracode, enterprises can use application security assessment to achieve code security and implement testing into their secure software development life cycle at key development milestones. For enterprises that want to improve SDLC security without sacrificing profitability or competitiveness, Veracode offers SecurityReview. SecurityReview combines static, dynamic, and manual testing capabilities and scans code after it has been compiled—at the binary level or "byte" code level rather than the source level, as other solutions do. This offers two distinct advantages: One, binary code analysis is more efficient, so vulnerabilities can be found more quickly and with fewer false positives. And two, binary code analysis is the most complete application security testing method because all code can be scanned regardless of origin. Source: www.veracode.com, 2009.
5. Cloud computing is a model for enabling convenient, on-demand network access to a shared pool of configurable computing resources (e.g., networks, servers, storage, applications, and services) that can be rapidly provisioned

and released with minimal management effort or service provider interaction. This cloud model promotes availability and is composed of five essential *characteristics*, three *service models*, and four *deployment models*. Essential characteristics:

On-demand self-service. A consumer can unilaterally provision computing capabilities, such as server time and network storage, as needed automatically without requiring human interaction with each service's provider.

Broad network access. Capabilities are available over the network and accessed through standard mechanisms that promote use by heterogeneous thin or thick client platforms (e.g., mobile phones, laptops, and PDAs).

Resource pooling. The provider's computing resources are pooled to serve multiple consumers using a multi-tenant model, with different physical and virtual resources dynamically assigned and reassigned according to consumer demand. There is a sense of location independence in that the customer generally has no control or knowledge over the exact location of the provided resources but may be able to specify location at a higher level of abstraction (e.g., country, state, or datacenter). Examples of resources include storage, processing, memory, network bandwidth, and virtual machines.

Rapid elasticity. Capabilities can be rapidly and elastically provisioned, in some cases automatically, to quickly scale out and rapidly release to quickly scale in. To the consumer, the capabilities available for provisioning often appear to be unlimited and can be purchased in any quantity at any time.

Measured service. Cloud systems automatically control and optimize resource use by leveraging a metering capability at some level of abstraction appropriate to the type of service (e.g., storage, processing, bandwidth, and active user accounts). Resource usage can be monitored, controlled, and reported providing transparency for both the provider and consumer of the utilized service.

Source: Draft NIST Working Definition of Cloud Computing, National Institute of Standards and Technology.

6 Carlota Perez, "Structural change and assimilation of new technologies in the economic and social systems," *Futures*, Vol.15, No.5, October 1983, 357–375.

7 *Geekonomics: The Real Cost of Insecure Software*, David Rice, Addison Wesley, 2007.

8 Source: http://www.deloitte.org/dtt/research/0,1015,cid%253D30239,00.html

9 Lisa Harrington, presentation delivered at the 2008 China Conference of the Council of Supply Chain Management Professionals, Shanghai, PRC.

10 Source: Bitran, Gabriel R., Gurumurthi, Suri, and Sam, Shiou Lin, "Emerging Trends in Supply Chain Governance," (January 2006). MIT Sloan Research Paper No. 4590-06. Available at SSRN: http://ssrn.com/abstract=882086

11 William Ulrich, http://www.systemtransformation.com/becoming_the_hub

fourteen
Minimizing Volatility in Service Supply Chains

Nathan Birckhead

Supply chain professionals who work for manufacturers, distributors, retailers, and other businesses that make and move hard goods might not think of the following as "real" supply chains:

- The consulting firm Accenture provides an operational analytics service tied to a specific physical supply chain. One of its clients is the St. Louis Transit System.
- The banking members of SWIFT (Society for Worldwide Interbank Financial Telecommunication) provide financial intermediary services to multi-enterprise global supply chains.
- Hewlett-Packard (HP) provides IT platform services that support the digital media supply chain.

These may not be traditional, product-based supply chains, but they are indeed "real." They are all examples of what we call "service supply chains." They have some characteristics in common with product-based supply chains, but in many ways they are quite different.

A *traditional supply chain* is a coordinated system of organizations, people, activities, information, and resources involved in moving a product in a physical manner from supplier to customer. Activities performed by some of the participants in a traditional supply chain transform raw materials and components into a finished product that is delivered to the end customer.

A *service supply chain* is a coordinated system of organizations, people, activities, information, and resources involved in delivering a service in a physical or virtual manner from supplier to customer. Activities performed by some of the participants in a service supply chain transform "work" into a virtual product—that is, a service—that is delivered to the end customer. There are two types of service supply chains:

- **Pure-play service supply chain:** This type of supply chain yields a service, in a stand-alone environment, that is not tied to a product-based supply chain. Some examples include utilities, telecommunications companies, and professional service consulting companies.
- **Hybrid service supply chain:** This type of supply chain works concurrently or sequentially with a traditional, product-based supply chain. Some examples include captive financing, warranties, call centers, and after-sales service and support.

Table 14.1 presents some examples of pure-play and hybrid service supply chains.

Table 14.1. Examples of different types of service supply chains. Pure-play service supply chains yield a service, in a stand-alone environment, that is not tied to a product-based supply chain. Hybrid service supply chains work concurrently or sequentially with a traditional, product-based supply chain.

Industry	Activity	Unit of inventory	Supplier	Example	Type
Telecommunications	Circuit provisioning	Circuit request	▪ Other telecoms ▪ Builders of facilities	Verizon	Pure-play
Personal computers and laptops	Technical support	Support call	▪ Technical support agents	Dell	Hybrid
Financial services	Procurement/port-folio management	Loan application	▪ Contract processing	Bank of America	Pure-play
Retail	Product support	Warranty	▪ Product servicing	Sony	Hybrid
Consulting (professional services)	Client engagement	Statement of work	▪ Internal resources ▪ Outsourced partner ▪ Offshore partner	Accenture	Pure-play

Source: Robert H. Smith School of Business, University of Maryland, 2009.

Service Supply Chains Present Unique Challenges

Service businesses increasingly are seeking to enhance competitiveness by applying supply chain management principles and best practices. These include visibility over multichannel demand signals, real-time collaboration among enterprises partnering within a formal business ecosystem, extended-enterprise IT network integration, and cross-enterprise workflow coordination and automation, among others.

But service supply chains present unique challenges, and not every aspect of traditional supply chains translates easily to them. Take the concept of inventory, for example. What is considered inventory in a supply chain that delivers services instead of tangible objects? For some types of companies, such as telecommunications or after-sale service, service requests are the inventory, and the service provider's focus is on internal process and/or workflow management. However, many of the traditional inventory principles also apply in the service model.

Another example: in product supply chains, the "bullwhip effect" causes demand signals to become amplified as they move further away from the source and upstream through the supply chain. Hoarding or "gaming" behaviors by key actors result in distortions in inventory orders and holdings across the entire supply chain. Contrast this with service supply chains, where bullwhip effects can cause networks to come to a grinding halt; think of overloaded telecom networks on holidays and summertime power-grid failures. The inability of telecom and electricity supply chains to adjust capacities to extreme demand volatility can lead to catastrophic consequences.

Demand forecasting is somewhat easier in hybrid models because demand is based on the product supply chain. Moreover, it is fairly easy to alter production and adjust a company's spend with its suppliers based on demand forecasts. But demand is especially difficult to predict in the pure-play type of service supply chain—imagine how hard it would be to forecast demand for consulting services, for instance. In some types of pure-play services, providers have to solicit information directly from consumers. Adding to the challenge is that variation is inherent in people-dependent service offerings, and as a result, there typically is more variation in lead times for delivery of services. This uncertainty affects suppliers as well, so that the performance of the entire supply chain is tied to the variability of customer demand.

Given this uncertainty, building a service-based supply chain that is both flexible and robust is of paramount importance.

Managing Quality, Visibility, and Control

Several practices can help service supply chains meet customers' requirements despite demand volatility. Two of the most commonly used are the Six Sigma statistical quality-control method and lean manufacturing techniques. Both of these methodologies, which stress continual improvement of performance and quality while eliminating waste, have been used in traditional manufacturing environments for quite some time. Some large companies, such as General Electric, have also had great success in applying them to the delivery of services.

Six Sigma was developed in the early 1980s by Motorola as a business management strategy, with the ultimate goal of improving product quality. It uses statistical analysis to measure variance from specifications and identify the sources of variability, with the ultimate aim of eliminating them. It stresses predictability, minimizing volatility, and identifying relationships within sub-processes. One of the major benefits of applying Six Sigma to service-based supply chains is that users gain a deep, data-driven understanding of the processes that support the supply chain and of how performance relates to customers' specifications and demands.

Lean manufacturing techniques promote flexible processes that are structured to meet customer demand while eliminating waste in the form of cost, time, labor, and material. Like Six Sigma, it is a complex methodology with its own vocabulary and process conventions. In very brief and simplified terms, lean techniques: define value from the standpoint of the end customer; identify all the steps in the "value stream" (the end-to-end process of creating and delivering the product), eliminating steps that do not create value; even out the flow of material and activities to minimize cost and effort; and respond to customer demand, "pulling" rather than pushing product through the manufacturing process.

Lean techniques are closely aligned with the Toyota Production System, but many companies have applied them in service industries. Lean is particularly beneficial for service supply chains because it addresses how to make processes flexible and agile to meet customer demands without incurring unnecessary costs—helpful indeed in an environment where demand volatility is a given.

There are several tools that can help provide greater control and visibility in the service supply chain. This section will highlight two of them: (1) failure mode and effects analysis (FMEA), and (2) simulation modeling.

Failure mode and effects analysis (FMEA) provides a mechanism for quantifying risk in a service supply chain. Each step in the process being evaluated is rated from 1 to 10 to reflect its risk attributes: how severe the effect of potential problems would be, how likely problems are to occur, and how easy they are to detect. The risk attribute numbers for each step are multiplied to get a risk prioritization number (RPN). The RPN serves as a guide for prioritizing mitigations. Figure 14.2 shows an example of an FMEA analysis sheet.

Simulation modeling software provides insight into the service supply chain by modeling the effects of upstream actions or performance on the interdependent factors and processes that influence the service supply chain. These might include key performance indicators, demand, capacity, throughput, cycle time, inputs, outputs, and so forth. A model can be "trained" using real data from the service supply chain so that it will be better aligned with the actual processes. The model can then be used to detect how sensitive the end-to-end supply chain process is to changes in certain factors. For instance, a company can run some "what if" scenarios to see how its supply chain would function if customer demand were to drop by 10 percent in the next two months.

The tools and techniques described above give supply chain managers visibility into performance as well as the ability to determine how to optimize the various components of the service supply chain. The following case study provides an example of how to apply some of the tools and applications that are commonly used to manage service supply chains.

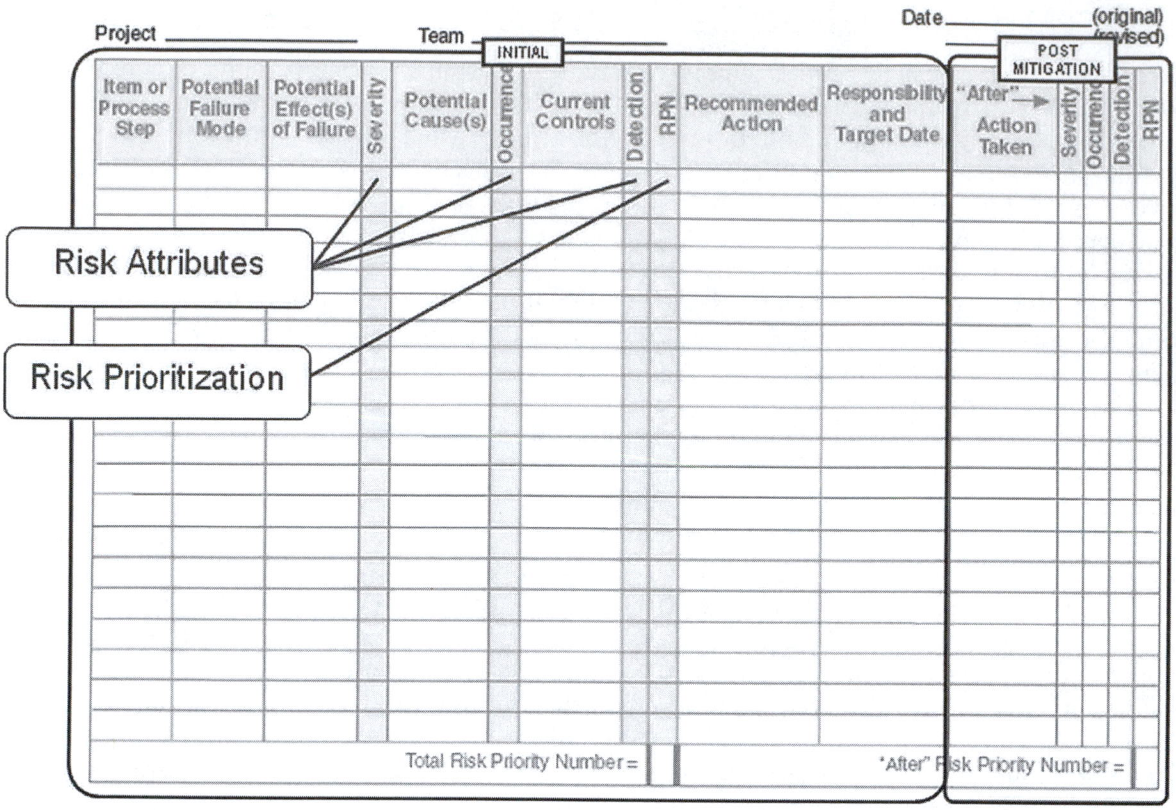

FIGURE 14.1 Failure mode and effects analysis (FMEA) worksheet. This type of worksheet is an effective tool for assessing risk and calculating its likelihood and potential impact. With this information, companies can prioritize risk mitigation actions.

Source: *Six Sigma Memory Jogger II: A Pocket Guide*. M. Brassard, L. Finn, D. Ginn, and D. Ritter, 1994, 2002, GOAL/QPC, Salem, NH.

RHS Telco: A Pure-Play Service Supply Chain Case Study

Robert H. Smith (RHS) Telco Company is a small, regional telecommunications firm that is looking to expand its regional footprint. It has a mixed customer portfolio of small and medium-sized businesses and consumers, and it is facing increased pressure from new entrants in the market (such as cable providers offering telephone service), incumbents (other telecom companies), and consolidation among regional telecoms.

RHS is under increasing pressure to cut its costs in order to compete with other companies in the industry that enjoy economies of scale. Its CEO believes that this is a huge threat for the continued existence of the company, and he does not want to be pushed out of the industry by the bigger players. Ideally, the CEO wants to dramatically increase market share so that RHS Telco can (1) utilize some economies of scale to stay competitive, and (2) attract the attention of other regional telecom companies for the purpose of consolidating. However, if RHS Telco makes the capital investment needed to support the increased demand that would come with greater market share, and sufficient demand fails to materialize, then it could well go bankrupt.

Table 14.2 illustrates RHS Telco's current supplier base. Figure 14.2 depicts RHS Telco's supply chain.

Currently RHS Telco receives 30 requests per day, but with a low standard deviation, or demand fluctuation of 2.5. Customers in this industry expect their requests to be filled within 10 days.

The executive team wants to greatly increase market share and increase demand to 110 daily requests (mean), almost four times the current demand. However, with the greater volume comes greater demand forecast risk, and the standard deviation increases to 20.

Table 14.2. RHS Telco's current supplier base. RHS Telco splits its business among five suppliers, which provide varying turnaround times and costs.

Supplier	Turnaround time	Marginal cost	Volume allocation
A	40 hr	$115	25%
B	35 hr	$125	30%
C (internal)	55 hr	$100	10%
D	40 hr	$115	20%
E	45 hr	$110	15%

Source: Nathan Birckhead for Robert H. Smith School of Business, University of Maryland.

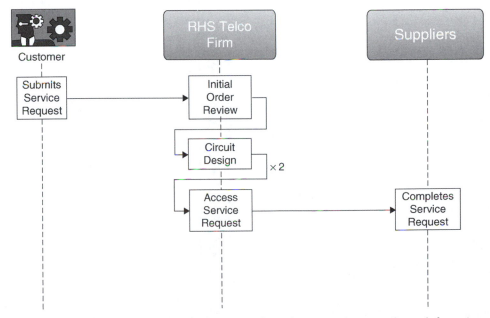

FIGURE 14.2 RHS Telco service supply chain. Customers' service requests move through four stages prior to fulfillment by one or more suppliers.

Source: Nathan Birckhead for Robert H. Smith School of Business, University of Maryland.

The CEO has authorized a $1 million budget to support this growth but has some concerns about the increased demand forecast risk and how that will affect operations. To address the CEO's concerns about the uncertainty of demand, two scenarios will be analyzed:

- *Scenario 1—minimize cost*: This scenario assumes that demand will not grow and will analyze what the service level would be with a bare-bones operation (one person in each department). If RHS Telco does not expect demand to increase and wants to stay competitive based on cost, then management might explore this option.
- *Scenario 2—maximize service*: This scenario focuses on building the service supply chain to maximize service. The primary question is: What would be the cost to maximize the service level (with no budgetary constraints)? If RHS Telco expects demand to grow as predicted and sustain at that level, it would explore this option of ramping up to meet the demand.
- *Scenario 3—optimal*: This scenario takes budget into mind, and will provide visibility to the service level based on demand assumptions noted above. Furthermore, this scenario will explore the tradeoffs between cost and service explored in Scenarios 1 and 2. If RHS Telco is very uncertain about the demand, it might explore this option.

Table 14.3. RHS Telco's baseline (current process). RHS Telco is barely meeting the 10-day customer lead-time specification, even with the current demand levels.

Baseline (Current Process)

	Initial Order Review	Circuit Design	Access Service Request	Network Provider A	Network Provider B	Network Provider C	Network Provider D	Network Provider E
resources	2	4	15	1	1	1	1	1
time (hr)	1	4	2	40	35	55	40	45
Allocation				0.25	0.3	0.1	0.2	0.15
Cost	$25	$100	$50	$115	$125	$100	$115	$110
Daily Capacity	16	8	60	0.2	0.228571429	0.145454545	0.2	0.177777778
Cycle Time	0.5	1	0.133333333	10	10.5	5.5	8	6.75
Avg Lead Time	9.783333333							

Source: Nathan Birckhead for Robert H. Smith School of Business, University of Maryland.

Table 14.4 The impact of cost and service scenarios on performance. When costs are minimized in Scenario 1, RHS Telco will not be able to meet current demand levels within the 10-day lead-time. Although the company is able to meet that specification in Scenarios 2 and 3, it can accomplish that more effectively in Scenario 3 while staying within the $1 million budget.

Scenario 1 (Minimize Costs)

	Initial Order Review	Circuit Design	Access Service Request	Network Provider A	Network Provider B	Network Provider C	Network Provider D	Network Provider E
resources	1	1	1	1	1	1	1	1
time (hr)	1	4	2	40	35	55	40	45
Allocation				0.25	0.3	0.1	0.2	0.15
Cost	$25	$100	$50	$115	$125	$100	$115	$110
Daily Capacity	8	8	4	0.2	0.228571429	0.145454545	0.2	0.177777778
Cycle Time	1	1	2	10	10.5	5.5	8	6.75
Avg Lead Time	15.15							

Scenario 2 (Minimize Service)

	Initial Order Review	Circuit Design	Access Service Request	Network Provider A	Network Provider B	Network Provider C	Network Provider D	Network Provider E
resources	4	10	1	1	1	1	1	1
time (hr)	0.85	3.4	1.7	40	35	40	40	45
Allocation				0.25	0.2	0.25	0.2	0.15
Cost	$25	$100	$50	$115	$125	$115	$115	$110
Daily Capacity	37.64705882	23.52941176	70.58823529	0.2	0.228571429	0.2	0.2	0.177777778
Cycle Time	0.2125	0.34	0.113333333	10	7	10	8	4.5
Avg Lead Time	8.566833333							

Scenario 3 (Optimal)

	Initial Order Review	Circuit Design	Access Service Request	Network Provider A	Network Provider B	Network Provider C	Network Provider D	Network Provider E
resources	2	9	1	1	1	1	1	1
time (hr)	0.85	4	2	40	35	40	40	45
Allocation				0.25	0.2	0.25	0.2	0.1
Cost	$25	$100	$50	$115	$125	$115	$115	$110
Daily Capacity	18.82352941	18	60	0.2	0.228571429	0.2	0.2	0.177777778
Cycle Time	0.425	0.344444444	0.133333333	10	7	10	8	4.5
Avg Lead Time	8.902777778							
Decisions								
Upgrade Operations	$600,000							
Hire Employees (5)	$375,000							
Train Dept	$25,000							
Total	$1,000,000							

Source: Nathan Birckhead for Robert H. Smith School of Business, University of Maryland.

Possible operational decisions and costs:

- Train employees for a 5 percent efficiency gain: $25k per department
- Hire new employees: $75k per team per employee
- Hire new employees: $75k per team per employee
- Invest in a new enterprise resource planning (ERP) system for 15 percent efficiency gain: $750k
- Invest in operations of internal network provider (C), leading to higher cost but shorter lead time, $600k (increase to 15 percent profit margin, cost: $115, time: 40 hours)
- Change volume allocations: A: 25 percent, B: 20 percent, C: 25 percent, D: 20 percent, E: 10 percent.

However, before applying these decisions and looking at the various scenarios, RHS Telco needs to establish a baseline of current operations. A simulation must be built to model current processes and their dependencies. This will not only depict how the current processes meet customers' demand but will also lay a foundation to apply Scenarios 1, 2, and 3, and forecast their performance. The simulation in Table 14.3 was based on RHS's Telco's process. As you can see, RHS Telco is barely meeting the 10-day customer lead time specification, even with the current demand levels.

Using the baseline, we are able to adjust the processes based on the attributes of Scenarios 1, 2, and 3. As noted in the scenario outcomes in Table 14.4, when costs are minimized in Scenario 1, RHS Telco will not be able to meet current demand levels within the 10-day lead-time specification. And although the company is able meet the 10-day specification in Scenarios 2 and 3, it can accomplish that more effectively in Scenario 3 while staying within the $1 million budget.

By modeling the current process and possible scenarios, not only is RHS Telco able to see how it is currently performing relative to customer specifications but it also is able to conduct scenario analysis and forecasting to predict how changes will affect the current process's capacity to meet customer demand.

The Right Tools and Techniques

Changing capacity, suppliers, and other aspects to meet customer and market demands is inherently quicker to implement and easier to predict in the service-based supply chain than it is in traditional, product-based supply chains. However, managing the service supply chain presents unique challenges compared to traditional supply chains. There is more inherent demand volatility, and in general, the supplier base is more difficult to manage and monitor. Because inventory is handled differently in the service supply chain, the focus turns to managing the many different but dependent processes that constitute the service supply chain. The tools and techniques reviewed in this chapter provide the service supply chain manager with the opportunity to gain visibility and a level of predictability by focusing on process management rather than on product management.

Part 4
When Things Go Terribly Wrong

fifteen
When Things Go Terribly Wrong

Gordon S. Cleveland, Patricia Cleveland, and John C. Schulte

Introduction

Gone are the days when one could *choose* whether to work in a risky environment; when the adventurous sought excitement in working abroad or in dangerous industries. Daily events demonstrate how a "normal" operation in an environment which rarely experiences uncertainty can suddenly be overtaken by unforeseen events—from extreme weather to civil unrest to medical emergencies. In fact, the increasing complexity and speed of modern life, combined with the interconnectedness of global business, has significantly increased the probability critical events will occur—i.e., events outside the normal management paradigms. Critical events can disrupt key processes and systems, supply chains and assets, and destroy life and/or property—as well as brands, careers, and reputations.

Because of the increasing frequency and, in some cases, severity of critical events, business leaders and managers must be well versed in risk assessment and incident management. They must develop a "toolkit" of reliable skills, networks, and practices they can call upon when critical events occur.

This chapter provides just such a toolkit in the form of the Incident Command System (ICS). First, we will describe some of the drivers shaping the new environment of risk and offer tools for identifying and assessing those risks. Next, we offer tools for developing and implementing a risk management/response plan. Using the worksheets, checklists, and tools provided, you will be able to apply the concepts of X-treme management to improve preparedness and response to critical events when they occur.

The ICS model succeeds as an incident management model, in part, because it includes and accounts for behavioral aspects relating to managing and responding to incidents and emergencies. The ICS model recognizes that conventional models of management and control often are inadequate to handle the complexities and uncertainties inherent in critical events. It also recognizes that management of critical events very likely involves coordinating, managing, and liaising with multiple agencies, organizations, and lines of authority—all of which adds to complexity and potential system breakdown.

A. The Human Response in Extreme Conditions

Behavioral factors in critical incidents and events are inescapable and add a reflexive complexity and degree of uncertainty to all plans and procedures. Management is not only responsible for directing and coordinating their employees' responses to emergency events; in many (most) cases, decision makers must also take into account the behavior of the "public"—whether customers and clients of the firm, neighbors in proximity to their operations and facilities, public officials or the media.

Analysis of human responses over a variety of historical disasters reveals patterns of behavior that are both unanticipated and counter-productive in survival of individuals and groups. In particular, the common assumption that people will panic, and create a rush for survival in which it is "every man for himself" is not, in fact, borne out in the accounts of a wide range of disasters. These include the September 11, 2001 attacks on the World Trade Center in New York, as well as the Virginia Tech. campus shooting rampage—during which there were remarkable acts of human kindness and mutual assistance, and a surprising lack of panic.

As Amanda Ripley notes in her book, *The Unthinkable,* people who have survived shipwrecks, plane crashes, and other disasters "all seemed to undergo a mysterious metamorphosis. They performed better than they ever would have expected in some ways and much worse in others."[1] In each of the cases recounted, ordinary citizens actually were the first responders on the scene, helping each other, accomplishing amazing feats with little or no formal preparation or knowledge of emergency procedures and methods, well before the "official" emergency responders arrived (p. xiii).

However, behavior in these events demonstrated other, more troubling patterns: Denial and inaction as the primary response to the first warning bells of an emergency is much more likely than panic. Ripley notes that, when confronted with an emerging incident—such as the plane hitting the World Trade Center tower—people more commonly respond by delaying action, to milling about, seeking out each other to discuss what's happening, collecting their belongings—in essence, to do everything except get out. She explains this surprising behavior as the result of a "normalcy bias," which arises from the way in which the human brain processes information by identifying patterns from the past to give meaning to the present.

When the situation is completely unfamiliar, though, these "normal" patterns based on prior knowledge are of little use. The tendency, therefore, is for people to gather together to seek validation of their perceptions—even if they have no prior knowledge to go on.[2]

A second behavioral pattern common to disaster response is that people look out for one another and cling to each other; they tend to remain in their social groups and in their positions within those groups, and their behavior mimics their normal roles in life. This tendency can lead to "group think," which can undermine an otherwise rational decision to save oneself. Rather than act independently, people seek out each other and follow blindly. Such behavior is well documented—recall the famous stories of passengers on the *Titanic* remaining at their tables as the ship sank, or Ripley's account of guests remaining at their table during a restaurant fire, and perishing as a result.[3]

Human perceptions of risk still are not well understood. The conventional view of management and economics for over a century is that people are rational economic actors, who seek out and apply information to guide their actions. Herbert Simon expressed this classical view clearly in his 1954 essay on applying mathematical models in social science, asserting the framework of the rational actor as the basis for economic and administrative theory, allowing for the explanation and prediction of social events as aggregated from the actions of individual actors.[4] Given the assumption of the rational actor choosing among alternative courses of action, the perception of risk would be a mental calculation between the possibility of something bad happening and the consequences if it does, and the decisions and actions one can bring to bear on the situation.

Conventional assumptions of humans as rational economic actors employing full information to assess risk and make decisions are increasingly being challenged in management, economics, and psychology, as seen in the emergence of the field of behavioral economics and current research in cognitive science. Research conducted at the Institut des Sciences Cognitives, provides empirical evidence, not only through behavioral studies, but through neuropsychological and neuroimaging data, that human decisions are strongly impacted by emotions.[5] Research conducted by Jennifer Lerner and her colleagues at the Harvard Kennedy School's Laboratory for Decision Science on the impact of emotions—especially fear and anger—on judgment and decision-making finds that when subjects are angry, they tend to be overconfident about their capabilities and the likelihood of a positive outcome, and that individuals regularly under-perceive risk in spite of warnings to the contrary.[6] Ripley noted the same discounting of risk and danger in her accounts of behavior in disaster situations, and argued that people employ "heuristic shortcuts" (pre-formed answers to "normal problems" based more on personal experience or conventional wisdom than analytical examination of information and alternatives),which tend to be more emotionally grounded, especially in uncertain situations.[7]

Given reasonable, tangible advice, however, people can be very receptive to warnings and instruction, as was observed in the 2005 Asian tsunami, when a schoolgirl remembered her lesson to run to high ground, saving the lives of those who followed her.[8] The schoolgirl's response illustrates the fact that the way in which people perceive and respond to risk is significantly influenced by training—or the lack thereof. Humans' instinctual, "hard-wired" psychological defense to threat and fear is a narrowing of vision and hearing—tunnel vision—with a resultant decrease in capability. This response can be mediated by experience and repeated, realistic training. Field research conducted by the Pittsburg Research Laboratory of the National Institute for Occupational Safety and Health (NIOSH) demonstrates that human behavior under traumatic stress incidents is mediated by stress and prior training and by prior performance under stressful conditions.[9]

For example, in the World Trade Center, the majority of the building's fire marshals had never actually left their own floor or the building during fire drills, and were unaware of the location of the fire exits and stairs. Although they were supposedly trained, they were trained only to await instructions.[10] In contrast to those who did not respond effectively under extreme conditions to stress and fear, risk and disaster, management can benefit from the example of Rick Rescorla, head of security for Morgan Stanley at the World Trade Center. Rescorla insisted upon training and practice for all staff and visitors, and made sure that everyone knew the location of the fire stairs and how to negotiate them by holding frequent unannounced fire drills.

The importance of training and preparation are clear. In the case of the attack on the World Trade Center, 2,687 Morgan Stanley employees—all but 13 colleagues—survived.[11]

As these examples illustrate, effective prior training and instruction provides "mental maps" (cognitive frameworks, viz Minsky) which give people the ability to (1) recognize what is happening in a situation, and (2) to build a repertoire of behaviors and actions to respond effectively to such situations. Minsky's classic theory of human cognition rejected a single basic principle or algorithm to explain human cognition, and instead posited a "society of mind"—a multifaceted set of structures and processes—organized around the concept of "frames," or chunks of memory, perception, reasoning, and language—to explain the workings of the human mind.[12]

Achieving mastery of performance and understanding of complex systems—particularly under stress and threat—takes discipline and commitment over time, creating through repetitive and structured training "mental maps" which can be reliably evoked under duress. Without these cognitive frameworks, a lay person lacking in education and training will fall back on "natural" human behavior, emotionally driven, unreflective, and reactive at best.

In other related research, an epidemiological study undertaken by the Center for Interdisciplinary Excellence in System Dynamics in 2003 describes results from a study of non-linear behavior in response to a disease outbreak which are very similar to those described by Ripley—a tendency to "freeze" (in this study, to self-quarantine) as an alternative to fight or flight. The authors argue that people's responses emerged from a combination of information flows which affected the population's perception of risk and were subsequently expressed in behaviors, which themselves became part of the phenomenon.[13]

Crafting well-designed plans and regulations is, therefore, only half the equation of predicting and managing incidents. Outcomes also depend to a great extent on the people within the system, from decision makers to the lay public. Not only is risk perceived differently amongst individuals, based upon their experiences; research conducted by Pidgeon and Kasperson demonstrates that the perception of risk is also impacted by the political and governmental context of the specific incident involved, and by the perceptions and beliefs of others in those contexts. Arguing that this contextual dynamic underlying perceptions of risk may also explain differences in public resistance or adoption of behavioral or policy changes, the authors call for a "genuinely new and integrated theoretical approach to risk, science, and governance, referenced to its appropriate societal and institutional contexts."[14]

Given these findings, it is clear that limits to these "control assumptions" mean that public behavior must be managed—and people do not like to be managed. They want to know what is going on, even if they do not understand it. They want to participate in decision making, which creates major communication challenges. Regardless of their educational background, training, and skills, people naturally try to figure out situations facing them, and create their own explanations. These must be taken into account in public interaction.

Managers are well aware that employees will comply more readily with regulation and requirements if they are involved in the process of devising these structures. It makes sense, therefore, that management engage employees in developing new methods and models for dealing with uncertain events and critical incidents as a way of overcoming natural resistance to top-down imposition of rules and regulations, or in a larger context, cooperation among otherwise independent agencies and individuals. This is where the methods and instruments developed by various agencies utilizing the ICS model can have a significant impact on business's ability to respond effectively to critical incidents and disasters.

Continuity of operations in a critical incident depends on the efficacy and predictability of plans and procedures deployed during response, as well as on the behaviors which enact these plans. In responding to critical incidents, the first task is to identify and analyze the risks entailed. These risks have the potential to undermine traditional management work roles and reporting relationships, especially under conditions in which the scope and/or complexity of the emergency exceeds the capabilities of the organization.

Additionally, significant uncertainties enter in when cooperation among organizational entities is required because, in many cases, lines of communication and authority must be established before individuals can be tasked to fill critical roles. The characteristics of the incident or emergency will determine the tactical and organizational needs. Therefore, it falls to management to determine the lines of accountability and responsibility to provide the necessary authority for decisions and actions undertaken outside the boundaries of normal operations. This is where the ICS concepts of *unity of command* and *formal delegation of authority* come into play. These concepts are time and field tested. They work, and are essential in conducting the rapid planning and organization required for effective response.

B. Preparing for Critical Incidents

Assessing Risk and Developing an Emergency Management Plan

The foundation of any critical incident management plan is an assessment, by agency/business decision makers and leaders, of the risks or vulnerabilities that potentially face an organization. A complete understanding of risk drives the level of emergency management and incident response planning needed.

There are a number of different processes and tools available to guide this risk assessment effort. One such methodology is the CARVER + Shock assessment tool used by some U.S. federal agencies. It was developed by the Director of the U.S. Army's Homeland Infrastructure Security Threats Office as a tool to assess the vulnerabilities to attack within a system or infrastructure.

CARVER + Shock was originally utilized as a targeting tool by U.S. Special Operations Forces to analyze quickly and thoroughly enemy critical infrastructure to identify a critical node against which a small, well-trained force could launch an attack to disable or destroy that infrastructure.

The U.S. Food and Drug Administration (FDA) and U.S. Department of Agriculture's Food Safety Inspection Service (FSIS) turned the focus of CARVER + Shock inward and used it to uncover previously unidentified weaknesses and evaluate potential vulnerabilities of farm-to-table supply chains of various food commodities.[15] The methodology also is used to identify risks and vulnerabilities for individual facilities (e.g., a food production facility) or processes.

Adoption of the CARVER + Shock tool has expanded beyond military- and food-related applications and is now also used to assess vulnerabilities in the supply chains of power and transportation industries.

By conducting a CARVER + Shock assessment of a production facility, supply chain, or process, the risk assessor can determine the most vulnerable points in their infrastructure, and focus resources on protecting them.

1. What is CARVER + Shock?

CARVER is a targeting prioritization tool that can be used to assess the vulnerabilities within a system or infrastructure to an attack or disaster. It allows the user to think like an attacker to identify the most attractive (vulnerable) targets for an attack.

The acronym stands for:

- *Criticality*—measure of public health and economic impacts of an attack.
- *Accessibility*—physical ability to access and egress from target.
- *Recuperability*—ability of system to recover from an attack.
- *Vulnerability*—ease of accomplishing attack.
- *Effect*—amount of direct loss from an attack as measured by loss in production.
- *Recognizability*—ease of identifying target.

Shock has been added to the original six to assess the combined health, economic, and psychological impacts of an attack on, or failure of, critical infrastructure nodes (for example impact on shareholder value or public confidence in a product).

The CARVER tool is designed to help organizations prepare for unforeseen emergencies that may not be directly connected with the functions of supply, production, and distribution of products, or other elements of supply chain management for a particular company or industry. An unforeseen emergency, in this case, might range from a 30 percent loss of workforce due to pandemic influenza, to the detonation of an improvised nuclear device at one of the large U.S. seaports. Such an event would cast a radioactive cloud potentially hundreds of miles downwind from ground zero.

Until effects of this event could be mitigated, transportation through the impacted area would come to a halt, the safety of personnel would become a first priority, public utilities would be impacted, storage and transshipment facilities would be out of service, and inventory would depreciate or expire.

The CARVER concept creates a method for thinking through the processes of one's business, as if vulnerabilities either were targets of sabotage or potential victims of disasters—of any kind. By identifying their vulnerabilities through an analytical method such as CARVER, organizations can then take the necessary steps to "harden" potential targets and prevent or significantly mitigate some or all of the effects of a potential event.

CARVER + Shock is similar in concept to the Supply Chain Operations Reference (SCOR) model developed by the Supply Chain Council and referenced earlier in this book. The SCOR model focuses on assessments associated with:

- Financial risks—supplier failure, customer default, bad debt, etc.
- Demand, supply, or market variability—unforeseen spike or drop in demand, market shifts, new technologies, etc.
- Quality risks—poor quality items, out-of-specification materials, embedded code errors, etc.
- Natural disruptions—severe weather, natural disasters, etc.
- Accidental disruptions—transportation accidents, production accidents, etc.
- Man-made disruptions—labor disputes, protests, etc.
- Malicious disruptions—tactical strikes, vandalism, hacking, etc.[16]

CARVER + Shock goes beyond these normal business-focused considerations. It enables risk assessment analysts to consider and prepare for catastrophic disasters beyond the scope of everyday business operations and risk, and drill down into the functional details of all-hazard risk assessment.

How to Use CARVER + Shock

How can managers and decision makers use the CARVER + Shock tool to assess and manage critical supply chain incidents? The first step in developing a CARVER + Shock analysis is to build a process flow diagram for the system to be evaluated. Then use the system to evaluate each of the seven CARVER + Shock attributes for each process flow diagram node. Using the "target" concept to visualize vulnerabilities, organizations can rank the attractiveness of a target on a scale of one to 10. This ranking is based on a sub-scale evaluation of targets for each of the seven attributes. Conditions associated with lower attractiveness (or lower vulnerability) receive smaller values (e.g., 1 or 2), whereas, conditions associated with higher attractiveness as a target (or higher vulnerability) rate higher values (e.g., 9 or 10). Table 15.1 provides a framework for this roll-up of values.

Evaluating or scoring the various elements of supply chain assessment for each of the CARVER + Shock attributes can help identify where an attack/failure is most likely to occur. The following attributes and scale offer an example for scoring the risk.

Criticality: A company might evaluate its supply chain and production operations to identify critical weaknesses which would be exacerbated by extreme or catastrophic events and result in significant economic impact (Table 15.2).

Accessibility: A measurement of the openness of the target or node to a threat, and the degree to which surveillance might control access. Table 15.3 provides an accessibility measurement matrix.

Recuperability: The time it will take for a specific system to recover productivity. The effect of a possible decrease in demand is considered in this criterion. Table 15.4 provides a matrix for gauging recuperability

Vulnerability: A measure of the ease with which a threat can cripple a node, or the supply chain as a whole. Table 15.5 offers a tool for assessing vulnerability exposure level.

Effect: A measure of the percentage of system productivity damaged by an attack or other catastrophic event. The effect is inversely proportional to redundancy or other back–up strategies built into the system (Table 15.6).

Recognizability: A target's recognizability is the degree to which it can be identified by an attacker or saboteur without confusion with other targets or components of a supply chain. Table 15.7 provides a way to rank a potential target's recognizability to an attacker.

Shock is the combined measure of the health, psychological, and collateral system-wide impacts created by a successful attack or disastrous event on the target or node. As adapted by the U.S.

TABLE 15.1. Scoring summary sheet for nodes across CARVER + Shock attributes

FOOD: _____

TARGET (Nodes)	CRITICALITY	ACCESSIBILITY	RECUPERABILITY	VULNERABILITY	EFFECT	RECOGNIZABILITY	SHOCK	OVERALL SCORE

Using the "target" concept to visualize vulnerabilities, organizations can rank the attractiveness of a target by attribute, using a scale of one to 10, with 10 being greatest impact.

TABLE 15.2. Criticality index. A matrix for evaluating the criticality of an incident

Criticality criteria	Scale
Loss of 90% or more of the total economic value, productivity, or deliverables for which you are concerned.	9–10
Loss of between 61% and 90% of the total economic value, productivity, or deliverables for which you are concerned.	7–8
Loss of between 31% and 60% of the total economic value, productivity, or deliverables for which you are concerned.	5–6
Loss of between 10% and 30% of the total economic value, productivity, or deliverables for which you are concerned.	3–4
Loss of less than 10% of the total economic value, productivity, or deliverables for which you are concerned.	1–2

TABLE 15.3. Criteria for assessing accessibility. A tool with which to assess how physically accessible "targets" are to attack or breach

Accessibility criteria	Scale
Easily Accessible (e.g., target is outside building and no perimeter fence). Limited physical or human barriers or observation capability. Attacker or promulgating event has relatively unlimited access to target or node. Multiple sources of information concerning location and vulnerability of target are easily available.	9–10
Accessible (e.g., target is inside facility, but unsecured). Observation and physical barriers limited. Only limited specific information is available regarding facility or location of target.	7–8
Partially Accessible (inside a facility, but relatively unsecured). Easily observed with some physical barriers to access. Only general, non-specific information is available on the facility or target.	5–6
Hardly Accessible (e.g., inside a secured part of a facility). Human observation and physical barriers with established means of detection. Limited general information available on facility or target.	3–4
Not Accessible. Physical barriers, surveillance, alarms. Defined means of intervention in place. No useful publicly available information concerning the target.	1–2

Case: According to a B-24 pilot present at the time, a World War II work release prisoner-of-war on the American Air Base at Brindisi, Italy, exchanged the signs in front of storage tanks for water and gasoline, resulting in the fuel tanks of a number of B-24 bomber aircraft being filled with water. Needless to say, considerable delays in the accomplishment of these bomber's missions resulted.

TABLE 15.4. Recuperability criteria. This figure provides a scale for assessing how long it will take to recuperate from a critical incident

Recuperability criteria	Scale
> 1 year	9–10
6 months to 1 year	7–8
3–6 months	5–6
1–3 months	3–4
< 1 month	1–2

TABLE 15.5. Vulnerability assessment tool. This figure provides a tool for gauging how vulnerable a site or physical assets are to disruption, destruction or damage

Vulnerability criteria	Scale
Easy for threat to destroy physical assets or totally disrupt activities.	9–10
Easy for threat to damage physical assets or disrupt activities.	7–8
30–60% probability for threat to damage physical assets or disrupt activities.	5–6
10–30% probability for threat to damage physical assets or disrupt activities.	3–4
Less than 10% probability for threat to damage physical assets or disrupt activities.	1–2

TABLE 15.6. Incident effect assessment offers a quick tool for evaluating the percentage of system productivity damaged by an incident

Effect criteria	Scale
Greater than 50% of the systems capacity impacted.	9–10
25–50% of the systems capacity impacted.	7–8
10–25% of the systems capacity impacted.	5–6
1–10% of the systems capacity impacted.	3–4
> 1% of the systems capacity impacted.	1–2

TABLE 15.7. Target recognizability index provides a tool for assessing how easily recognized a target is to a potential attacker

Recognizability criteria	Scale
Target is clearly recognizable and requires little or no training for recognition.	9–10
Target is easily recognizable and requires only a small amount of training for recognition.	7–8
Target is difficult to recognize or might be confused with other targets or components and requires training for recognition.	5–6
Target is difficult to recognize and might be easily confused with other targets or components and requires extensive training for recognition.	3–4
Target cannot be recognized under any conditions, except by experts.	1–2

FDA, Shock is considered to occur on a national level, and includes impact on major historical, cultural, religious, or symbolic targets, major loss of life, and costs ranging from $100 million to $100 billion. In business or supply chain models, Shock criteria might include the degree to which an event diminishes shareholder confidence, creates mass unemployment, or removes critical products or services from a broad range of other industries and businesses or the public sector. In the business sector these conditions and values could be highly variable, and Shock criteria would reflect variables determined by risk assessors from each supply chain management system.

Once the ranking on each of the attribute scales has been calculated for a given node within the supply chain system, the ranking on all of the scales can then be totaled to give an overall value for that node. This should be repeated for each node within a supply chain system. The overall values for all the nodes can then be compared to rank the vulnerability of the different nodes relative to each other. The nodes with the highest total rating have the highest potential vulnerability and should be the focus of countermeasure efforts.

Information derived from CARVER + Shock analysis contributes important input into Incident/ Event Complexity Analysis (ICA) discussed in the following section.

Response to Critical Incidents: Assessment vs. Management Plan

During an emergency or unplanned event, agency/business leaders often discover a written response plan does not exist, it is out of date, it does not address the current situation, or it is just not being used at the time of the current incident/event.

Because each of these events is outside of the "norm," it is important to train key personnel to develop and perform an emergency assessment or Incident/Event Complexity Analysis (ICA). The ICA can serve as a guide to manage a major event and also determine and document the level of management and the agency/business decision maker's time and attention required to respond. In addition, the ICA can identify the agency/business resources needed along with the safety and strategic issues that require mitigation. During major unplanned events or emergencies decision makers must also interact with local, state, or government response organizations involved in the event, in part to protect the valuable resources of the agency/business.

The ICA will help in developing incident objectives. These objectives can be employed in a management by objectives approach, to manage an incident or event (using the Incident Command System), develop an ICA, and assist the initial Incident Action Plan (IAP) process by clearly stating the situation and supporting the initial development of the incident objectives. The ICA process will help determine the size or scale of the incident or event (incident type) and the resources needed to manage and mitigate the incident or event. In a multi-agency or unified command environment, the ICA is used to provide a clear picture of the magnitude, complexity, and potential impacts of the anticipated or actual incident/event. The agency/business decision maker should certify the ICA decisions, once the analysis is completed.

2. Incident Complexity Analysis

Overview: What It Is

An Incident Complexity Analysis (ICA) is used primarily to determine the size or scale of the incident that has occurred. The ICA should be used by agency/business decision makers and Incident Commanders to evaluate emergency response incidents and determine the level of agency/business, local, state, or federal management organization required to meet the incident/event management objectives. The ICA also identifies resources, safety, and strategic issues that require mitigation. The assumptions for developing a complexity analysis are to:

- Facilitate assembling an efficient and effective organization during the early stages of the incident or event.
- Improve Incident Management Team or organization effectiveness as an incident becomes more complex.

The agency/business decision maker determines the complexity of an incident, its type, and recommends appropriate resources for its management.

Many factors determine the complexity of an incident, including size and potential growth of the incident/event, resources committed, resources threatened, safety, jurisdiction, management, and external influences. The following guidelines will assist in determining incident complexity.

The agency/business decision maker must understand the basic elements of incident complexity in order to recognize the magnitude of an actual or potential situation and make appropriate decisions regarding its management.

One of the first steps during an emergency or unplanned event is to determine the incident or event size, scale, and/or complexity. The National Incident Management System (NIMS) establishes uniform national standards that describe the different sizes or complexities of incidents/events. There are five major types of incidents as defined by NIMS, which we describe below.

Incident Type Descriptions

In a *Type 5 Incident*:

- The human resources or type of Incident Management Team required typically vary from two to six incident management personnel (see Figure 15.1).
- All Command and General Staff functions are not activated.
- The incident generally is contained within the agency/business jurisdiction/properties.
- An agency/business trained staff manages the operational aspects of this incident.

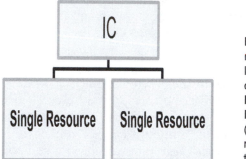

Most incidents are managed at the local level with a small organization. The Response Leader or Incident Commander (IC) and single resources perform the response actions.

FIGURE 15.1 Type 5 ICS Organization.

In a *Type 4 Incident*:

- The human resources or type of Incident Management Team required vary from a single individual to several people, a task force, or one or more strike teams (see Figures 15.2 and 15.3).
- The incident usually is controlled within 24 hours.
- The full complement of Command and General Staff functions are not activated.
- The agency/business decision maker participates in regular briefings of emergency response staff conducted by the Incident Commander(s).
- The agency/business decision maker ensures that a Delegation of Authority document is written and put into effect allowing for the transfer of authority for incident control from the agency/business decision maker to the Incident Commander(s), and that the Delegation of Authority and situation analyses are updated regularly.
- No written Incident Action Plan is required; however, an operational briefing is conducted and documented for all incoming incident management personnel.
- Agency/business decision maker provides a trained staff to manage the operational aspects of the incident.

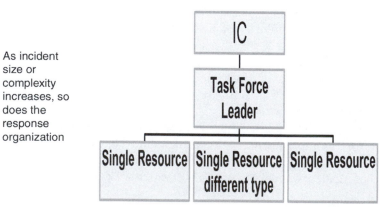

As incident size or complexity increases, so does the response organization

FIGURE 15.2 Type 4 ICS Organization.

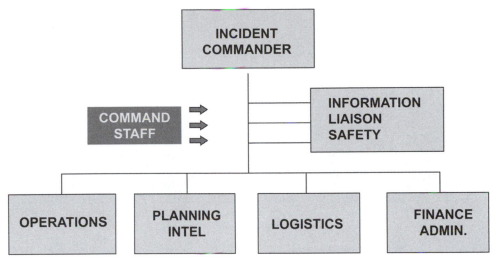

FIGURE 15.3 The ICS Command Staff.

In a *Type 3 Incident*:

- Some or all of the agency/business ICS Command and General Staff positions, or Type III Incident Management Team, may be activated (usually at the Division/Group Leader and/or Unit Leader level).
- The incident extends into multiple operational periods (multiple days/shifts).
- The agency/business decision maker ensures that a Delegation of Authority document is written and put into effect allowing for the transfer of authority for incident control from the agency/business decision maker to the Incident Commander(s), and that the Delegation of Authority and situation analyses are updated regularly.
- An Incident Management organization manages initial response with a significant number of resources and use extended resources until containment and/or control are achieved or until the initial response incident escapes the initial Control Area, at which time the situation is upgraded to a Type 1 or Type 2 Incident Management Team (IMT) and additional resources are mobilized for incident use.
- A written Action Plan is required for each operational period (day/shift).
- A qualified Operations Section Chief manages the operational aspects of this incident.
- Agency/business trained incident management personnel provide planning, finance, and logistics support to the incident.

In a *Type 2 Incident*:

- Most or all of the Command and General Staff positions or a Type II Incident Management Team are activated.
- The incident extends into multiple operational periods (days/shifts).
- A written Action Plan is required for each operational period (day/shift).
- Many of the functional units are needed and staffed.
- The agency/business decision makers participate in regular briefings of the incident management staff, conducted by the Incident Commander(s).
- The agency/business decision maker ensures that a Delegation of Authority document is written and put into effect allowing for the transfer of authority for incident control from the agency/business decision maker to the Incident Commander(s), and that the Delegation of Authority and situation analyses are updated regularly.
- Agency/business, local, state, and federal incident management operations and support personnel normally do not exceed 200 per operational period (day/shift), and total incident personnel do not exceed 500. (These numbers are estimates only.)

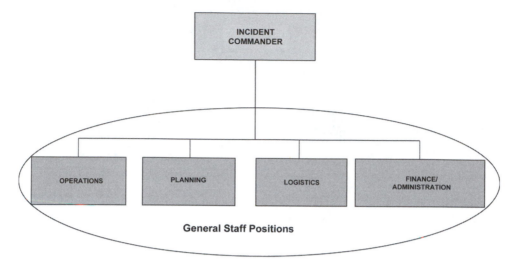

FIGURE 15.4 The ICS General Staff.

- Divisions are usually established to facilitate work assignments geographically.
- Agency/business, local, state, and federal (interagency) incident management personnel provide financial, planning, logistical, and operational support to the incident.

In a *Type 1 Incident*:

A Type 1 incident includes all of the criteria for a Type 2 incident in addition to the following:

- All Command and General Staff positions are activated.
- Agency/business, local, state, and federal incident management operations personnel often exceed 500 per operational period (day/shift), and total personnel usually exceed 1,000. (These numbers are estimates only.)
- Divisions and Groups are established, requiring qualified personnel.
- Branch activation may be required.
- Multiple Incident Command Bases may be required.
- The agency/business decision maker ensures that a Delegation of Authority document is written and put into effect allowing for the transfer of authority for incident control from the agency/business decision maker to the Incident Commander(s), and that the Delegation of Authority and situation analyses are updated regularly.
- The agency/business decision maker devotes greater amounts of time to interacting with Incident Command and General Staff in addition to participating in daily briefings and ensuring that the Delegation of Authority is updated regularly, as noted earlier.
- Use of an Agency/business Resource Advisor at the Incident Command Post is recommended.
- Because of the incident's high impact on the local office, additional staff resources are required for office administrative and support functions.
- A unified command structure is required.
- A representative from each of the involved jurisdictions shares in unified command and, at times, performs other functions. Collectively, the representatives direct the management of the incident to accomplish common objectives. Unified command should be established at the Incident Management Team level.

Completing the Incident Complexity Analysis

Most emergency events or incidents are controlled at the initial onset or extended stages using agency/business, industry, and local response resources. In those cases where the initial management response is unsuccessful and the incident extends beyond the capability of the agency/business, industry, local,

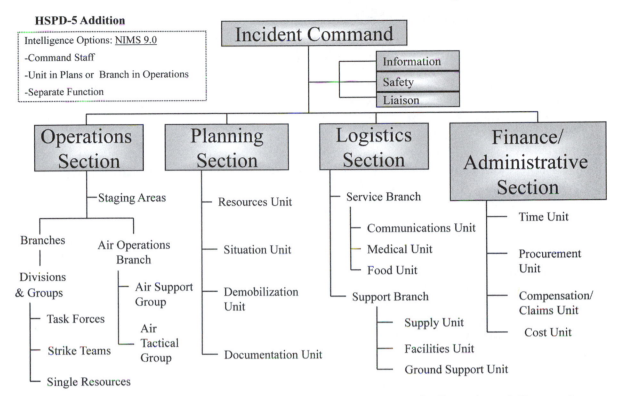

HSPD-5 Addition

Intelligence Options: <u>NIMS 9.0</u>

-Command Staff

-Unit in Plans or Branch in Operations

-Separate Function

FIGURE 15.5 Incident Command System Organization. On small incidents, the five major activities may be managed by a single individual who is called the Incident Commander or IC. Large incidents usually require each of the activities to be established as separate sections within the organization.

A basic guideline in ICS is that the person at the top of the organization is responsible for managing all functions until authority is delegated to another person. For example, the IC will perform all planning related activities until a Planning Section Chief and appropriate units and staffs have been established.

On smaller incidents where additional staffing is not required, the IC may directly manage all aspects of the incident organization.

ICS has complete internal flexibility. It can expand or contract to satisfy differing needs. This makes it very effective and efficient management system.

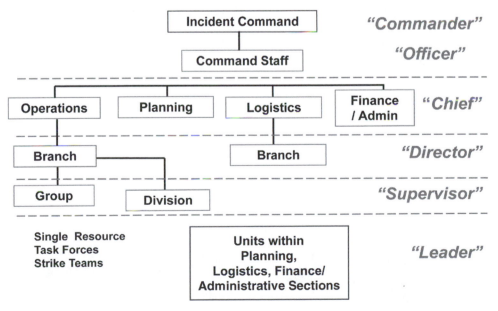

FIGURE 15.6 Position titles.

or state resources, the agency/business decision makers must conduct a complete situation analysis to evaluate alternatives and select a new strategy for managing all aspects of the incident. This is the stage where a comprehensive analysis of incident complexity determines the resources needed to implement the new strategy. The decision focuses on what type of resources or incident management team are needed, weighing the complexity of the actual incident or its potential to escalate against the recognized capabilities and limitations of the response resources or teams available on the scene.

The following guide offers a list of factors contributing to incident complexity. The agency/business decision maker is responsible for assembling a team of skilled personnel to perform an Incident Complexity Analysis, and for signing the Incident Complexity Certificate. The responsible ICA Team or Group Leader and team should analyze each factor specific to the actual or potential circumstances of an event/incident. The summary of that analysis will serve as a guideline to identify the complexity level of the incident and assign the appropriate type of incident management organization to it. Since the time required to assemble and transition an Incident Management Team to an incident may be as much as 24 hours, this analysis should consider both the current state of the incident and its probable state in 24 hours based on the spread or growth of the incident and mitigating actions of the current management.

The complexity analysis consists of a checklist based on eight categories of factors. Using a menu system for each category, the user indicates which factors are present in the current situation. After the checklist is completed, the user assigns an incident type, ranging from a low of "5" to represent Initial Attack, to a high of "1," representing the most complex situation.

Complete Methodology for Analyzing Incident Complexity

The following area and factors are a guide to analyzing event/incident complexity before ordering additional response resources or Incident Management Teams or replacing a response organization or team. The analysis is based on projections for the next operational period. Decisions on the type of team that is needed should be based on the number of "yes" answers. (Decision makers may determine some factors should be given more consideration than others.) The results of a series of checklists will be consolidated into an Incident Complexity Rating Worksheet which will provide an overall ranking of the incident complexity. As a rule,

- A Type III organization should be considered if eight or fewer individual factors receive "yes" answers, with one major area (A through H) having more "yes" than "no" answers.
- A Type II Team should be considered when there are more than eight individual factors or up to four majority areas that receive "yes" answers.
- A Type I Team should be considered if a majority of the five major areas have more "yes" than "no" responses.

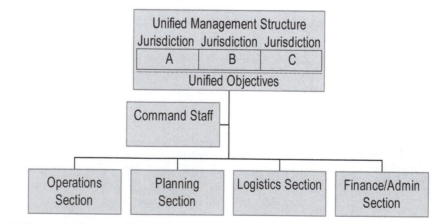

FIGURE 15.7 Unified command organization.

Use the checklist in Table 15.8 to analyze anticipated growth or spread of an incident. For each element check a Yes or No response.

Incident Complexity Rating Worksheet

Complexity Rating

The Incident Complexity Analysis provides a method to assess the complexity of the emergency or incident. The analysis is based on the number of positive complexity categories as determined in the eight checklist categories as shown in Table 15.9.

Incident Typing

1. If positive ("yes") responses exceed, or are equal to, negative ("no") responses on the checklists for any primary factor (A through H), and the primary factor should be considered as a positive response.

TABLE 15.8. Incident behavior growth or spread. Use the checklist to analyze anticipated growth or spread of an incident. For each element check a Yes or No response

A. Incident Behavior (Growth or Spread)	YES	NO
1. Incident behavior does *not* provide for any expected relief or reduction of incident conditions.		
2. Weather forecast indicates worsening conditions.		
3. Current or predicted incident behavior dictates defensive control strategies and/or increase in resource commitments.		
4. Other.		
Total		

B. Resources Committed/Incident Organization	YES	NO
1. 200 or more personnel assigned.		
2. Three or more (ICS) divisions deployed or needed.		
3. Operations organization exceeding the limits of span of control.		
4. A written Incident Action Plan (IAP) is required.		
5. A wide variety of specialized operations, support personnel or equipment is required.		
6. Heavy logistical support is required.		
7. Other.		
Total		

C. Values to be Protected	YES	NO
1. Population exposed or structures threatened, or potential for evacuations.		
2. Incident affecting or threatening more than one jurisdiction.		
3. Potential for a unified command organization.		
4. Threat to cultural value sites, major infrastructure, unique natural resources, and special designation areas.		
5. Sensitive political concerns.		
6. Unusual media interest.		
7. Other.		
Total		

(*Continued Overleaf*)

TABLE 15.8. Continued.

D. Responder Safety	YES	NO

1. Performance of responders affected by cumulative fatigue.
2. Command and General Staff are overextended.
3. Communications ineffective with tactical resources.
4. The facilities or environment in which personnel have to work are especially hazardous (physical, chemical, etc.).
5. Night operations will be necessary.
7. Access to work stations will be restricted physically or for security purposes.
8. Response personnel have been threatened by members of the public or special interest groups.
9. Other.

Total

E. Jurisdiction	YES	NO

1. Incident involves more than one business, agency, or geographic jurisdiction.
2. Incident control involves more than one administrative jurisdiction or local, state or federal agency.
3. High potential for numerous and/or complex claims (damages).
4. Different or conflicting management objectives exist between agency/business, geographic or administrative jurisdictions.
5. Disputes over responder responsibilities and authorities exist.
6. Other significant jurisdictional issues exist.
7. Environmental protection or other land use controversies present.

Total

F. External Influences	YES	NO

1. Controversial incident control policy is in effect or is a factor resulting in this incident's current condition.
2. Pre-existing controversies/relationships (past controversies are influential in developing current conditions).
3. Sensitive or high profile media relationships exist.
4. Potential concerns over land use and natural environment during and after the incident exist.
5. Sensitive political interests exist.
6. Other external influences exist.
7. Special interest group interest is high.

Total

G. Strategic Issues	YES	NO

1. Changes in objectives and strategy are needed.
2. Current Situation Analysis invalid or requires updating.
3. Incident will affect other ongoing programs.
4. Incident location presents significant logistical challenges.
5. Probability exists for long duration (beyond one month).
6. Duration and effectiveness commensurate with cost of response.
7. Indirect tactics are needed to manage the incident.

Total

H. Existing Overhead Incident Management Team (IMT)	YES	NO

1. Current IMT has managed two or more operational periods with little progress towards achieving objectives.
2. Existing management organization ineffective.
3. Current IMT is overextended (mentally, physically, emotionally, and organizationally).
4. Incident Actions Plans, briefing, etc, missing or poorly prepared.

Total

TABLE 15.9. Incident complexity analysis—major areas of concern checklist summarizes the major areas of potential concern in an incident

Summary of Major Areas	YES	NO
Incident behavior (growth or spread)		
Resources committed/incident organization		
Values to be protected		
Responder safety		
Jurisdiction		
External influences		
Strategic issues		
Existing overhead		
Grand total (max = 8)		

Grand Total	Incident Type	Complexity Rating
0	5 & 4	L
1	3	M
2–4	2	H
>4	1	H

Complexity Rating (circle): Low Medium High

2. If any three of the primary factors (A through H) are positive responses, this indicates the incident is or is predicted to be of Type 1 complexity.
3. Factor H should be considered last. If more than two of the items in factor H are answered yes, and three or more of the other primary factors are positive responses, a Type 1 team should be considered. If the composites of H are negative, and there are fewer than three positive responses in the primary factors (A–G), a Type 2 team should be considered. If the answers to all questions in H are negative, it may be advisable to allow the existing overhead or incident management personnel to continue action on the incident.

Each time an analysis is conducted, the agency/business decision maker should certify the result by filling out and signing the Incident Complexity Analysis Certification (Figure 15.8).

With an Incident Complexity Analysis completed and the certification signed, organized incident management can begin. Before describing the Incident Action Plan process it is important to describe the Incident Command System (ICS), its basic structures and some of the ICS history.

Each time an Incident Complexity Analysis is conducted, the agency/business decision maker should certify the result by filling out and signing the Incident Complexity Analysis Certification form.

A. Decision

     I have analyzed the _____ incident against the above factors and elements and have determined it to be a

     [ ] Type 1 incident

     [ ] Type 2 incident

     [ ] Other type of incident (specify under B below).

B. Comments, remarks relevant to decision –

C. Decision Certification –

 Agency/Business Decision Maker or ICA Leader

     Time and Date

D. Report received

     I have received and reviewed the Incident Complexity Analysis.

Time and Date

FIGURE 15.8 Incident complexity analysis certification.

C: Managing Incidents: What Is the Incident Command System (ICS)?

The ICS is a part of the National Incident Management System (NIMS) and works in concert with other parts of NIMS, including the Multi-Agency Coordination (MAC) System and Emergency Operations Center (EOC).

The Incident Command System (ICS) provides a common system for use in response to incidents of all types. ICS uses a standard organization structure, common terminology, and common planning methodology to promote communications, cooperation, and to meld different organizations to accomplish a common task (Figure 15.9). A few key points include:

- Federal agencies are mandated to use ICS through Homeland Security Presidential Directive (HSPD) 5.[17]
- Many states and local agencies have adapted ICS and follow HSPD requirements.
- ICS is an operational management system that defines the roles, activities, process, and structure of disaster response and recovery.
- ICS provides clear leadership, rapid mobilization, and deployment of resources, and also provides capabilities to ensure safety and success of operations.
- ICS consists of five functional components: command, operations, financial, logistics, and planning.

Under ICS, the number of personnel and applied resources increases as requirements increase.

There is a training curriculum developed to teach all levels of the Incident Command System. The current ICS national curriculum can be found through individual state emergency management offices or on the Department of Homeland Security, Federal Emergency Management Agency, and Emergency Management Institute website (at http://training.fema.gov/IS/NIMS.asp).

Exploring the Need for a Common Incident Management System

The complexity of incident management, coupled with the growing need for multi-agency and multi-functional involvement on incidents, increased the need for a single standard incident management system that can be used by all emergency response disciplines.

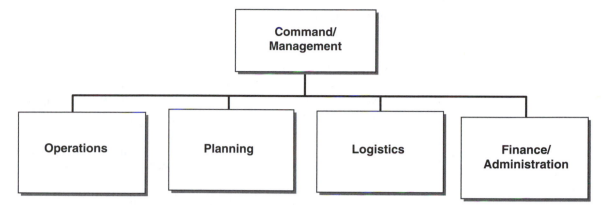

FIGURE 15.9 ICS functional components.

Emergency management and emergency management systems have been affected by factors such as:

- Population growth and spread of urban areas.
- Language and cultural differences.
- More multijurisdictional incidents.
- Legal changes mandating standard incident management systems and multi-agency involvement at certain incidents.
- Shortage of resources at all levels, requiring greater use of mutual aid.
- Increase in the number, diversity, and use of radio frequencies.
- More complex and interrelated incident situations.
- Greater risk of life and property loss from natural and human caused technological disasters.
- Sophisticated media coverage demanding immediate answers and emphasizing response effectiveness.
- More frequent cost-sharing decisions on incidents.

These and other factors have accelerated the trend toward more complex incidents. Considering the fiscal and resource constraints of local, state, and federal responders, the Incident Command System (ICS) is a logical approach for the efficient and cost-effective delivery of coordinated emergency services.

Some History of ICS

The concept of ICS was developed more than 30 years ago, in the aftermath of a devastating wildfire in California. During 13 days in 1970, 16 lives were lost, 700 structures were destroyed, and over one-half million acres burned. The overall cost and loss associated with these fires totaled $18 million per day. Although all of the responding agencies cooperated to the best of their ability, numerous problems with communication and coordination hampered their effectiveness.

As a result, in 1971 the USDA Forest Service (USFS) was tasked by Congress as the lead agency to develop a better system to manage emergency response.

ICS resulted from the obvious need for a new approach to the problem of managing rapidly moving wildfires. At that time, emergency managers faced a number of problems that are still common to most improperly managed emergency response actions:

- Too many people reporting to one supervisor.
- Different emergency response organizational structures attempting to work together.
- Lack of reliable incident information.
- Inadequate and incompatible communications.
- Lack of a structure for coordinated planning between agencies.
- Unclear lines of authority.

- Terminology differences between agencies.
- Unclear or unspecified incident objectives.

The standardized emergency management system designed to remedy these problems required many years of field testing to develop. The Incident Command System is the result of an interagency task force working in a cooperative local, state, and federal interagency effort. Early in the development process, four essential requirements became clear:

1. The system must be organizationally flexible to meet the needs of incidents of any type and size.
2. Agencies must be able to use the system on a day-to-day basis for routine situations as well as for major emergencies.
3. The system must be sufficiently standard to allow personnel from a variety of agencies and diverse geographic locations to meld it rapidly into a common management structure.
4. The system must be cost-effective.

Initial ICS applications were designed for responding to disastrous wildfires. It is interesting that the characteristics of these wildfire incidents are similar to those seen in many law enforcement, hazardous materials, and other all-hazards situations. Some commonalties include:

- Incidents can occur with no advance notice.
- They develop rapidly.
- Unchecked, they may grow in size or complexity.
- Personal risk for response personnel can be high.
- There are often several agencies with on-scene responsibility.
- Incidents can very easily become multijurisdictional.
- They often have high public and media visibility.
- Risk of life and property loss can be high.
- Cost of response is always a major consideration.

ICS applications and users have steadily increased since the system's original development. Some key milestones since ICS was first designed are:

- 1975: First ICS test implementation.
- 1980s: ICS adapted for all-hazard emergency and disaster response.
- 2001: ICS used by U.S. Forest Service and other responders to help manage the response to the terrorist attacks on the World Trade Center and the Pentagon.
- 2003: DHS takes ownership/responsibility of the National Incident Management and Incident Command Systems.

The complexity of twenty-first-century risks and threats were exemplified by the horrific events of September 11, 2001. Those events brought home the need and demand that all Americans share responsibility for vigilance and homeland security. All levels of government, the private sector, and nongovernmental agencies must be prepared to prevent, protect against, respond to, and recover from a wide variety of major events or incidents that exceed the capabilities of any single entity. These events require a unified and coordinated approach to planning and incident management.

To address this need, Homeland Security Presidential Directive 5[18] was issued by the White House in 2003. Management of Domestic Incidents (HSPD-5) establishes the national initiatives that develop a common approach to preparedness and response.

HSPD-5 identifies steps for improved coordination in response to incidents. It requires the Department of Homeland Security (DHS) to coordinate with other federal departments and agencies and state, local, and tribal governments to establish a National Response Framework (NRF) and a National Incident Management System (NIMS).

Develop an Incident Action Plan

The planning meeting described in this section outlines a process for engaging the agency/business leaders, Incident Commander (IC) and Incident Management Team (IMT) personnel in planning response activities that address relevant tactical, operational, and strategic needs.

The central tool for planning during a response to an emergency event or incident is orderly and systematic planning using a written Action Plan. The written Action Plan provides a coherent means to communicate the overall strategy and response objectives reached through this process. Every event or incident must have an Incident Action Plan based on clear, measurable, and attainable objectives, and prepared around a timeline called an operational period. A written Incident Action Plan may be required by agency/business policy. ICS provides standardized forms (ICS Forms) to aid in the development and writing of an Incident Action Plan.

Written Incident Action Plans provide a clear statement of objectives and actions, establish a basis for measuring work effectiveness and progress, and provide for accountability. They give specific tactical direction, and contain specific information pertinent and necessary for each operational period.

A typical operational period is 12 to 24 hours. More detailed, specific daily action plans listing resources, locations, and assignments, etc. may be needed depending on the scope. The Action Plan is prepared by the Planning Section Chief with input from the appropriate members of the IMT. The plan should be prepared/written at the outset of the response and revised continually (even daily) throughout the response.

The purpose of the plan is to provide all incident supervisory personnel with direction for actions to be implemented during the operational period, as identified in the plan. Objectives are used to develop and issue assignments, plans, procedures, and protocols; and direct efforts to support or attain the defined strategic objectives.

At the simplest level, all Incident Action Plans must have five key elements, as listed below. The ICS forms mentioned in this list are available on the book's companion website at http://www.routledge.com/textbooks/harrington. Click on "Chapter 15 Companion – Incident Management Forms."

- What do we want to do, and when do we want to complete it? (Objectives) Documented on an ICS 202 form.
- Who is responsible for doing it? (Organization) ICS 203 form.
- How will it be done? (Specific functional assignments) ICS 204 form.
- How will we communicate with each other? (Communications Plan) ICS 205 form.
- What happens if someone gets hurt? (Medical/Safety planning) ICS 206 form.

Emergency events/incidents vary in their type, complexity, size, and response requirements. The level of detail required in an Action Plan will vary according to these factors. The plan must be accurate and completely transmit the information generated during the planning process.

The plan must be prepared and distributed prior to the Incident Briefing or Morning Briefing and should be prepared for each operational period. (In operational periods lasting more than one day, successive Morning Briefings will be needed to revalidate and monitor progress of the Action Plan.) A planning process has been developed as part of the Incident Command System to facilitate the development of an Incident Action Plan in an orderly and systematic manner.

Figure 15.10 displays the planning process required to develop an Incident Action Plan. Following the planning steps will allow for the development of an Incident Action Plan in a minimum amount of time.

Although the Planning Section Chief is responsible for completing the Incident Action Plan, completion of the plan is a highly collaborative effort. Figure 15.11 outlines representative tasks and responsibilities.

After the agency/business decision makers and Incident Commanders set the objectives, each Section Chief has input requirements as indicated below:

Table 15.10. Functional planning responsibilities for Incident Management Team. This table describes the functional responsibilities allocated to responsible parties on the Incident Management Team.

Task	Responsible Party
Give briefing on situation and resource status	Planning Section Chief
Set incident objectives	Agency/Business Decision Maker/IC
Plot operational boundaries (geographic/functional)	Operations & Planning Section Chiefs
Specify tactics/work assignments for each geographic area or functional group	Operations Section Chief
Determine resources needed for each geographic area or functional group	Operations and Planning Section Chiefs
Specify facilities and reporting locations and plot on map	Operations, Planning and Logistics Section Chiefs
Place resource order(s)	Logistics Section Chief
Consider communications, medical, transportation planning requirements	Logistics and Planning Section Chiefs
Finalize and approve action plan	All incident management team members in agreement with Incident Commander

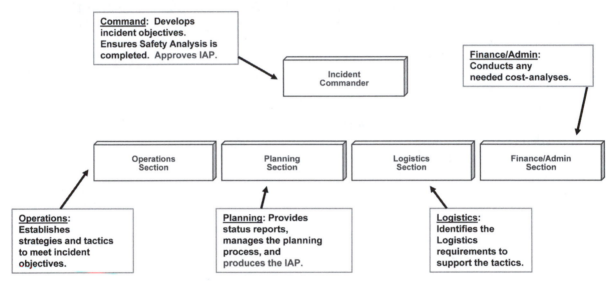

FIGURE 15.10 Who does what? Functional responsibilities of commander and section chiefs.

Incident Commander (IC)

- Provide general objectives and strategy.
- Provide direction or overall management.
- Provide or establish procedures for resource ordering, mobilization, and demobilization.
- Approve the completed Action Plan by signature.

Planning Section Chief

- Conduct the planning meeting and briefings.
- Coordinate preparation of the Action Plan.
- With Operations Section Chief, determine resource requirements.
- Determine Incident Management Team work assignments.

Operations Section Chief

- With Planning Coordinator, determine resource requirements.
- Determine field work/division work assignments and resource requirements.

Logistics Section Chief

- Establish the procedure for resource ordering.

- Place orders for resources and supplies.
- Ensure that resource ordering procedures are developed and made known to appropriate agency dispatch centers.
- Develop a transportation system to support operational needs.
- Ensure that the Logistics Section can logistically support the Action Plan.

Finance Section Chief

- Provide cost implications of objectives as required.
- Evaluate facilities being used to determine whether special contract arrangements are needed.
- Ensure that the Action Plan is within the financial limits established by the Incident Commander.

Set Event or Incident Objectives

The Incident Commander sets the objectives, within the limits of the delegation of authority. The overall objectives are not limited to a single operational period but will consider the total event/incident situation. The objectives state what will be accomplished.

Strategy, the general plan or direction for accomplishing objectives, is developed directly from the stated objectives for the response. The tactics, or individual work methods, outline how the strategy will be executed.

The Incident Commander establishes the general strategy to be used and states major policy, legal, or fiscal constraints in accomplishing the objectives and appropriate contingency considerations. Before finalizing the incident goals and objectives, the Incident Commander should provide a draft copy of the objectives to the Operations Section Chief. The Operations Section Chief should ensure that the goals and objectives are understood and they are realistic.

After discussion, the objectives are recorded on the Incident Action Plan form and delivered to the IMT Section Chiefs so they will know what the strategy is for the next operational period. The Planning Section Chief then prepares for the planning meeting.

Guidelines for Setting Objectives

Setting or re-affirming goals and objectives at the beginning of each operational period is a top priority of the Incident Commander. Here are three important guidelines:

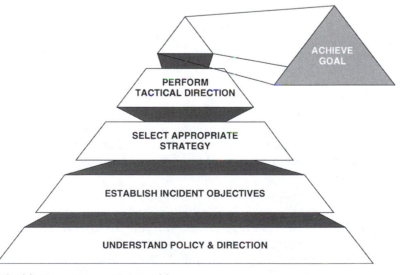

FIGURE 15.11 The incident management pyramid.

- Objectives must be clearly stated and measurable so the IMT can determine how much was accomplished during the current operational period.
- Objectives must be attainable given the personnel, equipment, supplies, and funding available during that operational period.
- Objectives must be broad and flexible enough for the IMT to achieve them the best way possible.

Setting Specific Tasks within the Objectives

Under each objective are specific tasks that need to be accomplished to complete that objective. Each task must be assigned to a specific person with a set due date. It cannot be overemphasized that for assigned persons to complete their tasks, they must be given adequate resources (including personnel) and funding commensurate with the task.

The Incident Action Plan may contain attachments addressing mitigation of specific factors in the field or at the event/incident site or as information documents. Factors and/or needs may include safety and security, communications, contact lists, maps, organizational charts, situation reports, etc. These attachments may be critical and may be quite complex within themselves. For example, a field Safety/Security Plan should contain specific security information and protocols including medical and evacuation information, emergency communications guidelines, trip planning, etc. A field Communications Plan would include radio use, call signs, frequency use, satellite communications, mobile phone use, etc.

Additional planning direction can be found on the NIMS Planning Process in the DHS National Incident Management System document published in December 2008.[19] The incident management pyramid (Figure 15.12) displays the stages of development of the incident management process.

Supply Chain Management

The National Incident Management System (NIMS) and Incident Command System (ICS) utilize a standardized set of supply chain processes and procedures called Resource Management. Resource Management involves the coordination and oversight of personnel, tools, processes, and systems that provide incident managers with timely and appropriate resources during an incident.

What Is Resource Management?

Resource management under NIMS is based on:

- Providing a uniform method of identifying, acquiring, allocating, and tracking resources.
- Classifying kinds and types of resources required to support incident management.
- Using a credentialing system tied to uniform training and certification standards.
- Incorporating resources contributed by private sector and nongovernmental organizations (NGOs).

Resource management involves coordination and oversight of tools, processes, and systems that provide agency/business decision makers and Incident Commanders with the resources they need during an incident or event. To assist agency/business decision makers and incident/event managers, NIMS includes standard procedures, methods, and functions in its resource management processes. By following the standards established by NIMS, resource managers are able to identify, order, mobilize, dispatch, and track resources more efficiently.

Five key principles underlie effective resource management:

1. Advance planning: Preparedness of organizations working together before an incident to develop plans for managing and using resources.
2. Resource identification and ordering: Using standard processes and methods to identify, order, mobilize, dispatch, and track resources.

3. Resource categorization or typing: Categorizing by size, capacity, capability, skill, or other characteristics to make resource ordering and dispatch more efficient.
4. Use of agreements: Developing pre-incident agreements for providing or requesting resources.
5. Effective management: Using validated practices to perform key resource management tasks.

Defining and Categorizing Resources

In NIMS and ICS applications, incident resources consist of all personnel and major items of equipment available or potentially available for assignment.

Resources can be described both by *kind* and by *type*.

A. Kinds of Resource

The kind of resource describes what the resource is, e.g., patrol vehicle, search and rescue (SAR) unit, helicopter, fire engine, ambulance, crane, etc. The kinds of resources can be as broad as necessary to suit the incident application.

B. Types of Resource

The type of resource describes a performance capability for that kind of resource. For example, a Type 1 helicopter will carry up to 16 persons. A Type 3 helicopter will carry up to five persons.

Resources are usually typed by a number, with Type 1 being the highest capability or capacity; Type 2 the next highest, etc. When referring to personnel resources such as Incident Commander, SWAT Team or Incident Management Teams, the Type 1 resource has the highest level of training, experience, and self-sufficiency and is most suitable for the most complex assignments.

The specific capability of the resource must always be clearly spelled out in the type descriptions.

There are three distinct advantages to typing resources:

1. In Planning: Knowing the specific capabilities of the various kinds of resources helps planners decide the type and quantity of resource best suited to perform activities required by the Incident Action Plan.
2. In Ordering: Ordering resources by type saves time, minimizes error, gives a clear indication of exactly what is needed, and reduces nonessential communications between the incident and the off-site order point.
3. In Monitoring Resource Use: An awareness of the type of resource assigned enables the manager to monitor for under-or-over-capability, and make changes accordingly. Careful monitoring of resource performance can lead to the use of smaller or less costly resources, which can result in increased work performance and reduced cost.

Certification and credentialing help ensure that all personnel meet a minimum level of training, experience, physical and medical fitness, or capability for the position they are assigned to fill.

Resource managers use various resource inventory systems to assess the availability of assets provided by public, private, and volunteer organizations. Resource managers identify, refine, and validate resource requirements throughout the incident or event using the standardized planning process in ICS which will identify:

- What and how much is needed.
- Where and when it is needed.
- Who will be receiving it?

Because resource requirements and availability will change as the incident evolves, all entities must coordinate closely, beginning at the earliest possible point in the incident. Requests for resources or supply items that the Incident Commander cannot obtain locally must be submitted through the agency/business office or Emergency Operations Center using standardized resource ordering procedures.

Resource managers use established procedures to track resources from mobilization through demobilization. Resource tracking and mobilization are directly linked. When resources arrive on-scene, they must check in to begin on-scene in-processing and validate the order requirements.

Importance of Maintaining Resource Status

On any incident, the effective management of resources is vital. The ability to select the right resource for the task to be done is essential to accomplish the job properly, ensure resource safety, and remain cost-effective. Maintaining status of all resources assigned to the incident is an important aspect of resource management. For this reason, it is strongly recommended that the various kinds of resources used within ICS be typed whenever possible.

In addition, not all resources at an incident may be usable at any given time. For a variety of reasons, some resources may be temporarily out of service or placed into an available (ready) but not assigned status.

Under the NIMS and ICS, managers should plan for demobilization at the same time that they begin the mobilization process. Early planning for demobilization facilitates accountability and makes transportation of resources as efficient as possible.

The NIMS describes the Recovery process as the final disposition of all resources. During recovery, resources are rehabilitated, replenished, disposed of, or retrograded.

Reimbursement provides a mechanism for funding critical needs that arise from incident-specific activities. Processes and procedures must be in place to ensure that resource providers are reimbursed in a timely manner. Together, each of these resource management processes creates an integrated, efficient resource management system.

Processes and Procedures for Resource Management

The Principles of Resource Management

Basic management principles that apply directly to the resource management processes include:

- Planning
- Organizing
- Directing
- Controlling.

Planning

Planning is the management process of evaluating the situation, determining objectives, selecting a proper strategy, and deciding which resources should be used to achieve those objectives in the most efficient and cost-effective manner. In ICS, resource planning is ongoing and directed toward operational periods.

Organizing

Organizing is a continuation of the management process after planning, whereby the Incident Commander brings essential personnel and equipment resources together into a formalized relationship. The organization chart found in the Incident Command System and which is an integral part of the Incident Action Plan is the mechanism for grouping functional units into a cohesive general organization. Providing essential staffing is also considered a part of the organizing activity.

Directing

Directing is the process of guiding and supervising the efforts of various resources toward the attainment of specified incident control objectives. A very important part of directing incident resources is providing proper motivation, leadership, and delegation of authority.

In ICS, providing direction is accomplished by assigning responsibility and authority for specific activities as appropriate throughout the organization. This accomplishes several objectives:

- Use other people's knowledge and skills.
- Complete the tasks without unnecessary delay.
- Enhance training and personnel development.
- Provide a more meaningful work environment.

Controlling

Controlling involves evaluating the performance of an organization and its components, and applying the necessary corrections to make sure that the performance is constantly directed toward accomplishing the established objectives. The steps in establishing controls over the resource management process at an incident involve:

- Establishing standards of performance based on acceptable norms.
- Comparing the actual results with the established standards.
- Taking corrective actions as necessary.

An important part of controlling in ICS is the continuing assessment of the adequacy of the Incident Action Plan.

Incident Resource Management

Managing resources safely and effectively is the most important consideration at an incident. The incident resource management process includes several interactive activities.

- Establishing resource needs.
- Resource ordering.
- Check-in process.
- Resource use.
- Resource demobilization.

Establishing Resource Needs

A. Planning for Resource Needs

Sound planning to determine resource needs is essential at all stages of an incident. It is particularly critical during the initial stages. Mistakes made at this point may compound and complicate all further actions. In the Incident Command System, there is an effective planning process that provides a framework for determining the resource needs at all levels of the organization.

Planning Meeting Activity Checklist

Operational Planning provides information on:

- Incident work location.
- Work assignments.

- Kind and type of resources needed.
- Current availability of incident resources.
- Reporting location.
- Requested arrival time for additional resources.

The Operational Planning Worksheet (ICS Form 215) is a standardized planning tool used during the planning meeting to collect and display critical information. By using the worksheet, planners can quickly:

- Determine total resources required (e.g. 25).
- Subtract the number on hand (−12).
- Determine additional resources needed (13).

The ICS Form 215 can also quickly help to identify surplus resources which may be released.

On larger incidents, the Operational Planning Worksheet should always be used to determine what tactical resources are needed.

B. Organizing for Resource Needs

In ICS, the Incident Commander organizes the incident by bringing essential personnel and equipment resources together into a formalized and cohesive relationship. The ICS organization developed for each operational period establishes essential chain of command relationships, and provides the framework for all resource assignments on an incident. Personnel resources are assigned to functional areas within ICS Sections based on experience, training, and past performance. Equipment resources consist of both the equipment and the personnel to operate the equipment. This includes aviation resources.

Resource Ordering

A. Acquiring Resources

Most incidents will have an initial commitment of resources assigned. Resources can include key supervisory personnel (often referred to as management) and personnel and equipment assigned as tactical resources. As incidents grow in size and/or complexity, more tactical resources may be required and the Incident Commander may augment existing resources with additional personnel and equipment. As a consequence, more supervisory and support personnel may be needed to maintain an adequate span of control. The planning for additional resources now becomes more complex.

On large, complex incidents extending over several operational periods, many resource orders may be executed.

1. Resource Ordering from the Incident

At any incident, the procedure for ordering additional resources will depend on what parts of the incident's organizational structure have been activated at the time the ordering is done.

2. Responsibility for Ordering Resources

Within the ICS organization, there are three organizational elements authorized to place resource orders. If the incident organization is small and General Staff positions have not been filled, the Incident Commander will personally request the additional resources from the agency/business office or dispatch center. If the Logistics Section Chief position has been filled, then the Logistics Chief has the delegated authority to place the resource order after the order has been approved by the Incident Commander.

On larger incidents, where the Logistics Section contains a Supply Unit, the Supply Unit has the authority to place the approved resource order.

Final approval for ordering additional resources, as well as releasing resources from an incident, is the responsibility of the Incident Commander.

3. The Resource Order

Resource orders are communicated from the incident to an agency/business office or dispatch center. Even though different formats may exist, every resource order should contain the following essential elements of information:

- Incident name.
- Order and/or request number (if known or assigned).
- Date and time of order.
- Quantity, kind, and type. Include special support needs as appropriate.
- Reporting location (specific).
- Requested time of delivery (specific, not simply ASAP).
- Radio frequency or communication system, information to be used.
- Person/title placing request.
- Callback phone number or radio designation for clarification or additional information.

B. Resource Ordering

The resource order is normally prepared at the incident, approved by the Incident Commander, and transmitted from the incident to a central location, typically the jurisdiction or agency/business dispatch center.

Check-in Process

ICS has a simple and effective resource check-in process to establish resource accountability at an incident.

As responders arrive, they must be separated from spectators, volunteers, and victims by securing a perimeter around the incident. The inner perimeter allows the organization to:

- Establish resource accountability.
- Control access.
- Ensure safety of the public.
- Establish a working environment for responders that is as safe and secure as possible.

Incident security requires:

- Distinguishing agency personnel who have been dispatched from those who self-dispatched.
- Identifying and credentialing (providing incident identification that allows access to the incident) officially dispatched mutual aid resources.
- Establishing controlled points of access for authorized personnel.

The Resources Unit will establish and conduct the check-in function at designated incident locations. If the Resources Unit has not been activated, the responsibility for ensuring check-in will be the Incident Commander's or Planning Section Chief's.

Utilizing Resources

In the ICS, there is both a chain of command (the organization) and a unity of command (each person has one person to report to). These two factors provide the basis for effective resource management and personnel accountability. Supervisory personnel direct, guide, monitor, and evaluate the efforts of subordinates toward attaining specific objectives. Resources, whether they are tactical resources assigned to the Operations Section, or personnel assigned to support the overall operation, are always directed by a designated supervisor or leader.

Resources Performance Evaluation

This step monitors, evaluates, and adjusts the performance of the organization and its components to ensure that all efforts are directed toward achieving the specified objectives. Performance standards for personnel and equipment resources are based on accepted agency norms. These should be communicated and/or reaffirmed prior to assignments. Results must be constantly evaluated against the standards, and corrective action taken if required.

Performance standards will vary in their form and content from agency to agency. They can include job aids, task books, policy and procedure guides, evaluation checklists, etc.

The specified objectives that are to be achieved must also be reviewed as a part of this process to ensure that they continue to be realistic and valid.

Demobilizing Resources

At all times during an incident, the Incident Commander and General and Command Staff members must determine when assigned resources are no longer required to meet incident objectives. Excess resources must be released in a timely manner to reduce incident-related costs, and to free resources for other assignments. On larger incidents, the planning for demobilization should begin almost immediately and certainly well in advance of when demobilization actually takes place.

The process of demobilizing resources generally begins at the Operations Section level, where the need for continued tactical resources will be determined. When tactical resources are no longer needed, other parts of the organization can also be reduced.

A. The Process of Demobilization

On single-agency and/or smaller incidents, the planning and the process of demobilization may be simple and will not require a formal written demobilization plan or a Demobilization Unit to prepare it.

On large incidents, especially those which may have personnel and tactical resources from several jurisdictions or agencies, and where there has been a good integration of multijurisdiction or agency personnel into the incident organization, a Demobilization Unit within the Planning Section should be established early in the life of the incident. A written demobilization plan is essential on larger incidents.

In order to determine excess resources and begin the demobilization process, it will be necessary for each part of the ICS organization to evaluate the continuing need for both personnel and tactical resources. Resources no longer needed within each section should be reported to the Section Chief as soon as it is determined that the need no longer exists. The Demobilization Unit, if established, may recommend release priorities for the Incident Commander's approval based upon continuing needs both on and off the incident.

Agencies will differ in how they establish release priorities for resources assigned to an incident. Also, the process for demobilization will vary by application area. Participants at an incident should expect to see and accept differences as reflected by agency policy.

B. The Demobilization Plan

An incident Demobilization Plan should contain five essential parts:

- General Information (guidelines).
- Responsibilities.
- Release Priorities.
- Release Procedures.
- A Directory (maps, phone listings, etc.).

Key Resource Management Considerations

Safety, personnel accountability, managerial control, adequate reserves, and cost are all key considerations when managing incident resources.

A. Safety

A basic principle of resource management is that resource actions at all levels of the organization must be conducted in a safe manner. This includes ensuring the safety of:

- Responders to the incident.
- Persons injured or threatened by the incident.
- Volunteers assisting at the incident.
- News media and the general public who are on scene observing the incident.

Current laws, liability issues, and future trends will continue to place additional emphasis on personnel safety.

B. Personnel Accountability

The ICS provides a unity of command structure which allows supervisors at every level to know exactly who is assigned and where they are assigned. If the management process is followed, and the principles of ICS maintained, all resources will be fully accounted for at all times.

C. Managerial Control

ICS has a built-in process which allows resource managers at all levels to assess performance constantly along with the adequacy of current action plans. Strategies and actions to achieve objectives can and must be modified at any time, as needed. Information exchange is encouraged across the organization. Direction is always through the chain of command.

D. Adequate Reserves

Assignment of resources to various incident facilities (the Incident Base, camps, and staging areas) provides the means to maintain adequate reserves. Reserves can always be increased or decreased in Staging Areas to meet anticipated demands.

E. Cost

Incident-related costs are always a major consideration. The Incident Commander must ensure that objectives are being achieved through cost-effective strategy selection, and selection of the right kind and right number of resources.

The Finance/Administration Section's Cost Unit has the responsibility to:

- Obtain and record all cost information.
- Prepare incident cost summaries.
- Prepare resource use cost estimates for planning.
- Make recommendations for cost savings.

The Cost Unit can assist the Incident Commander in ensuring a cost-effective approach to incident resource management, and should be activated on any large or prolonged incident. Resource managers must be constantly aware that the decisions they make regarding the use of personnel and equipment resources will not only affect the timely and satisfactory conclusion of the incident, but also may have significant cost implications.

Facilitating Transfer of Responsibilities

Once the decision is made to mobilize an Incident Management Team, the following guidelines can facilitate the transition of incident management responsibilities from the local unit to the incoming team. This includes the briefings that must be provided by the agency/business decision maker and the Incident Commander(s) for the Incident Management Team.

Although some information will be conveyed in writing and some orally, the provision of all briefing information—as well as the information itself—will be documented. A written Delegation of Authority is to be provided by the agency/business decision maker to the incoming Incident Commander at the initial briefing.

Transfer of Command Responsibilities

The local team or organization in place at an incident site should remain in charge until the incoming Incident Commander and Management Team members have been briefed by their counterparts, a written Delegation of Authority has been signed, and a mutually agreed-upon time for the transfer of command has been established. The Incident Management Team will specify times of arrival and transfer of command and will discuss these time frames with the incoming Incident Commander(s). The initial response personnel or IMT should complete the following tasks prior to the arrival of the incoming team:

- Determine the Incident Command Post/base location.
- Order basic office and field support equipment and supplies for incident response, including suitable office space.
- Secure an ample supply of appropriate maps of the incident site and surrounding areas. (This is critical.)
- Determine the Incident Management Team's transportation needs, and obtain the necessary vehicles.
- Schedule a time and location for the initial briefing of the Incident Management Team by the agency/business decision maker.
- Obtain necessary information for use in the agency/business decision maker briefing.
- Obtain necessary communications equipment.

The briefing by the agency/business decision maker, assisted by the Incident Commander(s), should take place as soon as the incoming team's Command and General Staff have been assembled, preferably at a location away from the incident. The Incident Situation Analysis (see below) and the signing of the written Delegation of Authority should be completed prior to the briefing.

Incident Situation Analysis

The agency/business decision maker should provide the incoming Incident Commander(s) with an Incident Situation Analysis—a written overview document that includes, at minimum, the following:

- Incident/Event status/information.
- Name of the incident and number(s) of businesses, states, counties, and premises involved.
- The incident(s) approximate size, location, and jurisdictions (e.g., businesses, state, Tribal, or county) and corresponding jurisdictional land status.
- Name of the current Incident Commander.
- General weather conditions at the incident site(s).
- Incident/Event characteristics.
- Populations at risk.
- Current objectives, strategies, and tactics.
- Location of the Incident Command Post and/or base locations.

- Other uses of resources that might have an impact on the incident.
- Local participation in the team organization in terms of resources and agency/business representatives.
- Any relevant information about the existing or anticipated unified command organization.
- The names and skills of technical specialists assigned to the incident.
- Priorities for control.
- Procedures for dealing with the news media.
- Political considerations.
- Agreements or memorandums of understanding in effect.
- Any other agencies' human resources or representatives who are already responding to the incident.
- The desired date and time for the team transition to occur.
- A summary of safety issues, including accidents to date; the status of accident reports; the names of areas with existing or potentially hazardous materials; and the names of local, state, and agency/business Safety Officers.
- An overview of operations and planning considerations, including strategies, tactics, and any unusual local conditions in the vicinity of the incident; preplanning information available for use by the team; reporting requirements for the Agency/Business Incident Status Summary; the status of the current team; the status of local agency personnel; agency/business capabilities for the support of the team's operations; agency/business rest-and-rotation policies; and agency/business demobilization concerns.
- An overview of logistical considerations, including transportation routes; the ordering system to be used; the procurement unit in place or requested; personnel food services; available sleeping facilities; local medical facilities; the nearest treatment and medical evacuation facilities; contact information for local law enforcement agencies; and a summary of any contacts already made with local law enforcement personnel.
- An overview of the financial and administrative situation, including fiscal limitations and constraints; any cost-sharing arrangements affecting the incident; the name of an available contracting officer; the potential for claims/injuries; the name of the Incident Business Advisor assigned to the incident; the Service and Supply Plan; agency/business business management requirements; whether a Buying Team and Payment Team have been requested; local business contacts; the incident financial package requirements; and a printed list of local contractors (e.g., firms that may be called upon to help with activities or services).

Delegation of Authority

As mentioned, the Delegation of Authority allows for the transfer of authority for incident control from the agency/business decision maker to the Incident Commander(s). An Incident Management Team may initiate incident control actions only after the Incident Commander has received a written, signed Delegation of Authority from the agency/business decision maker.

The Delegation of Authority will contain specific, measurable objectives to be accomplished by the Incident Management Team as well as any limitations to the team's authority. Measurable objectives will provide both the agency/business decision maker and the Incident Management Team with a means for continually evaluating control actions so that necessary adjustments can be made as the incident progresses.

Human Resource Guidelines

An effective response to an emergency incident/event typically involves significant effort on the part of considerable numbers of personnel. Suggested guidance on various human resource issues that may arise in this regard is provided below.

Work/Rest Guidelines—The Incident Management Team should ensure that all personnel are provided a 2-to-1 work-to-rest ratio (i.e., for every two hours of work or travel, one hour will be provided for sleep and/or rest). The Incident Commander or the agency/business decision maker will document and approve any proposed justification for work shifts exceeding 12 hours (including travel time) after the first operational period (day/shift) and will include this in the daily incident records.

Length of Commitment—To provide for safe, efficient, and effective support of incident/event control and containment operations, policies on length of assignments should been established. The following suggested policies should apply to all ICS incident response personnel, including temporary, managerial, or support staff:

- Incident assignments should not exceed 21 days (excluding travel). In situations in which objectives are close to being met, exceptions to this policy may be necessary to allow for the smooth transition of work to replacement personnel. The Incident Commander(s) and agency/business decision maker(s) will monitor such situations and agree jointly on any assignment extensions.
- The Incident Commander should document any assignment that exceeds 21 days, gain the approval of the agency/business decision maker for it, and include the justification for it in incident records. However, no assignment should exceed 30 days (excluding travel). Back-to-back assignments must be considered carefully in light of the health, readiness, and capability of the staff resource. The health and safety of incident personnel will not be compromised under any circumstances.
- In making incident assignments, supervisors must consider when the requested individual's last day off occurred—prior to mobilization—in order to optimize the individual's readiness and capabilities for the assignment.
- The length of the commitment of state personnel and personnel from other cooperating agencies and partners may be specified in existing agreements and will take precedence over this suggested guidance. In any case, the safety and welfare of staff resources always should be paramount.

Incident Status Reporting

As mentioned, the Incident Management Team must provide the agency/business decision maker with a report on the status of an incident at least once every 24 hours.

Incident status is reported via the Incident Status Summary or other summary, depending on the requirements of the agency/business decision makers involved. Time frames should meet local, agency/business decision maker requirements.

Releasing an Incident Management Team

Preparing to release an Incident Management Team—either at the end of a rotation or at the end of an incident—essentially involves procedures that are the reverse of the transfer of authority and operations *to* the Incident Management Team. The agency/business decision maker must approve the date and time of the release.

Releasing a Team at the End of a Rotation—Before an outgoing Incident Management Team is released, the incoming Incident Management Team should be allowed ample time to phase into the work of the outgoing team. The outgoing team should not be released from duty until agreed-upon objectives for the team have been met and until management activity and the workload are at levels that the incoming team reasonably can be expected to assume.

Releasing a Team at the End of an Incident—Criteria for deciding to release an Incident Management Team at the end of an incident include the following:

- The agency/business objectives have been met.
- Most operational personnel and resources not needed for incident activities have been released.

- The Incident Command Post has been closed down or reduced in staff or is in the process of closing down.
- The Planning Section Chief has prepared a draft of the incident summary (including both the work that has been accomplished and the tasks that remain) for use by the Incident Management Team in a close-out briefing for the agency/business decision maker.
- The Finance/Administration Section Chief has resolved most of the known finance issues. Arrangements have been made for the transfer of financial records and remaining tasks to the agency/business administrative personnel.
- Resource rehabilitation work (e.g., repair of any property damaged as part of the incident/event work) has been completed or done to the satisfaction of property owners.
- Personnel performance ratings, including ratings for temporary personnel, have been completed.
- The Incident Management Team has provided the agency/business decision maker with a final (close-out) briefing.

The agency/business decision maker should receive a final briefing by the Incident Management Team and should rate the performance of team members as soon as possible after their release. Should an Incident Management Team be unable to follow some of the above procedures because of emergency conditions or other issues, the assigned Incident Commander(s) and staff will work with members of the agency/business to obtain the information necessary to make an effective, organized transfer of operations and authority.

Team Evaluation and After-Action Review

After the demobilization of the Incident Management Team, the agency/business decision maker should conduct a Team Evaluation and an After-Action Review. These documents are described below.

Team Evaluation—the agency/business decision maker should complete a written evaluation of the Incident Management Team no later than three months after demobilization of the team. Ideally, this evaluation should be completed not at the time of the closeout review but rather after sufficient time has elapsed so that incident cost documentation, claims processing, demobilization procedures, and rehabilitation activities have been completed and can be evaluated thoroughly. During this time, the agency/business decision maker also can gather information with which to evaluate the Incident Management Team's effectiveness with cooperating agencies and partners, the communications media, and neighbors.

The Delegation of Authority, which includes objectives established and updated as necessary by the agency/business decision maker, will serve as the primary standard against which the Incident Management Team is evaluated. The agency/business decision maker will provide a copy of the evaluation to the Incident Commander and will retain a copy for the final incident package containing the incident files and other documentation.

Other factors to consider in a written evaluation of an Incident Management Team include:

- How orderly was the transition of work from the agency/business local unit to the Incident Management Team and from the Incident Management Team back to the local unit?
- How well were human resources managed?
- Were personnel safety records accurate, complete, and current?
- How closely did budget projections predict actual fiscal performance?
- Was property accounted for and its security controlled?
- Were costs well documented?
- Were claims investigations and documentation complete?
- Was optimal use made of reporting systems?
- Were relations with the communications media handled effectively?
- Was interaction with cooperative agencies and partners, local unit staff, neighbors, and support units helpful and effective?

- Was financial and payment documentation accurate and complete?
- Was demobilization conducted in an orderly manner?
- Was the final report package complete?

After-Action Review—In addition to the team evaluation, the agency/business decision maker should conduct an After-Action Review to document lessons learned and to suggest modifications to current policies and procedures for the improvement of future emergency response endeavors. The review should be conducted with the assistance of the key members of the Incident Management Team as well as agency/business leaders and representatives of industries involved.

Summary

Successful incident management at all levels of complexity requires clear, open, honest communication and the cooperation of all involved. The establishment of standards for effective communication and resource deployment and the development of criteria for levels of incident typing are designed to facilitate a better understanding of the nature of effective incident response and the priority agency/business decision makers place upon it.

The After-Action Review Process

When developing a plan for emergency management, and the standard operating procedures to be utilized while responding to an emergency or event, it is important for agency/business leaders to know what has happened in the past. Which processes or procedures were successful and effective and which were not? An effective way to begin collecting that information is through an After-Action Review (AAR). The AAR process can be very formal and detailed or basic and informal.

Here's what a simple After-Action Review might look like:

What was planned?

- Review the primary objectives and expected actions or outcomes planned.

What actually happened?

- Review the daily or event actions:

   — Identify and discuss effective and ineffective performance.
   — Identify barriers that were encountered and how they were addressed and mitigated.
   — Discuss all actions or processes that were not standard operating procedures, or those that introduced safety concerns or cost.

What did happen?

- Discuss the reasons for any ineffective, unsafe, or costly performance. Concentrate on *what* not *who*.

What can be done next time?

- Determine how to apply lessons learned in the future.
- Develop Standard Operating Procedures and processes for future incidents.

Developing Standard Operating Procedures

The use of Standard Operating Procedures (SOP) by agency/business leaders can provide several benefits. First, agency/business intent will be communicated to all individuals in the organization. Second, SOPs provide consistency in the way you provide guidance as a leader. Third, SOPs provide subordinate employees with the desired outcome or end state and allow them to use their discretion if decisions need to be made.

SOPs can provide agency/business leaders with the framework to conduct business safely by allowing them to focus on critical decisions instead of routine ones, thus enhancing their decision-making ability in stressful or emergency situations. Finally, SOPs provide a mechanism to identify needed changes, implement agency/business policy, enhance training, describe desired performance, and a way to evaluate operational performance. The result of SOP usage is improved operational efficiency, greater accountability, and increased safety.

SOPs are not meant to limit the ability of agency/business personnel to make decisions. In fact, if developed and implemented properly, SOPs will provide the desired end state and allow agency/business decision makers a great deal of flexibility in their decision-making processes.

SOPs also set the standards for basic organizational operations. A variety of tasks such as rules of engagement, use of the risk management processes, and communication procedures can be addressed through the development and implementation of Standard Operating Procedures.

This planning guide and reference will assist in developing, implementing, and maintaining SOPs in one of two formats. The first is a stand-alone document. You may wish to develop specific standard operating procedures for very specific situations. If multiple stand-alone SOPs are developed an SOP manual should be considered.

The second format is a Unit/Functional Operations Guide. By creating this document the agency/business or unit/functional leader can outline what is expected of each employee in the performance of his or her duties. The operations guide will provide the framework for each member to know what is expected of them and how they are to accomplish those tasks.

Standard Operating Procedures

The following information describes some key actions in the development, implementation, and evaluation of SOPs. This process is useful in the development of single Standard Operating Procedures or for the development of an agency/business or unit Operations Guide.

Task Analysis

A task analysis can be summarized as asking basic questions about your agency/business or function and making a list of factors that will influence your SOPs.

- What areas of my operation need SOPs?
- What situation am I trying to clarify?
- What processes or procedures do I want my unit to use for a given situation?
- Is the development of an SOP the answer to these questions or should I resolve these issues in another manner?

Steps in Developing the SOP

There are eight basic steps in the SOP development process.

1. Build the Development Team.
2. Provide Organizational Support.
3. Establish Team Procedures.
4. Gather Information and Identify Alternatives.
5. Analyze and Select Alternatives.
6. Write the SOP.
7. Review and Test the SOP.
8. Approve the SOP.

In many circumstances the SOP development team will be a single person or perhaps two members of the agency/business or function. It is important to take a few minutes to identify alternatives and analyze each, then select the best method. Keep in mind that just because your agency/business has always done something in a specific manner, does not mean that it is the way it should be done in perpetuity. Take the time to select the best alternative since the SOP should be one that stays with your organization for a long time. Remember, you do not always have to reinvent the wheel. Your peers will face most of these same situations as well. Ask them how they handle specific situations and share SOPs. Some questions to ask during a SOP development are:

1.   Is the proposed procedure realistic? Can it work in the agency/business, in the function, etc?
2.   Can the procedure be readily implemented given the current resources of the agency/business?
3.   Will training be required?
4.   Will new equipment be needed?
5.   Does the procedure comply with agency/business policy and guidelines?
6.   How will this procedure impact individual agency/business employees?
7.   Will the procedure survive outside scrutiny?

Writing the SOP

A standardized format for SOPs streamlines the writing process. Additional benefits include ease of revision or updating and enhanced usability. Regardless of the format, several items are usually included in any single SOP. A sample single SOP format can be seen below (Figure 15.12). Single SOPs should be incorporated into a comprehensive SOP Manual or as an appendix to an agency/business operations plan.

- A numbering system—Important for reference, usability, and integrating SOPs into an overall manual.
- Effective date—Date the SOP is officially adopted for use by the agency/business. This may be different from the date of issue.
- Expiration/review date—Important for ensuring the currency of SOPs by establishing a date for periodic review and revision, if needed.
- Title.
- Description of purpose or rationale statement—Describes the purpose of the SOP, why it is needed, and what it intends to accomplish.
- Authority signature(s)—Indicates that the SOP was properly created, reviewed, and approved by the agency/business decision makers.
- Scope—Describes situations for which the SOP was created and the intended audience.
- General procedures—The body of the SOP; sets forth broad procedural guidelines for operations.
- Specific procedures—Specific actions necessary under the SOP to mitigate a situation safely.
- References—Source material used to create the SOP.

Agency/Business Name:

Revised:

Scope: This Standard Operating Procedure applies to all Agency/Business personnel conducting......

Purpose: The purpose of this SOP is to standardize the ....

Procedure:

Approved by:

Effective Date:

FIGURE 15.12 Example standard operating procedures format.

Implementing the SOP

Implementation includes all the steps that an agency/business takes to introduce the SOP to users and make it an integral part of normal operations. The implementation process should be designed to ensure that:

- Everyone is informed about the new or modified SOP and understands the significance of the change.
- Copies of the SOP are distributed as needed and readily accessible to all potential users.
- Personnel know their roles and have the knowledge and skills necessary to implement the SOP safely and effectively (including an understanding of consequences for failing to comply).
- A mechanism exists to monitor performance, identify potential problems, and provide support in the implementation process.

Training Needs Assessment

To determine training needed for implementation of a new SOP ask the following:

1. Who needs to be trained in the new or revised SOP?
2. What instructional content should be covered? What training methods will be most effective? Will a simple agency/business meeting with distribution and discussion of the new SOP be adequate?
3. How will understanding and competence be evaluated?
4. How long will the training sessions take? How will training be scheduled and administered?

Training: Scheduling and Administration

Keep in mind that training is a critical component of the SOP implementation process. Training is the means by which the SOP becomes a useful and intuitive operational tool. Some procedures will not require extensive orientation and are self-defining; others will require more explanations and definition. Even the best SOP will be ineffective or could be dangerous if agency/business members are not capable of carrying it out. It is up to agency/business decision makers to ensure that each employee understands the SOP and is capable of carrying it out.

Some questions to ask when preparing for training are:

1. What training materials are needed? Who will prepare them?
2. Who can teach this material effectively?
3. What time frame is appropriate for initial training and refresher training?
4. Can this training be integrated with other training or unit activities?
5. What facilities, special equipment, and supplies are needed?

Evaluation

Every SOP should undergo a periodic review. Evaluations may initially be needed more often. The goal of an evaluation is to assess the results of the SOP, a task that requires asking the following questions:

- What were employee abilities, behaviors and actions before the SOP was implemented?
- What administrative or operational problem was the SOP designed to address?
- Was the new SOP fully implemented, or were there unexpected barriers to full implementation?
- How did employee abilities, behaviors, and actions change after introduction of the SOP?
- Were the changes in abilities, behaviors, and actions the same as were intended?
- Was the purpose of the SOP accomplished?
- Is the need for the SOP still current? Is the present SOP the best solution?

Operations Guide

You will find that following the process outlined for the development, implementation, and evaluation of SOPs is helpful in the development of an Agency/Business Operations Guide as well. Start at the beginning by conducting a task analysis and walk through the process, bypassing those steps which do not apply to your situation. It is important to note that an Operations Guide, like a stand-alone SOP, is only as effective as your ability to communicate its purpose, use, and individual accountability in its application.

The following list is a suggested format for an Operations Guide along with typical material it contains. You may find that your agency/business may have specific needs that are not addressed here and you should adapt this format as necessary.

- Cover page with document title, agency/business name, and date.
- Table of Contents.
- Vision Statement and Expectations.
- Policy.
- Alcohol and Drug Policy.
- Vehicle or Equipment Use.
- Facilities Maintenance.
- Administration.
- Injury Reporting.
- Mission or Incident Assignment Responsibilities.

Being Prepared

Emergency management officials and professionals are acutely aware of the need for prior resource planning and management of information and resources to support rapid and effective response to fast-moving critical incident situations. Recent events have raised awareness of the general public to the kinds of hazards they may confront in their "normal" lives, and the need to be better prepared to take care of themselves and their families. Business managers and administrators—indeed, anyone with responsibility for an enterprise—can especially benefit from expanding their management knowledge and skills to include methodologies such as CARVER + Shock assessment and Incident Complexity Analysis.

This chapter has provided a detailed overview of some of these valuable concepts, systems, and processes, and showed how business leaders and managers can use and adapt these concepts to their "management toolkits" for planning and management of future events and emergencies affecting their operations.

This chapter has also reviewed some of the literature which illuminates the way "real people" actually behave in emergency situations, as a more realistic grounding for designing emergency systems and training. The realization that first responders to most critical incidents are "ordinary people" lends urgency to the need to expand the reach of these risk assessment and response methodologies. It is encouraging that there is a growing body of experience and research, and a robust methodology which can be employed at many levels to better prepare decision makers—and ordinary citizens—to respond effectively.

Business leaders and managers must be able to assess and determine the size, scope, and complexity of events or emergencies that occur. We have described the methodologies and processes of risk assessment offered by the CARVER + Shock assessment tool and the Incident Complexity Analysis. Both are proven tools with worksheets and checklists that will aid business leaders and managers in the risk assessment task.

We have discussed and described additional systems and processes that will support business leaders and managers in organizing and managing events and emergency incidents. The Incident Command System (ICS) is used to manage all types and sizes of emergency and planned events worldwide. The ICS description includes a short history of ICS, the incident planning process, and the primary positions used in an ICS organization. We discussed the importance of resource management and the primary steps and processes used to manage and evaluate the resources used on an event or emergency incident.

Finally we described the processes that can be used to conduct an After-Action Review and to develop Standard Operating Procedures. Business leaders and managers can use these to improve emergency management response procedures and, more importantly, to build capacity within their business or organization.

Using the systems, worksheets, checklists, and tools provided, managers and decision makers at all levels will be able to apply the concepts of "Management in Extremes" to improve preparedness and response to critical events when they occur.

Notes

1 Amanda Ripley, *The Unthinkable: Who Survives When Disaster Strikes—and Why*, Crown Publishers, New York, 2008, xi.

2 Ibid., 9.

3 Ibid., 114–115.

4 Herbert A. Simon, "The Mathematical Reduction of Rationality: Some Strategic Considerations in the Construction of Social Science Models," reprinted in Leonard I. Krimerman, *The Nature & Scope of Social Science: A Critical Anthology*, Appleton-Century-Crofts, New York, 1969, 555; from "Mathematical Thinking in the Social Sciences", ed. by Paul Lazerfeld, Free Press, New York, 1954, 388–406.)

5 Giorgio Coricelli, Raymond J. Dolan, and Angela Sirigu, "Brain, Emotion, and Decision-making: The Paradigmatic Example of Regret," *Trends in Cognitive Sciences*, Vol. 11, Issue 6, pp. 258–265, June 1, 2007, Elsevier.

6 J.S. Lerner, and L.Z. Tiedens, "Portrait of the Angry Decision-maker: How Appraisal Tendencies Shape Anger's Influence on Cognition," *Journal of Behavioral Decision-making*, 19, pp. 115–137.

7 Ripley, p. 31.

8 Ibid., p. 48.

9 Kathleen M. Kowalski-Trakofler, Charles Vaught, and Ted Scharf, "Judgment and Decision-making Under Stress: An Overview for Emergency Managers," *International Journal of Emergency Management*, Vol. 1, No. 3, 2003, pp. 278–289.

10 Ripley, p. 18.

11 Ibid., p. 210.

12 M. Minsky, "A Framework for Representing Knowledge," MIT AI Lab Memo 306, 1974.

13 John F. Heinbokel, and Jeffrey Potash, "Endogenous Human Behaviors in a Pneumonic Plague Simulation: Behavioral and Psychological Theories as Small 'Generic' Models," ISDC-2003_Report of the Center for Interdisciplinary Excellence in System Dynamics.

14 N. Pidgeon, R.E. Kasperson, and P. Slovic, "Public Perceptions of Risk, Science and Governance," *Science in Society*, 2003; J.X. Kasperson, R.E. Kasperson, N. Pidgeon, and P. Slovic, "The Social Amplification of Risk: Assessing Fifteen Years of Research and Theory." In N. Pidgeon, R. Kasperson, and P. Slovic (Eds.), *The Social Amplification of Risk* (pp. 13–46), London: Cambridge University Press, 2003.

15 USDA Food Safety and Inspection Service and Food and Drug Administration, *An Overview of the CARVER Plus SHOCK Method for Food Sector Vulnerability Assessments*, July 18, 2007.

16 Logistics Management Institute and the Supply Chain Council, *Using SCOR Model for Supply Chain Risk Management*, January 31, 2009.

17 Department of Homeland Security, "Homeland Security Presidential Directive 5," http://www.dhs.gov/xabout/laws/gc_1214592333605.shtm#1

18 Ibid.

19 Department of Homeland Security, *National Incident Management System*. FEMA Publication P-501 (Catalog Number 08336-1). Washington, DC, 2008.

Part 5

Summing Up

sixteen
The Science of Opportunity

Lisa H. Harrington

Definition: X-treme Supply Chain Management (X-SCM): the science of governing global supply chains experiencing instabilities of unprecedented amplitude, frequency and duration.

In deciding to produce this book, we took on a tremendous challenge. We and our contributing authors made a pact to bring our expertise to bear in order to break new ground—to develop a new science for managing supply chains in an extreme world. This new science—X-SCM—is both the theory and practice of mastering change that is occurring on a scale and level not previously experienced.

This book and its associated online tool kit aim to give supply chain managers the arsenal they need to not just survive change, but to thrive on volatility. X-SCM is based on a systemic approach to building the capability and depth to rapidly assess risk and respond appropriately and cost-effectively to it.

We tackle supply chain risk and volatility on all fronts: the physical supply chain, the financial supply chain, the cyber supply chain, and the service supply chain.

Organizations everywhere continue to struggle under the burden of applying old supply chain management models to a new world. Volatility has become a systemic condition—the norm rather than the exception. But traditional supply chain management models are not up to the task of dealing with this reality. Their static, reactive nature precludes rapid adaptation. Thus, they are doomed to repeat the react-and-recover cycle over and over again.

Only by applying the new science of X-SCM—as Cisco has done so successfully—can enterprises break out of this cycle.

Clearly, the multidimensional supply chain requires a well-thought-out *enterprise risk management strategy and roadmap* for change management. This book and online tool kit and simulations represent the best multimedia package available today for understanding and learning how to manage extreme supply chain change.

The spirit of the new science of X-SCM is hopeful, not fearful. It sees opportunity in risk, not just danger. It sees the new science of supply chain volatility management as a powerful way in which enterprises can embrace, be prepared for, and capitalize on rapid change—no matter what its source.

As we go forward into a world where extreme volatility is the norm, let us take to heart the wisdom contained in the following quote:

> The only way to approach a period in which uncertainty is very large and one cannot predict the future is not to predict but to experiment and act inventively and exuberantly.[1]

Note

1 C.S. "Buzz" Holling, quoted in Homer-Dixon, Thomas, "Our Panarchic Future," March 2008, Worldwatch Institute, Washington, DC.

Appendix: Supply Chain Risk Literature Review

Below is a listing of literature relating to supply chain risk.

Anupindi, R., and R. Akella. "Diversification under supply uncertainty," *Management Science*, 39(8) (1993): 944–963.

Baiman, S., P. Fischer, and M. Rajan. "Information, contracting, and quality costs," *Management Science*, 46(6) (2000): 776–789.

Baird, L.S., and H. Thomas. "What is risk anyway?" In R.A. Bettis and H. Thomas (Eds.), *Risk, Strategy, and Management*, JAI Press, Greenwich, CT, 1990, pp. 21–52.

Cachon, G.P. "The allocation of inventory risk in a supply chain: Push, pull, and advance purchase discount contracts," *Management Science*, 50(2) (2004): 222–238.

Chen, F., Z. Drezner, J.K. Ryan, and D. Simchi-Levi. "Quantifying the bullwhip effect in a simple supply chain: The impact of forecasting, lead times, and information," *Management Science*, 46(3) (2000): 436–443.

Choi, T., and J. Liker. "Bringing Japanese continuous improvement approaches to US manufacturing: The roles of process," *Decision Sciences*, 26(5) (1995): 589–620.

Cyert, R., and J. March. *A Behavioral Theory of the Firm*, Prentice Hall, Englewood Cliffs, NJ, 1963.

Davenport, T. "Putting the enterprise into the enterprise system," *Harvard Business Review*, 76(4) (1998): 121–131.

Dean, T., and R. Brown. "Pollution regulations as a barrier to new firm entry: Initial evidence and implications for future research," *Academy of Management Journal*, 38(1) (1995): 288–303.

Droge, C., J. Jayaram, and S. Vickery. "The ability to minimize the timing of new product development and introduction: An examination of antecedent factors in the North American automobile supplier industry," *Journal of Product Innovation Management*, 17(1) (1999): 24–40.

Eisenhardt, K. "Agency theory: An assessment and review," *Academy of Management Review*, 14(1) (1989): 57–74.

Ellram, L.M. *The Role of Supply Management in Target Costing*, Center for Advanced Purchasing Studies, Tempe, AZ, 1999.

Faisal, M.N., D.K. Banwet, and R. Shankar. "Supply chain risk mitigation: Modeling the enablers," *Business Process Management Journal*, 12(4) (2006): 535–552.

Finch, P. "Supply chain risk management," *Supply Chain Management*, 9(2) (2004): 183–196.

Hallikas, J., V. Virolainen, and M. Tuominen. "Risk analysis and assessment in network environments: A dyadic case study," *International Journal of Production Economics*, 78(1) (2002): 45–55.

Handfield, R.B. "The role of materials management in developing time-based competition," *International Journal of Purchasing and Materials Management*, 29(1) (1993): 2–10.

Hartley, J.L., and T.Y. Choi. "Supplier development: Customers as a catalyst of process change," *Business Horizons*, 39(4) (1996): 37–44.

Hartley, J., J. Meredith, D. McCutcheon, and R. Kamath. "Suppliers' contribution to product development: An exploratory survey," *IEEE Transaction on Engineering Management*, 44(3) (1997): 258–267.

Hendricks, K., and V. Singhal. "An empirical analysis of the effect of supply chain disruptions on long-run stock price performance and equity risk of the firm," *Production and Operations Management*, 14(1) (2005): 25–53.

Kannan, V., and K. Tan. "Supplier selection and assessment: Their impact on business performance," *Journal of Supply Chain Management*, 38(4) (2002): 11–21.

Kary, T. Is there a silicon lining from Taiwan's earthquake? CNET News, 1999.

Kleindorfer, P., and G. Saad. "Managing disruption risks in supply chains," *Production and Operations Management,* 14 (2005): 53–68.

Koufteros, X., M. Vonderembse, and W. Doll. "Concurrent engineering and its consequences," *Journal of Operations Management,* 19(1) (2001): 97–115.

Koufteros, X., M. Vonderembse, and W. Doll. "Integrated product development practices and competitive capabilities: The effects of uncertainty, equivocality, and platform strategy," *Journal of Operations Management,* 20(4) (2002): 331–355.

Kraljic, P. "Purchasing must become supply management," *Harvard Business Review,* 61(5) (1983): 109–117.

Krause, D.R. "The antecedents of buying firms' efforts to improve suppliers," *Journal of Operations Management,* 17(2) (1999): 205–224.

Krause, D.R., and R.B. Handfield. *Developing a World-Class Supply Base,* Center for Advanced Purchasing Studies, Tempe, AZ, 1999.

LaBahn, D.W. "Early supplier involvement in customer new product development: A contingency model of component supplier intention," *Journal of Business Research,* 49(3) (2000): 173–190.

Larson, P., and J. Kulchitsky. "Single source and supplier certification: Performance and relationship implications," *Industrial Marketing Management,* 27(1) (1998): 73–81.

Lee, H.L., and C. Billington. "Materials management in decentralized supply chains," *Operations Research,* 41(5) (1993): 835–847.

Lee, H., V. Padmanabhan, and S. Whang. "Information distortion in a supply chain: The bullwhip effect," *Management Science,* 43(4) (1997): 546–558.

Lee, H.L., K.C. So, and C.S. Tang. "The value of information sharing in a two-level supply chain," *Management Science,* 46(5) (2000): 626–643.

Lee, H.L., V. Padmanabhan, and S. Whang. "Comments on 'Information distortion in a supply chain: The bullwhip effect.' The bullwhip effect reflections," *Management Science,* 50(12) Supplement (2004): 1887–1893.

Lockhart, M., and L. Ettkin. "Vendor certification: Seven steps to a better product," *Production and Inventory Management Journal,* 34(1) (1993): 65–69.

Logan, M.S. "Using agency theory to design successful outsourcing relationships," *International Journal of Logistics Management,* 11(2) (2000): 21–32.

Luce, R., and H. Raiffa. *Games and Decisions,* John Wiley & Sons, New York, NY, 1957.

Marcussen, C.H. "The effects of EDI on industrial buyer-seller relationships: A network perspective," *International Journal of Purchasing and Materials Management,* 32(3) (1996): 20–23.

Mentzer, J.T. et al., "Defining supply chain management," *Journal of Business Logistics,* 22(2) (2001): 1–25.

Michalski, L. "How to identify vendor risk," *Pharmaceutical Technology,* 24(10) (2000): 180–4.

Mitchell, V.W. "Organizational risk perception and reduction: A literature review," *British Journal of Management,* 6(2) (1995): 115–133.

Newman, R. "Single source qualification," *Journal of Purchasing and Materials Management,* 24(2) (1988): 10–17.

Newman, R. "Single sourcing: Short-term savings versus long-term problems," *Journal of Purchasing and Materials Management,* 25(2) (1989): 20–25.

Newman, R., and J. McKeller. "Target pricing: A challenge for purchasing," *International Journal of Purchasing and Materials Management,* 31(3) (1995): 13–20.

Newman, W.R., M. Hanna, and M.J. Maffei. "Dealing with the uncertainties of manufacturing: Flexibility, buffers and integration," *International Journal of Operations and Production Management,* 13(1) (1993): 19–34.

Noordewier, T.G., G. John, and J.R. Nevin. "Performance outcomes of purchasing arrangement in industrial buyervendor relationships," *Journal of Marketing,* 54(4) (1990): 80–93.

Norrman, A., and U. Jansson. "Ericsson's proactive supply chain risk management approach after a serious sub-supplier accident," *International Journal of Physical Distribution & Logistics Management,* 34(5) (2004): 434–456.

Raz, G., and E. Porteus. "A fractiles perspective to joint price/quantity newsvendor problem," *Management Science,* 51(11) (2006): 1764–1777.

Robertson, T.S., and H. Gatignon. "Technology development mode: A transaction cost conceptualization," *Strategic Management Journal,* 19(1) (1998): 515–531.

Sanders, D.R., and M.R. Manfredo. "The role of value-at-risk in purchasing: An application to the foodservice industry," *Journal of Supply Chain Management,* 38(2) (2002): 38–45.

Shapira, Z. *Risk Taking: A Managerial Perspective,* Russell Sage Foundation, New York, NY, 1995.

Sheffi, Y. "Supply chain management under the threat of international terrorism," *International Journal of Logistics Management,* 12(2) (2001): 1–11.

Sheffi, Y. *The Resilient Enterprise: Overcoming Vulnerability for Competitive Advantage,* MIT Press, Cambridge, MA, 2005.

Smeltzer, L.R., and S.P. Siferd. "Proactive supply management: The management of risk," *International Journal of Purchasing and Materials Management,* 34(1) (1998): 38–45.

Starr, M., and D. Miller. *Inventory Control: Theory and Practice,* Prentice Hall, Englewood Cliffs, NJ, 1962.

Steele, P.T., and B.H. Court. *Profitable Purchasing Strategies: A Manager's Guide for Improving Organizational Competitiveness through the Skills of Purchasing*, McGraw-Hill, London, 1996.

Stump, R.L. "Antecedents of purchasing concentration: A transaction cost explanation," *Journal of Business Research*, 34(2) (1995): 145–157.

Tang, C. "Perspectives in supply chain risk management," *International Journal of Production Economics*, 103(2) (2006): 451–488.

Tomlin, B. "On the value of mitigation and contingency strategies for managing supply chain disruption risks," *Management Science*, 52(5) (2006): 639–657.

Tsay, A.A., and W. Lovejoy. "Quantity flexibility contracts and supply chain performance," Manufacturing and Service Operations Management, 1(2) (1999): 89–111.

Tullous, R., and R. Utecht. "Multiple or single sourcing?" *Journal of Business and Industrial Marketing*, 7(3) (1992): 5–18.

Wagenaar, W.A. "Risk taking and accident causation." In J. Yates (Ed.), *Risk Taking Behavior*, John Wiley & Sons, New York, NY, 1992, pp. 257–281.

Walker, G., and D. Weber. "A transaction cost approach to make-or-buy decisions," *Administrative Science Quarterly*, 29(3) (1984): 373–391.

Walton, L.W. "Telephone survey: Answering the seven Rs to logistics research," *Journal of Business Logistics*, 18(1) (1997): 217–231.

Wasti, S., and J. Liker. "Risky business or competitive power? Supplier involvement in Japanese product design," *Journal of Product Innovation Management*, 14(5) (1997): 337–355.

Watts, C., and C. Hahn. "Supplier development programs: An empirical analysis," *International Journal of Purchasing and Materials Management*, 29(2) (1993): 10–17.

Williams, S., M. Zainuba, and R. Jackson. "Affective influences on risk perceptions and risk intention," *Journal of Managerial Psychology*, 18(1/2) (2003): 126–138.

Wynstra, F., A. Van Weele, and M. Weggemann. "Managing supplier involvement in product development: Three critical issues," *European Management Journal*, 19(2) (2001): 157–167.

Yates, J.F., and E.R. Stone. "The risk construct." In J. Yates (Ed.), *Risk Taking Behavior*, John Wiley & Sons, New York, NY, 1992, pp. 1–25.

Zsidisin, G.A. "Defining supply risk: A grounded theory approach," Proceedings from the Decision Sciences Institute Annual Meeting, San Diego, CA, 2002.

Zsidisin, G.A. "Managerial perceptions of supply risk," *Journal of Supply Chain Management*, 39(1) (2003a): 14–26.

Zsidisin, G.A. "A grounded definition of supply risk," *Journal of Purchasing and Supply Management*, 9 (2003b): 217–224.

Zsidisin, G.A. "An agency theory investigation of supply risk management," *Journal of Supply Chain Management*, 39(3) (2003c): 15–27.

Zsidisin, G.A., and L.M. Ellram. "Supply risk assessment analysis," *PRACTIX: Best Practices in Purchasing and Supply Management*, 2(4) (1999): 9–12.

Zsidisin, G.A., L.M. Ellram, J.R. Carter, and J.L. Cavinato. "An analysis of supply risk assessment techniques," *International Journal of Physical Distribution & Logistics Management*, 34(5) (2004): 397–413.

Zsidisin, G.A., and M.F. Smith. "Managing supply risk with early supplier involvement: A case study and research propositions," *Journal of Supply Chain Management*, 41(4) (2005): 44–57.

Appendix to Chapter 5

Additional Readings on Supplier Risk

C. Araz and I. Ozkarahan, "Supplier evaluation and management system for strategic sourcing based on a new multicriteria sorting procedure," *International Journal of Production Economics*, 106(2) (2007): 585–606.

R. Calantone, R. Garcia, and C. Droge, "The effects of environmental turbulence on new product development strategy planning," *Journal of Product Innovation Management*, 20(2) (2003): 90–103.

S. Chopra and M.S. Sodhi, "Managing risk to avoid supply-chain breakdown," *Sloan Management Review*, 46(1) (2004): 53–61.

M. Christopher and H. Lee, "Mitigating supply chain risk through improved confidence," *International Journal of Physical Distribution & Logistics Management*, 34(5) (2004): 388–396.

K. Demeter, A. Gelei, and I. Jenei, "The effect of strategy on supply chain configuration and management practices on the basis of two supply chains in the Hungarian automotive industry," *International Journal of Production Economics*, 104(2) (2006): 555–570.

F. Fiedler, "A contingency model of leadership effectiveness," *Advances in Experimental Social Psychology, Vol. 1*, New York: Academic Press, 1964, pp. 149–190.

E. Fredericks, "Infusing flexibility into business-to-business firms: A contingency theory and resource-based view perspective and practical implications," *Industrial Marketing Management*, 34(6) (2005): 555–565.

A. Gingsberg and N. Venkatraman, "Contingency perspectives of organisational strategy: A critical review of the empirical research," *Academy of Management Review*, 10 (1985): 421–434.

L. Giunipero and R. Eltantawy, "Securing the upstream supply chain: A risk management approach," *International Journal of Physical Distribution & Logistics Management*, 34(9) (2004): 698–713.

The Hackett Group, "Dow Chemical Company: Supply risk management process is key to improving safety and security," *Performance Studies* (The Hackett Group, October 9, 2007), http://www.thehackettgroup.com/research/results.jsp?fn=109168997

Ç. Haksöz and A. Kadam, "Supply risk in fragile contracts," *Sloan Management Review*, 49(2) (2008): 7–8.

J. Hallikas et al., "Risk management processes in supplier networks," *International Journal of Production Economics*, 90(1) (2004): 47–58.

R.B. Handfield and K. McCormack, *Supply Chain Risk Management: Minimizing Disruptions in Global Sourcing*, Auerbach Publications, Boca Raton, FL, 2007.

M. Hillman and H. Keltz, "Managing risk in the supply chain—A quantitative study," AMR Research, 2007.

D. Kandemir, A. Yaprak, and T. Cavusgil, "Alliance orientation: Conceptualization, measurement, and impact on market performance," *Academy of Marketing Science Journal*, 34(3) (2006): 324.

C. Koo et al., "Do e-business strategies matter? The antecedents and relationship with firm performance," *Information Systems Frontiers*, 9 (2007): 283–296.

M. Kotabe and J.Y. Murray, "Global sourcing strategy and sustainable competitive advantage," *Industrial Marketing Management*, 33(1) (2004): 7–14.

B. Ritchie and C. Brindley, "Supply chain risk management and performance: A guiding framework for future development," *International Journal of Operations & Production Management*, 27(3) (2007): 303–322.

A. Rubinson and J. Jablecki, "Enhancing supplier performance management for more profit, less risk," *Supply Chain Management Review* (2008).

B. Slobodow, O. Abdullah, and W.C. Babuschak, "When supplier partnerships aren't," *Sloan Management Review,* 49(2) (2008): 77–83.

C. Tang, "Perspectives in supply chain risk management," *International Journal of Production Economics,* 103(2) (2006): 451–488.

B. Tomlin, "On the value of mitigation and contingency strategies for managing supply chain disruption risks," *Management Science,* 52(5) (2006): 639–657.

R.J. Trent and R.M. Monczka, "Achieving excellence in global sourcing," *Sloan Management Review,* 47(1, (2005): 24–32.

P. Trkman and K. McCormack, "A conceptual model for managing supply chain risk in turbulent environment," *International Journal of Production Economics,* 119(2) (2009): 247–258.

A Z. Zeng, P.D. Berger, and A. Gerstenfeld, "Managing the supply-side risks in supply chains: Taxonomies, processes and examples of decision-making modeling." In E. Akcali, J. Genues, P. Pardalos, and H.E. Romeijn (Eds.), *Applications of Supply Chain Management and E-Commerce Research,* Springer, New York, 2005.

Appendix to Chapter 11

A Simple Supply Chain Diagnostic for Times of Upheaval

Accelerating volatility and complexity of supply chains have made it increasingly difficult to design a coherent set of processes and technologies that is up to the task. We offer this simple diagnostic as a starting point for how to get started in your journey to create a "chaos-tolerant" supply chain, to use Gartner's term.

Product/Division

- Do you have multiple product/service lines that are managed separately but sold through the same channel or to the same customers? If so, what is the customer/partner experience like? Who owns the overall customer experience?
- Do you have multiple business units/divisions that are managed separately but sold through the same channel or to the same customers? If so, what is the customer/partner experience like?

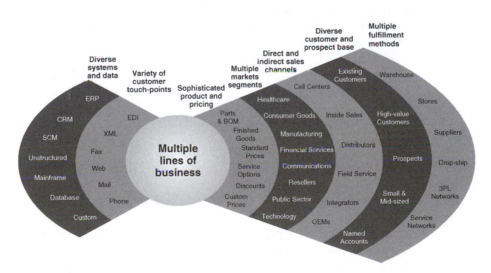

FIGURE A11.1 Supply chain diagnostic for times of upheaval.

How does management get visibility across the silos? Is there a single customer master? Who owns the overall customer experience?

- Are the products produced, sold, and distributed the same way using the same systems, processes, and employees? If different, are they enabled with different systems and processes?
- Do you sell service products as well as discrete ones? Are they sold together? If so how is that enabled?
- Are some products built/assembled to order or require selection of options or features? How is that supported and do they need expert advice to complete valid orders?
- Do you sell third-party products or fulfill customer orders directly from suppliers or third-party warehouses? How well does that work?
- Is there a strategy to bundled products across LOB to increase the share of wallet?
- Does your company grow by acquisition or by adding new product lines? How many in the last three years? How are they integrated from a selling perspective (catalog, OM, billing)?

Market/Region

- How many market/segments do you sell to? How often do you add new ones? How different are they in their buying preferences and service requirements? How do you support those differences?
- Are there different product catalogs and options by segment? Who owns the customer catalog? Is it a different group than the one that manages the customer master or manufacturing BOM? How well does that work?
- Are Marketing and Sales organized by segment or by product/division? How is that managed from the customers' perspective?
- How does price vary by segment or customer? How complex is it? How is that managed and how often does it change?
- Do promotions and marketing vary by segment or customer? How is that delivered and how often does it change?
- How are configurable and service products priced? How many possible SKUs are there and how are they booked in the ERP system?
- Are the sales force or channel partners using complex pricing and quoting (rebates, national account pricing, special pricing overrides, price protections) to gain and retain business? How is that managed? Are approvals, reconciliation, and statement charge backs an issue? How well does it stand up to SOX audits?

Sales Channel

- Do you use both direct and indirect channels to sell? How does that vary by product/division, segment, or geography?
- Are there different internal organizations to support each channel and geography? Do they each have there own processes, P&L, and support systems? How well does that work?
- How often do you launch a new channel or geography?
- Does each group have their own call centers? Is turnover, training, and productivity an issue? Is there a plan to consolidate them across the LOB?
- How satisfied is the business with the job the channel partners are doing? How do you collaborate with partners to serve customers better?
- Do you provide tools or services to support channel partner selling? What tools do the partners feel that they lack?
- Do the same customers buy from multiple channels? Do you or the customer have visibility on orders across channels? What is their buying experience like? Do they get multiple invoices?
- Are the EU and APAC business and sales process the same as in the NA? Does everyone use the same systems or different ones?

■ Does the level of maturity/adoption of technology vary by channel or geography? Are the plans to normalize globally?

Customer Segmentation

- Do you have different "grades" or levels (A, B, C) of customers? Do you treat or service them differently? How is that handled now? What is the revenue breakdown by customer segment? Are you looking to grow any particular segment? If so, how?
- Does your organization or your channel partners sell directly to consumers and business customers? How do you support both types?
- How are new customers acquired? How are prospects targeted? How is that personalized?
- Do you have national or global accounts/contracts? How are they set up and managed? What happens when they buy through a channel partner?
- Are customers satisfied with how they are serviced? Are they asking for new service capabilities? Is that true for all channels, geographies?
- How do customers compare/select you over your competitors? Do you have any plans to change that?

Order Channels

- How many call centers do you currently run? How are they segmented? Can they all sell multiple products or just a single product line? Would it be beneficial to consolidate them or allow cross-selling?
- Do customers conduct business using multiple communication channels (phone, fax, mobile, email, Web, XML, EDI)? Are you equally capable, flexible, and cost-effective regardless of the method?
- How do the orders get into the back office system? Are they placed into more than one? How is that handled?
- Is the system used to capture, validate, and place the orders common across the communication methods? Do some methods create bottlenecks or excessive errors?
- How are customers using procurement systems like Ariba supported?
- Do you have to syndicate product data and prices to customers and partners? Is it in an industry standard form (UCCNet, PIES) or is it proprietary by customer?
- How do you support selling scenarios that involve multi-party transactions like bundling, brokering, 3rd-party fulfillment?
- Is self-service available for customers track and change orders and their accounts?
- Do customers have to deal with different systems and process by channel, product, and geography? Are there plans to improve the current state?

Systems

- What type and how many ERP instances do you have? When were they installed? How did that go? Are there plans to consolidate?
- How many processes (special pricing, order validation & consolidation) are handled outside the ERP system?
- Can you support the entire inquiry to cash process in your current systems without manual hand offs?
- Are the systems and processes adaptable to the product, segment, channel, geo, or do they have to conform to the supported flows?
- Do your system limitations limit the way you service your customer or the types of new selling programs you would like to execute?
- When you acquire a new company do you retain their systems or consolidate them into yours? How long does that take?

- What type of Web presence do you have? How and when was that accomplished? Do changes require IT involvement?
- What is the lead time to get IT projects done?
- How is internal (product master) vs. external product data (sales catalog) managed? Is it stored in more than one system?

Index